The NEW Handbook
of
Cognitive Therapy
Techniques

The NEW Handbook
of
Cognitive Therapy
Techniques

RIAN E. MC MULLIN, PH.D.

W. W. Norton & Company
New York   London

For information about permission to reproduce selections from this book, write to
Permissions, W. W. Norton & Company, Inc. 500 Fifth Avenue, New York, NY 10110

The text of this book is composed in Nofret and Eras with the display set in Mramor
Manufacturing by Haddon Craftsmen
Book design and desktop composition by Justine Burkat Trubey

Library of Congress Cataloging–in–Publication Data

McMullin, Rian E.
The new handbook of cognitive therapy techniques /
Rian E. McMullin. — [Rev. ed.]
p.   cm.
Rev. ed. of: Handbook of cognitive therapy techniques / Rian E. McMullin.
New York: Norton. 1986.
"Norton professional book."
Includes bibliographical references and index.
ISBN 0–393–70313–4
Cognitive therapy Handbooks, manuals, etc. I. McMullin, Rian E.
Handbook of cognitive therapy techniques.
RC489.C63M36   1999
616.89'142—dc21   99-16390   CIP

W. W. Norton & Company, Inc. 500 Fifth Avenue, New York, N.Y.
www.wwnorton.com

W. W. Norton & Company Ltd., 10 Coptic Street, London WC1A 1PU

3 4 5 6 7 8 9 0

Contents

103901

Preface

THIS CLINICIAN'S HANDBOOK is for the practicing therapist. It is not a textbook on theory or research. I presume the reader has already learned the basic theoretical knowledge of cognitive therapy and has read one or more of the many fine books available on the subject, such as the works of Albert Ellis (1995, 1996), Aaron Beck (1993, 1996), Michael Mahoney (1991, 1993a), Donald Meichenbaum (1977, 1994), or Arthur Freeman (Freeman & Dattilio, 1992).

I wish to give the practicing therapist an immediately usable guide. While writing each section, I maintained a precise focus: I pictured the reader as an experienced therapist facing a full caseload each day. What would therapists need to know to try one of the techniques with an upcoming client? What problems might they encounter? What snares might present obstacles? Is there a handout they could give their client? How well would a session's transcript give therapists a feeling for the technique? What examples would best help therapists to try the technique the next day with one or more of their clients?

This book is a how-to reference for therapists and counselors who render service in a variety of settings (public and private clinics, schools, hospitals, and corporate health centers). It is designed to target practitioners wanting to enhance their effectiveness with clients in need of cognitive therapy.

Although based on my earlier work, Handbook of Cognitive Therapy Techniques (Mc Mullin, 1986), this book is a considerable revision of the earlier text. I added three chapters on teaching the basic concepts, discovering the client's beliefs, and grouping the clients key cognitions. These sections were omitted in the first edition because this information was presented in my 1981 publication (Mc Mullin &

Giles). Since this earlier work is no longer readily available, I have added some of the information to the present handbook.

I expanded the presentation of cognitive change techniques by tripling the size of the countering section and subdividing it into three chapters because further clinical experience has shown me that clients respond differently to different types of counters. The perceptual shift section also has been rewritten and expanded to three chapters so that the therapist will have a clearer idea about how to use these interventions.

I added two new chapters on resynthesizing historical and cultural cognitions because these techniques have taken on more importance in recent years. All practice techniques have been grouped in one chapter to make it easier for the reader to use them. I have dropped three chapters and subsumed some of the information into other sections where they are more relevant. I added two sections on counseling clients with drug and alcohol problems and working with severely mentally ill patients. I dropped the research appendix because extensive research in the last ten years has provided strong support for cognitive therapy (J. Beck, 1995; Dobson, 1989; Elkin et al., 1989; Shea et al., 1992), making the appendix superfluous. Finally, I added a short chapter on the philosophical foundation of cognitive restructuring therapy.

The main change in the book is the increased number of clinical examples. Most of the letters I received from therapists about my earlier works showed that readers like clinical stories because they help the practicing therapist to understand how to apply the techniques. In order to convey the flavor of cognitive therapy, I tripled the examples, dialogues, transcripts, and stories. All the cases are true, but I have changed names and other information that would reveal the identity of the client. In the tradition of a handbook, rather than a textbook, I included instructions to clients, patient handouts, parts of client manuals, examples of homework sheets, and many figures and illustrations. Transcripts of sessions were edited to avoid unnecessary repetition and to make oral communication more readable.

I included only those techniques that my colleagues and I have used extensively with a variety of clients. This handbook is not simply a survey of all cognitive techniques developed by all counselors who call themselves cognitive therapists. Although the overall philosophy of the book is cognitive–constructionistic rather than rationalistic (Ellis, 1988b; Guidano, 1991; Mahoney, 1988, 1991, 1993b, 1994;

Neimeyer, 1993), I was interested only in usable techniques, not those that simply fit a specific theoretical model. I discuss cognitive behavioral techniques as well as rational emotive behavior therapy procedures. If I found a technique helpful with the variety of clients my colleagues and I have counseled, I included it.

If the reader finds one of his or her favorite techniques not included, it is because we did not find it useful, were unaware of it, or because we arbitrarily employed another approach.

I take full responsibility for the techniques described in this book. They were developed over 27 years of therapy experience with different types of clients from many different cultures. However, these techniques, like all psychotherapeutic procedures, developed from the common pool of published reports and books and from discussions among colleagues. I have attempted to give credit for a technique, or an aspect of a technique, when I could identify its origins, but years of practice, and free-flowing creative thought have made it impossible for me to always pinpoint the exact source. If I have slighted someone in my references, it is unintentional and I apologize for the oversight.

OUTLINE

The main emphasis of the first edition was on the last step of cognitive therapy—helping clients to change their damaging beliefs, to shift their perceptions from being destructive and harmful to being more promotive and useful.

The present edition is more comprehensive in that it includes the full range of techniques that cognitive therapists need to work with clients. The techniques are presented in the approximate order therapists use when counseling clients.

While universities thoroughly train mental health professionals to help clients, after graduation we are still ill equipped to converse with "real" people. Often we attend four years of undergraduate college, five years of graduate or medical school, and one or two years of post-doctorate internship or residency. During these eleven years of training, we read hundreds of professional books and thousands of research articles, all for one purpose—to help us counsel future clients.

The only difficulty with all of this university education is that we spend most of our time talking to college professors and fellow professionals. Consequently, by the time we see our first real clients, our language has become so enmeshed with jargon and incomprehensible lingo that many clients have difficulty understanding us.

When we start our practices, many of us talk in an academic, graduate/medical–school dialect like the following:

> The purpose of this initial diagnosis is to ascertain the intensity of various pathological symptoms. We, of course, will be empirical in our search, and will cast a glancing eye at etiology.

Predictably, the client's response is, "What?" or "Huh?" It takes some of us years to learn to say, "How do you feel? What's bothering you?" or "How may I help?" In the examples, scripts, and dialogues of this handbook, I have tried to use the vernacular whenever I could to show the style of communication my colleagues and I have learned to use with clients.

The handbook can be read by going to the chapter most pertinent to readers' needs, but most readers would find it helpful to review the finding beliefs chapters (1 through 3), and to be familiar with the basic, cognitive change chapters (4, 5, 6, 7, and 11). I include a summary of the chapters to help readers make their selections.

Chapter 1, Teaching the ABCs, gives techniques, examples, and instructions about why cognitions are important and how they cause emotional and behavioral problems. Understanding this is crucial, because most clients come into counseling with the belief that their problems are caused by almost any variable other than their thoughts. It is necessary to show clients that their cognitions are relevant to their problems.

Chapter 2, Finding the Beliefs, is also crucial for all later techniques. Here we go into great detail about how to find specific cognitions that may be associated with a client's problems. Ten different types of cognitions are presented and the methods to identify them are described.

Chapter 3, Groups of Beliefs, discusses how to develop a master list of client cognitions, how to trace them in terms of life themes, and how to develop a cognitive map of the core beliefs that need to be addressed to lessen the client's emotional and behavioral problems.

If therapists correctly accomplish the procedures mentioned in the first three chapters, they will have the foundation for the rest of the therapy. If the client accepts, at least in part, that cognitions are relevant, the therapist can develop a list of the most important cognitions, and if the client understands how thoughts are related, then the therapist is prepared to move to the last step of cognitive therapy—how to change the client's beliefs.

Chapter 4, 5, and 6, Countering Techniques, cover cognitive change techniques. The three chapters discuss changing the clients' internal language. Each chapter presents a different countering technique. *Chapter 4, Hard Countering,* discusses how to teach forceful disputing and challenging. *Chapter 5, Soft Countering,* describes how to pair relaxing and noncatastrophizing emotions to change thoughts. *Chapter 6, Objective Countering,* shows how to use counters devoid of intense emotional associations.

Chapters 7, 8, and 9, Perceptual Shifting Techniques, cover changing clients' overall patterns of perception, not just their individual beliefs. These three chapters discuss each technique: *Basic, Transposing,* and *Bridging.*

Chapter 10, Historical Resynthesis, describes the third type of change technique and involves reevaluating cognitions from the past by resynthesizing them. These approaches remove the historical routes for many of the client's present destructive beliefs.

Chapter 11, Practice Techniques, provides a series of techniques to help clients make cognitive changes habitual. These practice methods enable clients to master their new cognitions.

Chapter 12, Adjuncts, presents focusing, a component underlying all effective cognitive procedures, and offers suggestions for using cognitive restructuring with specialized clinical populations such as seriously mentally ill patients, drug and alcohol addicted clients, clients who sabotage counseling, and clients in crisis.

Chapter 13, Cross-cultural Cognitive Therapy, helps clients differentiate their own attitudes from those taught to them by their cultural reference groups. This process helps clients isolate what they believe from what they have been taught to believe.

Chapter 14, Philosophical Underpinnings, offers a brief explanation of some of the philosophical foundations for cognitive restructuring therapy.

Chapters are based on the same outline and each includes: basic principles underlying the cognitive technique, the specific steps to implement it, real examples of how it has been used in clinical practice, problems to look for, and advice on how to obtain further information about the technique.

ACKNOWLEDGMENTS

I dedicate this book to Robyn Strike, the young woman I met while living and working in Australia. Her warm companionship enabled me to write this book. Her name is now Robyn Strike Mc Mullin.

I also wish to thank Terri Klein for polishing the manuscript and Susan Munro, my editor at Norton, for her help. As always, I thank my two daughters, Linda and Michele, for their encouragement.

The NEW Handbook
of
Cognitive Therapy
Techniques

Introduction

IN THE EARLY 1970S, I became interested in cognitive therapy while counseling agoraphobic clients at an east coast liberal arts college. The case of one of the first clients I saw after finishing graduate school provides a frame of reference for the techniques offered in this book.

I'll call this client "Ed." Before Ed came to see me, he had seen five other therapists but his problem hadn't lessened. He had panic attacks, but didn't know why. On the surface he appeared above average. He was bright, verbal, well–read, highly educated. But constant, powerful panic attacks made Ed miserable. At times they were so strong that he had to leave work and spend the rest of the day in bed. His panic attacks continued for many years. They ate away at his life, causing his happiness to deteriorate. He lost his intimate relationships, he accepted jobs way below his ability, and he retreated from people until he ended up alone, hiding from the world.

Ed tried in vain to find explanations for his misery. As an adolescent, he conjured up a new theory every week. One week he decided he wasn't cool enough, so he watched James Dean movies in search of a hero to imitate. The next week he claimed he was too passive, so he tried to act like John Wayne. One time he even bought a book about self–analysis and tried to dig up some deeply repressed memory. Another time he concluded he wasn't spiritual enough, so he read the *Lives of the Saints* and prayed for five hours a day, straining to become holy. None of these approaches worked. He abandoned each attempt after a couple of weeks.

His neighbors had their own explanations and loved to tell him their pet theories. One woman, who had studied macrobiotic diets, proclaimed, "It's all the grease you're eating, all that junk food. If you followed the diet in this book I'm reading, you would feel right in no time." Another suggested that Ed learn tae kwon do to become more masculine. A third, the neighborhood's amateur biochemist, determined that Ed was hypoglycemic.

As Ed got older he turned to therapy to seek an explanation for his panics and misery. His first therapist told him he was repressing his sexual feelings. The panics continued, so the therapist suggested he must be repressing aggression. When the panics still continued, the therapist kept searching for something else Ed was repressing. The second therapist hypnotized Ed and gave him some posthypnotic suggestions that he was worthwhile and safe. Ed felt good for a couple of hours, but when the trance faded he quickly regressed. The third counselor didn't offer an explanation; he just reflected Ed's feelings. The fourth gave Ed two tapes: one to relax and one to become assertive. The tapes ended up canceling each other out. The last therapist just handed Ed some medication that made him feel that he was floating on a cloud all day. His panics didn't leave; they just rattled around inside the medication box in his head.

Ed felt as miserable as ever when he came to see me, his sixth therapist. I didn't know what was causing his panic attacks either, so I decided to examine Ed's history. Ed described all the major events that had happened during his childhood. He said it was happy. His family never worried about money, but his parents didn't spoil him and made him earn his allowance. He did well in school, played several sports, and had several friends. All in all, his past seemed more positive than most people's. We searched carefully for some critical event, some key that might explain what had happened to him. But as we examined his history, we found nothing remarkable—no unusual frustrations, no severe traumatic events, no overwhelming disappointments or sadnesses. His frustrations and experiences were typical of most people.

So where did his panic attacks originate?

Initially I thought there might be some Freudian–like, unconscious reason, or possibly some biological, hereditary imbalance. But none of these panned out. Finally, I decided to take one last look at Ed's history and search for a more obvious explanation.

Although Ed's life experiences were positive and unremarkable, there was something unusual about Ed's tone of voice when he described certain events. I decided to probe into the history again, focusing this time on Ed's beliefs, and to ask him pointed questions about what he *thought* of the event, rather than just about what had happened.

Ed paid attention to two events in his past: the time he felt rejected in grade school; and the time his first girlfriend left him for another man. The following is a recreation of the session, based on my case notes.

Session 1

> ED: So, when I went to grade school some of the kids didn't like me much. I didn't seem to fit in.

My usual response to this type of statement was "That must have hurt," or some other empathetic communication. But this time, since we had been over the same thing so many times, I decided to try something different.

> THERAPIST: So what if they didn't like you? Why was that so terrible?

I had thought this way for weeks, but my graduate school training about never challenging clients directly made me reluctant to say it. Because the official techniques were simply not working, I decided something different was called for.

> ED: So what! You must be kidding! It's terrible for a kid not to fit in.

Since I had abandoned the empathy approach, I decided to go all the way.

> THERAPIST: Why?
> ED: You are supposed to be the psychologist. Come on! What are you talking about? Kids need others to like them.
> THERAPIST: So you say. But what's so terrible about them not liking you? Did they beat you up, or throw stones at you, or what?
> ED: No, of course not. I just wasn't liked as much as most of the other kids.
> THERAPIST: Okay. Sure, it may have been unpleasant, but you said you had some other friends, so what did it really matter that you weren't super popular with everybody?
> ED: Because it meant that I was different from the other boys.
> THERAPIST: Excuse me! How do you think you were different?
> ED: I felt like I must be some kind of weirdo, or a nerd or something.
> THERAPIST: Just a moment. You have told me for several sessions that you felt different from the other boys. Okay, maybe you were. But now you imply that this difference was bad. You suggest that there was something wrong with you for being different—that the difference proves you were inferior in some way.

Why? Why couldn't your difference indicate you were superior?

ED: Well, if I was better, then I would have been popular. Right?

THERAPIST: Wrong! Kids reject anybody who is different. They don't differentiate between someone who is different because he is superior or different because he is inferior. The most popular person in school is the one who fits in the best. A Mozart or Einstein would be rejected as much as a no-hoper. Maybe more, because the other kids would be envious.

ED: I'm no Einstein or Mozart!

THERAPIST: No. However, you don't have to be hugely different to be rejected. The pressure to conform in adolescence is so powerful that peers will detect even small differences and attack kids who fail to submit to the will of the adolescent subculture. Adolescent groups may pride themselves on not conforming to the adult world. But inside the group itself, adolescents are very conforming. No human association acts more rigidly or treats nonconformists more intolerantly than an adolescent peer group. They can be very cruel. They don't tolerate boys or girls who don't fit in; they simply cast them out of the group. There are no exceptions. There is no appeal.

ED: So how might I have been different, even in a positive sense?

THERAPIST: You have already told me. You were a lot smarter than the other kids. When they read comic books, you read your sister's college books on astronomy, or philosophy, or a classic novel, right? Their comic books bored you. You thought the things your peers watched on TV or in the movies were silly. You liked classical music and read Ibsen's plays when you were ten. Remember the time you hid a copy of Agamemnon in a comic book so that the other boys wouldn't find out what you were reading? So, you were different all right—without a doubt. That difference wasn't the problem. You simply possessed a more inquiring mind than most boys—far more. You brought the problem to life when you judged this difference as inferior, when you concluded you lacked something that the other boys had. Really you had something that other boys lacked.

ED: It never occurred to me that I could have been different in a positive, rather than a negative, way. At that time and since then, I always took my difference as a sign of inferiority.

THERAPIST: That's the way your peers evaluated you, but do you have to evaluate yourself in the same way?

ED: Well no. I guess not.

Session 2

THERAPIST: So you were a senior in high school when "Betsy" left you for "Mongo" the sailor. That's painful for all young men. But again, why did you feel so horrible that you contemplated suicide? Almost all young men and women are rejected at some time in their dating career, but it doesn't totally destroy their lives.

ED: I discovered for the first time that no normal woman would ever want me.

THERAPIST: Whoa! Stop! Where does that conclusion come from? Maybe she left because "Mongo" was better looking or had more money.

ED: Well, Mongo was a navy recruit those days so he didn't have much money, and he was one of the ugliest men I ever saw, and . . .

THERAPIST: Okay, maybe she left you because she liked men in uniform—any man. Or maybe she preferred "Mongo" being on a ship all the time because then he wouldn't be around to bother her; or maybe he had a hairy wart on his left ear, and she loved hairy warts. Who knows? But good heavens, Ed, where did you come up with the conclusion that since she didn't want you, no woman ever would?

ED: I don't know; it's just the way I felt.

THERAPIST: No, not felt . . . *thought!* It's just the way you *thought.*

We reviewed the other events in Ed's history and came to the same conclusion. His experiences weren't special, but his interpretations were. He exaggerated, catastrophized, distorted, and twisted almost every major event that had happened to him. It became clear that his problem was not complicated or esoteric—it was really quite simple. His thinking was twisted. Ed's problem wasn't his unconscious, biology, diet, early upbringing, or anything else; it was his attitude.

So we decided to work on changing his thoughts and to forget about the rest. Ed improved, but not as remarkably as is usually described in books like this. For instance, he didn't get up at the end of the session and say, "God bless you, doctor. I am cured, cured!" Instead he fought the concept, and kept going back to the "I stink" scenario. Gradually, however, and with small steps, he did change. He started to focus on his thoughts rather than the events. And his panic attacks lessened both in frequency and intensity.

Occasionally, I get a card from him. He says he gets a panic attack only every six months or so and that it is a flash panic (an alarm reaction for only two or three seconds). He tells himself, "Same old garbage," and it goes away.

While I was counseling Ed and other clients like him, other colleagues were coming to the same conclusions. We started to read the theories and techniques of cognitive-semantic therapists, particularly the works of Albert Ellis and Aaron Beck. Together we developed our own brand of cognitive therapy. This new therapy started to grow, as other psychologists had similar experiences with clients. Today, many therapists spend most of their sessions working with clients' beliefs.

Encounters with thousands of clients like Ed have taught me this truth: *If we change our thoughts, we change ourselves.*

ONE

Teaching the ABCs

Cognitive therapy focuses on thoughts. Emotions, behavior, and the environment are all considered important, but the distinguishing feature of cognitive therapy is its concentration on the client's beliefs, attitudes, and cognitions.

The first step in any cognitive therapy is to teach clients the importance of thoughts. Therapists must show clients that beliefs, philosophies, and schemata can cause powerful emotions and behaviors, and that to reduce or eliminate negative emotions, clients must change their beliefs. This is not a casual process; therapists need to use a systematic method to explain these principles.

Before clients can employ cognitive techniques effectively, they must be convinced that their beliefs are connected to their problems. Initially, most clients don't think so. They may blame genetics, parental mistreatment, traumatic childhood experiences, bad luck, the hostile intent of others, an ill-formed society, or an insensitive, incompetent government. They accuse everybody and everything—except their own cognitive processing—for their emotional pain.

The reason for their omission is evident. Their thoughts occur so rapidly and seem so ethereal that many clients don't notice that they are thinking anything at all. All they perceive is the environmental trigger (which is objective, concrete, and readily discernible) and the emotional response (which is palpable and strongly felt). Transient, nebulous thoughts are usually ignored in the process.

It can take much convincing for clients to see that the faint little voice they hear inside their heads may be the culprit, but this convincing must take place if clients are to cooperate with cognitive therapy.

TEACHING THE BASIC FORMULA
Principles

Although you can teach clients the core concepts of cognitive therapy by using several methods, one of the quickest and most direct is to reserve the first cognitive session for instruction. The first session is usually the most effective time to present the key formulas and basic vocabulary to the client. Arrange an individual tutoring session or run a group class when you have several beginning clients.

Method
1. If possible, devote the entire session to the topic. Teach clients that there are two contrasting ways to explain why people feel emotions and why people act in certain ways.
2. Present the older theory that emotional and behavioral responses are caused by something in the environment. Most clients believe this theory is correct.
3. Next, explain the new theory that *thoughts* about things, not the things themselves, elicit feelings.
4. Provide the client with a series of examples that compare and contrast the two theories. Show that the same environmental situation can be interpreted in several different ways, and that it is the interpretation, rather than the situation, that is most important.

The Formula

This is a typical first session script that I have used with many clients. Although it appears to be a monologue, it is actually an interactive dialogue in which the therapist and client are constantly checking back and forth while each concept is being explained. I provide a written version of this to clients at the end of the first session.

> To solve your problems you must know the cause of them. This sounds so obvious that it may not seem worth mentioning, but many people ignore the obvious and try to discover causes in a helter–skelter way, until by luck they stumble across an answer, or more likely, they collapse from exhaustion and conclude that the problem is unsolvable.
>
> Emotional problems are the same as other kinds of problems. If you don't correctly identify the source, you will waste effort working on fixing things that won't change how you feel.

But how do you find the cause?

The fields of psychology and psychiatry have so many differ-ent theories about the causes of various emotional problems that it is easy to get confused. To clear things up, let's start with two simple formulas. Learning and memorizing them now will save you much time and effort later on.

Old Formula

A ———————————————▶ **C**

(Draw this for your client during the session.)

- Each letter stands for a different thing.
- A stands for an activating event: the situation you are in, a trig-ger in the environment, a stimulus, anything that starts off the whole process of reacting.
- C stands for either your emotions or your behavior. Cs are the consequences of A. They can be a feeling or an action.

The old theory asserts that As cause Cs—that situations in your environment cause feelings inside you and cause you to act in certain ways.

To see how this works, picture this.

Imagine one Sunday afternoon you are sitting in your chair reading the paper when suddenly you start feeling anxious. The fear is strong, seems real, and it bothers you. You know the C immediately. You feel it. Your heart is beating faster, your breath-ing is rapid and forced, and you feel hot and are perspiring. You have a desire to get up and move around, or even better, to run. It's hard to just sit there in the chair but there's no place to run and nothing to run from. This is the C in our formula—fear. Of course Cs can be any emotion—anger, sadness, panic, frustration—but for our example let us say you are feeling anx-ious.

The question that would probably leap into your mind this Sunday afternoon is, "Why? Why am I suddenly feeling scared about something, and what am I scared about?"

The old formula offers an answer. It is your A—the situation you are in. It's what a sound video camera would record if it were viewing your situation with no interpretation and no feel-ing. The camera would only record the sights and sounds that were occurring while you were sitting in your chair. Was the television or radio on? What was showing? Were you reading the paper? What were you reading? Were other people in the room and, if so, were they talking or looking at you? Where you eating or drinking something? What were the sounds outside? Were you looking at something or staring off into space? All these and more are the As.

Now according to this old formula, you would look at your As to see what is causing your fear. The old theory suggests that some A caused your fear, and that if you look very carefully you may be able to find the A. Once you do, you only need to remove the offending A and your fear should dissolve.

This A–causes–C theory is so popular that we hear it all the time. How many times have you heard people say, "You really made me angry," "he got me upset," or "the news really depressed me"? All these statements imply that some outside As caused us to feel some inside Cs. The idea is so universal that it seems like common sense. But is it true?

No! Outside things exert little power over us. Our senses make us aware of the outside world. If we close our eyes or cover our ears the outside world disappears and its effect on us is minimal. If we can't detect an object with one of our senses, the object can't make us laugh or cry, run away, or sing or dance. Outside things have no magical powers—they can't sneak inside our heads and create our feelings. The simply sit in sensory darkness waiting to be observed by us.

The correct formula is what follows. It is simple and has been stated many times before, but it is so essential to our understanding of ourselves that it is worth memorizing. It was created by one of the world's most famous psychologists—Albert Ellis. Others have tried to improve upon it, but it is still one of the best ways to explain the keystone of cognitive therapy.

The new formula is:

$$A \longrightarrow B \longrightarrow C$$

(Draw this for your client.)

- B stands for cognitions, beliefs, and attitudes.

As you can see, we have added an additional letter: B. It stands for our beliefs about the situation, and the thoughts, images, imaginations, perceptions, conclusions, and interpretations that we tell ourselves about A. Mostly, B stands for our brain—how our brain takes the raw information about the As and molds this raw data into patterns, schemata, themes, and stories.

Almost all of your emotions and behavior can be understood by this new formula. So instead of simply looking at your As, look at what you are telling yourself about them.

Practical Examples

In the first session we often go over the following examples one at a time until our clients understand the principles.

Example 1

A = Bill's boss called him into his office and criticized him for turning in a report late.

B = Bill told himself that the criticism was unfair because his secretary hadn't typed the report in time.

C = Bill felt angry.

We tell clients, "You may think the boss's criticism caused Bill's anger, but in truth it's what Bill believed about the criticism that counts. Had he thought the criticism valid, he may have felt guilty or worried, but anger was felt only when his brain fabricated the abstraction that the criticism was *unfair.*"

Example 2

A = Barbara looked at her body in the mirror.

B = She thought she looked fat.

C = She felt depressed.

Some would think that the visual impact of seeing a fat body is the culprit. Who wouldn't be upset?

Many people. Barbara had to first accept that there is an ideal female weight (a cultural standard that constantly changes), and she must have believed that she had an obligation to be this weight. The origin of this sense of obligation is a mystery.

She must also have concluded that she crossed an imaginary line into what she arbitrarily believes is an unacceptable weight, and she needed to tell herself it's terrible to be over this line. The effect of her reflection in the mirror pales in comparison to her huge mental creations. Her brain causes her depression, not her weight.

Example 3
A = John felt a pain in his stomach
B = He thought it might be stomach cancer.
C = He had a flash of panic.

Even something as basic as pain is interpreted by our brains (Freeman & Eimer, 1998). If your muscles are sore after a heavy workout, you may judge the pain as a sign that your workout was successful. The pain of childbirth may be far greater than the pain of disease, but the latter is far more onerous than the former because the brain interprets the two pains in quite different ways—one brings forth life; the other may destroy it.

In these three examples, we explain to our clients that the A–B–C formula is the key to the causes of their emotions. When they feel an unpleasant emotion and want to know what causes it, they can use the formula to find out. The formula can ultimately help them to change the upsetting emotions that cause ongoing disruption in their lives.

Comment

There are numerous alternative formulas to Ellis's A–B–C formula, many of which are more complicated. For example, Teasdale and Barnard's interacting cognitive subsystems (ICS) provide a comprehensive conceptual framework (Teasdale, 1993, 1996; Teasdale & Barnard, 1993). Aaron Beck (1996), Mahoney (1993a) and even Ellis himself (Ellis, 1988a, 1995, 1996) have extended the formula.

I have attempted to use all of these formulas with my clients, but I have found that almost all clients understand, remember, and use the simple A–B–C formula better than any of the more complicated ones.

It is not essential that clients be convinced about the efficacy of the A–B–C theory at this early point in counseling. In fact, most clients will be skeptical. Furthermore, they may not entirely understand it. In cognitive restructuring therapy, a direct challenge of clients' theories early on is avoided. However, it is critical to secure an agreement that the A–B–C view may have some merit and that it is reasonable to consider it further. To help persuade the clients in the first few sessions, give A–B–C examples taken from other people's situations, not from the client's own life. This way, clients don't have to defend their own theory, and they can tacitly join you in seeing the mistakes others have made in their thinking. These examples can pave the way for establishing the truth behind the theory.

After the first session, we give the homework assignment on page 13 to our clients.

HOMEWORK

(Hand in at the beginning of Session #2)

NAME_____

ASSIGNMENT 1. Study pages 1-7 in *Talk Sense to Yourself* (Mc Mullin & Casey, 1975).

ASSIGNMENT 2. Read chapters 1 and 2 from *A Guide to Rational Living* (Ellis & Harper, 1998).

ASSIGNMENT 3. The following examples describe six A-B-C situations, but the Bs are not present. You are to guess what thought (B) must be included to connect the situation (A) with the emotion (C). Identify the (A) and (C) for each of the following, and write in the (B).

1. Alfred's boss criticized him for coming to work too late. Alfred then felt depressed.

2. Mary came to two therapy sessions and quit because she thought it wasn't working.

3. Susi had a stomach pain. Then she started to feel scared.

4. Joe was caught in a speed trap and got very angry.

5. Jane was embarrassed when her friends saw her crying at a romantic movie.

6. Fritz got violently angry when a clerk asked for identification while he was cashing a check.

ASSIGNMENT 4. Write five examples from your own life where your thoughts (B) caused you painful emotions (C). Describe these examples in terms of A-B-C.

1. A.
   B.
   C.
2. A.
   B.
   C.
3. A.
   B.
   C.
4. A.
   B.
   C.
5. A.
   B.
   C.

Further Information

Some of the examples and the homework assignment evolved from my earlier works (Casey & Mc Mullin, 1976, 1985; Mc Mullin & Casey, 1975).

Donald Meichenbaum is one of the major contributors to cognitive therapy. He is the founder of cognitive behavior modification (Meichenbaum, 1977, 1993) and cognitive stress inoculation training (Meichenbaum, 1985) and has most recently specialized in posttraumatic stress disorders (Meichenbaum, 1994). He emphasizes the importance of providing clients with an early, clear, distinct framework for therapy. He suggests that this conceptualization and structure play an important role in helping the client to understand the change process, and should precede any specific treatment interventions. See Meichenbaum (1975, 1993), Meichenbaum and Deffenbacher (1988), Meichenbaum and Genest (1983), Meichenbaum and Turk (1987).

PROVIDING EVIDENCE THAT BELIEFS PRODUCE EMOTIONS

Principles

After the therapist presents the initial formulas and some brief examples in the first session, the hard work begins. It takes more than formulas or lectures to persuade clients about the power of cognitions; therapists need to provide proof. Most clients enter counseling with such strongly held opposing views that it requires more than the authority of the therapist to convince them of the key principle of cognitive theory. I have found the following exercises helpful in securing the client's cooperation.

Method 1. Create an Emotion Now

Therapists can show their clients how their beliefs, not their environments, create particular emotions. The therapist needs to demonstrate how clients can make themselves feel happy, not by changing anything in their surroundings, childhood, or biochemistry, but only by changing what they think.

To do this, give a complete description of any scene that has several sensual anchors. The more senses the client can use while imagining the scene the better. For obvious reasons the scene should be pleasant rather than aversive. You can create any scene you wish but the following is a good example. Tell your client to imagine this scene as vividly as possible.

> Imagine for a moment that you are walking along a tropical beach. It's the middle of summer and very warm. It's late in the afternoon. The sun has not yet begun to set, but it's getting low in the horizon. You feel the cool, hard-packed sand beneath your feet. You hear the cry of sea gulls and the roar of ocean waves in the distance. You can smell and taste the salt in the air. As you continue to walk, the sky turns gold and amber. There is an after-glow of crimson glistening around the palm trees. The sun is beginning to set into the ocean. The sky turns blue and turquoise and envelops you in a deep purple twilight. A cool breeze comes off the ocean. You lie down on a sand dune and look up at the night sky. It's a brilliant starry night. You feel surrounded by the cosmos. A deep sense of calm and peace overtakes you. You feel at one with the universe. (Adapted from Kroger & Fezler, 1976)

Explain to your clients that if they felt calm while you read this to them, it is because their imagination created the calm. Their biochem-istry, unconscious, present environment, or early experiences were the same before imagining this scene as during. Only their thoughts changed.

If hearing the passage didn't produce a sense of calm, this is also due to their imagination and what they said to themselves. While hearing the passage, "I am walking on a tropical beach," instead of thinking about the beach, clients might have thought, "No, I'm not! I am really sitting at home in a chair." Or while reading, "It's in the mid-dle of summer and very warm," they may have told themselves, "Non-sense, it's freezing cold outside."

The scene doesn't create their feelings, their thoughts do. What they heard doesn't matter—only what they thought. Their thoughts could have created any emotion they desired. They could have created anger if they thought, "Last time I walked on a beach I was with Fifi before she left me for that bum, Bruno." Or fear: "A cool breeze comes off the ocean . . . but then the poisonous jellyfish start creeping onto the shore, dragging their slimy bodies behind. They encircle me, waving their rancid tentacles at my legs, grabbing, grasping for me. I run but can't escape."

To create any emotion, all they had to do was focus on a thought to produce it. Explain this to your clients, and say, "It's not the words, the environment, your early childhood experiences, or your bio-genetic makeup that creates these feelings. Rather, it's the picture your brain paints. You are the artist. Your emotions are your own creations."

Method 2. Imagine Changing Another Person's Bs

A different type of scene may convince other clients about how mighty their thoughts are. The following story presents a hypothetical person called Fred. Therapists can either tell this story or create one of their own.

Imagine that you see a man named Fred walking down a road. He is normal and average in every way—not exceptional, not insane, no more neurotic than anyone else. He is a salesman in a local department store and has a wife and two kids. On Thursdays he bowls with his friends and on Saturdays coaches little league football. Sometimes he drinks too much when he goes to parties with his neighbors and starts arguing too loudly about some political issue, but he doesn't drink much usually, and generally is a rather mellow guy. His sex life with his wife is good, not as exciting as in the early days, but his wife seems content. He is a good parent, spends more time with his kids than most fathers do, corrects them when they are wrong and comforts them when they are sick. He is reasonably popular. He has the knack of getting along with different kinds of people—his fellow salesmen at work, the janitor, his bowling friends, his neighbors.

Now let's suppose we do something to Fred. Imagine that we have figured out the exact chemical component of a belief. By this I mean that we've found the chemical composition of a thought like "the world is flat," and the chemical component for the opposite thought, "the world is round." (We recognize that this is pure fantasy. Thoughts have physical representation in our brains, but they aren't chemical compounds. Still, follow the fantasy.) Now imagine that we've broken down thousands of beliefs into their chemical compositions and have put them into syringes that we could inject into people.

Let's say we want to inject a particular thought into Fred—one thought, not a whole bunch of them. Once injected, this thought will take root; Fred can never remove it for as long as he lives. We don't do anything else to Fred—we just inject him with this one thought.

We pick a thought at random, let's say a vial of *"I need everybody to like me in order for me to be happy,"* and we insert it into our tranquilizer gun and wait for Fred to walk by our house. Finally, one Saturday afternoon as he walks by we shoot him with the thought.

If we follow Fred, we won't notice any difference in him—at least not for a while. If we looked very close, we may see some little things; his gait may have changed a little. Where before he just sauntered along, now he seems to be more hesitant. He worries about how other people are walking and starts to imitate them.

We follow Fred for the rest of the day and into the evening. It is Saturday night, and he and his wife have gone to a neighborhood party. Fred likes these parties, and is usually one of the most popular guys there. But this time he isn't. He seems nervous, he doesn't know who to talk to, and stands there fumbling with his hands. A friend asks Fred's wife if he is feeling sick. Two of his neighbors are having their monthly argument about gun control and ask Fred what he thinks. He answers, "Well there are really two sides to every question, and we shouldn't jump to conclusions too quickly." The neighbors look strangely at Fred, who has never acted so unsure of himself before; he usually just comes out with his opinion. His neighbors shake their heads and walk away.

Later that night Fred and his wife go to bed. He wants to make love but he is indirect and unsure of himself. He tells her at least five or six times, "You know if you're tired I understand." She persistently reassures him that it will be all right. But Fred is uncomfortable making love. He keeps asking, "Is it all right for you?" and he wonders if he is a good lover.

The next morning, he has difficulties at football practice. A boy's father asks him to play his son Mervine more often—he isn't a very good player, doesn't practice, never bothers to learn the plays, and fumbles a lot. But Fred is afraid to say no, and puts one of his starters (whose father isn't there) on the bench. Mervine fumbles three times and the team loses badly.

If we jump several years ahead, we notice Fred has developed other problems. He is having trouble in his marriage because he developed erectile difficulties and hasn't been able to make love for over a year. He went to a therapist and told him, "It's like watching myself perform."

Fred also has an ulcer. He works extra hours at the store to please his boss. The football team got a new coach after they lost six games in a row. He hasn't been invited to parties for a long time, but he knows his friends are still having them. He has tried several different types of tranquilizers, but they haven't helped.

You see what has happened—our little injection has changed Fred totally. The thought we implanted, "I need everybody to like me to be happy," is one of the core cognitive determinants of what psychologists call social phobia. By injecting it into Fred we have ruined his happiness—he has become a people-pleaser, a social phobic.

It may seem strange that one thought can cause so much misery, but the thought we injected is particularly damaging. It destroys what makes Fred so unique and turns him into a social puppet. He loses his individuality and wanders around trying to please everybody. Curiously, instead of getting people to like him, the thought causes the opposite reaction. People lose respect for somebody who doesn't express his own opinions or who is afraid to take sides on an issue. The thought makes Fred act like a wimp. Others see that there is nobody left inside but a mirror reflecting whatever is projected onto it.

Of course, we don't have vials of beliefs or an injection gun. However, thoughts can be injected just as quickly, just as deeply, and just as devastatingly in less fanciful ways that we will describe in our counseling.

Method 3. Dreams and Hypnotism

Dreams also show the power of clients' thoughts. When the client dreams, the outside environment is the bedroom. This reality remains the same no matter what clients are dreaming. When they have a nightmare, their fear is clearly not coming from their environment (their bedrooms); it is coming from their dreams. If dreams switch, then the emotions produced by them also switch. Dreams are Bs also, just like clients' thoughts, but they are thoughts that clients beget when their senses are reduced, and they are focused on propriocep-tive rather than extroceptive stimuli.

The successfulness of hypnotic induction reveals that there are few A causes C situations. The cortical area of the brain is even involved with processes that appear immediate and automatic, like pain. The subjective pain experienced when pricking your finger on a needle seems like a clear example of an A–C situation. A—the needle—

directly causes C—the pain. But hypnosis shows that even this is an A–B–C state. If you suggest to hypnotized subjects, "Your hand is in cold water and quite numb; you can feel nothing," the subjects won't feel their finger being pricked. While under hypnotic analgesia, people still feel a kind of stimulation, but they don't describe it as "pain." Many subjects describe it as a sensation that is neither positive nor negative. Of course, subjects' ability to block pain is based on their capacity to accept the reality of the hypnotist's suggestion.

Hypnotism and dreams show that what clients imagine is more important to their emotional state than what is real. If they dream they are in a ship sinking in the North Atlantic after colliding with an iceberg, they will feel all the terror that the passengers on the Titanic felt, and the reality that they are lying safely in their bed will not change these emotions. If they imagine they are five years old swinging on a swing, they will feel all the exhilaration of flying through the air; it doesn't matter that they are an adult lying on a hypnotist's couch. What is real to us is what our brain says is real.

Method 4. Physical Evidence

For clients with more linear processing styles or with poor imaginations, a more factual approach may be useful. For such clients we present the physiological aspects of the A–B–C theory. We start by showing a cartoon picture of a brain with the following labels (Figure 1.1).

FIGURE 1.1 Cognitive and emotional areas of the brain (Casey & Mc Mullin, 1976, 1985)

We also suggest that more educated clients read *Descartes' Error* by Antonio Damasio (1994). In his book he describes the neurological path of emotions. The process begins with our conscious, deliberate consideration of the A. We first reflect on the situation; we judge the content of the event of which we are a part. We evaluate its consequences to ourselves and others. These cognitive evaluations are represented in our sensory cortexes (smell, hearing, and vision). Next, our brain takes these representations and compares them to other situations of a similar type that we have experienced before. The prefrontal area of our brain automatically searches for associations and pairings in our memory. "Have we been in this situation before? Is it something to worry about? What happened the last time we faced a situation like this?"

This entire process is cognitive. All of these are Bs. Though these cognitions are instantaneous (often lasting less than a second) and involuntary, they are all occurring in the cortex and prefrontal areas of our brain. Once these cognitive processes are completed, then and only then is the biochemistry of complex emotions made active. Automatically, these cognitive conclusions (in the prefrontal areas of our brain) signal the emotional areas of our brain (the amygdala, the anterior cingulate, the autonomic nervous system, and the brain stem, among others) to start up. It is then that we "feel" an emotion. People who have physical damage to their prefrontal lobes cannot generate emotions, and thus cannot experience the ensuing feelings. Physiologically, Bs are the major components of our emotions.

Method 5. Best Examples from the Client's Own History

Most clients already know the power of Bs from their own histories. It is helpful to remind them of what they already know. Ask them to remember a time when they were greatly bothered by something, something that overwhelmed them and upset them but that no longer has that power anymore—something that they have gotten over. Ask them to focus on this earlier event and to identify the A and the C. Have them picture the situation until it becomes clear in their minds, then ask them to identify the Bs. What did they tell themselves when they got so upset? Finally, have them focus on what they believe today. What are they telling themselves now that they didn't believe before?

Most clients learn that the most damaging thing about the earlier event was not what happened, but what they said to themselves about it. The effects of an event may end quickly, but their self-statements at the time are far more long lasting; the effect of their conclusions can be devastating, and may last a lifetime. Help your client to see that it was not the trauma that caused their problems, it was their B.

Method 6. If the B changes, the C changes.

Give your clients some A–B examples. Hold the situation (A) as a constant, but vary what they say to themselves. Ask them to identify what emotion would be created by the different thoughts (B). You can describe the examples to your clients, include them in homework assignments, put them in a pamphlet, program them on a computer, or show them on slides in group sessions. Here are some examples:

1. Imagine you are sitting in the cafeteria at work and you see two colleagues talking in whispers and occasionally glancing in your direction. What you feel is dependent on what you tell yourself. If you think, "How terribly rude they are talking about me behind my back," you will feel angry. If you think, "They must have found out about the mistake I made yesterday on the Hutchinson account," you will feel guilty. If you believe they are planning a surprise party for your birthday next week, you may feel happy. The A is the same in all cases. Your Bs alone produce the different emotions.
2. This example comes from Hauck (1980). Imagine that while reading this book you suddenly look down and see a snake coiled around your legs. Unless you like snakes you will probably be upset. Impulses from your brain send neural chemical messages that produce endocrine and other responses in your bloodstream. These signal your muscles and limbs and cause you to have a startled response. If someone asks you why you are upset you may breathlessly point to the snake.
   This looks like a clear A–C situation. You see the snake, A, which causes you to become afraid at C. But if someone comes over, picks up the snake and shows you that it is a rubber snake, will you still be afraid? In most cases, probably not. What is the difference? The A is the same; you still see the snake lying at your feet. The difference in what you feel is only your thought. In the first case, you probably instantaneously thought several things: "It is a snake. It is real. It may be poisonous. It could harm me." Remember, although it can take several seconds to read these thoughts, you could have thought them all in a millisecond. In the second situation you

thought, "It's a toy snake. Toy snakes can't hurt me. I have no reason to be upset." Seeing the snake didn't make you feel anything at
all; it's what you said to yourself about what you saw that made the
difference.

3. Consider these various Cs in response to the same A.

> A = You have an appointment with a close friend but he
> is an hour and a half late.
> C = You are afraid.

What would you have to say to yourself at B to ignite your fear?

> B = "He has been in an accident, and may be hurt."

or,

> C = You are angry.

What would you need to think to create this?

> B = "How rude of him to keep me waiting without calling
> me."

or,

> C = You are depressed.

What would cause you to feel this?

> B = "I guess he thinks so little of me that he doesn't feel the need
> to show up on time."

The A is the same in all the examples. The only variable that could
cause the different emotions at C is what you told yourself at B.

Method 7. Create an Emotion Directly

1. Have your clients practice shifting their emotions slightly by simply
   changing their thoughts. Direct them to make themselves feel
   happy, slightly sad, amused, proud and self-confident, safe and
   content, and to try rapidly switching from one feeling to another.
   This exercise should be done for five minutes a day. (See rational
   emotive imagery in chapter 8.)
2. Ask your clients to observe people who are acting in ways they
   consider odd or unusual, and to consider what those people might
   be telling themselves that makes them act in those ways. What
   would they have to believe in order to behave in such a strange
   manner themselves?

Comment

It would be overwhelming for clients to go through all of the methods just mentioned, but it is useful for the therapist to learn all of them, because you cannot be sure which method will be most persuasive for a particular client.

The best examples are those that the client creates. These have the advantage of being personally significant and thus have built-in persuasive strength. The therapist should encourage clients to think of their own examples of how Bs cause Cs.

Further Information

One of the most efficacious books for relaxation images is *Hypnosis and Behavior Modification: Imagery Conditioning* (Kroger & Fezler, 1976).

See Damasio (1994) or Gregory (1977, 1987) for information on brain physiology for the lay person

Cognitive therapy for management of pain has been explored by Baker and Kirsch (1991), Cipher and Fernandez (1997), Litt (1988), Meichenbaum and Genest (1983), Scott and Leonard (1978), Sternbach (1987), and Turkat and Adams (1982).

Rational emotive behavior therapy (REBT) therapists provide some of the most effective analogies of cognitive principles that you can use with your clients. They are unusually clear and image forming. Pay particular attention to the works of the REBT therapist Paul Hauck (1967, 1980, 1991, 1994).

In some of my earlier books, I provide a number of metaphors and images that therapists can use. See Casey and Mc Mullin (1976, 1985), Mc Mullin, Assafi, and Chapman (1978), Mc Mullin and Casey (1975), Mc Mullin, Casey, and Navez (1979) (in Spanish), Mc Mullin and Gehlhaar (1990a), and Mc Mullin, Gehlhaar, and James (1990).

HOW POWERFUL ARE ENVIRONMENTAL FORCES?
Principles

Despite the therapist's best efforts in teaching the A–B–C principles, many clients still insist that certain environmental forces (As) are so powerful that they override the effects of any perception or thought. The As they suggest as most powerful are physical environment, early childhood experiences, biochemistry, unconscious, and heredity.

These As are powerful, but as stated earlier, their ability to influence people and dominate lives is based on how people cognitize them rather than the As themselves. Heredity, biochemistry, and early childhood experiences are no different from other As. They are triggers or stimuli, but they don't control a person. In other words, they may incline people to act, but they don't *make* them act. Strong predisposition created by early childhood experiences, physical condition, biochemistry, or heredity can often be offset or mitigated by the client's Bs. The following methods and examples show how.

Method

1. Tell the patient about someone you know who has conquered a severe childhood experience.
2. Give an example of a person whose thoughts and attitude overcame a severe physical handicap.

Example 1. Overcoming Bad Childhood As: The Story of Anna

One of my first clients was a woman I'll call Anna. She was an older woman who had entered counseling for general anxiety and depression. She had suffered through one of the worst childhood experiences anyone could imagine.

Anna had been born in a small Russian town before World War II. When the Germans invaded her village, they enslaved the townspeople and forced them to work for the Third Reich. Partisans living in the surrounding area were sabotaging army supply lines, and the Germans decided to make an example of the village.

Early one evening SS troops rounded up everyone in town—men, women, and children—and marched them to a ravine. Anna and her mother were dragged along with the rest. The Nazis forced the villagers to huddle in a gully. They then lined up machine guns on the outer edge and fired. While people were screaming and trying to climb out, Anna's mother pushed her underneath the falling bodies. The dead and dying on top of her shielded Anna from the bullets.

All night long she hid there. She was soaked with blood, and people moaned all around her. After several hours, the moaning stopped. Everyone was dead but Anna, and she felt too terrified to leave.

The next morning people from a neighboring village searched for relatives among the slain. They heard Anna whimpering and frantically dug through the bodies, following the sound of her crying until they uncovered her. They carried Anna home and gave her food and comfort. She was the only survivor of the village, and hundreds of partisans spent months taking care of her, moving her from one town to another and hiding her from the SS. Finally they arranged to smuggle her out of Russia through the underground. She settled in the U.S., where she lived with some distant relatives.

For years Anna suffered from horrible nightmares. Friends repeatedly suggested she see a therapist but she resisted—at last she called me.

I obviously couldn't erase the appalling event that had happened to her, but I could help her to change the way she looked at it. Instead of focusing on the experience, we concentrated on her beliefs, and we searched for a new viewpoint to cope with her ancient pain. We examined the broad, sweeping problems all people face. We discussed our deeply felt values about philosophical and religious subjects such as life and death, and good and evil.

After a while the sessions helped. She would always feel some pain, but Anna had learned to accept what had happened. This was the key. She had accepted that sometimes bad things happen to good people for no reason. She agreed that she didn't deserve it, that she had done nothing to cause it, and that there was nothing she could have done to prevent it. But most importantly, she learned to accept that many times the universe isn't the way she would like it to be. It can be nasty and painful, and it has no obligation to be different from what it is. When she could accept living in this kind of universe, her anxiety and depression shriveled up, and she became happier.

Anna's story teaches us a great truth. Human beings have an amazing ability to adapt. No matter how bad our childhood or how horrible our experiences, we can rise above all of these and free ourselves by changing the way we look at life.

Example 2. Overcoming Bad Physical As

Consider this example of a person who overcame a severe physical condition. The event took place a few years back in the New York marathon. The race had finished hours before, and it was late in the evening. The TV was showing interviews of the day's winners, and almost as an aside, the camera panned to a live shot of a man who was still on the course. He was without legs, pushing himself on a board. His hands were bandaged and bloody, but he continued to push with everything he had. He was on back streets, and only a few people were watching—an older couple, a man coming home from work, a homeless man sitting on a curbside. Six or seven adolescent kids, looking like they'd be more at home in a gang than watching a race, also looked on.

As he was coming up the street, the few people present acted embarrassed for him. Everyone but the adolescents, who appeared to be mocking and taunting him, looked away, pretending they didn't see him.

The man seemed to ignore them all, and kept looking straight ahead, pushing with all his might. But as he passed the people and they looked at his face, they must have seen his expression, or suddenly understood what the man was doing, because a remarkable thing happened. All of the people who had been ignoring or mocking him started to cheer—not just polite cheering, but shouting and screaming at full volume, encouraging him to continue. They were jumping up and down, running next to him, pleading with him to keep trying, patting him on the back. The street kids were cheering louder than anyone else, and it wasn't phony, mocking cheering—it was gut–busting, soul–driving, powerful cheering.

Why the change? Why did they suddenly stop mocking him and start cheering him? We don't know, but we can guess. We can imagine that the spectators may have recognized that this man was doing everything he could just to finish the race. He was putting every effort, every bit of energy he could muster to keep on going, and it was this energy and spirit that they understood and recognized and admired and cheered. The man was still handicapped, but his spirit rose above it all and made his physical impairment inconsequential.

Comment 1

Our two examples reveal that coping with powerful As (whether they be traumatic childhood events or physical handicaps) uncovers an important principle about people. After offering these two examples to our clients, we often explain the principles by giving them the handout, "Why As Aren't Everything."

Counteracting the importance of A can be very therapeutic in itself, particularly for clients who have had to cope with severe environmental or physical handicaps. Posttraumatic stress disorder victims often have to cope with feelings of helplessness; this is caused by having been exposed to forces beyond their control. For such people, a few short examples are not sufficient to overcome the thought that the As are just too powerful to be coped with. Therapists may find it ben-

HANDOUT: WHY As AREN'T EVERYTHING

Ultimately the greatest payoff for being human is not in having a
wonderful childhood, winning a race, or living a calm, tranquil life.
Nor is it based on heaps of money, fame, more pleasure than pain, or
the promised reward of a better life hereafter. The real payoff may be
in pouring all of our being into reaching a goal, whether it is winning
a race, or accepting a horrible childhood, or living through a traumatic event. The immature human only sees the immediate gain or
loss in each situation, but the person who knows the pain of life
seeks the long-term reward. The reward for Anna and the marathon
man is grander than the immediate reinforcement of the moment. It
is the ultimate payoff of using all of our energy, all of our ability, all of
our strength for one grand final push, striving for a goal until we
reach it or we die trying. The goal is irrelevant, and reaching it is as
well; it's the striving that counts.

eficial to assign books that illustrate human beings overcoming adversity by changing and enhancing their beliefs (see section on further information for some examples).

Homework

At the end of the A–B–C sessions, we give all clients the homework assignment on p. 29. No matter what additional homework is assigned, they continue this homework throughout the rest of the counseling

Comment

There is a danger that therapists should be aware of while teaching the A–B–C theory and the power of belief—some clients may overdo it. Suggestible clients, with the aid of unscrupulous counselors, media hype, or wishful thinking, may come to believe that humans can control everything simply by exercising the power of the mind.

This happened to Johnny, an adolescent client I saw years ago. He had been a member of a quasi–religious cult that taught only one principle: You can control anything with your mind.

"Virtually anything," he reported. The elders of the cult had told him that he could acquire everything he wanted if he learned to control his thoughts. He could change the weather, gain great wealth, stop wars, cure famine—anything at all. All he needed was to have faith and to believe that he could.

Johnny spent a year testing the principle; he tried to stop his tennis elbow from acting up, he strove to materialize ham sandwiches when he was hungry. Of course, he didn't succeed. When he went back to the elders, suggesting that perhaps they were wrong, they shook their heads and said he didn't have enough faith. They insisted, "You must have absolutely *no* doubt whatsoever. If you doubt even a little, this uncertainty will obliterate your power." They also expressed their disappointment that he was not turning out to be the type of novitiate they had hoped for.

Johnny went out and tried again, this time even harder. No ham sandwiches appeared, and he became poorer rather than richer because of all of his donations to the cult. As for his tennis elbow, he had stopped noticing the pain when the migraine headaches he began getting grabbed his attention.

For two years Johnny tried to find sufficient faith to make his thoughts powerful enough, but he never succeeded. Because he felt

HOMEWORK

Name _____

If you wish to try to help yourself with the material given to you in counseling, the first step is to learn to distinguish As, Bs, and Cs. In practice, people find the C first, then the A, and lastly the B. Each day, do the following:

1. Identify the strongest negative emotion you have had during the last 24 hours. You may have had many, but choose the strongest. Look for emotions such as fear, sadness, or anger. Allow yourself to focus on the emotion. Let it emerge until you can feel it distinctly but at a low level.

2. Next, search for the A. What was occurring right before you felt the emotion? Be sure not to include any of your thoughts at this point. An A is what a sound motion picture camera would pick up if it were observing the scene. The camera wouldn't interpret what it saw; it would simply record it.

   To find the As, you may need to pinpoint the exact time that you felt the emotion. If the time is not readily apparent, review your activities for the last 24 hours. Begin when you woke up and visualize in detail what you did. Keep reviewing the day until you first noticed the emotion. When you find the correct time, review everything going on around you when you were feeling the emotion. What were you looking at? What sounds did you hear? Were there any smells or tastes present? Were there any internal sensations you were having right before the emotion occurred, such as an upset stomach, or an arm pain, or a feeling of dizziness?

3. Finally, find the B. What did you tell yourself in the situation that caused you to feel the emotion? In most cases you will have told yourself many things. Try to find them all. In time you will have a list of your most common beliefs, but for now you will have to guess. You will know that you've found the right belief if the thought serves as a bridge between the A and C. If you can imagine everyone with that belief feeling the same emotion then you are probably correct. If someone would have had the thought but wouldn't feel the emotion, then you haven't found the right belief.

4. Continue to do the above procedure. Survey your emotions for a week or more. Later, when you feel a strong emotion, find the A-B-C. Record what you find. Over time you will discover that the same situations, beliefs, and emotions keep showing up. You will then be able to find your patterns of thinking.

guilty for failing, he sought counseling. I told him that the elders' ideas were absurd. Thoughts are indeed powerful, but not that powerful. The elders had twisted cognitive therapy beyond all recognition.

I wrote out the following response for Johnny and discussed it with him.

> Every human being lives in two spheres—the inside and the outside. What happens in one sphere *cannot* influence the other unless you build a bridge connecting the two. Your thoughts are in the inside sphere—that is, they are inside your body. Your beliefs and attitudes can influence anything that is also occurring inside your body. Since your spinal cord connects your brain to various bodily systems, your thoughts can be very powerful. Your thoughts can produce changes in your digestive system and cause stomach problems; your respiratory system and produce asthma or hyperventilation; your cardiovascular system and accelerate your heart or blood pressure; your endocrine system and secrete hormones that produce panic, rage, or despair; your defense and lymphatic system and reduce your ability to withstand disease and infections; your muscular system and cause migraine headaches or low back pain; or your reproductive system and make you aroused or impotent.
>
> But your brain is not connected to ham sandwiches, the stock market, unlimited bank accounts, weather systems, or the combined military–industrial complex of nations. These things are in the second sphere (outside of you) and all the thinking or wishing (inside of you) won't change this sphere.
>
> If you want to change the outside sphere and make a difference on this planet, you had best build a bridge—a bridge between your inside and your outside. And you already have one. It's called behavior and it means action. It may take the form of physical energy, speaking, or writing. Unlike the mind–power drivel, your methods of affecting your world are not dramatic, exciting, or quick, but they do accomplish results. To achieve power, you have to be willing to put away mind games and get down to some hard, concrete work.

Further Information

Spangler, Simons, Monroe, and Thase (1997) found that As (negative life events) were not a crucial factor in how well clients succeeded with cognitive therapy.

Some of the great classics in literature are based on people's ability to surmount overpowering forces by changing beliefs. The therapist can make his or her own selections, but we are impressed with *Man's Search for Meaning* by Victor Frankl (1980) (Frankl's logotherapy is one of the precursors to cognitive therapy) and *The Diary of Anne Frank*. Many novels and stories are inspirational because they describe how humanity can rise above their As.

LEARNING THE CONCEPTS
Principles

One hour a week of explaining cognitive principles to clients is hardly sufficient to improve the efficacy of cognitive therapy, especially if clients continue to think in their former ways for the other 167 hours of the week. For the cognitive approach to be understood and retained, clients need to practice the new type of thinking after they leave your office. We have found several methods effective in improving clients' retention of the material.

Method 1. Client Manuals

We give manuals to all clients who attend individual or group sessions. They are very helpful—almost essential, in fact—in reinforcing the ideas presented in the sessions. Informal surveys show that clients double their retention of session material when they can review it in corresponding manuals. You may use published manuals (Figure 1.2) or those of other therapists. You may find it is most helpful to create your own manuals that more closely reflect your own counseling style.

We wrote these manuals (in Figure 1.2) to address different client problems. *Talk Sense to Yourself* (Mc Mullin & Casey, 1975) and its Spanish translation (Mc Mullin, Casey, & Navas, 1977) addresses general adult anxiety and depression. *Straight Talk to Parents* was written for parents having difficulty with their children (Mc Mullin, Assafi, & Chapman, 1978). *The Lizard* is a beginning manual that discusses alcohol problems (Mc Mullin, Gehlhaar, & James, 1990). The fifth manual is more advanced and for addicts and alcoholics (Mc Mullin & Gehlhaar, 1990a). These manuals parallel our individual and group sessions; if a session covered methods of changing damaging beliefs, the client is told to read the manual's section on eliminating an irrational thought.

All of the manuals are written in the same style. They cover the most important points of each therapeutic session and they are interactive in a program–learning fashion so that the client can practice what has been presented in therapy. They are short (50 pages or less) and they include as many illustrations and cartoons as could be managed.

Method 2. Outside Readings

With the financial limitations presently placed on therapeutic sessions by HMOs, it is essential that clients learn as much information as they can outside of the counseling hour. Self-help books can save valuable session time for both therapists and clients. Unlike the manuals, they don't provide a step–by–step outline of in–session material; they do provide more detailed information about some concepts or exercises that can be better digested outside of the therapeutic hour. Because of this, therapists often assign both the manuals and a chapter from an appropriate self–help book for the next session. Other therapists may have their own favorites, but over the years our clients have nominated the following cognitively–oriented self–help books as the most beneficial.

Ranked first is one of the most popular self–help books published. Written by Albert Ellis and Robert Harper, the book now has three editions: *A Guide to Rational Living* (Ellis & Harper, 1961), and its revisions, *A New Guide to Rational Living*, 2nd Edition (1975), and *A Guide to Rational Living*, 3rd Edition (1998). Ranked second is one of the first books that explained to the public some basic principles of cognitive therapy—*Your Erroneous Zones* (Dyer, 1993). Number 3 presents a combinations of different cognitive approaches—*Feeling Good: The New Mood Therapy* (Burns, 1980, 1989). Number 4 is a newer book by Dr. Ellis—

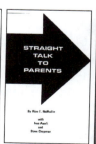

FIGURE 1.2 Client manuals

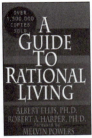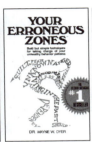

FIGURE 1.3 Most popular self-help books

How to Stubbornly Refuse to Make yourself Miserable about Anything, Yes, Anything (Ellis, 1988a). Number 5 is a specialist book for marital counseling that was not generally popular but that our marital therapy clients liked—*A Guide to Successful Marriage* (Ellis & Harper, 1961).

Method 3. Multimedia, Audio, Videotapes, Cartoons, and Computer Programs

When teaching the A–B–Cs and other aspects of cognitive therapy, therapists should use as many learning aids as possible. A client's ability to comprehend and retain verbal material is limited, but if the therapist transforms the information into visual cues, retention is increased. This section that you're reading illustrates this principle; instead of simply listing the bibliographic references to manuals, self-help books, slides, and cartoons, I have shown the actual illustrations. With these visual cues is it not easier to remember what was read?

Slides. The key points of all the therapeutic sessions can be put on slides. The *Cognitive Restructuring Therapy Package, Revised* (Casey & Mc Mullin, 1976, 1985) illustrates 54 slides used in our group sessions.

Video and audiotapes. One of the best sources for audio and videotapes is the Albert Ellis Institute for Rational Emotive Behavior Therapy, 45 E. 65th St., New York, NY 10021, (800) 323–4738, E-mail: orders@rebt.org.

The American Psychological Association offers many useful books, films, and tapes. See their website: http://apa.org/books/.

Cartoons. You can identify the key concepts of your therapy and capture them in succinct cartoons that will significantly help your client remember your concepts. Long after what you've said about a particular subject has been forgotten, your cartoon will be remembered and will help clients cope with troublesome situations. Our clients have reported that the following cartoons (Figure 1.4) have been the most useful to them.

Computers. Therapists can also illustrate their concepts through the use of computers. Computers now accompany most of our individual and all of our group sessions. Computers have the advantage of being more flexible than other teaching methods; for individual therapy sessions, the therapist can have a second monitor for clients to view the therapist's concepts and their own responses immediately. For group therapy we generally run the whole session from a laptop computer connected either to an LCD projector or to a large-screen TV through a TV scan converter. The therapist can use an electronic marker to illustrate the main points shown on the screen.

Computer software, such as "Ideas that Make You Feel," by Martin Sandry (1992), is available to help clients learn concepts. Therapists can also create their own programs by using a scanner and digital camera. Scanning self-help manuals, cartoons, homework assignments, or key principles of their therapy for clients to review on their own computers can also be helpful.

One of the major benefits of using computers in therapy is that it saves the therapist's time and the client's money. If a computer with an interactive program is placed in the therapist's waiting room, clients can learn certain key principles before or after a counseling session. Teaching clients as much as possible with computers reserves the more expensive therapy sessions for individualized instruction. For example, the principles discussed in the present chapter (basic formulas, A–B–C analysis, etc.) can be more readily taught to clients with a computer program than by the therapist, but the information in the chapters that follow (finding a client's specific Bs or selecting individual cognitive change techniques) is better covered in face–to–face sessions.

Clients can also use computers to practice some of the cognitive change techniques. Clients can carry palmtop computers to monitor their thoughts, to practice their counters (see chapters 6 and 7), or to prompt the use of certain cognitive restructuring techniques (see Newman, Kenardy, Herman, & Taylor, 1997).

Comment

The learning methods presented are adjuncts to therapy; they do not replace the necessary encounter between the therapist and the client.

FIGURE 1.4. Therapeutic cartoons (1. Mc Mullin & Casey, 1975; 2. Mc Mullin & Gehlhaar, 1990a; 3. Mc Mullin, Assafi, & Chapman, 1978; 4. Mc Mullin, Gehlhaar, & James, 1990)

Further Information

Neimeyer and Feixas (1990) found that clients who were required to do homework with their cognitive therapy did better than clients who had the same therapy without homework.

Newman and colleagues (1997) effectively used palmtop computers with panic–disorder clients and found the results comparable to regular cognitive behavioral therapy. Computers have been shown to aid in the implementation of a number of cognitive restructuring techniques (Buglione, DeVito, & Mulloy, 1990; Chandler, Burck, Sampson, & Wray, 1988; Selmi, Klein, Greist, Sorrell, & Erdman, 1990).

Extensive research has been done on the effectiveness of manuals and self–help books (known as bibliotherapy) as an adjunct to the client's regular therapeutic sessions (see Gould, Clum, & Shapiro, 1993; Jamison & Scogin, 1995; Scogin, Jamison, & Davis, 1990; Smith, Floyd, Scogin, & Jamison, 1997; Wehrly, 1998).

Possibly the best guide to good self–help books is *The Authoritative Guide to Self-Help Books* (Santrock, Minnett, & Campbell, 1994). It not only lists the books but also rates their usefulness. For some of the best books out now, see Ellis (1995), Ellis and Lange (1995), Ellis and Tafrate (1997), Freeman and Dewolf (1993), and Freeman, Dewolf, and Beck (1992).

Michael Free (1999) has 12–session multimedia psychoeducation program. His book contains all the materials needed to conduct the group: overheads, homework, fully scripted mini–lectures, exercises, guidelines for checking homework, handouts, and masters for visual resources that can be directly photocopied.

TWO

Finding the Beliefs

THE BASIC A–B–C FORMULA is simple. What is not simple is having clients apply it to their lives. Clients experience the greatest difficulty with finding the correct B. Many clients pick the first cognition that could be even vaguely connected to their emotions, and they then spend their time and energy trying to change it. Later they may discover that they have wasted their efforts because they picked the wrong thought.

To find the correct cognitions, clients first need to learn that B stands for many types of internal processes. Bs are not just a subvocal language or images that clients generate. These are Bs, but Bs are also much more. To give clients even a rough idea of the diverse types of cognitions Bs encompass, we hand out the following list.

- Self–talk
- Self–efficacy
- Perception
- Selective attention
- Selective inattention
- Attributions
- Labels (words and phrases)
- Explanations
- Explanatory style
- Categories
- Cognitive maps
- Self–demands
- Life themes
- Mental associations
- Cognitive conditioning
- Self–concept
- Images
- Selective memory
- Gestalt patterns
- Themes and stories
- Superstitions, imaginations, judgments
- Conclusions
- Self–instruction
- Assumptions
- Reifications

- Internal scripts
- Prototypes
- ICMs (idealized cognitive models)
- Personalized myths
- Informational processing
- Neural networks

- Linguistical prototypes
- Pattern connections
- Brain organization
- Cognitive schemas
- Gestaltens
- Primal modes

Therapists can help clients make sense of this long list of labels by explaining that these Bs all occur at different times. Like dominoes falling, each one of these mental processes triggers the next one until they gather enough force to cause clients to feel a certain emotion or act in a particular way.

$$\frac{A \qquad\qquad C_e \quad C_b}{B \quad B \quad B \quad B \quad B \quad B \quad B \quad B \quad B} \longrightarrow$$

A = activating events or stimuli
Bs = different kinds of beliefs and cognitions
Ce = emotional reaction—what we feel
Cb = behavioral reaction—what we do

EXPECTATIONS

Principles

Some Bs occur before the event (A) appears. They are often broad philosophies or ways of looking at the world that feed into how clients regard the event.

$$\text{———}|\text{———————— A ——————— } C_e \text{ ——— } C_b \text{ ——→}$$
B

Expectations

Expectations are what clients require of themselves, others, and the world itself. They are the slide rules that clients use to decide whether they succeed or fail, the demands they place on themselves about how well they should perform. Clients may have too high or too low expectations about themselves, about others, or about the world. When clients require that they reach what they expect, expectations become demands.

Often, unrealistic expectations are the sole cause of clients' emotional problems. Perfectionist clients make impossible demands and set their expectations so high that they can never measure up. These clients may always feel like failures. They may become suicidally depressed because they receive a grade lower than they were expecting in a class, or they may become terrified if they can't control certain internal processes. For example, the key expectation for many agoraphobics is: "I must keep from getting anxious, or if I get anxious I must reduce it right away." Other clients endure constant anger because they expect everyone to act in a just and rational way and then get angry when people don't. Some depressed clients' expectations are so low that they give up any endeavor without trying.

Before an A even takes place, clients enter the event carrying a heavy load of expectations and demands that will determine whether they view the A as good or bad, a success or failure, positive or negative. The intrinsic worth of the A is unimportant; it is assessed only through the colored glasses of clients' expectations.

Method

1. Have clients focus on a problem situation and imagine it until it is sensed clearly.
2. Have them decide what the best outcome could be for the situation, and ask them to record their answer on a ten-point scale. The scale is anchored by what clients imagine the best and the worst things are that could happen in their life. For example, winning a Nobel prize (10) could be compared to being diagnosed with terminal cancer (0).

(0) |_____|_____| (10)
worst life event   (5)   best life event
(Draw this for the client.)

3. Have clients imagine the best and worst possible outcomes in the problem situation and mark their scores on the scale.

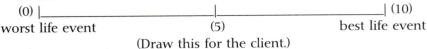
worst outcome   best outcome

4. Have your clients decide where the just-reasonably-acceptable (JRA) point is. Explain JRA as, "What outcome would you consider just reasonably acceptable—the minimum necessary for you to consider the event barely positive."

worst outcome   JRA   best outcome

5. Finally, have your client fill out a variety of scales for different problem situations using the same procedure. You will then be able to
establish what expectations, self-demands, or entitlements they are
using to judge themselves and others.

These scales will establish the various points on the client's slide
rule of expectations. Observe how the client's measuring scale differs
from most people who have faced similar situations. For example, the
following scales show various distortions.

All–or–nothing Thinking

worst   best

The end points on the scale are too far apart, too extreme. There is
a large difference between the best and worst possible outcome.
Clients who score in this way often catastrophize and dramatize. They
believe that either something wonderful or something terrible will
happen, even in mundane situations. For example, a pre-med student
faced with getting a B minus in a chemistry course imagines not getting into medical school and spending the rest of his life wandering in
city alleys eating out of garbage cans.

Depressed Thinking

worst   best

This scale is too narrow—both scores are in the negative zone.
Some depressed clients see little difference between the worst and best
outcome. For these clients even the best outcomes are negative; there
is little to motivate them to strive to achieve their goals.

Perfectionist Thinking

|_____X_____|_____ JRA ___X_____|

The JRA is too far to the right, and almost equivalent to the best
outcome. This scale is symptomatic of perfectionist clients, who allow
no room for error. If they don't get the best, they feel like failures.
Also consider whether your clients would draw the scales differently for others than for themselves. For example, angry clients often

require others to achieve a much higher JRA (toward the best out-come). They demand better behavior from others in various situations than they expect of themselves.

Example

Having expectations that are too high can create lifelong problems. Years ago, my colleagues and I worked with a type of client whose prob-lem turned out to be quite baffling. These clients had strong feelings of inadequacy and very low self-esteem, and would attack themselves unmercifully. They believed themselves totally worthless and suffered from depression so strong that they often contemplated suicide.

We had diagnosed these clients as having inadequate personalities, but informally among ourselves we often called these people "INPS" Clients ("I'm nothing but a piece of shit" clients). We were being nei-ther cruel nor cavalier; we simply believed the INPS label described the clients' problem more accurately. It wasn't that these clients were really inadequate people; it was that they thought they were.

Other therapists had tried to help them by attempting to boost their dismally low self-esteem, persuading them to like themselves and encouraging them to stop their self-attacks. Little worked.

A client named Al was a typical example. He thought he was totally rotten inside and couldn't find one positive thing about himself that he liked. He believed himself ugly despite the fact that women kept chatting with him and making passes. He thought he was uncaring, but on the weekends he took out fatherless boys for the Big Brothers organization.

His negative attitude caused him a great deal of pain and produced insomnia and hypersomnia. He became antihedonic, had recurring crying spells, and frequently thought about suicide, which he had attempted twice.

Al's self-perceptions were totally irrational, but even more confus-ing was the way that he responded to any attempt to change his atti-tude. He generally acted weak and passive, but when therapists tried to reform his belief he would fight them as hard as he could, relin-quishing his wimpy, passive demeaner and fighting any suggestion that he wasn't a totally worthless individual. At times he became hos-tile and aggressive toward the idea that he might be adequate, insist-ing and even demanding that he was worthless. He simply wouldn't tolerate any suggestion that he wasn't one of the most despicable human beings on the planet.

This client's belief was a puzzle. He was in a great deal of pain and knew that it was his attitude that was causing it, yet he did everything he could to hold on to his self-depreciating belief.

The problem was finally resolved by identifying Al's expectation of himself. His core philosophy was that he was an Einstein. This was not just a wish but a firmly felt attitude. He became upset when other people treated him as an ordinary mortal; it bothered him when he had to do such mundane things as balancing his checkbook or taking out the garbage.

What bothered Al more than anything was his own discouragement about himself. Every time he made a mistake he would attack himself unmercifully for making stupid errors, until after a while he was consumed by depression and turned into an INPS.

"It's bad enough for anyone to make mistakes," he would say, "but it's intolerable for me (an Einstein) to keep making them."

What's more despairing than a person with the capacity of an Einstein living the life of an ordinary mortal and having no one in the world recognize his exceptional worth?

Friends unwittingly fed Al's attitude by trying to boost his ego; this simply raised his expectation even further, making the contrast between his real and ideal self even larger. The result was that Al felt more depressed.

Al believed he was inferior because of his self-demand and self-expectation; he knew that his real achievements in life didn't measure up on his perfectionist expectations. Each time he attacked himself he reinforced his belief that he really was an Einstein, albeit an Einstein who kept messing up. From his perspective, if he stopped the self-attack he would be admitting that he wasn't special.

The approach we took in counseling was not to prop up his flagging ego, but rather to focus on his belief that he was an Einstein.

Comment

Cognitive restructuring therapy differs from other cognitive approaches in that it is crucial to gather the list of client beliefs, attitudes, and philosophies first. Only after the list is complete should the belief systems be challenged; any earlier challenge will prompt the client to defend them, argue against the therapist, and be far more reticent about telling the therapist any more of his or her private expectations. This results in an inaccurate or incomplete list of the client's self-demands.

The therapist should remember that the placements of Bs on the timeline are more descriptive than theoretically precise. Self demands and many other Bs can be placed at other locations; some Bs, such as self–concept, may exist all along the timeline.

Further Information

Safren, Juster, & Heimberg (1997) discovered that expectations are crucial to various forms of cognitive psychotherapy. Whittal & Goetsch (1997) found that the expectation of suffering a panic attack was significantly related to agoraphobia.

Some early studies support the importance of expectations on the effectiveness of reinforcement (Farber, 1963; Gholson, 1980; Spielberger & DeNike, 1966; Weimer & Palermo, 1974). In these studies, reinforcement didn't change behavior unless the subjects' expectations were taken into account. If subjects expected a greater reinforcement than they received, they in turn treated the actual reward as a punishment.

SELF–EFFICACY

$$\text{———}|\text{———} \quad A \text{———————} C_e \text{———} C_b \text{———}\longrightarrow$$
$$B$$
$$\text{self–efficacy}$$

Principles

Alfred Bandura (1995) and his colleagues have noticed that clients' beliefs about succeeding are crucially important in determining whether clients reach their goals. What they accomplish is based on what they think they can accomplish. Efficacy is inversely related to expectations; expectations that are too high often lead to a reduced sense of being able to accomplish goals—low self–efficacy. Clients judge that they do not have the power to reach their own high demands.

Most of the literature on self–efficacy emphasizes the damage of low self–efficacy, but in recent years self–efficacy that is too high has been targeted as equally damaging. Examples of this variety are alcohol– and drug–dependent clients who mistakenly believe that they have the ability to control the use of drugs ("I can stop after a couple of drinks") and psychotic patients who believe themselves able to control their hallucinations through willpower alone.

Method

1. Have the client relax and focus on a particular A–C problem situation.
2. Ask the client to predict his or her ability to successfully solve the situation. Have him or her place the prediction on a continuum. (You may use the same continuums drawn for expectations.)

|_____|_____X___|
low chance of success   high chance of success

"I am 90% certain I can control my anger even when my wife yells at me."

3. Tell the client to switch the prediction and notice how it changes the feeling. For example, "Imagine that you were only 10% sure that you wouldn't hit your wife when you got angry. How would you feel then about continuing your arguments with her, and what would you feel about your past assaults?"
4. Go through a variety of situations to establish the client's mean self–efficacy. Is it too low or too high?

Example: The Story of Mike

This case is a good example of self–efficacy that is too high.

A client, Mike, could not maintain good relationships with women and had a history of failed love encounters. Despite possessing some skills and much creativity, he wasn't successful at work because he refused to do the menial tasks concomitant in any position; he would usually be fired. He had emotional problems that were initially minor but built into powerful upheavals because he was incapable of tolerating even the smallest frustration. Mike felt like an emotional mess.

Mike's problems had many causes, but a major contributor was inappropriate self–efficacy. He was the youngest in a large family, and his mother had suffered two miscarriages prior to his birth. The doctor had warned her that bearing another child might kill her, but she liked motherhood and desperately wanted one more child. To the surprise of his father, mother, and the medical profession, Mike was born. His mother then had a hysterectomy assuring that he was her last.

Mike was an attractive baby and was treated like a prince by every–

one in the family—particularly his mother. When Mike started to form his self-efficacy, he looked in the mirror his family was holding and saw the reflection of a special child, adored by his family and treated as royalty. He knew nothing about his mother's miscarriages, her hysterectomy, or that he was the last child possible. All he knew was that he was not like other boys; he saw himself as a unique gift from God.

Life was pleasing for Mike until he went to school, where the other children treated him like a normal human being rather than a prince. His schoolmates didn't need him as his family did, but he didn't understand this. All he knew was that he wasn't receiving special treatment. He got angry with his peers and demanded that they serve him properly, but this further enraged them, so they teased and ridiculed him. He became the brunt of their practical jokes. This just made Mike feel worse; he became angrier and made more demands. Soon a vicious cycle had developed until Mike had no friends at all. He became a social isolate.

The treatment Mike received from his classmates might have made him wonder whether there was something wrong at home, but it didn't. Instead Mike concluded that something was wrong at school. He decided that his schoolmates were jealous of him because they recognized how special he was and how inferior they were.

He continued this way throughout his life. When his girlfriends didn't treat him as his mom had, it was obvious to him what was wrong—wrong girlfriend! He spent most of his adult years searching for a woman who had enough sense to treat him properly; he never found her. He once told me, "With women's liberation, it's really hard to find a good woman nowadays."

When Mike experienced normal fears, frustrations, and petty annoyances, his reaction was one of rage. "It's unfair that life is so hard on me; something is wrong; it shouldn't be this way. I have the right to get everything I want!" When a sales clerk did not wait on him immediately he would throw a temper tantrum and walk out of the store.

Mike's problem was fairly clear. He had what I call the "Prince in Disguise Syndrome"—he believed that he had special power and was entitled to extraordinary treatment from the world. His self-efficacy was so high, distorted, and unrealistic that it kept him from accepting the normal frustrations that we all have to deal with. Instead of coping, he just sat there feeling cheated. His attitude was created by the warped sense of self-efficacy he had learned from his family.

Comment

Because they are closely connected, self–efficacy is usually discussed with self–expectation; they are synergetically related. For example, high expectation low self–efficacy is one of the most damaging combinations. Depressed clients often have very high self–demands accompanied by little hope that they can achieve them.

In practice, we often have patients rate both variables on the same continuum as shown below.

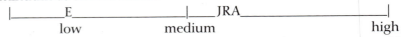

|_____E_____|___JRA_____|
low   medium   high

"Show me on the scale what you would consider a just–reasonably–acceptable result (JRA). Now mark down what result you think you can achieve (efficacy)." Clients who viewed their problems in this way would feel despondent. They would see little reason to try since their expectation of success was so far from an outcome that would be even minimally acceptable.

Further Information

Albert Bandura researched the concept of self–efficacy and is the major theorist and writer in the area. See Bandura (1977a, 1977b, 1978, 1982, 1984, 1995, 1997; Bandura, Adams, Hardy, & Howells, 1980; Bandura, Reese, & Adams, 1982; Bandura & Schunk, 1981; Schwarzer, 1992). Some behaviorists have argued that self–efficacy is concomitant with goal–directed behavior, but not a cause (Hawkins, 1992; Hayes 1995). Bandura counter–argues that self–efficacy is a central and important determinant of human behavior (Bandura, 1996).

SELF–CONCEPT

self-concept

Principles

Self–efficacy and expectations can be grouped into what has traditionally been called self–concept. There is probably no need to include self–concept as a separate category since its components combine the two Bs of self–efficacy and expectations, but the literature and history of this variable are so massive that it does deserve a separate listing.

A person's self-concept precedes environmental stimuli. It is one of the most powerful Bs that determines how people act, and a key determinant of whether they feel that their lives are happy or miserable.

Emergence of Self-Concept

Developmental psychology suggests that the self-concept emerges gradually during infancy. Infants' worlds begin as a bizarre, buzzing confusion. They have instincts that cause them to grab, suck, cry, or wet, but not much else, and their self-idea and perception of the environment are merged into one aggregate; Mommy and baby are one, the bottle and hand are one. There are few separations.

As babies begin to differentiate the outside world, they break things down into Mommy and not-Mommy—then Daddy, nasty older brother, and Pat the cat come along. The rest of humanity emerges as "none of the above."

Carried along with this other awareness, a different type of cognizance emerges—the self. Initially the self is just another object that infants begin to notice—an amorphous mass of hunger, sounds, strange smells, and movements whose impressions seem closer to them than other things in their environment. Infants don't have the concept that these things belong to them. Eventually, these closer things start gathering around a concept we later call "self." Other sensations are separated into not-self.

As the self-concept emerges, other aspects are gathered, including emotions. "This thing called self is fearful, happy, hungry, or angry." Of course infants don't have these words, but the feelings are present and are identified as belonging to them rather than to someone else.

While the child is still at a young age, a very important thing takes place: the self starts gathering an overall value. Children start placing a positive or negative worth on this self: "This is a good self. This is a bad self. This is a flawed self. Others have better selves. This is an evil self. This self has merit. This self is worthless. This self is sick."

This valuing process is crucial, because children start acting according to the value they have assigned themselves. If they judge the self as bad, they start acting badly. If they think they are incompetent, they act incompetently. Instead of passively responding to the environment, this valued self starts changing the environment and reaffirming itself. For example, the incompetent self withholds effective action, fails on more tasks, and views these failures as further evidence of incompetence. Over time these ratings become self-fulfilling prophecies.

The value clients have assigned to themselves can have huge staying power, and can last throughout their life unless they actively do something to change it. Their value becomes the central structure through which they filter all they feel, think, do.

Where does this rating come from? How do they form their self-worth? There is one probable answer. People learn their value by absorbing the rating of others. When they are children they cannot accurately appraise their own merit; at 7 or 8, children are not capable of making an objective judgment. So those around them are the mirrors through which they judge who they are. Others show them what they are worth or not worth. If their important others accept them, they judge themselves as worthwhile and the self becomes acceptable. But if these others treat them as if they are evil or bad, they interpret themselves as evil and that the evilness lives inside them.

It is at this point that the problem occurs. If others don't judge accurately, children's perceptions of their self-worth are distorted. Parents' insecurities and problems may cause a perverted or warped reflection. The child is too young and inexperienced to know that their important other's mirror isn't accurate. A child does not deduce, "I am not a bad child. My mother spanked me because she is a histrionic personality who is upset because she is no longer the center of attention." The spanked child will naturally conclude that something is wrong with him, not with his mother. In the end, the child accepts what is reflected back as true, and adopts this distorted view of self.

Method

Although there are many measures of self-concept that may be of some use, probably the more valuable method for the cognitive therapist is to abstract the self-concept from the list of Bs gathered from the client.

1. Complete the client's master list of beliefs (discussed in chapter 3).
2. Select the Bs that directly refer to self.
3. Find the positive or negative valence the client reveals with each of these beliefs. For example, the B, "The world is a big and dangerous place," demonstrates a self-concept of, "I am weak and helpless." This attitude would be negative self-valence.

Example: The Story of Cynthia

Cynthia was born into a dysfunctional family, and when she started to form her self-concept at around age 7, the family was in a constant state of uproar. Her father was an alcoholic and sexually abused her when he was on one of his binges. Her brother was a cocaine addict and beat her when he was going through his withdrawal rages. Her mother was an enabler who kept the family together by minimizing all of the problems and pretending not to notice that the family was blowing up around her. The mother felt totally worthless as a human being and clung to only one principle—keep the family together, no matter what.

Cynthia's self-concept formed in this terrible environment. She concluded, as most children would, that there was something horribly wrong with her. "I must be one of the worst people on the planet to be treated so badly," she thought.

As outside observers, we can see that Cynthia was wrong. We know it wasn't her fault that she was beaten, abused, and ignored. We know that her family was pathological. But Cynthia didn't see it this way. Her only mirror was the reflection her family gave her. Therefore, her self-concept was distorted.

When her father sexually abused her, she assumed that she was to blame. When she later learned about sex, she decided that she must have been a bad, evil girl—a slut, cheap and dirty. The one time she talked to her mother about her dad's abuse, her mother told her that she was lying, that she was not to make a big thing of it, and to shut up. Cynthia couldn't have understood that her mother was in the terminal stages of denial, that she could only survive by pretending everything was fine.

Cynthia didn't know that her family's sickness had twisted her view of herself; she didn't know that her family was dysfunctional. Seven years old and on the receiving end of mountains of hate, disgust, and abuse, she concluded that she was the cause of it all.

This mistaken self-perception was built on and enhanced over the years. She had survived by turning off her emotional switches and becoming stoical. The family, achieving a level of perversion that only chemically dependent families can reach, judged her demeanor as strength. Not having any other person with even the appearance of strength, the family turned to her for support. She became the family's hero and head nurse; she was substitute wife for the father, confidante for the mother, parent to her brother—all at the age of 14. She sacrificed her adolescence in a doomed attempt to keep her disintegrating family together; by the time she was 22, she had made three suicide attempts.

Clients' views of themselves are at their cognitive centers; they are what makes them tick. Through their self-image they see all the world and all the people in it, and it is this view that can make life happy or turn it into a private concentration camp.

Comment

In the discussion of expectations, self–efficacy, and self–concept, I have mentioned that clients can have too high as well as too low self–esteem. While it is difficult for some professionals to accept that clients can have erroneously high self–esteem, Martin E. P. Seligman offers a meaningful discussion about some of its effects:

> Feelings of self–esteem in particular, and happiness in general, develop as side effects—of mastering challenges, working suc-cessfully, overcoming frustration and boredom, and winning. The feeling of self–esteem is a byproduct of doing well. Once a child's self–esteem is in place, it kindles further success. Tasks flow more seamlessly, troubles bounce off, and other children seem more receptive. There is no question that feeling high self–esteem is a delightful state to be in, but trying to achieve the feeling side of self–esteem directly, before achieving good commerce with the world, confuses profoundly the means and the end.
>
> This is just what makes the California report on self–esteem so gaseous. It is true that many school dropouts feel low self–esteem, many pregnant teenagers feel sad; many young drug addicts and criminals feel self–loathing, and many people on welfare feel unworthy. But what is cause and what is effect? The California report, with its "vaccine" recommendations, claims that the feelings of low self–worth cause the school failures, the drug use, the dependence on welfare, and other social ills. But the research literature shows just the opposite. Low self–esteem is a consequence of failing in school, of being on welfare, of being arrested—not the cause. (Seligman, Reivich, Jayucox, & Gillham, 1995, pp. 33–34)

Further Information

Seligman has done extensive work on the positive and negative effects of self–concept to develop his theory of learned helplessness and learned optimism (Seligman, 1975, 1994, 1998; Seligman, Reivich, Jayucox, & Gillham, 1995). Bromley (1977) explores the development of the self. Guidano has been one of the major cognitive theorists examining self-concept from a developmental perspective (Guidano, 1987, 1991; Guidano & Liotti, 1983). In addition, Carl Rogers (1951, 1959) and George Kelly (1955, 1980) made self-concept the core of their theories.

ATTENTION

attention

Principles

Some cognitions precede environmental triggers while others follow them. But attention is the type of cognition that occurs at the same time that the A occurs. In fact, this type of mental process helps decide what is and what is not an A.

People's identification of As is based on which elements they focus on and which they ignore. The raw information received through their senses is a myriad of sights, sounds, smells, tastes, and feelings—viewed alone, these are random and incomprehensible. Their brains make sense out of this kaleidoscope of data by forming raw stimuli into patterns.

People's brains tell them what to see and what not to, which sound to pick out from the masses of sounds, which smell to identify, which taste to ignore, and which physical sensation will alarm them. If their brains choose to disregard some incoming information from their senses then the information ceases to exist for them. What affects them from the outside world is based on what their brains have told them to pay attention to.

Method

1. Instruct your clients to create a mental picture of what is bothering them the next time that they feel upset. If they can they should make a sketch of the key components.
2. Next, direct them to create another mental picture with a different focus. This will be difficult, because they will want to keep returning to their first image. Encourage them to keep practicing, to keep changing their focus. After a while they may discover that what they see is fairly arbitrary and based on what they choose to see.

Example

I asked an agoraphobic woman who was afraid of leaving her house to draw what it was like when she left her territory. (Figure 2.1).

Her drawing illustrates how she perceived herself and what she focused on. When she tried to leave her house, she felt trapped, as if she were in a box. The box would get smaller as she traveled farther away from home, and the pressure would build until she feared exploding or going insane. She focused her attention on her anxiety and the feeling of being trapped. The more she focused on her body sensations, the more scared she became. This client was helped when she was able to shift her attention to the outside—the surrounding environment.

Comment

What clients attend to is one of the most difficult cognitions to discover. Most clients are unaware that there is anything else that they could focus on in a situation. They believe that the environment (either internal or external) is causing them to focus on things in the way that they do. They deny selecting what they attend to, or what they extract from the kaleidoscope of stimuli, and suggest that the stimuli force them to look and focus in the way that they do.

An anxious client automatically focuses on his fears the minute he

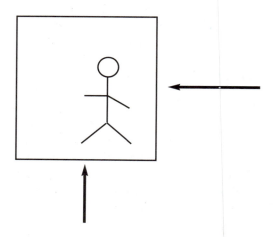

FIGURE 2.1 Drawing by agoraphobic client

feels the least bit of anxiety. A depressed client believes that once she experiences sadness and the sense of hopelessness, she can focus on nothing else. An angry patient says that his anger overwhelms him, making consequences and objectivity something he cannot think about. One of the first lessons to teach clients about attending behavior is that it is not forced upon them; they select it.

Further Information

Attentional processes are important in social cognitive theory (Bandura, 1977a, 1996) and modeling theory (Bandura & Barab, 1973). Chemtob, Hamada, Novaco, and Gross (1997) found that altering attentional focus was important in reducing anger in PTSD patients. Aaron Beck and his colleagues have discovered that attentional focusing is a major component in increasing anxiety and depression (Beck 1967, 1975, 1993; Beck, Emery, & Greenberg, 1985; Judith Beck, 1995, 1996).

SELECTIVE MEMORY

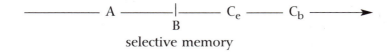

selective memory

Principles

The next cognition on the timeline occurs immediately after attending to the A. The human brain searches through long- and short-term memory to find any experience that may match what it is perceiving. While trying to interpret stimuli, clients subvocally ask themselves, "Have I seen something like this before? What did it turn out to be then? Was it dangerous, should I be alarmed?" This search is crucial. If clients have never encountered the stimulus or something like it before, they don't know how to react to it. They feel confused and alarmed until their memory scan finds a match.

The difficulty with memory is that it is highly selective and often grossly inaccurate. Memory is not like a storage box that holds snapshots of past events—recalling something is not the same as pulling out an album folder and searching through old photographs. When clients remember a past event they are recreating the past anew. It is their present impression of the past, not the actual past, that their memory search uncovers.

Clients' memories consist of millions of events, impressions, feelings, and thoughts. Their memories exist like a giant tapestry so large that they can only see parts of it. The part they focus on is always a very small piece of the total cloth, and what they recall is often biased depending upon what they desire to remember and what they wish to feel at the moment. Clients often select the most reinforcing memory for the situation at hand. If they feel angry, they choose to remember previous times when they got revenge. If they're lonely they recall the closeness and comfort they once had. If they feel weak they reminisce about the times they felt strong and exercised power, even if such a time never actually happened.

They call up from their memories the events that fit their current mood. Many clients who feel unhappy about the present choose to remember positive things from their past. Their childhood appears rosy: They remember the birthday presents, the romances, the achievements; they selectively forget the sicknesses, the disappointments, the broken hearts, and the pain.

Each time that clients remember, they change the past; they repaint what happened a long time ago with present brush strokes. The new picture is based on present feelings, thoughts, desires, and wishes. The actual past has long since ceased to exist for them; it disappeared in the distant past time and can no longer be accurately retrieved.

Some clients object to the idea that their picture of the past is based on present feelings, thoughts, desires, and wishes. They may ask, "Isn't the past the past, what happened, happened? How can I change something that doesn't exist anymore? Isn't the past total and complete just the way it is?"

Rationally this is true; the past is unalterable, but the client's memory of the past can be changed. The client's view of the past is quite incomplete. Nobody can remember things exactly the way they were—human memory is too poor for that, and is selective as well. We remember what we choose to remember and forget what we choose to forget.

Method 1

Explain the principles of selective memory to your clients. You may wish to offer a description similar to the handout on selective memory that we give to many of our clients.

Method 2

1. *Vague remembering.* Ask your clients to remember a past event, not to recall all of the details but simply to allow the overall memory of the event to emerge. Have them write down or audio record what they recall.
2. *Relaxation.* Next, have them relax. Teach them systematic relaxation, or have them listen to a nature tape or relaxing music.
3. *Meticulous remembering.* Have them imagine traveling back in time to the early scenes. Pick a specific scene to focus on. Tell them to use all of their senses to fill in the scene: Vision—what colors, lighting, objects, movements, perspective do they see? Sounds—can they hear people talking? Do they hear background sounds, music, people talking in the next room, traffic outside? Smells—what odors do they notice? Kinesthetic—are they moving or standing or lying down? Emotional—are the feelings happy? sad? angry? scared? In what combination and strength? Go through each step; don't jump ahead or generalize. Use as much detail as possible. Their memories may be stimulated by using aids such as photos, diaries, or letters. Remind them of what other events were happening at this time. Use any cues that may remind them of this earlier time.
4. *Record.* Jot down what they remembered.
5. *Compare* the first remembrance (vague remembering) with the last (meticulous remembering). What did they fail to remember? What did they forget?

Example

Clients' memories can be so inaccurate that they may recall events that never happened. One client spent many hours discussing the time her uncle sexually abused her when she was ten. When she did the meticulous remembering part of the exercise she recalled that her uncle had died before she was six. She had never actually been abused at all, but her best girlfriend had, and she had empathized so completely with her that she later imagined that it had happened to her.

Other clients remember an event that they read in a book or saw in a movie, but later forget the source and think it happened to them. There is a famous case of this type—Bridey Murphy (Bernstein & Barker, 1989). Under hypnosis she recalled living in Ireland in a previous lifetime. Some people checked her description of the Irish village

HANDOUT: SELECTIVE MEMORY

Whenever you start reminiscing about your past, about the great experiences you had in high school, about your first love or about the wonderful time you had living in Akron, Ohio, you had best be careful, because your memories may be fooling you. You may have created a fantasy that never existed because you selectively screened out all of the contrary themes, emotions, and experiences that did not fit with the mood you were trying to strike. Fooled by this distortion and taking it for the truth, you experience this fabricated past as real.

Sometimes your distorted memory of the past creates your present unhappiness. In such cases, the only way to become content in the present is to force yourself to remember the past more accurately. Only if you recall your history in the most unbiased, unprejudiced, dispassionate manner will the lessons of your early experiences be able to guide you.

It is best to choose your past carefully.

and found her reports to be amazingly accurate. Her case was used as evidence for reincarnation. Later a reporter discovered that she had learned these stories from an elderly woman who had lived in the Irish village as a child. When Bridey was five she had sat on the old woman's porch and listened to the old woman's stories about Ireland.

Clients have been taken back to their pasts by using age–regression hypnosis. They have revealed the details of some earlier events, such as a birthday party at age 7, or the first time they met a future spouse. Under hypnosis they reported the events in great detail, and were sure that their recall was accurate, but when their memories were checked against objective data such as photographs, diaries, or relatives' reports, the recall was found to be grossly inaccurate.

A client, Diane, remembered her first marriage with great fondness. She had been married four times, and spoke about how kind, hand–some and strong her first husband was. She spent years regretting the loss of the relationship and kept trying to find him. This regret had only begun after her fourth marriage was failing; before that time she hadn't thought about him at all. We checked with some of her old friends and found out that her first husband had been a horror. He drank much of the time, cheated on her constantly, couldn't hold down a job for more than a few months, wouldn't come home for days, and physically abused her.

How could she have failed to remember all of this?

When her fourth marriage was failing, she had tried to comfort her–self by recalling at least one good relationship in her life. Since she hadn't had one, she created one in her memory. She recalled only the few good things about her first husband and had totally forgotten the many bad things.

Comment

Memory work may be traumatic for clients because of the powerful emotions that are often associated with earlier experiences. In the begin–ning stages of cognitive therapy, the purpose is only to collect memories rather than to examine them carefully or attempt to change them.

Further Information

Mark Williams (1996a, 1996b) is one of the major authors empha–sizing the importance of memory in cognitive therapy. He broadens the concept into four types: fact, behavioral, event, and prospective memory. Our emphasis here is most similar to what he calls semantic memory, where "damaging experiences create vulnerable attitudes and assumptions that become encoded as laws of nature in semantic memory" (Williams, 1996b, p. 111).

Biases in selective memory have been shown with panic disorder (Cloitre, Shear, Cancienne, & Zeitlin, 1994; McNally, Foa, & Donnell, 1989), social phobia (Lundh & Ost, 1997), generalized anxiety (MacLeod & McLaughlin, 1995), and depression (Beck, 1975, Beck, Rush, Shaw, & Emery, 1979). A good research review is Symons and Johnson (1997).

ATTRIBUTION

$$\text{————} A \text{————} \overset{|}{\underset{B}{}} \text{———} C_e \text{———} C_b \text{————}\rightarrow$$

attribution

Principles

A very important cognition appears next on the timeline—attribution. The Latin root of the word reveals its meaning: Attribution comes from the past participle of *attribuere*, meaning to bestow or assign. This is what clients do to the perceptual world they experience. They bestow or assign causes and effects to what they sense. They neither find nor discover causes; they create them. They guess at the cause of almost every event that they experience. Their attribution may be totally wrong—it may be a superstition and have nothing to do with the real cause—but they will choose one just the same.

Our clinical experience suggests that most clients pick the wrong cause most of the time. Whether they're searching for the cause of their panic attacks, why they got divorced, why they can't handle alcohol, or why they keep returning to a mental hospital, most patients misattribute the cause and consequently misdirect their activities to solve the problem. One of the aims of cognitive restructuring therapy is to help clients ferret out real causes from superstitious ones.

Method

1. Focus on clients' particular A–C situations.
2. What do they believe are the causes of the problems?

3. Have them use their imagination and picture all the other possible causes they can think of. Practice until they each can make a large list.
4. Help them look for the objective evidence both for and against each cause on their list. Pick the cause that has the most positive and least negative evidence.

Example

Attributions are a crucial B, and they make an important difference in how events effect clients. Attribution is the difference between whether clients judge themselves responsible for their behavior or not.

Imagine a man driving down a street late at night. A teenage boy suddenly runs into the road from behind some buses, the man slams on his brakes, but it is too late; he can't stop and hits the boy, killing him. Whether this man is guilty of murder or an unfortunate participant in a terrible accident is totally dependent upon the motive that a jury attributes to him. If they believe that he did everything he could to avoid the accident, they will rule him innocent. If they think he steered his car into the boy and tried to hit him, they may convict him of murder. If he was drinking alcohol they may judge him guilty of manslaughter, a type of in-between guilt. No matter what the jury's attribution, the event remains the same, the boy is dead and the man killed him. But what will happen to the man, whether he spends the rest of his life in prison or is immediately released, is dependent upon the jury's attribution and their attribution alone.

In a sense, clients are all amateur jurors. They look at their responses, notice what happened just before they acted, and guess about the cause. They do the same when looking for explanations for others' behavior. Unfortunately, people are often poor jurors, and their guesses are often wrong. People rarely take steps to distinguish real causes from random coincidences. Whatever explanation jumps into their minds initially is often what they judge is the cause, and they rarely look further. Most of the time, their attributions come from some private superstitions they have never investigated.

Comment

Many clients are strongly insistent that their attributions are correct. They vigorously assert that there is no other possible cause. When the therapist asks, "How can you be so sure?" They answer, "I just know it." They are very reluctant to use any rational or empirical process to examine other possibilities.

A direct attack by therapists against these assertions usually fails. Clients simply assume that the therapist is wrong, doesn't understand the situation, or wasn't there and has no way of knowing. A more effective approach is to depersonalize the search for causes by having clients discover other explanations for themselves (see alternative interpretation section in chapter 6).

Further Information

For two comprehensive books on the attribution process, see Graham and Folkes (1990), and Kelley (1972). Attribution is related to the words clients use—particularly the verbs they choose—to describe events. See Cheng and Novick (1990), Corrigan (1992), Rudolph and Forsterling (1997) for a more comprehensive explanation of the connection between language and attribution.

An excellent study by Linda Bobbitt demonstrates that attributional style is not a personality trait but rather based on the context of different situations. The results of her studies indicated that people attribute differently depending upon whether the situation is social or competitive in nature (Bobbitt, 1989).

EVALUATIONS

$$\text{———————} A \text{———} C_e \text{—}|\text{—} C_b \text{———————} \longrightarrow$$
$$B$$
evaluations

Principles

This timeline shows a separation between the emotion (C_e) and the behavior (C_b). Most clients don't recognize this disjunction. They assume that once they feel an emotion a behavior automatically and instantaneously follows. There are, however, at least three types of cognitions intervening between feeling something and acting on it. First is the client's cognitive evaluation of the emotion. Whenever clients feel scared, sad, or angry, they immediately judge how bad the feeling is; they appraise whether the emotion is mild and manageable or horrible and catastrophic.

The intensity of any emotion is in part dependent upon how it is cognitized. Some clients exaggerate every emotion. They tell themselves, "It is terrible that I am tense. I can't stand feeling sad. It is horrible that I get frustrated." All of these negative emotional evaluations create an extremely low frustration tolerance. If clients tell themselves that they can't stand something, this belief will keep them from wishing to tolerate the feeling. It is not because they couldn't stand it, but simply because they told themselves that they wouldn't be able to. If clients tell themselves that they can't endure being tense or scared, they may, upon feeling the slightest tinge of tension, try to escape from the A in order to remove the feeling they have judged as a horrible, terrible, and catastrophic. If they tell themselves it is distressing to feel tension but not dangerous, or that it is unfortunate to be sad but not horrible, or that it is displeasing to feel annoyance but not appalling, then they will feel upset but will not engage in any extreme behaviors.

Albert Ellis, the grandfather of all cognitive therapies, distinguishes between two types of evaluations (Ellis, personal communication, May 2, 1986). He states that clients can evaluate emotions either rationally or irrationally, and that this determines how they are motivated to cope with the A. Rational evaluation of emotion includes frustration, sorrow, annoyance, regret, and displeasure, and may range on a scale of intensity from 1 to 99. The irrational type of evaluation begins at 101 and goes to infinity. Emotions such as depression, anxiety, rage, despair, hostility, and self-pity fall on this scale. This type of evaluation causes the problems for clients because they have created emotions without limit; they have turned regret into despair, fear into terror, annoyance into rage. To solve this self-created problem, clients had best practice countercatastrophizing and bring their evaluations back into the world of normal limits.

Method

1. Help clients make a list of ten events from their past that greatly upset them.
2. Help them to record on a continuum from 1 to 7 how upset they were about the event. On this continuum, the event is rated a 6.

damage   upset

1 ——— 2 ——— 3 ——— 4 ——— 5 ——— 6 ——— 7
slightly upsetting   horrible & terrible

3. Next, have clients record on the continuum how damaging the event actually turned out to be. This continuum shows a rating of 2.
4. The difference between the two scores is how much your client catastrophizes. (+4).
5. Remind your clients that the next time they are upset they would do well to remember how much they exaggerate and practice adjusting their fear to a more realistic level.

Example: The Story of Betsy

Clients' evaluations of emotions sometimes become so twisted that they can change a positive emotion into a negative one just through their thinking. An example is the case of Betsy.

Betsy was a young student in her first year of college. She visited me when I was a therapist working in a college counseling center. She told me that strong emotions were overwhelming her. She couldn't describe exactly what she was feeling, since she had never felt these emotions before, but she was terrified of them. She felt very upset and thought she couldn't cope any longer; she feared losing her mind. Her feelings had started a few months earlier, right after she had arrived on campus as a freshman.

We searched for a cause by exploring her background. Betsy had an unusual history. Her mother and father were severely handicapped throughout their lives, but she was not. Although her parents' severe handicaps limited their activities, she described them as warm and caring, and said that she'd had an otherwise normal and positive childhood.

Finding nothing in her past, we explored the present. Her college environment was satisfactory. She lived in the dorms with a friendly roommate, was popular with her fellow students, had gone on several dates, and enjoyed social functions on campus. She wasn't homesick, her parents were pleased she had gone to college, and her brother and sisters took care of her parents so she felt no guilt about leaving home. She viewed her classes realistically, was an excellent student, and found the courses interesting but not too difficult. She had no medical problems.

We searched and searched but everything seemed to be fine. This attractive young lady was doing well in school, had friends, no problems at home, had lived successfully away from her parents for several months, but felt suddenly attacked by overpowering feelings she couldn't control. What was causing her to be so upset?

Our discussion of evaluation provided the answer. Her problem was not with her emotions but with the way she evaluated them. Any of her evaluations could have been the problem, but only one turned out to be crucial.

She had evaluated her upset emotions in the same way that I had, and had assumed, as most people would, that the core emotion underlying everything must have been negative. Most of us would assume that the horrible and catastrophic feelings Betsy described were anxiety, depression, guilt, anger, or some other aversive state. These are the emotions that bother us, so we naturally conclude that these must have been the emotions bothering Betsy. But when I tried to resolve her presumed negative emotion through relaxation training, supportive counseling, and desensitization, it didn't work. It was only later that I discovered that the emotions that scared her weren't negative at all—they were positive!

Strange at it may sound, Betsy had evaluated her happy feelings as negative. Because of the way she had been brought up and the time she had spent taking care of her handicapped parents, she'd never enjoyed her youth. She'd had few friends because of her household responsibilities, hadn't dated, and had never done things just for the fun of it. Her life hadn't been negative, but it had been immensely dull and deprived of excitement. Because Betsy had no parallel life to compare hers with, she hadn't known that life could be fun. Now, after a few months of college, she was being bombarded with stimulation—new friends, success in school, dating. Her excitement was so new and unexpected that it felt terrifying. Having rarely experienced excitement before, she didn't know how to cope with it; it was so new and so unexpected that she panicked.

Solving her riddle helped solve her problem. Instead of helping Betsy to suppress her emotions, we taught her to accept them. She was shown that excitement is a pleasure to be enjoyed rather than a terror to be avoided.

Comment

Most clients' evaluations of their emotions are subtle. They place twists and spins on their emotions that keep them from coping with their feelings. Over the years, I have heard the following twists.

"I shouldn't feel this way."

"It's wrong that I have to feel this."

"It's dangerous to feel."
"I should be able to control this emotion and make it go away."
"If I don't get rid of this feeling, it will take over and control me."
"I can't stand this feeling."

Further Information

Ellis and the rational emotive behavior therapists are the major group of counselors that have emphasized the importance of clients' evaluations. Ellis's well-known phrase of "terrible, horrible, cata-strophic," represents clients' mistaken evaluation of the damage of an emotion. See Ellis (1962, 1985, 1988a, 1995, 1996; Ellis & Dryden, 1996; Ellis & Harper, 1961, 1971, 1975, 1998; Ellis & Lange, 1995; Ellis, Gordon, Neenan, & Palmer, 1996; Ellis & Tafrate 1997; Hauck, 1994).

Extreme evaluations of social situations are the key to social fears and social phobias (see the review article of Heimberg & Juster, 1995).

SELF–INSTRUCTION

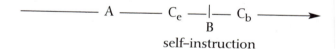

self–instruction

Principles

The second belief that occurs between the emotion (C_e) and the behavior (C_b) can also occur anywhere on the timeline. I call this B the inner teacher. Clients describe this cognition as having an ongoing dialogue with themselves, as if they had an adviser inside their heads talking to them. This inner voice may be loud or soft, intrusive or in the background, but when clients pay attention to it they can usually hear it. One client described it as, "like having your own private tutor inside your head."

Most clients report that they can carry on a long, involved dialogue with themselves about what they should do when they feel scared, get angry, or feel depressed. Their teacher speaks to them between the emotion and behavior and may tell them to run away, hit somebody, or pretend that nothing has happened.

Other times, their inner voice focuses on something totally differ-ent, like telling them what to eat for dinner, reminding them to tune up their car on Saturday, or berating them for having erred on a busi-ness project. Clients have a stream-of-conscious dialogue going on all of the time, even during the counseling session. They don't often men-tion it or reveal its contents, trying instead to narrow their responses to the therapist's questions or to the direction of the therapy session. Sometimes it is useful to have them report on this ongoing dialogue (the voice inside their head). Reassure your clients that having an inner dialogue isn't a cause for concern. Everybody has a voice or inner teacher. Although they can focus their attention on only one task at a time (like listening to you), their brain still processes other undigested thoughts, images, and experiences. It's like having two computers going at once—one listening to you and the other think-ing about other things. It's normal for everybody, but this ongoing dialogue can reveal some key attitudes that the client has not dis-cussed.

Method

1. People constantly have an internal dialogue with themselves. They talk to themselves continuously, giving advice, making evaluations, trying out new strategies, and teaching new principles. To access this ongoing dialogue, therapists can employ Aaron Beck's princi-ple of automatic thoughts.
2. Tell your clients that when they are not doing anything in particu-lar they should focus on their automatic, internal chatter. Have them write down what they are thinking. Or, if they need help, you can write it down with the clients in one of your sessions. You need to continue to probe past the first few responses to allow all of the thoughts to emerge. Tell clients not to report in the way that they usually do. Don't try to make complete sentences or keep irrele-vancies or distractions out, don't censor the thoughts for grammat-ical or personal reasons. Have them write down everything exactly as the automatic thought occurs.
3. Ask them to put their writing away for a few days and bring it to your next session. Help them relate their writings to the core thoughts that you have gathered.
4. Keep clients' spontaneous writings. They will provide you with a good snapshot of their internal processing.

Example

Clients often have nasty voices talking to them. One client had a voice like Cinderella's stepmother. It kept yelling, "You stupid, lazy slob! You haven't done anything with your life. You haven't had a relationship with a man that's amounted to anything. What a rotten piece of garbage you are and always will be."

Another client had a teacher so mean that we called it, "The Nazi in Her Head." It would cruelly attack her for the slightest mistakes. I suggested that she fire the old teacher and hire a new one.

A millionaire businessman client had a voice that would never let him succeed. It kept shouting, "You think you're God's gift to the world because you're rich, don't you? Well, you aren't anything. You can make all the money in the world, but you will always be a classless bum."

Although many people have nasty teachers, now and then therapists come across an inner voice that is too kind. George, a heroin addict, had a teacher that was a cross between Pollyanna and a Little Sister of the Poor. It would tell him, "Don't worry about those nasty old cops arresting you for holding up a liquor store again. It's not your fault; it's just that you had a bad childhood. Deep down inside you are still a good boy, poor dear." What he really needed was a teacher with the temperament of a Marine drill sergeant who would keep him in line and make him face all the misery he had inflicted on others.

Comment

Where do clients' inner teachers come from? How do they pick them? Many clients can identify the source. They often recognize the teacher's tone of voice and can picture a person speaking to them. Sometimes they hear a parent or other relative, or they picture a school teacher, doctor, or coach they once knew. Other times they imagine an historical figure like Abe Lincoln or a literary character like Hector. Preadolescent children pick fantasy figures such as Johnny Quest, or Super Friends: Wonder Woman, Superman, and Aquaman (Mc Mullin, 1999). Why people choose one teacher over another is still not clear. The inner teacher is usually chosen at an early stage of life, probably preadolescence. This is such a traumatic time for most people that they feel the need for guidance, and if it isn't available from the outside they create their own from the inside. A boy who feels weak often creates a Rambo-like teacher to make him strong. This is his mind's way of teaching him what he thinks he needs to learn in order to be tough. A boy who wishes to please his father but feels he isn't succeeding may bring his father inside his own head to give him private instruction. An adolescent girl who feels lonely may create a kindly grandmother teacher to give her the emotional chicken soup she wants.

There is nothing wrong with people creating these teachers to help them when they are young. The problem occurs when the client doesn't know when to retire the teacher and hire a new one. The heroin addict's soft teacher may have been helpful when he was little because he grew up in an abusing family and needed to create a caring person to help him cope with a hostile, unloving world; the nurturing inner voice helped him then. But when George became addicted to heroin he needed a different voice—a tough, streetwise guide who could help him fight a serious drug addiction. This was beyond his kindly grandmother teacher, but he never fired her; she had tenure.

With the therapist's help, clients can replace their teachers. One sign that therapy is succeeding is a client's report that a different voice is advising. In most cases bad voices are replaced by good ones. New teachers start to say things like, "You didn't succeed, but it was a good try." "I know you feel bad, but hold on; it will pass." "Keep working on it, you'll make it."

One client replaced his Genghis Khan–type teacher with a group of wise elders. One was a Buddhist monk, another was Albert Schweitzer, and the third was his kindly old grandfather whom he had hardly known. Whenever he felt sad, he closed his eyes, relaxed, and imagined those three people sitting with him and giving him advice. They would sometimes debate about what he should do and he would sometimes argue back, but he felt that they cared for him and he usually found their advice useful.

Clients don't really have a teacher inside; the voice they hear is their own, or at least another part of their own brain. If they hear a nasty voice they had best get rid of it—if it's a good teacher giving wise advice, they should listen.

Further Information

Tracking automatic thoughts was made famous by Aaron Beck. He developed extensive procedures for counting them, helping clients develop an awareness of them and shifting them (see A. Beck, 1975, 1993; Alford & Beck, 1997; and J. Beck, 1995).

A major contributor to the concept of client self-instruction is Donald Meichenbaum from The University of Waterloo in Canada (see Meichenbaum 1975, 1985, 1993).

THE HIDDEN COGNITION

$$\text{————— A ——— } C_e \text{ —|— } C_b \text{ ———→}$$
$$B$$
hidden belief

Principles

The third cognition between emotion and behavior is a belief I call the hidden cognition. It is hidden because most clients are not aware of its existence. The B occurs after clients feel an emotion, but immediately before they engage in a behavior (between C_e and C_b). Most clients don't notice this cognition because it is so rapid. They experience it as a vague impression, an undigested conception often occurring before they can put it into words. Though short, it can be very powerful.

What is this B?

It is an instantaneous decision to carry a feeling through to a behavior, like a nonlinguistical whisper in which a client thinks, "Yes, I should," or "No, I shouldn't."

Most clients deny having this cognition. They believe that there is no break between feeling and acting, and that once they feel something the emotion immediately forces them to take a specific action. They suppose that they have no choice but to act. According to the A-B-C formula, this is like asserting that emotions at C_e cause behavior at C_b. Clients usually say something like, "I got so scared I had to run away," "Because I felt so depressed, I couldn't get out of bed," or "I felt so angry that I had to hit him."

Method

1. Ask your clients to focus on the last time that they acted impulsively. It is the behavior, not the thought or emotion, that you are looking for. Pick a time where they slammed a door, or cursed at someone, or ran away from some danger.

2. Help your clients search through their memories to see if they can find those instantaneous thoughts and key cognitions that gave them permission to act. Some possible thoughts you may find:

> I must express my feelings.
> I can't control it.
> It's the right thing to do.
> I can get away with it.
> I am not responsible; something made me do it.
> I should do it.
> I have to do it.
> I can't keep from doing it.
> I want to do it.

3. Focus on one of your client's thoughts and switch it to see if you have found the right cognition. Have your clients imagine that they believed the opposite thought. Get them to picture the scene as vividly as they can. Then ask them, "Would you have behaved in that way if you believed this opposite thought?" If the answer is no, they would not have engaged in the behavior, then you have found their hidden cognition.

Example

The clients who probably deny the hidden cognition most frequently are the batterers—men who assault their wives or girlfriends. "She made me so angry that I hit her." The man is asserting that his feeling of anger (C_e) directly caused him to hit the woman (C_b). He is claiming that he had no choice in the matter—that it happened against his will. It's similar to claiming temporary insanity, or saying "the devil made me do it." He denies the existence of a cognition that occurs between his feeling and his action.

This claim is an inaccurate assertion. Emotions don't make clients act in a certain way. They may incline people to act, they may motivate them, but they don't make them respond. Between the emotion and the action they tell themselves something; they make an assertion. This assertion may be almost instantaneous. They are probably not aware of it, but it is there nevertheless. The battering man may assert to himself, "Yes, I can," or "She can't stop me," or "She deserves it," or "It will feel good to hurt her," or "I can get away with it and nothing bad will happen to me if I do." Whatever his assertion is, after he gets angry and before he hits his wife he gives himself some sort of permission to go ahead and do it, and the therapist can usually identify that brief cognition.

What assurances do we have that this cognition exists? How can we be sure there are intervening thoughts between clients' feelings and clients' actions? The evidence is that clients can act in totally different, often contradictory ways while immersed in the same feeling state. The battering husband who claims his anger made him hit his 5'2", 110-pound wife will not take a swing at a 6'5", 280-pound armed policeman who is investigating the assault. He may be even angrier with the officer for interfering in his domestic matter than he was with his wife, but his anger will not reach fruition. Why? If his emotion causes the behavior, shouldn't he attack the officer?

The answer is that his cognition, his self-assertion, was different in the two situations. With his wife he may have told himself, "She's little. She can't hurt me. Nothing happened the last five times I hit her." But with the officer, he may tell himself, "He could beat the hell out of me. Maybe I'd better cool it." It is not surprising how easily clients can keep their emotions from leading to certain behaviors when the behavior may be severely and instantaneously punished.

Another example of people who don't believe in the hidden B are addicts. Many chemically-dependent clients believe that unpleasant emotions drive them to use drugs. They say, "I felt so depressed, angry, or scared I just had to take a drug to feel better." They blame the emotion for making them use.

We have told addicts that believing that emotions drive them to use is an excuse, a self-con (Mc Mullin & Gehlhaar, 1990a). Emotions, no matter how strong or intense, don't drive anybody anywhere, much less to abuse drugs. Emotions don't know how to drive; they just sit there and bubble. Addicts don't choose to be addicted, but they do choose to take drugs, choose to go along with the craving, choose to respond to their emotions by taking a drug. Addicts have a hidden cognition that occurs between the craving and the using. The cognition takes the craving and turns it into action. If the hidden cognition is changed, no action will occur. The recovering alcoholic who says, "No," to his craving will not drink. The assertive man who says, "No, I won't hit her," will not strike his wife no matter how greatly he is angered. People may not be responsible for feeling an emotion but they are responsible for acting on it. Feeling may be an automatic or conditioned reflex, but action comes from our choices and past reinforcements rather than our reflexes.

Comment

It may seem that the question about emotions causing behavior is ontological and better answered by philosophers arguing about free will and determinism, or by lawyers arguing culpability in a court-room. But as therapists we are faced with clients trying to free themselves from destructive behaviors that are destroying their happiness. We don't need to answer these philosophical–legal questions, but we do need to help our clients stop their self–destructive behaviors.

Only by carefully examining your clients' cognitions will you confirm that clients do have an intervening cognition after they feel but before they act. Simply asking a client, "What did you tell yourself before you hit your seven–year–old son?" will almost always get the same response: "I didn't tell myself anything. I just got angry and hit him." If you ask this client to imagine the scene in detail, he will see the appearance of the hidden cognition. Tell him to use all of his senses until he feels absorbed by the scene. How did his son look? What were the other sights and sounds? What did he feel? Then at the crucial point, switch the hidden cognition. If he was thinking, "It is no big deal. I didn't hit him that hard," you should help him change his focus. For example, say:

> In this situation, you were focusing on your own feelings of anger. This time imagine the situation while focusing on your son's feelings of terror. You can do this by remembering vividly how you felt at the same age when your father hit you. Do you recall how it felt? Take a few moments and try to remember it. Good. Now imagine the situation again, but this time feel your son's terror. Do you still feel it was no big deal? Do you still believe that you had no choice but to hit him?

One final note: I have occasionally counseled clients who adamantly, consistently, and angrily denied having any thought intervene between their emotion and the destructive behavior. They claim vehemently that they were helpless victims of their uncontrolled passion. Without exception, when I learned more about the circumstances, I discovered that they all had an external reason for their denial. Sometimes the reason was legal: "If I admit to thinking something, I will be admitting I was responsible." Sometimes the problem was guilt: "It would be my fault." To help these clients accept their hidden cognition, it was always necessary to shift the reinforcements until the rewards for accepting the cognition outweighed the rewards for denying it.

Further Information

Hauck (1980, 1991, 1992, 1998) was one of the first writers to identify the hidden cognition. Ellis (Ellis, McInerney, DiGiuseppe, & Yeager, 1988) labels these beliefs as facilitive in the sense that they facilitate drug and alcohol use for the addicted patient. Aaron Beck (1996) agrees that there is an activation mode that may predispose the person to certain action.

EXPLANATORY STYLE

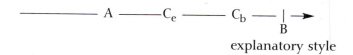

explanatory style

Principles

The last B in the timeline follows the others cited earlier. After the activating event occurs and clients have searched their memories, attributed a cause, and labeled their feelings, after they've evaluated their feelings, advised themselves, and acted, clients form a conclusion. They make some sense or meaning of the event by summarizing the experience, telling themselves why it happened, and figuring out what they can do about it in the future. They may say, "Well, this just proves what a rotten person I really am," or they may conclude, "I had some bad luck this time and made some mistakes, but I'll practice and do better in the future."

Eminent psychologist Martin Seligman and his colleagues discovered that people's explanations about why bad things happen are highly indicative of how they will cope with the same situation in the future. Seligman defined three important types of explanatory styles: internal versus external; stable versus unstable; global versus specific. Individuals who explain negative events with internal, stable, or global cognitions were more likely to get depressed and develop "learned helplessness" (Seligman, 1975, 1994, 1996). The first explanatory style, internal, refers to thinking that biochemistry or a personality trait, rather than a bad environment or bad training, caused the problem. Global style refers to accepting that the problem involved most of their life situations and wasn't specific to one situation, and stable refers to thinking the problem would stay with them for a long time. Any of these three assessments are likely to lead to depression.

It is useful to determine whether your clients are viewing their problems through one or more of these attitudes.

Method

1. Have your clients make a list of their central problems. Example: "I have trouble in relationships."
2. Help them decide how many of these problems are long–term and not likely to change. Example: "I will always ruin relationships" versus "I am having trouble right now."
3. How many general problems rather than specific ones? Example: "I will never have a good relationship with any man" versus "I had difficulty relating to Fred."
4. Do your clients believe that they cause their own problems, or do they think some outside force has created them? Example: "There is something wrong with me for having relationship problems" versus "I have bad luck in relationships."
5. Help your clients to search for alternative explanations. If they have judged their problem to be internal and permanent, transpose it to external and temporary. Do the same if the clients have judged their problem as outside them and transitory. Notice the difference it makes in how the client feels and which emotions arise.

Example: The Stories of Delma and Suzanne

To understand how these explanatory styles work, consider the cases of Delma and Suzanne. Both clients were divorced, and the circumstances of their divorces were very similar. Delma felt as if she had been through an earthquake. The ground of her emotional support was totally shaken, she felt lost and adrift, and she had contemplated suicide. Suzanne, however, experienced only a short period of grief and loss, quickly started dating again, and felt much happier than she had when she was married. What was the difference between these two women?

They had very different explanatory styles. Delma thought, "It was my fault we got divorced" (internal blame); "I will never find anyone else" (stable); "Nobody will want me now" (global); "I will live the rest of my life alone and destitute" (permanent). Suzanne thought, "Free at last. Free at last. Thank God almighty, I'm free at last."

In order to counsel clients like Delma it is necessary to invert their explanatory style. Therapists might consider saying:

> Your spouse had something to do with your divorce; it was not caused by some hypothetical flaw in you alone. Maybe your chemistry together wasn't suitable or maybe he wasn't mature enough to be married, or maybe he was extremely difficult to live with. It just didn't succeed with him (specific). Your sadness will not last forever (unstable or temporary).

When Delma's explanatory style changed, her depression was significantly reduced.

Comment

Counseling chronically mentally ill clients or gamma addicts that their problems are externally caused, narrow, and only temporary will make them incalculably worse, because you will encourage them to deepen their denial. To be helped, these populations need to accept that they have a real problem that is inside of them rather than in the environment, and that their problem won't simply go away in a couple of weeks (see the sections on treating seriously mentally ill patients and cognitive restructuring therapy with addicted patients in chapter 12).

This teaches an important lesson about all cognitive techniques. Our cognitions are like paintings that our brains draw of the world. They are our interpretations of the realities we face. But all images are not of equal value or of equal utility. Everything is not totally subjective. There is an outside world projecting itself on the canvas of our minds that we all must face. The closer our mental painting's image is to the image on the outside, the more adaptable we are and the better we can cope with life. Early attempts to create the same cognitive self-affirmations for all clients were shown to be vacuous because the reality that each client faces is different. What works for one client doesn't necessarily work for another. Nothing replaces knowing the person directly and working individually with each client.

So which type of explanatory style is best: believing that our problems are temporary, specific, and external, like the depressed client should do, or believing that our problems are permanent, global, and

internal, like the addict or psychotic should do? The answer is as obvious as it is ancient:

God grant me the serenity to accept the things I cannot change,
Change the things I can,
And the wisdom to know the difference.

Further Information

Martin Seligman created the concept of explanatory styles and has
expanded it into a major therapeutic intervention (see Buchanan &
Seligman, 1995; Petersen, Maier, & Seligman, 1995; Seligman, 1975,
1994, 1996; Seligman & Johnson, 1973). Bobbitt (1989) shows that
explanatory style is a state rather than trait–dependent.

THREE

Groups of Beliefs

In THE EARLY DAYS OF cognitive therapy, when it was called cognitive-behavioral therapy, Bs were often considered as individual covert stimuli producing emotional and behavioral responses. Taking the lead from the behavioral roots of the therapy, theorists viewed cognitions as either conditioned stimuli paired with emotional responses (as in the classical paradigm) or as discriminating stimuli paired with behavior and reinforcements (as in operant theory).

Nowadays one doesn't hear much of this theory; cognitions are more likely to be viewed in groups, gestalt patterns, schemas, and ways of organizing thoughts than as individual triggers. At the heart of modern cognitive therapy is the collective arrangement of clients' cognitions rather than the quantitative assembly of disconnected data. The emphasis now is on how clients creatively transform data, how they gather raw bits of perceptual and memoric information and sculpt them into intricate patterns, themes, and stories, and how clients create their own conceptual world.

There are many methods of discovering clients' cognitive patterns, but this chapter discusses those that we have found to be most useful.

CORE BELIEFS
Principle

At the base of most emotional problems is often one core belief. It is the keystone B that holds up the other beliefs. These core attitudes may anchor many of the client's psychological problems. Only a few key attitudes can cause all of the damage.

Therapists have known for some time that client's beliefs are multilayered. Clients have surface beliefs and underlying ones. These cognitions are psychologically related. Therapists can explain these layers to their clients by drawing the inverse pyramid pictured in Figure 3.1.

At the top of the pyramid are surface thoughts, the beliefs that clients are aware of and that they usually reveal to others. When clients are asked what they are thinking, they usually pick out one of these surface beliefs. At the bottom of the pyramid are clients' core assumptions or core beliefs. These are not readily apparent to clients or to others, and therapeutic work is required to uncover them. It's not necessarily true that these beliefs are unconscious or that clients fear uncovering them (this is probably true of only a small percentage of clients' beliefs, although therapists from a psychodynamic orientation would disagree). But core beliefs are so basic, so fundamental, that clients may not be aware that they have them. It is analogous to a fish not being aware of water because it has lived in water all its life and has never been out of it. It doesn't know that water exists. Likewise clients who have always lived with a core belief may not be aware of its existence.

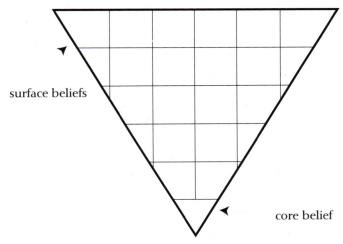

FIGURE 3.1 Reverse pyramid

Method

Finding your client's core beliefs is important for all later work. Cognitive therapy is effective only if the therapist is working on the correct core beliefs.

1. Relax your clients for five minutes. Give them a transition from their concentration on external events and change their focus to internal events.
2. Turn the clients' focus toward the A. Have them imagine as clearly as they can the situation that they are concerned about. Have them use all of their senses (vision, hearing, smell, taste, kinesthetic) to make the A as vivid as they can.
3. While your clients have the A clearly in mind, focus on their C^e, their emotions. What emotion emerges while imaging the A? Ask them not to make up an emotion; let it come in whatever way it comes. Let them feel it.
4. Now ask the clients to focus on their thoughts. Ask them, "What are you telling yourself right now about the A that makes you feel the emotion at C? Let the first thoughts that pop into your mind emerge." If you need to, take a quick break and write the belief down, then return to your clients' mental focusing. (At this point you accept clients' surface beliefs.)
5. Keep their belief clearly in mind and ask clients the questions, "So what if . . . ?" or "Why does it matter that . . . ?" Keep asking the same questions until you find their core answer. It's important to listen to clients' answers and to wait for their imagination to originate a thought. (You may find it useful to write the whole process down in order to help you keep track of your client's answers.)

Example

A businessman client of ours was worried about giving talks to large professional audiences. We followed these steps to help him find his core B.

1. We asked the client to sit back, relax, and turn his attention inward.
2. The client pictured himself standing at the podium in a lecture hall with many professional people staring at him. He heard the murmurs of their conversations, smelled the coffee brewing, noticed how it felt to rest his arms on the podium and to hear the crackle in the sound system.

3. He turned his focus inside and noticed the tension and tightness in his chest. He felt scared.
4. When he changed his focus to his thoughts, the first one that popped into his head was, "They may not like my speech."
5. We then engaged in the following dialogue:

QUESTION: So what if they don't like your speech?
ANSWER: Then they won't respect me.
QUESTION: What does it matter if they don't respect you?
ANSWER: If they don't respect me, I will feel bad.
QUESTION: Why will you feel bad?
ANSWER: If I don't have everybody like me, I feel bad.
QUESTION: Why do you need everybody to like you?
ANSWER: Because I don't like myself, and I need to prop myself up with others' positive impression of me.

"I don't like myself," was the core belief. To eliminate his fear of public speaking, we addressed this belief.

Comment

Clients usually have a series of core beliefs connected to a series of inverted pyramids. In any particular A–C situation, several pyramids may be activated, causing different emotional and behavioral responses.

When trying to change beliefs, it is usually best not to work on the core belief first. It is too far away from the client's immediate awareness, and often not acknowledged. It is also more connected to an integrated network of other core beliefs; this makes it far more difficult to extract from the entangled web of beliefs. Cognitive therapists usually work from the surface of the pyramid downward, only tackling core beliefs after the client has shown some skill with the surface thoughts.

Further Information

The technique described has been called the downward arrow technique. (The origin of this label may have come from one of my earlier works—Mc Mullin & Giles, 1981, pp. 42–48—in which we used downward arrows to illustrate the process.)

Guidiano and Liotti have done some of the best theoretical work on core beliefs. They call them the "metaphysical hard–core" and explain them as the deep, relatively indisputable, tacit self-knowledge that people develop during their lives (Guidano & Liotti, 1983, p. 66). They are metaphysical because they are not based on experience, logic, or reasoning; they are core unproven assumptions (also see Guidano, 1987, 1991).

Judith Beck uses a core–belief worksheet to monitor the progress of changing negative core beliefs (J. Beck, 1995, 1998).

Core beliefs are a major component of Aaron Beck's theory and are related to what he calls "protoschemas" (Beck, 1996, pp. 11–5).

LIFE THEMES
Principles

Where do clients' core beliefs come from?

According to most clients, they come from the big, important things, those major, life–shattering events that happen to all of us. Whether it be the death of a parent, the time they were injured and went to the hospital, or the day their brother or sister was born—the event seems crucial in the formation of their personalities.

Although these events are important, we found that it is not the big swirling things that create clients' core beliefs, it's the little insignificant things. Clients can trace many of their problems back to what seems like a trivial event. Maybe it's the time they didn't receive the special gift that they wanted for Christmas, or when they couldn't find their mother in the supermarket, or the night they forgot their lines in the Easter play, or the time they went to the party and nobody asked them to dance.

Trivial experiences can pack so much punch that they haunt clients for years. Some theorists have suggested that these little events impale people because they symbolically represent some deep, underlying human conflict. For instance, a client may remember stepping in duck droppings because he associates it with incestual desires during potty training. But a simpler explanation may be called for.

Events are not critical because of what happened to clients but rather because of what they *concluded* about what happened. They may recover from a traumatic event like the death of their grandmother if they conclude that Grandma had a full, rich life and is living with God in heaven. But they may never get over the death of their pet goldfish if they conclude that God shouldn't let goldfish die since He didn't create a goldfish heaven for them to go to.

It's not the strength of the experience that makes the event critical; it's the brute force of the client's conclusion. Clients' deductions about tiny things can be enormous. It's as if they are walking down one path in life when they trip over a pebble and suddenly turn down a totally different road. These conclusions become life themes that serve as road maps guiding them through life.

Method

Because of the importance of these events and the life themes that form from them, cognitive therapists should make a list of the most significant experiences in a client's life—not significant from the outsider's point of view but from the client's. The therapist should collect three lists: 10 critical incidents from childhood, 10 from adolescence, and 10 from adulthood. Discuss each event in great detail, paying close attention to what the client concluded happened. The client's attributions are the key—some clients have held to erroneous conclusions years after the event occurred.

List of Critical Events and Life Themes

1. Construct a list of the 30 most critical events that have happened in your client's life. Don't only choose negative events (like the death of a loved one); pick the turning points in their lives that could be positive or negative (like earning a degree or getting married), or pick events that may not seem significant to the outside observer. If they are important to the client, include them. You need three lists: 10 incidents from the client's childhood, 10 from adolescence, and 10 from adult years.
2. Compile the incidents in terms of As and C_es. What happened and how did the client feel?
3. Once you have collected their thirty A–C incidents, try to find the core Bs for each one. What did they tell themselves at that time that got them so upset? It's not what they think of it now, it's what they thought about it then. What did they conclude about themselves or about others or about the world because of this event? In finding their Bs, remember to look for the different types of beliefs mentioned in the previous chapter: expectations, attributions, labels, self–instructions, etc.
4. Go back through the client lists starting with childhood and working through to adult, and look for the recurrence of the same theme

or Bs. The words for the theme may have changed over the years. As a child they may have concluded, "I'm no good because I can't play baseball." As an adolescent, "I'm no good because I don't have a pretty girlfriend." As an adult, "I'm no good because my company won't promote me to a leadership position." The words are different but the life theme is the same—"I am inferior as a male." Make a list of these beliefs.

Master List of Beliefs

As the final exercise in gathering your client's beliefs, develop a master list of beliefs. This list should include the major Bs you have gathered from all of your other exercises. There should be at least 30 or more items on the list and it should be as comprehensive as you can make it.

Number each thought and write it out separately. Don't worry about the wording for now; you can correct it later. The only mistake you can make is not to include all of your client's Bs. You cannot have too many on the list—if you duplicate some thoughts you can cull them out later.

Most of the counseling techniques we use in cognitive restructuring therapy are based on this master list.

Example 1

Over the years, many faulty life themes have been gathered from clients. Here are some examples.

Albert was a *C* student in grade school. This average performance was hard on him because his older brother and sisters had been the top students in their classes. One term he had tried as hard as he could in his math class. He previously had never received more than a *C minus*, but this time, through hard work, he was able to get a *B+*. When he received his report card, he ran home to show his dad. After glancing at it, his dad said, "That's okay, son. Now, if you just put in a little more effort, you can earn an *A* next time." That was it; it was all his dad had said. From this "little" event, Albert formed some big conclusions.

- "If you don't do things perfectly, you might as well not do them at all."
- "To be worthwhile, you have to be the best."
- "I can never be the best in everything, so I can never be worthwhile."

Example 2

Consider a client I'll call "Marina." She entered therapy because she was afraid to be alone. She felt terrified whenever she was by herself. As a result she collected friends and tried to get enough of them so that she had an ample supply. She stockpiled boyfriends also, and was afraid to end any relationship in case she ran short. At parties she would have all of her boyfriends lined up on the couches, sitting and staring at each other. It made her feel secure, but it put a strain on the festivities.

Marina made a list of her critical events. She could find no instances where a parent or someone else had abandoned or left her as we might suspect. She did find a few minor experiences that most children have had: she had chicken pox at the age of 6 and remembered her mother sitting up all night for several nights; she lived on a busy street and her father had warned her repeatedly that she should never cross the street by herself, and she was told never to go to parties by herself because her two older sisters had gotten pregnant before they'd gotten married.

The conclusions and life themes she formed from these incidents were not minor. From a whole series of petty incidents, she developed the following life philosophy:

- "The world is a big and dangerous place, and I am weak and help-less."
- "I need other people around me to be safe."

With this philosophy she had never allowed herself to be alone, and had surrounded herself with as many people as she could for safety.

These two examples show that many emotional problems have the same source—little events with big conclusions. These conclusions start adding up in clients' lives and form their life themes. Over time these life themes become the road maps that clients use to navigate their life experiences. If their themes are distorted they get off course and end up in the wrong place.

Comment

One of the most useful and important techniques in cognitive therapy is gathering your clients' life themes. Take as much time as is needed to develop a comprehensive list. This process is very revealing to your clients; they start to see how they have misinterpreted many situations based on the same ancient cognitive mistake. Most of the remaining clinical time is usually spent working on changing these life themes rather than working on idiosyncratic beliefs that only occur in limited situations.

Further Information

Life themes have been an important concept in psychology for some time. Csikszentmihalyi and Beattie (1979) review some of the earlier theorists such as Berne (1961, 1964), Erickson (1982), and Erickson and Rossi (1981). Later work can be found in Guidano (1991) and Freeman (1993, 1994), and Freeman, Simon, Beutler, and Arkowitz (1989) who reveal that life themes and personal schemas may be formed by how people resolve the various life crises they must face.

One of the major developers of the principles of life themes is Jeffrey Young. He calls them schemas rather than life themes and has created a therapy with schemas as the primary focus—schema-focused therapy. His approach goes into more detail about schema domains and developmental origins. It is best to read him directly (Bricker, Young, & Flanagan, 1993; McGinn & Young, 1996; Young, 1992, 1994; Young, Beck, & Weinberger, 1993; Young & Rygh, 1994).

COGNITIVE MAPS
Principles

Cognitions are like pieces in a jigsaw puzzle. The individual pieces, though essential, don't reveal the complete picture. We see our clients' compositions only when we put all of the pieces together. Our clients respond to the story and overall theme rather than to the subparts that make up these stories.

Method

1. Assemble a cognitive map from your client's master list of beliefs. You can do this by taking each thought on the master list and comparing it to every other thought. Ask yourself and your client, "How are the thoughts alike? How are they different? Which thought comes first and which follows?" For example, if a client's list includes the thoughts, "I am an evil person," and "I need to be perfect," determine how these two thoughts are related. Trying to be

perfect may be an attempt to make up for feeling evil. Feeling evil may result from failing to live up to perfectionist standards.

2. Record the relationships among the thoughts on a graph or cognitive map (see figures 3.3 and 3.4).

3. In a session go over the map with your client and make any changes suggested. You may explain the principles by using the drawing and explanation in figure 3.2.

   This drawing illustrates how a cognitive map works. Each dot represents an individual thought and the 8 dots can be combined to form a surface pattern. However, on closer inspection there is also an underlying pattern that can be seen—a cube. A cognitive map is not the individual dots or surface pattern, but the underlying cube they form. Once seen, we react more to the cube than the dots. In the same way, we pay more attention to the total pattern of beliefs than to any individual one.

Example

People with different emotional problems have different cognitive maps. On the basis of extensive experience with a variety of clients' problems, cognitive restructuring therapists have identified the map in figure 3.3.

This kind of cognitive map clearly demonstrates why a client would have panic attacks. Many clients grew up being overprotected. They learned to think that the world was a dangerous place and that they

FIGURE 3.2 Necker's Cube (Bradley & Petry, 1977)

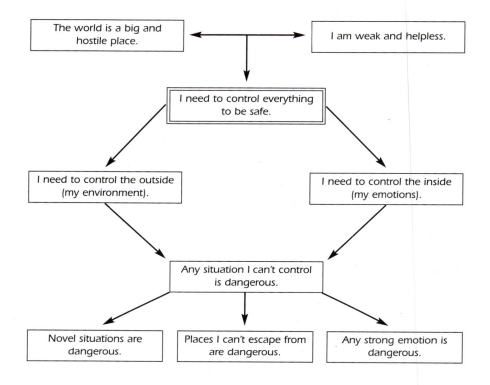

FIGURE 3.3 Cognitive map for clients with panic reactions

were too weak and helpless to take care of themselves. To compensate, they tried to control everything—the outside environment and their inside feelings—only then did they think they could be safe. It didn't work; they were unable to control everything so they started to have panic attacks. Whenever they were faced with a situation in which they weren't in full control, whether they were passengers in someone else's car or sat in the front row at church, or felt any strong emotion such as pleasure, anger, or sadness they would panic. The more they tried to control their fears, the more they feared. Their cognitive maps caused a vicious circle.

Other clients with other problems have different cognitive maps. Clients who are chemically dependent often show the pattern in figure 3.4.

At the heart of their cognitive maps, addicts deny the existence of a chemical problem. Extending outward from this base they paradoxically believe that they can control their use ("I can stop after a couple

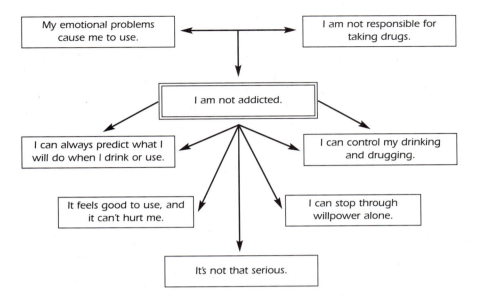

FIGURE 3.4 Cognitive map for chemically dependent clients

of beers") while thinking that they aren't responsible ("My bad child-hood causes me to snort cocaine").

Comment

There are many other types of cognitive maps. Each of the hundreds of psychological problems has its own map, and every person has his or her own variations. It is essential for the therapist to accurately map the key components of each client's cognitions.

Further Information

The cognitive–map concept comes from one of my earlier books (Mc Mullin & Giles, 1981, chapter 7). Although they do not use the term, many cognitive therapists discuss the pattern of cognitions connected to various clinical problems (Beck, Emery, & Greenberg, 1985; Beck, Freeman, & Associates, 1990; Dobson & Kendall, 1993; Ellis, 1996; Foy, 1992; Freeman & Reinecke, 1993). Young integrates clients' schemas into a map using the Schema Conceptualization Form (Young, 1992). Dattilio (1998) and Freeman and Dattilio (1992) discuss the SAEB system, which provides a structured outline of cognitions and emotions connected to panic attacks.

FOUR

Countering Techniques: Hard

A SINGLE THEORY UNDERLIES all cognitive restructuring techniques that employ countering. The theory is this—*when a client argues against an irrational thought and does so repeatedly, the irrational thought becomes progressively weaker.*

This theory does not assume that countering one thought with another can magically change an emotional–physiological state. Rather, it presumes that the counterthought might elicit affective conditions, which in turn reduce negative emotions or remove the stimulus triggering emotions.

The roots of countering are found in the realm of philosophy rather than psychology. Disputing, challenging, and arguing are all ancient methods, older than Plato's dialogues. These techniques are used by virtually everyone in all kinds of situations—from barroom arguments about religion to presidential debates.

This section on countering is subdivided into three chapters, each describing a different type of countering. Chapters 4 and 5, on hard countering and soft countering, describe techniques that pair emotional states with cognitions to produce attitude change. Hard countering deals with assertive emotions; soft countering deals with relaxing ones. Chapter 6, on objective countering, describes techniques that attempt to disconnect emotional states from belief modification.

Principles

Hard counters are cognitions that go against irrational thoughts. A hard counter can be one word ("Nonsense!"), a phrase ("Not true!"), a sentence ("Nobody at this party cares if I'm not good at charades"), or an elegant philosophy ("My purpose in life is not to be as popular as I can, but to develop my own potential, even if others disapprove").

The ideal hard counter is a philosophy that pulls in a hierarchy of values, perceptions, and experiences, drowning the damaging thought in powerful currents flowing in the opposite direction. Short phrases or slogans can be useful when they are tied to a counterphilosophy— not because they have the strength to overcome the irrationality, but because they are quick reminders of the philosophy itself. The therapist should help the client form counters that are grounded in such a philosophy.

Method

1. Help clients identify hard counters for each irrational thought. Make sure they oppose the irrational thought forcefully. For example, "It is impossible to succeed in everything you do" is a better counter than "It is often quite difficult to succeed in everything you do."

2. Have clients develop as many counters as possible; 20 counters are twice as good as 10.

3. Make sure the counters are realistic and logical. Cognitive restructuring therapy does not subscribe to the power of positive thinking, in which people often tell themselves positive lies. Instead, we stress the power of truthful, realistic thinking, asking clients to say true things to themselves, not just things that sound nice. For example, although it may feel good to think that "life gets better with each passing day," it's not true; some days things get worse.

4. Instruct clients to dispute irrational thoughts repeatedly. Months may be needed for this technique to be effective, and many clients balk at this investment of time, saying they've already tried the technique to no avail. After exploring what the clients' previous efforts were, the therapist usually discovers that they have argued with themselves for an hour or two. What clients must understand is that they may need to argue against a belief as many times as they have previously argued in its favor. It may take an hour a day for a year or more to overcome a lifelong core belief.

5. Ensure that each counter is in the same mode as the irrational thought. Pair visual irrationalities with countervisualizations, linguistic errors with linguistic counters, angry beliefs with compassionate ones, passive thoughts with assertive ones, proprioceptive

irrationalities with proprioceptive realities, etc. For example, a client who fears tall buildings because she pictures them falling over will be better helped by a countervisualization of a building constructed on the rock of Gibraltar than by a linguistic argument that buildings don't fall over. When the counter is of the same modality and logical type as the irrational thought, it is more likely to have a disruptive impact.

6. Attack all of the clients' irrational beliefs, not just some of them. It's important to tie the counters to all of the cognitions that produce emotional responses. As shown in the chapters on finding beliefs, if major beliefs have been missed, the therapist may be unsuccessful in reducing emotions.

Example

At one point in my career, I worked in a small town where few other psychologists practiced, and I often received calls from the editor of the local newspaper inquiring about various psychological issues. One particular call stands out. The editor needed a quote for an article about cabin fever. Before he hung up he asked if I could offer one suggestion he could give his readers so that they might avoid psychological problems. I answered that there were many suggestions; picking just one would be difficult. But he pursued his request, asking for one central cause, one common theme underlying most emotional problems, just one! I said I would think about it and get back to him.

Some time later I phoned back with the most central cause I could think of. I said, "Most people who have psychological problems have them because they don't *run to the roar.*"

At first he didn't understand and may have thought there was something wrong with me. Then I told him a story I had read many years before:

The daughter of a missionary lived on the Serengeti plains in Africa. She had grown up around lion prides and noticed that, with regard to their older members, they acted differently from other species. While other animals left their elders to die when they could no longer catch their own game, the lion prides didn't; they used them to assist in the hunt. The pride would trap antelope and other animals in a ravine, assembling young lions on one side and the old, clawless, toothless lions on the other.

The old lions would then roar as loudly as they could. The animals in the ravine would hear the roar and run in the opposite direction, straight into the waiting group of young lions. (theme comes from Bakker, 1982)

The lesson for the antelope was clear, though few were left to benefit from it. Had they run to the roar, they would have been safe; but they were too afraid of the noise. By running away from the sound of danger, they ran into the danger itself.

The story may not be true, but it is helpful nonetheless because it symbolizes a serious problem that most clients have. They turn away from whatever it is that they have a difficult time facing—they run away from the roar.

Anxious clients run from fear, trying to find a calm, safe place to hide on the planet. If they are afraid of flying, they avoid planes. If they fear crowds, they stay home by themselves. If they are scared of water, they avoid swimming in lakes and oceans. Their fears never diminish; they only increase. The more they run, the more afraid they become.

Depressed clients run from the belief that they are the same as everyone else. It may sound strange that many depressed people are arrogant; it would seem to be the opposite. But many therapists have found that beneath the depression, their clients harbor the curious expectation that they are supposed to be perfect, and their depression arises when they find out that they aren't. So they run from the reality that they aren't demigods but instead fallible human beings like everyone else.

Alcoholics and drug addicts run away at a feverish pace, refusing to accept that they are addicted. They fight the truth and hope to get away with it. They see other people drink in moderation and think they can do the same; they refuse to accept that they are biochemically different from others. Alcoholics and other addicts can lose everything—their families, jobs, and health—but they keep pretending they can use drugs or alcohol safely.

The solution to these problems is the moral of the lion story that I tell all my clients. *Stop running away!* If clients faced their problems, they could solve most of them. Had the water-phobic client approached water, put his feet in the surf, paddled around in the shallow end of swimming pools, and forced himself to sit in row boats, his phobia would have been conquered years ago. Had the depressed woman categorically accepted herself as a fallible human being, she would not have become depressed when she made mistakes. And had the chemically dependent client completely accepted that he was inextricably hooked, he could have finally figured out that he must stop.

What is the lesson for all clients? *Run to the roar!*

What follows are various methods of teaching your clients to face and attack their beliefs.

COUNTERATTACKING

Principles

Hard countering is an emotional process as well as an intellectual one. Therapists can pair emotions with beliefs, and they can use their clients' strong emotions to change beliefs directly.

I use an analogy to explain to clients how strong emotions can help them change their damaging beliefs. I call it the "Melted Wax Theory."

> Consider, for a moment, that thoughts are like wax impressions in your brain. They are often formed when we have a strong emotion like fear or anger. These emotions act on your thoughts like heat, causing them to liquefy and reform into new beliefs.

> When the heat of high emotional arousal has dissipated, the thought is solidified. To change the belief you have to either chip away at the wax impression, which takes a long time, or reheat the wax so the thought can be remolded. If you get angry and assertive enough with irrational thoughts, it is like heating them up so that they can be poured into a new mold.

The intensity of emotion the client invests in a counterattack is the key to its success. Disputing is most effective when the client attacks a thought with emotion in a high state of arousal. The expression of emotion virtually eliminates the repetitious, mechanical parroting that so often renders counters ineffectual. It is often helpful to encourage the client to be angry before you initiate the counterattack. After all, the irrational beliefs have caused all of the client's emotional pain—why should they be treated tenderly? Frequently only an aggressive attack can elicit a strong enough emotional level to overturn an irrational thought.

Method

1. Develop a list of hard counters.
2. Help the client counter forcefully. The client should practice the counterattack technique in front of you, modeling your behavior until a comparable level of intensity is achieved. Gradually shape the client's responses toward a dramatic attack with intensity and energy.
3. The therapist can strengthen the counterattack by encouraging clients to use physical exertion, progressively contracting their muscles. Initially, clients counterattack while their muscles are limp, then slightly tensed, then strongly contracted. Frequently the client's emotional arousal parallels physical arousal.
4. Clients also strengthen their counterattacks through voice modulation, gradually sharpening their voices and increasing the volume. The counterstatement can at first be said nasally and softly, then normally through the mouth, then somewhat loudly while filling the upper part of the lungs, then very loudly, with the lungs filled with air. As with physical exertion, the voice becomes an analogy for the client's level of anger.

Example 1: The Story of Philip

Philip, a young man, entered counseling after attending a therapy class I had given. Despite being an accomplished football player, sturdy, and 6'5", he was extremely shy with women. The class had helped him generally, but he still couldn't ask a woman for a date. He had no difficulty being assertive with men and handled male confrontation appropriately. After completing his cognitive map, we isolated one central belief: He thought women were weak, fragile creatures who must be protected by men. He viewed himself as a complete lummox, a Baby Huey who could step on the sensitive toes of these delicate people.

Philip's personal history indicated that his father had taught him this belief. Apparently, the father feared that his son's large size would make him too aggressive with women—a problem the father had experienced himself when growing up. As a result, he taught his son to be extremely careful not to hurt women. The lesson had been so effective that Philip hadn't dated for two years and was so nervous around women that he said practically nothing in their presence for fear of bruising their delicate feelings. As a result, women rejected him out of hand as an extremely dumb, though attractive, jock.

As we went through the usual cognitive preliminaries, the client developed a long and accurate list of counterarguments against his core thought. However, when he tried to use them he would counter so passively that his arguments were ineffective. It was at this point that we decided to use counterattacking.

I introduced the technique as follows:

> I am your boxing coach but I can't get into the ring with you because the ring is inside your head. Your opponent is the core belief that women are extremely fragile. This belief has been beating you up for years, making you inordinately shy around women and preventing you from developing normal relationships. Even though you know the belief is false, you haven't convinced yourself. You've hardly been fighting at all, and on those rare occasions when you do fight, you do it so weakly that the belief easily overpowers you. It keeps giving you a black eye. You must start defending yourself and fight back whenever this belief enters your head. You can't appease it. It's like dealing with any other bully. The more you give in, the more ferociously it will come back next time to beat on you. You must start attacking the belief as hard as you can.
>
> Initially the thought will be stronger than you and will win the fight. But if you persist, you will gradually become stronger and it will become weaker. After a while you will begin to win some of the time, then most of the time, until finally it won't come back anymore. Let's get started with your first boxing lesson.

Example 2: The Story of Bess

The following example concerns Bess, a client who was afraid of fainting. I demonstrated the following to her so that she could use physical exertion in her counterattacks:

> I would like you to do something that will help you understand how to counter with emotional energy. Let's pick a thought that has caused you some problems. You have said that you are afraid that if you get anxious you will faint. Now, what would be a good counter for that thought? (Bess chose the counter, "I never have fainted from anxiety.") Very good, a good counter. But it's not

enough to simply have a good counter. How you say it is also very important.

Now, just for practice, I would like you to say the counter, but say it through your nose. I know it seems silly and feels a little bit embarrassing, but please go ahead, say your counter nasally. (Pause.) Very good. Now I would like you to say the same counter, but this time say it with your mouth. (Pause.) Now fill the upper part of your lungs and say it with more force. (Pause.) That's fine. Now this time make it as powerful as you can. Fill all your lungs with air, make your body rigid, and say the counter with as much force as you can. (Pause.)

Excellent! That last one was a counter. All the others were not. The words were right, but there was no force behind them. In the future when I speak of countering, I mean the last type. Whenever you counter, do it as hard as you can.

Comment

This technique is useful in helping passive clients, and it is the treatment of choice for many depressed patients. However, it must be used carefully, as it may backfire with especially anxious clients or seriously disturbed patients. Since the technique accelerates clients' emotional level, it sometimes causes anxious clients to become even more fearful or psychotic patients to become more agitated. In these cases soft countering is more appropriate.

It is also crucial that clients attack their beliefs rather than themselves. Tell your clients that it can be helpful if they call their irrational thoughts silly, stupid, or ridiculous, but it's important not to call themselves names for believing them. Explain that they believe the thoughts because they have been taught to, and that anyone with their same background and experiences would have believed them.

Although it takes a long time for most countering techniques to weaken irrational beliefs, counterattacking occasionally produces dramatic reversals. I have seen several clients quickly remove beliefs they had held for years because they became intensely angry at their thoughts.

For example, one client kept quitting her job whenever she had an anxiety attack. This woman had been through years of long-term therapy, but nothing seemed to help—until she got thoroughly fed up with her situation. One afternoon, after she quit her third job that year, something unusual happened. She changed what she said to herself. Here's how she described her self-talk:

I'm really getting tired of this. Here I am again in the same place for the same reason. I'm upset because I'm afraid I'll go crazy and I think quitting work will safeguard my sanity. It's really stupid! I'm messing up my life, spending a lot of money, worrying people who care about me. It would probably be better if I just went crazy. Then I could spend my whole life running away like a chicken with its head cut off. This stinks! If I get scared again, I get scared. So what, big deal! I'm tired of running. I won't run anymore! If I go insane, the hell with it!

The next week she got another job—the best she could find. That was 15 years ago. She never left because of anxiety again.

Further Information

The relationship between strong emotions and cognitions has been researched for over 30 years. See the classic research of Schachter and Singer (Schachter, 1966; Schachter & Singer, 1962) and their more recent theoretical work (Morowitz & Singer, 1995; Schachter & Gazzaniga, 1989; Singer, 1995). Also review Arnold (1960) and Plutchik (1980).

Albert Ellis has clients practice their counters on tape in order to produce vigorous, forceful, and persistent countering (see Ellis, 1998). Arthur Freeman and Aaron Beck have done extensive work on anxiety and panic disorders (Alford, Beck, Freeman, & Wright, 1990; Beck, Emery, & Greenberg, 1985; Beck & Zebb 1994; Freeman et. al. 1990).

COUNTERASSERTION
Principles

Assertion training has been in practice for over 30 years and almost all therapists are familiar with the approach. Assertion classes explain the various components of the technique: how to use eye contact, how to express oneself spontaneously, how to exhibit assertive body posture, how to demonstrate a well-modulated voice. While it takes months of practice to gain the skill, some people are able to make permanent behavioral changes, so assertion training can be helpful. But the classes may not touch the deeper problem for some clients, who return to being passive when they finish the classes.

Being assertive with *others* is useful and can help clients improve their relationships, but clients may find assertion more useful if they are first assertive with *themselves.*

Method

1. Teach clients the core principles of assertion training. Help them to become assertive with themselves before they practice being assertive with others. For example, tell a patient who criticizes himself because he made a bad investment, "There are four different ways you can handle your mistake. You can be:

   (a) *Passive.* Ignore your mistake and pretend it didn't happen. This is not useful because you will probably keep making the same mistake and will not reach your financial goals.

   (b) *Aggressive.* Attack yourself. Blame yourself unmercifully for being so stupid for spending the money. This approach will cause pain, lower your self-esteem, and make it less likely that you will take *any* investment chances in the future.

   (c) *Passive-aggressive.* You can get back at yourself indirectly by getting drunk, overeating, and intentionally make worse investments. This is damaging; not only do you not reach your goals, but you have also played hide and seek with yourself so you are no longer sure what mistake you have made.

   (d) *Assertive.* Be honest with yourself that you made a mistake. Identify the error as one of judgment rather than one of character. Specify the nature of the error, i.e., 'I accepted what the agent said without checking it out.' Describe what you will try to do differently in the future, i.e., 'I will always check future investments with an independent source.' This approach makes it more likely that you will reach your goals without having all the negative, distracting emotions stirred up by self aggression."

2. Practice. Many practice techniques may be effective, but the most useful ones for self-assertion are role-playing and taped rehearsal.

   (a) *Role-playing.* Make a list of typical conflict situations with which the client is faced. However, unlike in standard assertion training, the conflicts should be internal, not external. Then have the client practice the four different types of internal responses out loud. Ask the client to notice the different emotional feelings that each approach produces.

   (b) *Taped rehearsal.* Clients practice their self-assertive responses on a tape recorder until they are satisfied with their content and tone.

3. *Inner Teacher.* As the last part of self-assertion training, describe the

analogy of the inner teacher in sufficient detail (see the section on self–instruction in chapter 2). Help your clients find their "teachers," identify their origins, and, if necessary, help them fire their old teachers and hire new ones.

Examples

On the outside, most cocaine addicts are extremely aggressive. They will fight the world to get their next hit: the police, their spouse (if they still have one), their mother. They will steal, embezzle, con, assault, and sell their bodies. One addict told me he would sell his soul for a gram of cocaine if anybody would take him up on the offer. They are clearly aggressive people when they have their craving, which is most of the time. On the *outside* they are anything but passive.

But on the *inside* many addicts are wimps. Burt, a client of mine, was a cocaine addict who rarely resisted his craving. Whenever his desire welled up he yielded, caving in totally to the impulse without putting up any resistance. When the craving ordered, he obeyed, and meekly surrendered without a whimper.

Burt needed to learn self–assertion. I told him to look at his cravings for drugs in the same way he would imagine being assaulted by a bully—an interior bully who had been beating him up for 10 years. He had never resisted this bully, never learned to fight back. He would accept such excuses as, "One hit can't hurt me. I can control my use. I need it to feel better. I'm addicted because I had a rotten childhood. My emotional problems cause me to use too much."

I told him to start fighting the bully. Tell him off. Get assertive. He ended up writing down the following assertion and carrying it in his wallet. It said:

I will never stop at one hit, never have, never will. Since I've been using, my life has been totally out of control. My emotional problems or rotten childhood or any other reason I dream up is just another excuse to use drugs. The real reason I keep using is because I am a romping, stomping, tromping junkie. If I don't like what my addiction brings me, I can work on it, get help, stop using, and turn my life around. If I don't want to work on it then I must accept the consequences. It's my choice. So choose! Every–thing else is just bullshit.

Some clients are the opposite of Burt: passive on the outside but horribly aggressive on the inside. Another client, Sara, was an extremely passive person. Her friends described her as one of the mousiest people imaginable; she embodied meekness. She spoke in a whimper and constantly had to be asked to speak up. But incredibly, in her conversations with herself she spoke in a monstrous, ruinous way. Her self–attack was so vicious that it was surprising that she stood it. One time, after locking her keys in her car, she shouted at the top of her voice, "You worthless, syphilitic, bitch, slut, cunt!" She told me that had anyone else spoken this way to her, she would have tried to pluck her eyes out, but she continually accepted these monumental obscenities from herself.

It was useless to teach Sara to be assertive with others when she was beating the worth out of her self. I told her she was wrong to treat herself so badly. She had rights like anyone else and was a worthwhile human being, deserving of respect and kindness not just from others but, more importantly, from herself.

Sara's self obscenities were making her miserable. Although getting along with others was very important, it was far more important for her to get along with herself. She needed to learn self–courtesy, good self–manners, and well–behaved self–talk.

Sara practiced her internal dialogue until she got it right and it helped. She never had to do any how–to–be–assertive–with–others training because she didn't need it. Once she began treating herself with respect, she found it fairly easy to stand up for her rights in front of others.

Comment

Sara's case points out the problem with assertion training and many other techniques that simply aim to change how clients behave. Clients act as they think and think as they act. They can change their behavior perfectly and follow a prepared script, but they may revert back to their old ways very quickly if they haven't changed their attitude.

Burt was aggressive toward others because he believed himself a hero. According to his self–description, he was God's favorite, a special creation for whom a little thing like drugs couldn't be a problem. This attitude kept him assaulting others and refusing to admit that he couldn't handle cocaine. Similarly, Sara was passive externally because internally she hated herself. How could she feel otherwise when she accepted the viciousness of her own attacks?

Clients' passivity or aggressiveness may be rooted in their self–concept. How can other people respect them when they don't respect themselves? How can they like themselves if they hate everybody around them? Their attitude and behavior combine and revolve around each other. It's a constant feedback loop; one affects the other. It is impossible to work on one and leave the other unchanged. If clients are passive, they need to resolve their belief that they are unworthy or inferior. If they are egotistically aggressive, they need to examine why they believe themselves so superior.

Further Information

The classic works on assertion training are well known. Most famous is *Your Perfect Right* (Alberti & Emmons, 1995). Review the authors' professional edition (Alberti, 1987) and their manual for assertion trainers (Alberti, 1990, with 1995 supplement). A new revision is available of a well-known assertion book for women (Butler, 1992). You may find it useful to review an assertion book with a strong cognitive component (Paris & Casey, 1983) and a client handbook of assertion used by mental health workers (Rees & Graham, 1991). Hauck describes several assertion strategies he uses in a cognitive framework (Hauck, 1992, 1998).

DISPUTING AND CHALLENGING
Principles

Rational emotive behavior therapy (REBT) employs a more free-floating style than other countering techniques presented in this chapter. In REBT, the counselor focuses on irrational thoughts as they occur in the client's conversation, and client and therapist work together to dispute and challenge false thinking. The style enables the counselor to stay in touch more fully with the client's immediate concerns, because the therapist follows the client's agenda. In contrast, the standard cognitive restructuring approach is more structured and more closely follows the therapist's regimen.

Traditional REBT uses a Socratic approach in which the therapist directs the client's attention to a series of logical questions leading to the faults underlying the client's thinking. The counselor probes freely into key areas of irrationality, reflects and reinforces the client's rational discoveries, and provides information.

REBT is used in cognitive restructuring therapy as an adjunct rather than as a basic technique. It usually accompanies other, more structured approaches.

Method

1. Keep in mind that, although unstructured, REBT does use certain established components at different stages of the therapeutic process.
2. Help the client focus on the central irrational thought causing the anxiety, guilt, anger, or depression.
3. Probe into the evidence against the belief.
4. Dispute the client's catastrophizing (i.e., "it's terrible, horrible, and catastrophic that . . . ") and self–demanding aspects of the client's thinking ("I must, ought to, and should . . . ").
5. In most cases don't give counters directly. Rather, use incisive questions to help the client discover his or her own counters.
6. Encourage the client to dispute and challenge irrational thoughts whenever they occur. Some formal practice each day is suggested. A tape recorder is often helpful (see Ellis, 1998).
7. You may find it helpful to develop a mental set for the use of REBT by listening to a therapeutic session by Albert Ellis or one of his colleagues.

Example

Examples of the REBT style are so numerous in the literature that another example would be superfluous. I recommend Ellis's books, *Better, Deeper, and More Enduring Brief Therapy*, (1995) and *Growth Through Reason* (1971), which presents seven verbatim cases in REBT. Even better, however, are recordings of REBT therapeutic interviews, which can be ordered from the Albert Ellis Institute for Rational Emotive Behavior Therapy, 4S E. 65th St., New York, NY 10021–6593 (orders@rebt.org). These tapes are from the professional tape library and are available only to qualified therapists.

Further Information

The literature on REBT is truly extensive. The catalog from Ellis's Institute for Rational Emotive Therapy lists the major publications. If the reader is not familiar with REBT, the following sources provide a comprehensive review: Ellis (1962, 1971, 1973, 1975, 1985, 1988a, 1988b, 1991, 1995, 1996, 1998); Ellis and Abrahms (1978); Ellis and Dryden (1996); Ellis and Grieger (1977); and Ellis and Harper (1961, 1975, 1998); Ellis and Lange (1995); Ellis and Whiteley (1979); Ellis, Wolfe, and Moseley (1966); Ellis and Yeager (1989); Ellis and colleagues (1996).

For REBT methods with more specialized client populations, see the following: for children, Hauck (1967) and Ellis, Wolfe, and Moseley (1966); marital, Ellis and Harper (1971), Ellis, Sichel, Yeager, DiMattia, and DiGiuseppe (1989); sex therapy, Ellis (1975); addictions, Ellis and colleagues (1988) and Ellis and Velten (1992).

FORCING CHOICES

Principles

There is a truth that many experienced therapists have learned, but don't often mention to the public. While it usually takes at least 10 years of experience with thousands of clients to discover, most therapists are reluctant to discuss it in their books, write about it in their journals, or mention it to their colleagues. It is one of the more regrettable, sadder aspects of being a therapist and it causes a great deal of stress to many mental health professionals.

What is this truth? Simply this: *Clients don't change until they have to.* Most clients change only in small, painful steps if they change at all; no matter what techniques therapists give them, many clients will continue to suffer through their problem until some crisis forces them to make a choice. Even then, during the crisis, clients will avoid choosing for as long as possible, and will escape from choosing to change for as long as they can. They will postpone the inevitable until they absolutely, positively cannot avoid it anymore. This is sad, because clients end up enduring additional emotional pain and waste additional time unnecessarily.

A good metaphor I give my clients in explaining the process of change is that of a river. I ask them to picture their beliefs as if they were in a river flowing toward the ocean: as long as their cognitions are flowing freely along with all the currents, whirlpools, and eddies of their life experiences, they are healthy. But as soon as their cognitions become rigid and customary, the river becomes stopped up and they become stagnant. They stop growing and changing. The dam they build becomes so strong that only extreme pressure will break it.

Clients will do everything they can to avoid choosing to break through the dam and change their beliefs. Like a river, they will try to flow around beliefs by overflowing the banks. Only when all escapes are blocked and the river has no place left to go, only when the pressure gets strong enough, will the dam break and the client's cognitions flow freely again.

We therapists often mishandle blockage problems. We try to immediately reduce the pressure against the dam to help the client feel less anxious or frustrated. We do this with good intentions; we want to make our clients feel better. We teach relaxation and prescribe tranquilizers and antidepressants. We hospitalize them; we allow their relatives to visit, to comfort and soothe—all are attempts to reduce their pain. But this comforting and soothing may be accomplished at the cost of keeping some clients from breaking through their dams. Pressure, stress, and pain are not always bad. They show patients that something is wrong, something is hurting. Clients need to identify the hurt and correct it, not just tranquilize it.

Though it is difficult, it's often best not to push our clients' hurt and pain away as quickly as we can. Despite the empathy that we feel, we may help them more by allowing them to feel the pain—this will propel them to choose to break through the dam.

Pure weariness develops the strength needed to attack the cause of problems rather than just the painful symptoms. When clients are ready, therapists should help by blocking escape routes; refusing to tranquilize all their pain helps to prevent them from running from the problem to get temporary relief. Four principles summarize the essential components of forcing therapeutic change.

Method 1

1. The old, damaging perception must be painful for clients. It must be a reservoir of anxiety, depression, or anger, creating a condition from which clients want to escape.
2. Clients must be aware of a reasonable, alternative cognition, a new perception. This alternative B must be important and relevant so that the client will seek it after the old cognition has been destroyed.
3. Clients must feel trapped by their old thought. They must come to believe that the only way out of the trap is to choose to change their attitude. The pain associated with the old belief should not be reduced or made so tolerable through drugs or other ameliorative

strategies that it is possible for clients to hold onto their mistaken belief.

4. It is essential that therapists don't add to the client's problem. The natural consequences of the old attitude should trap the client in the present situation. The therapist should not place an artificial impediment in the way.

Method 2

1. Find a core mistaken belief that is generating a major share of the client's pain. For example, the client may believe his or her purpose in life is to fulfill imaginary "oughts," "musts," and "shoulds."

2. Counter the client's mistaken beliefs, introducing as many persuasive contrary views as possible. For example, "oughts" and "musts" don't exist except in the minds of human beings. The world just is. It has no "oughts," "shoulds," or "musts" in it.

3. Contrive a situation or exercise, covert or in vivo, in which the client faces only two choices: believing in the old perception or shifting to the new. For example, suggest a situation in which two "musts" of equal strength oppose each other, and both produce strong negative effects.

4. Do your best to help your client face the conflict. If you encourage or provide an escape route that doesn't require clients to change their beliefs, they will take it.

5. At the peak of the conflict, identify the shift to be taken and encourage the client to make the shift.

Example 1: The Story of Kate

Kate was married to a drunken, drugging, abusive, philandering husband for 15 years. He spent days away from home with other women, neglected their children, couldn't hold down a job, physically abused her many times, and gambled all of her money away. His malevolence was obvious to everybody. He was hated by all Kate's friends and relatives, who constantly advised her to leave him. Unfortunately, she could never bring herself to do it.

She had a thousand excuses. She blamed herself and kept hoping that she could straighten him out. She went to marital counseling but her husband refused to attend. She tried to get him to attend AA meetings, but he went just once and left, saying he didn't like it. She left self–help pamphlets around the house hoping that he would read them but he threw them away. Whether he was arrested, fired, or had spent their money, she would accept him back as if nothing had happened.

It was obvious to all what she needed to do. He was a monstrous husband, and since she couldn't change him, she either had to accept the horrible marriage or leave. Everybody she knew, male and female, young and old, told her to leave, but she kept trying to escape the obvious by going to different doctors, ministers, or therapists. She read every pop psychology book on "how to fix your marriage," "how to straighten out your husband," "how to be a total woman," "how to be a sensual wife," "how to save a failing marriage." Nothing helped and things got worse.

She had a 10-year-old son named Billy who suffered along with her. One night Kate's husband came home drunk again, and started to yell at her because the dinner was cold. The yelling became louder and louder and Billy overheard the fight as he had overheard many fights before. He saw his father hit his mother, which had also happened before, but this time Billy couldn't stand it and jumped on his father's back, holding on, trying to protect his mom. His father threw Billy off and Billy fell down a flight of stairs. He lay unconscious at the bottom while his father rushed out of the house cursing. Kate called the ambulance and took Billy to the hospital. He had a mild concussion.

One would think this would have been the last straw for Kate, but it wasn't. She denied that her husband was to blame. When he came home several days later, she accepted him back and told her friends it had just been an unfortunate accident.

Her friends knew better. One of them called social services and reported the incident, and all of the other abuse that had been going on for so many years. Social services investigated and found the husband to be an unfit and dangerous parent. The court ordered him to leave the house and forbid him to see the children until he had totally stopped all drinking and drugging for one year, had successfully completed an anger-management class, and had received individual therapy. He could occasionally visit his wife and children if he complied with all of these orders.

At the same time, social services told Kate that she must not allow her husband to live at home. If she violated the order it would be grounds for them to send her children to a foster home.

But Kate still wouldn't choose. She told the workers she would be willing to enter counseling treatment, go to classes, or do anything else so that her husband could remain in their home. She tried to fight the decision legally, wrote letters to the local paper, hired her own lawyer, and tried to sue, but nothing worked. The child protection agency and the courts would have none of it.

Kate ignored the order. She sneaked her husband back into the house and hid him whenever social service personnel visited, but this became increasingly difficult as the social workers became suspicious, and would sometimes arrive unannounced. Things went along this way for some time, until one Sunday afternoon.

Kate was home alone. Her children were visiting their grandmother and her husband was on the other side of town drinking beer and watching football with some buddies. She was sitting alone in the living room, thinking about all of her problems. She realized that eventually social service would make an unexpected visit and discover her husband living at home. She would either lose her husband or lose her children. She felt trapped, panicky, and in complete despair; she seriously contemplated suicide, but quickly abandoned the idea. After panicking all afternoon, she suddenly jumped up, went to the phone, and made three phone calls. She called her husband and told him that he had to leave the house immediately. She phoned the police and had a restraining order taken out in case he came by. Finally, she called her lawyer and told him to file immediately for a divorce.

Later, she told me that Sunday had been the turning point. She ended the whole thing that one afternoon, and never went back on her choice or doubted it for a moment. She followed through on all her threats. Her husband *did* violate the order but was prosecuted and placed on probation. Upon receiving a threatening letter from him, she immediately called his probation officer. She obtained her divorce and started to date attractive, responsible, nondrinking men. She never regretted her choice, never felt sorry for her ex-husband, and never doubted herself for a moment about leaving the relationship. And all this occurred one uneventful Sunday afternoon when *Kate chose to break through her dam.*

Example 2: The Story of Daniel

The case of another client, Daniel, further illustrates the process. Daniel was a person who feared going crazy, and this fear dominated his life. He was afraid that someday his emotions (particularly tension and anxiety) would become so powerful that they would make him go crazy. He wasn't sure exactly how stress could make one's brain snap, but he was certain it could happen. He vividly pictured himself locked in a padded cell, confined in a straitjacket, lying in the back ward of a dirty, broken-down, mental hospital, screaming day after day, month after month, with nobody in the world giving a damn. It terrified him.

He did everything he could imagine to avoid losing his mind. He visited a dozen doctors, tried all kinds of tranquilizers and avoided watching any movie or TV show or reading any novel that discussed insane people. He tried to keep his fear from escalating by living alone in his house so that others couldn't upset him. He spent most of his day watching mild sitcoms on TV. He didn't like them, but at least they didn't make him afraid.

Still, no matter what he tried he would still occasionally get anxious, and when that happened he would rush to the phone and call his therapist, demanding admission to the local hospital. There he would be sedated until the fear went away. He'd had himself admitted five times in two years.

Late one winter night Daniel was lying on the couch with the TV on, half asleep but still vaguely aware of the sights and sounds around him. Suddenly he started to feel anxious. He sat up, concerned, and looked around for the cause. Finally he noticed that the television was tuned to a talk show about ex-mental patients who were describing their experiences in full and gory detail. He quickly got up and changed the channel, but it was too late; he had heard too much. He was unable to block his fear, and it quickly grew into a full-fledged panic attack.

He tried everything he could to reduce it. He rushed to his medicine cabinet to take some tranquilizers, but the bottle was empty. He remembered he had hidden a reserve bottle in case he ever ran out, but he'd forgotten where it was. He rummaged desperately through all the cabinets, closets, and boxes in his apartment, but he couldn't find them anywhere.

He went to emergency plan #2. Despite the late hour, he called his therapist but found no answer, then remembered that he was out of town. He tried phoning some of his past therapists, but reached answering machines or found that their phones had been disconnected. He tried calling two different 24-hour crisis lines, but both told him not to worry about it. He scrambled for someone else to call, knowing that though he had lost his friends through the years, he still had some relatives who might help. He phoned them and woke them up, but after years of hearing Daniel cry wolf, they were tired of his panics. They didn't appreciate being woken up in the middle of the night, and told him he would have to handle the problem himself.

His fears rising to a maximum, he rushed out of the house, jumped into his car and drove as fast as he could to the emergency room of the county hospital. But when he arrived he found that there had been an ice blizzard on one of the major freeways and twenty–five cars had been involved in a pileup. The hospital staff was running around trying to help the accident victims and he was told that they didn't have time to see him.

So there he was—*trapped*. He had no place to go, no one to call, nobody to turn to. Deciding that since he was going to panic he might as well do it at home, he got into his car and drove back to his apartment. He sat in his living room chair, turned the lights off, and waited for his brain to snap and to go insane. He sat there for two hours, letting the waves of panic flow over him.

Later on Daniel described what had happened to him as he sat waiting. (This dialogue is reconstructed from his report.)

> I was sitting there with waves and waves of panic, exhausted, terrified, with no place to go and no one to turn to. I was waiting to go crazy. But suddenly out of nowhere, I jumped up and started to talk to myself out loud. I talked louder and louder until I was shouting at myself. I said, "Who the hell cares if I go insane? It couldn't be any worse than what I'm feeling now. My life hasn't been worth a bucket of shit for the last ten years. I'm not married, I don't have any girlfriends, I can't hold a job, and I've been on medical disability for the last 10 years. I have no friends, my relatives can't stand me, and my therapists are tired of me. So who the hell cares? This isn't a life. I don't have to fear losing anything, because I have nothing left to lose. There is no reason to protect myself anymore. It doesn't matter what precautions I take—they don't work, so what difference does it make? I've had it. The hell with it all. If I'm going to go insane, I'm going to go insane, but I'm not going to escape anymore. There is no place to escape to, anyway. If I'm ultimately going to end up a loony, I might just as well have a good time before I do!"

Afterwards he got up, walked out of the house and went to an all–night restaurant where he had the biggest, gooiest pizza he could find. He ate the whole thing, then went to an all–night movie and didn't return home until dawn.

This was Daniel's turning point. Having been faced with a crisis from which there was no escape, Daniel chose an alternative B and he never looked back. His panics subsided, and he tried to live life to the fullest. He began to travel and took some classes in school. He looked for a job and started to date. Some time later he found his hidden pills, but immediately threw them away in disgust. At the end of a year he was a totally different person and almost never got anxious. All of this can be traced back to that winter night when *he chose to break through his dam.*

Comment

These two stories are representative of many cases. How could Kate hold onto such a terrible relationship for all those years and then, suddenly, immediately end the relationship without any regrets or backward glances? How could Daniel, after years of fear, break through in one dramatic evening?

Possibly the best explanation for both metamorphoses is the principle mentioned in the beginning of this essay: *People don't choose to change until they have to.* Once they are forced to make the decision, they rarely look back. They may have stayed rooted in their problems for years, favoring palliatives and pain over the big decision, but when they are completely trapped and have no escape left, they create their own change.

The therapist may wonder when to use this technique. Our experience has found that it should be used after the other CRT techniques have been taught. Clients should know that it is their beliefs, not their environments, that are causing emotional distress; they should have identified the specific thoughts causing the distress, and they should have a very clear idea of what replacement belief is rational and realistic. Then and only then will this technique lead to constructive changes.

Obviously, this technique should not be used with clients who have suicidal tendencies or who are likely to cause physical harm to themselves or others in response to their emotional pain.

In theory, forcing choices is an oxymoron. If choice is forced, it is not a choice. The intent of the technique is not to eliminate all choices but to narrow them to two: choosing to put up with the problem or choosing to change.

Further Information

Existential psychotherapy was an early promoter of the importance of client choice and self-responsibility. Clients are encouraged to take the necessary risks to try to actualize their potentials (Frankl, 1959, 1972, 1977, 1978, 1980; May, 1953, 1981).

William Glasser, founder of reality therapy, developed a psychotherapy grounded on client choices (Glasser, 1998). He asserts that we choose all we do and that acting and thinking are voluntary activities (Glasser 1989, 1998).

CREATING DISSONANCE
Principles

Clients unify their thoughts coherently, though not necessarily correctly. If they begin with an absurdly irrational assumption, they then interpret all subsequent data in light of that mistaken beginning, with the primary goal of consistency rather than accuracy. Accompanying the unified schema is a feeling of consonance—that all is right and logical in the world even if their unhappiness persists. That consonance, however, is like a jigsaw puzzle—disturb one element in the pattern and the pieces no longer fit together. The pattern becomes incoherent, and the earlier feeling of consonance is replaced by a feeling of dissonance.

Clients attempt to maintain consonance even though the schema itself causes emotional distress, because dissonance is even *more* stressful to them, and could result in an anxiety attack. The effect is tantamount to saying, "It's all right to be unhappy, if the reality is that this is your only alternative in life." Even though it depresses them, clients will hold to the perception that they are sick because their behavior and attitudes are based on that perception; they will defend their "sick" assessment despite overwhelming contradictory evidence. The key here is that their "reality" is a fabrication, a product of clients' mistaken beliefs about themselves and the world around them.

One method of changing the mistaken reality that forms the background for clients' unhappiness is to attempt to show them the inconsistency in their thinking. The method by which this is done includes pointing out that their feeling of consonance is an illusion, that their patterns of thinking are full of contradictions, and that their thoughts can't possibly be true. Although clients will argue against such a confrontation, the therapist's persistence will create more and more dissonance in their mistaken cognitive system.

Once this dissonance reaches a certain point, the whole schema will be thrown into disarray, and clients will be compelled to adjust it to gain a new feeling of consonance based upon their new perception. It is essential that the formation of a more rational synthesis be carefully managed. Remember that the client's primary goal is consistency: It is just as easy to adopt a *consistent* pattern that is only half as erroneous as their original pattern as it is to adopt a totally correct pattern. The burden is upon the therapist to insure that the consonance–dissonance–consonance transition concludes with the most functional reality possible for the client.

Method

1. Ask your clients to present their schema about themselves and their view of the world. They can have a specific schema or a general one. While the clients are discussing their views, the therapist takes very careful notes recording the principles, evidence, and support the clients give.
2. Ask a series of carefully prepared questions aimed at challenging the client's prepared schemes. Instead of asking questions leading to counterarguments, prepare probes intended to throw the client into dissonance.
3. The client will usually defend the schema by giving excuses and by coming up with new rationales. You must continue to ask questions that create doubt about the client's formulations. In all cases, maintain the client's dissonance until the client resynthesizes the schema. It is important that you don't answer the probes for the client.
4. As the client moves to embrace a new, unified schema, monitor carefully to insure that this new perception does not encompass the seeds of future unhappiness.

Example 1

SCHEMA: I must constantly guard against catching germs.
PROBE TO CREATE DISSONANCE: How do you keep from breathing them?

SCHEMA: If I don't engage in this ritual (counting my steps when I walk to my car), I will get into a car wreck.
PROBE: Maybe you are using the wrong ritual. Perhaps the correct ritual is not to count. How would you know? How many accidents were you in before you began this ritual?

SCHEMA: It is terrible when others reject me.
PROBE: When you reject others, is it terrible for them?

SCHEMA: Other people are causing all my problems.
PROBE: How are you going to stop others from doing this?

SCHEMA: The only way I can be happy is by taking care of everybody who needs it.
PROBE: Where will you get the power to take care of everybody?

SCHEMA: My parents' values are correct. I must follow them.
PROBE: Are your parents' values better than other parents' values? Are they the same as other parents' values? If they aren't, are all other parents *incorrect*? How do you know which parental values are correct?

SCHEMA: If you are assertive, people will hate you.
PROBE: Do they love you now when you are passive?

SCHEMA: The only way to be happy in life is to be tough and hard, and not to let people take advantage of you.
PROBE: If you act that way, why would anybody want to love you?

SCHEMA: Women keep pressuring me for a deep commitment. They won't grant me my independence. They keep getting angry with me.
PROBE: If you were a woman, would you date yourself?

Example 2: The Story of Carol

We can further illustrate creating dissonance with the story of Carol, a middle-aged female client. She was referred to me by her medical doctor because she had a phobia about getting cancer. Generally speaking, this is not an abnormal fear, but in her case it was. Rather than worrying, which would have been useful, she obsessed over it, which wasn't. She consulted doctors repeatedly and became terrified if she found a pimple; she spent hours each week examining herself.

Carol knew the best specialists and received expert examinations. These practitioners all found the same thing—nothing. They reassured her about every mole and pain and told her they were certain that she had absolutely nothing to worry about. But every time they added the habitual "Of course we will keep an eye on it," Carol felt shattered. She ignored the "nothing to worry about" and "we are certain" phrases and focused instead on the hint of future problems. She left the doctors' offices more upset than before, convinced that they were being kind to her and that they weren't telling her the truth.

Carol came to a few sessions of therapy, and although it helped her in other ways, it didn't significantly reduce her phobia. She had a counter to every one of my arguments. If I asked, "Why are you diagnosing yourself when all the experts say you are clear?" Carol would answer, "I know how many times doctors tell the patient they are certain, even though they have severe doubts." I would say, "Look at how much your worrying costs you. You don't reduce your chances of getting cancer by one iota. All you do is make yourself miserable by agonizing." She would reply, "You must catch cancer at its very earliest stages. If you don't, you could be out of luck." If I said, "You have been searching for years and competent physicians have never found anything." Carol would respond. "But there is always a chance I will!"

And so it continued. She sabotaged every counter her doctors and I could think of. One day, after she had been raging about the horrors of dying of cancer, how unfair it would be if she got it, and how the medical profession was incompetent because they hadn't found it, I became frustrated and inadvertently created dissonance by saying,

"Big deal. So you get cancer and die. What's so God awful terrible about dying anyway? No matter what you do, no matter how much you try to protect yourself, no matter how hard you look for signs, go to doctors, and get examined, it's all going to fail anyway. Because sooner or later, no matter what you do, you are going to die—maybe not of cancer but of something, for sure. What's so terrible about that? Do you think the universe will stop when you die? I don't mean this insultingly, but what makes you so precious? Do you think that God is counting on your help? Do you think that the universe can't get along without you?"

Carol felt I was unsympathetic, but I had made my point; she began to think about my questions and her fears. For a time she thought that it wasn't death she was afraid of but the pain of dying. She concluded that that didn't wash when she realized that she could die suddenly and without suffering. She realized that even if the worst happened and it took her several months to die, her total pain for those months would not add up to a fraction of the pain she was creating for herself by worrying and anticipating it for forty years.

So why was Carol so afraid of death?

Later we learned that my dissonance–creating question about whether the universe couldn't get along without her was her core belief. Rather than being afraid of the act of dying, she was afraid of not existing. The idea that she would someday cease to be was intolerable to her; she did not believe in a hereafter, so her present life was all she had. She feared that after her death only a few people would mourn her. Her family might shed some tears, and the funeral might be full of prominent people who would come to grieve, but that would be it. In a short time few people would think of her. She would become a fading picture in a family album that few could identify. After 150 years nobody would remember her at all. Everybody who knew her would be long dead and it would be as if she had never existed at all.

This was Carol's fear, and in a strange, paradoxical way it gave her life the meaning and purpose she was so afraid of it lacking. As long as she existed she could still, "Rage, rage against the dying of the light." Giving up her fear would be like surrendering to oblivion.

There are many clients like Carol who can accept the pain of death but not the shame of it—the shame of meaninglessness.

They ask me, "What's the point? Why go through all the pain and suffering of living when there is no purpose? Death makes life nonsensical. With death everything a person does in life becomes insignificant, trivial, puny, not worth a rap." Looked at in this way, life can appear meaningless. The human race is three million years old, and the billions of people who lived on this planet before us seem gone, forgotten. The principle holds true that whether looking at earth's inhabitants of one million years ago or one thousand years ago, names and accomplishments seem to disappear. Countries and empires are gone, as are much of art, architecture, and philosophy. A handful of names has endured, yet we have no real impression of the people behind the names, of who they were or what they did. Most of the past is wrapped up in fables and fantasy.

As for the common people who preceded us, no matter how rich, how successful, wise, beautiful, creative, or strong they were, their births, struggles, and deaths are all gone and forgotten.

This was Carol's original dilemma: the idea that life appeared pointless, without significance or purpose. Once we had identified the problem, we were able to work toward consonance. Through counseling, Carol came to the conclusion that life is neither hopeless nor meaningless—that hidden inside the apparent oblivion of all the people who came before is a purpose that she couldn't see by trying to look at one individual's life. Carol found that by stepping back and viewing the human species as an entirety and across time, she could see that *the human race is progressing,* advancing, and moving forward, and that all people are part of the progression. She saw growth and advancement against ignorance, superstition, disease, poverty, and injustice.

Carol was finally able to see that she could contribute by trying to make things just a little bit better. She came to view herself as part of the human tide moving forward and to believe that no life was meaningless, including her own.

Comment

Clients will defend their mistaken realities against all attacks, even if these realities are a fundamental source of misery for them. Some can even take a certain pride in their unique constructions, and feel that abandoning their philosophy would be a sign of weakness or, ironically, a show of irrationality. For the more adamant victims of this disorder, paradoxical counseling techniques might be more helpful. Dissonance is painful, and the use of this technique is a classic example of having to "hurt" the client to help the client. Fortunately, the very nature of the disorder ensures that the hurt will be brief, for the moment the foundations of the mistaken reality begin to crumble, clients move quickly to replace them. The therapist need only make sure that its replacement is as error–free as possible.

Some clients don't need the help of the therapist to resolve their dissonance. They can often resolve it themselves by reassessing their own values and desires.

Further Information

Cognitive dissonance theory has been examined in a large number of publications (see Aronson, 1980; Festinger, 1957, 1964, for the original work). Wicklund and Brehm (1976) provide an early summary, and Schachter and Gazzaniga (1989) have a recent review of much of Festinger's theory. Schauss, Chase, and Hawkins (1997) provide a behavioral analytic interpretation of dissonance.

COGNITIVE FLOODING
Principles

Another form of hard countering is flooding. It places clients in the presence of a very aversive conditioned stimulus (CS) and does not allow them to escape. If they stay in the setting long enough, the emotional conditioned response (CR) is often lessened or removed. There have been many explanations for this effect. One view is that fatigue gets paired with the CS, thus counterconditioning it. Another is that extinction eliminates the CS because the unconditioned stimulus (UCS) never occurs. A third view is that reactive inhibition sets in.

A cognitive explanation of flooding suggests something different. Flooding can be understood in terms of removing a conditioned avoidance response. Avoidance is a major component of any fear or anxiety. Once clients feel the emotion, they will desperately look for a way to run from potentially problematic situations, even if it is not clear what they are running from.

Although escaping makes them feel safer and leads them to believe they have demonstrated some measure of control over the event, their running away actually increases their fear, since they don't stick around long enough to prove or disprove the validity of their fears. There are two possible consequences for clients placed in situations from which they cannot escape: either the damage will occur or it will not. Only by staying in the situation will they find out. Therefore, the solution to overcoming catastrophic fears is to immerse oneself in the danger and see if the catastrophe happens. It is the ultimate experiment.

It is important that clients be prohibited from escaping if the experiment is to work. If clients are permitted to escape before the experiment is completed, they will conclude that it was their escape that saved them. If they are allowed drugs, a drink, a counselor's soothing words, or any other support or cop–out, they will determine that it was this variable that kept the catastrophe from happening. Without the proper controls, the client will never be able to see that their beliefs were irrational in the first place, and the likelihood that they will attempt to escape again will be increased.

A variety of flooding approaches are summarized below.

Method 1. Image Flooding

1. Have your clients imagine, in vivid detail, the feared scene and accompanying irrational thoughts.

2. Continue until the CR naturally subsides.
3. When clients have irrational fears, instruct them to feel the emotion until they get tired of doing so.
4. Clients should make themselves afraid at various times during the day by imagining the same scene with the same thoughts again and again.
5. The therapist may find it helpful to use hypnosis in a flood–relax–flood–relax sequence.

Method 2. Verbal Flooding

Have your clients discuss, in great detail, all of their past trauma experiences. Go through every incident many times until your clients are tired of talking about them.

Method 3. Focused Flooding

This is the same as the other methods, except that clients focus on CRs exclusively. Clients try to recreate all of the physical sensations connected with the anxiety—rapid heartbeat, queasy stomach, disorientation, and difficulty in breathing. They continue until the symptoms naturally decline. Fear is experienced as deliberately as possible.

At least three half–hour sessions are usually necessary for this technique.

Method 4. Negative Practice

Have your clients say all their irrational thoughts repeatedly until they feel tired, bored, and annoyed. Stop the practice only when they absolutely refuse to think about them anymore.

Method 5. Hierarchy

1. Help your clients make a hierarchy of their most–feared situations and most–feared associated thoughts.
2. Imagine the least upsetting item on the list vividly with full emotional effects. Continue until the client has no CR while picturing the situation.
3. Move to the next item on the hierarchy and repeat the process.

Example: The Story of Justin

A modified form of flooding was used successfully with another client afraid of being insane. Justin was a psychological hypochondriac. He was very knowledgeable about certain aspects of psychopathology, and had read *DSM*-II. Each time he got upset he would look in the book and pick out the psychological problem he was having that day. Over a 10–year period he had diagnosed himself as manic, psychotically depressed, sociopathic, obsessive compulsive, anorexic and bulimic (whenever he lost or gained a few pounds), and an explosive personality (when he was angry).

He traced the origins of his anxiety to his college years, when he had taken some marijuana for the first time after being goaded into it by an acquaintance. The drug had been laced with a hallucinogenic, and when he began to hallucinate, he panicked. He stayed awake for 24 hours, moving back and forth, in and out of panics. The next day, when the acquaintance told him that the marijuana had been laced, his panic immediately subsided. He thought the drug caused the fear and didn't worry about it after that.

About a year later, Justin was sitting in a beginning psychology class listening to a lecture on the psychological effects of drugs. The instructor said that those who have panic reactions while taking marijuana are probably prepsychotic, or at the least have borderline personalities. That night he began to get scared, and by morning he had a full–blown panic attack. His panics stayed with him on and off for 10 years. He had periods when he felt no anxiety, but whenever he read or saw something that reminded him of insanity the fear would resurface. He couldn't watch TV shows about people having nervous breakdowns; he was terrified when he watched the movie *One Flew Over the Cuckoo's Nest*. He couldn't stand reading science fiction about strange people on strange planets, because he would start to think himself strange as well.

His core belief was easy to identify—he knew it himself: "I am close to being insane. At any moment, stress could make me flip over and become permanently psychotic." We can consider his belief as a conditioned stimulus as shown on the next page.

> Note: In classical conditioning the contiguity (the close association of CS and UCS in time) is considered important. In cognitive conditioning, the contingency (the mental connection of one event with another, no matter what the time frame) is all that

is necessary. In the above example contingency was present but contiguity was not. See Schwartz (1978) and Rescorla (1967) about the distinction.

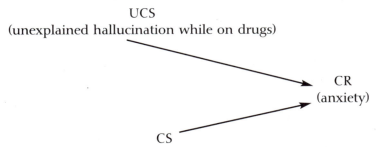

UCS
(unexplained hallucination while on drugs)

CR
(anxiety)

CS
(association a year later that he may be prepsychotic)

Justin had gone to many counselors and had tried many techniques to no avail. Finally, we decided to use flooding. He was instructed to take off three mornings over three successive weeks. He was to allow at least five hours for the technique.

Each time he was told to lie in his bed with only a dim light shining in from the next room. He had to lie there for five hours, with all distractions removed. He could accept no phone calls, the radio and TV had to be turned off, he couldn't get up and walk around, read a book, or distract himself in any way. His entire focus and environment was to be mental.

Justin was told not to fight the fear of going crazy and not to avoid it in any way during his flooding time. Instead, he was to concentrate on the idea of going insane, feel the anxiety intensely, and maintain the fear for as long as he was able during the five–hour period. Whenever he caught himself getting tired, he was to redouble his efforts and continue to think about going crazy. He was to keep the thought at a maximum level. After each session we set an appointment for him to discuss his experience.

His first session was difficult. For the first three hours he panicked—not continually, but in waves. He said that he must have had at least eight panic attacks. When he felt the fear, he desperately wanted to run out of the bedroom. The only thing that kept him in the bed was this thought:

I have been scared for 10 years; my life is going nowhere. I have lost my most important relationships and have not grown in my career, all because of this fear of going insane. If this fear is true, I will go insane. But what of it? It would happen sooner or later anyway, why not today? Today is as good a day as any other to become psychotic. If it is not going to happen, well, let me find that out now.

For the first three hours he feared insanity, but for the next two he had trouble keeping his mind on the fear. His mind started to wander; he began to think of what he was going to have for dinner, where he was going to go on his vacation, a new car he needed to buy. Near the end of the five hours he was glad to stop. The whole exercise was boring him.

Justin's next two sessions were easier. He had trouble thinking the belief and only had two or three waves of panic. He got bored more quickly and he felt little anxiety about insanity. In the final session, the thought didn't bother him at all. He spent most of the session thinking of other things. He couldn't force himself to think about it because it seemed silly.

Flooding didn't cure Justin as quickly or as easily as this account suggests. It took him several months of practice at overcoming occasional panic attacks before the problem was solved. As Justin described it later,

> The fear wasn't the same anymore. The edge seemed to have been taken off of it. Since the flooding, I knew the fear was just bullshit. I knew the thought was just a silly superstition. It took me a while to be sure, I had to keep on testing myself, but somewhere inside I knew.

My last report from Justin, many years later, was very positive. He would occasionally get some mild fear about insanity, about every year or so, because he let his thinking get lazy. But he reported that he could easily get rid of it with a little cognitive work.

Comment

The key to all flooding techniques is for clients to remain in the feared scene until their bodies naturally reduce the CRs. If they escape without completing the flooding, the fear increases.

Flooding is one of the last techniques used in the cognitive restructuring repertoire because the technique is quite painful.

Of course, for flooding to be appropriate, therapists must be certain that no real UCS can occur in the flooding procedure. It is common sense not to flood schizophrenic clients who are afraid of hallucinating or depressive patients who are afraid of committing suicide.

Further Information

Flooding and implosive therapy, although primarily behavioral rather than cognitive techniques, may be based on removing a conditioned avoidance response. The most comprehensive work on the subject is Boudewyns and Shipley (1983). Also see Stampfl and Levis (1967) for implosive therapy.

Related techniques are negative practice, massed practice, implosion, and reactive inhibition.

Wolpe (1958, 1969, 1973) discusses image flooding and its variations. The most comprehensive review is in Marshall, Gauthier, and Gordon (1979). Dunlap (1932) first discussed negative practice.

External, reactive, and conditioned inhibitions have been offered as noncognitive explanations for flooding. See Rescorla (1969) and Zimmer-Hart and Rescorla (1974). Also see Clark Hull's (1943) theoretical discussion of sEr and Ir, and Rescorla (1967) and Schwartz (1978) for more theoretical examination.

COGNITIVE AVERSIVE CONDITIONING
Principles

Aversive conditioning is a form of hard countering in which the therapist teaches clients to punish their own irrational beliefs. The theory is that if aversive stimuli are paired with false beliefs, clients will be less likely to think them, and the thoughts will be less likely to elicit conditioned responses. This is the opposite of reinforcing a rational belief—instead of eating a candy bar for thinking a rational thought, the client might be encouraged to take a dose of castor oil for thinking a negative thought.

Many stimuli can negatively sensitize irrational thoughts; these include negative beliefs, images, emotions; unpleasant physical sensations (like shock), nausea, muscle strain; and unpleasant behaviors. If there are enough pairings, and if the stimuli are aversive enough, the thoughts themselves will be experienced as unpleasant.

Method 1. Self-Punishment

1. Use the client's master list of beliefs.
2. Record the major types of situations in which the client is likely to have these thoughts. Each situation should be described with a specific scene and in enough detail so that the client can clearly visualize it.

3. Have the client imagine one of the scenes with its accompanying irrational thought; when it is clearly in mind give him or her the following instructions.

> Okay. Now I would like you to imagine the worst possible consequences of thinking this irrational thought. What bad things have occurred because you have thought this way? What pain has this thought given you? What good things have been removed or never happened? What has it done to your self–esteem? What has it done to your relationships? How has it hurt your life? I would like you to imagine all these things happening simply because of your irrational thought. Don't just *think* about the bad things, but *picture* them until they are clearly in your mind, so that you can feel the negative emotions.

4. Repeat the aversive scene at least three times with each irrational thought. If you wish, have your client say out loud what he or she is imagining so that you can help to make the scenes as aversive as possible.
5. Audiotape the exercise and instruct the client to listen to the tape three times a week for several weeks.

Method 2. Standard Aversive Images

1. Standard images of vomiting, a snake pit, spiders, or being despised by everyone can be used. Interweave the images with the irrational thoughts so that the two become closely associated. For example, one client had low self-esteem and was frequently depressed because she was dependent on others. She manipulated others so that they would manage her finances, plan her vacations, and direct her life. We used the following aversive script.

> Imagine that you are having many problems in your life that need to be corrected. Your car is broken, your sink is clogged up, you haven't gotten a pay raise in three years, and you're overdrawn at your bank. For three years you have gone with a man who says he is not ready to marry.
> You start thinking: "Somebody needs to take care of me. I need somebody to solve these problems. I am too fragile to cope with life." As you think these thoughts, you begin to get a queasy feeling in your stomach. You feel nauseous. Small

chunks of food come to your mouth and taste bitter. You swallow them back down.

You start thinking of getting someone to help you, someone who will call the bank or find a plumber. But the thought makes you feel sicker. Your eyes water. Snot and mucous from your nose are running down into your mouth. Your stomach is turning. You think about calling your ex-husband so that he can take care of you, and about asking your mother to call your boss to complain about your not getting a raise, but these thoughts cause you to feel very sick. You start to vomit. You vomit all over yourself. It starts dripping down your legs onto the floor. You think again of how somebody must take care of you and you vomit even more. There are yellow and brown stains all over your clothes.

You start having the dry heaves. You can't stop retching. It feels like your insides are about to come out.

2. The best aversive images are those selected by clients, based on their own idiosyncratic fears and disgusts. Have clients describe the most disgusting, detestable experiences they have ever imagined happening to them. You can make a brief hierarchy. Then, using the above interweaving method, tie these aversive images to their irrational thoughts.

Method 3. Physical Aversion

Have the client imagine the irrational thought. When it is clearly in mind, associate with it an external aversive stimulus such as a mild finger electrical shock or a snap of a rubber band. Other options are tensing up the stomach muscle, holding one's breath, noxious smells like sulfur odor, or strenuous, painful physical exercise. A thought and an aversive sensation must be paired repeatedly in order for the thought to become noxious.

Method 4. Red Taping

Red taping allows clients to engage in the negative thinking, but only after they have performed a variety of aversive activities. Pick a belief that clients are obsessed with, such as: "I am sick and inferior to everyone." Instruct them that they are permitted to think this thought only after they have earned the right to do so. To earn the right, they must do the following: exercise for 15 minutes, drink three glasses of water, record the time and place where they will permit themselves to engage in their obsession, and write out every nonobsessive thought they have for at least 20 minutes. Only after performing these tasks are they permitted to obsess for 10 minutes. If they want another 10 minutes, they must do the same routine again. The response cost becomes so expensive that after a while most clients prefer to skip the 10 minutes of obsessing.

Method 5. Removing Positive Stimuli

Another form of aversive conditioning entails the removal of something positive. The effect is similar to associating a negative stimulus to the belief. The removed positive variable can be one of many things: needed relaxation; a pleasant image, a positive emotion, or a positive belief—any or all might be removed the moment your client succumbs to the irrational belief. In the literature this technique is often called covert response cost or negative punishment.

Like other covert sensitization procedures, a large number of repetitions is often needed. Clients practice with the therapist as well as at home by listening to tapes of the exercise.

Method 6. Negative Labels

Words are symbols of larger concepts, and these symbols often have a negative connotations that produce aversive emotional responses. By associating negative labels to the clients' irrational thoughts, therapists can help them develop a negative response to the thoughts themselves.

Whenever clients think or express the irrational thought, they should say these words to themselves: dumb, lame, muddled, asinine, bird–brained, childish, inane, absurd, foolish, nonsensical, ridiculous, laughable, ludicrous, idiotic, meaningless, preposterous, half–baked, groundless, inept, vapid, boring, monotonous, drivel, lame–brain, babble, dense, oafish, gullible.

Sometimes you may ask the clients to identify their thought by the negative label, e.g., "I had my idiotic thought yesterday, but I didn't have the lame–brain one," or "I got upset again when I had the monotonous thought that others are better than me." As in all aversive conditioning, it is essential that clients label their thoughts, but not themselves, as negative, e.g., "I am smart, but this thought is idiotic."

Comment

Whenever therapists use aversive techniques to change thoughts, they run the risk of clients' attaching negative feelings to more than just the targeted variable. Clients can start feeling negative about therapy, the therapist, the counseling technique, or themselves. It is essential that the therapist provide exact discrimination training to keep the aversive associations from generalizing to other stimuli.

As in the case of positive reinforcers for positive thoughts, negative pairing with negative thoughts must be commensurate with the offending thought. Clients must not feel that they should chop off an arm for a relatively minor transgression.

Most aversive techniques are used in conjunction with escape conditioning. See the next section of this chapter for an explanation.

Further Information

A great deal of research has been done on aversive conditioning. Although most of it has not been cognitively oriented, the reader can easily make the necessary adaptation. Cognitive aversive techniques have been used successfully for the treatment of obsessive thoughts (Hoogduin, de Haan, Schaap, & Arts, 1987), but much of the research shows mixed results as to the effectiveness of the behavior procedures. See particularly Barlow, Agras, Leitenberg, Callahan, and Moore (1972), Barlow, Leitenberg, and Agras (1969), Barlow, Reynolds, and Agras (1973), Brownell, Hayes, and Barlow (1977), Cautela (1966, 1967, 1971a, 1971b), Hayes, Brownell, and Barlow (1978), Singer (1974), Thorpe and Olson (1997), O'Donohue (1997). Some authors have suggested that there are always procedures superior to aversive techniques (Lavigna, 1986).

Originally, I called this technique "self-punishment" (Casey & Mc Mullin, 1976, 1985; Mc Mullin & Casey, 1975).

COGNITIVE ESCAPE CONDITIONING
Principles

Escape conditioning is most often used in conjunction with aversive techniques. Any stimulus that removes an aversive state becomes a negative reinforcer. If the therapist has conditioned clients to feel pain whenever they think a particular irrational thought, they can then be taught to escape this pain by thinking a rational thought. The rational thought would therefore be more likely to occur, while the irrational thought would decrease in frequency.

The full aversive–escape paradigm is often called covert sensitization, and it can be diagrammed as follows. In the example, an animal is conditioned to fear a red light because it has been paired with shock. The shock is removed if the animal presses a lever that switches the light to green. Thus the lever pressing and the appearance of the green light are negatively reinforced and are more likely to increase in frequency.

What is true for a behavior like lever pressing is also true for thoughts. In the cognitive example the rational thought allows the client to escape from the pain elicited by the irrational thought. The irrational thought (NS) becomes less likely to occur, while the rational thought (CS) increases in frequency. As a result, the rational thought is negatively reinforced.

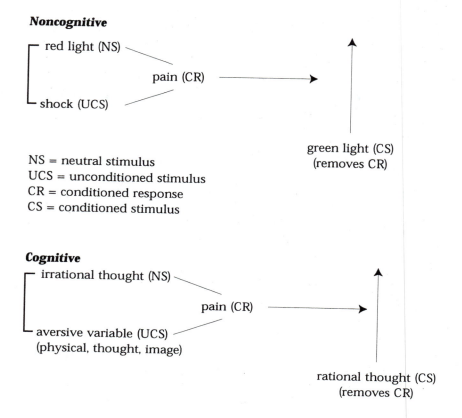

Noncognitive

red light (NS)

pain (CR)

shock (UCS)

green light (CS)
(removes CR)

NS = neutral stimulus
UCS = unconditioned stimulus
CR = conditioned response
CS = conditioned stimulus

Cognitive

irrational thought (NS)

pain (CR)

aversive variable (UCS)
(physical, thought, image)

rational thought (CS)
(removes CR)

Method 1. Relief from Aversive State

Connect an aversive stimulus to a negative belief. You can use self-punishment, aversive images, physical aversion, or negative labels. (See previous section on cognitive aversive conditioning.)

After the aversive state is created, have your clients think the realistic, rational thought. When it is clearly in mind, remove the aversive state immediately. If a finger shock has been used to create the aversive state, immediately remove it upon the presentation of the rational thought. If a negative image is presented, the image is changed to a positive picture as soon as the rational thought occurs. For example, in the aversive conditioning example mentioned earlier (the vomiting scene interwoven with the irrational thought, "Somebody needs to take care me," pp. 122–123) the following escape scene was presented.

> You are still feeling extremely nauseous. You are about to vomit again, but then you start thinking about how you really can take care of yourself; you can solve your problems on your own. You can fix the car and the sink, and you can correct the overdraw problem at your bank. You can confront your boyfriend and your boss. Immediately, you start feeling better. You take a deep breath, and your lungs and stomach start clearing. You walk out of your house and feel the fresh clean air. You feel the warm sun. There is a gentle breeze. You lie down on soft, mossy grass, underneath a willow tree, relaxing as you contemplate your strength and how you can solve your problems by yourself. You walk back into your house and open all of your windows. You clean everything, scrubbing floors, walls, rugs, and furniture. You throw away your vomit–stained clothes and put on new, fresh, crisp ones. You start thinking of how you will handle all your other problems yourself, just as you handled these. You make a resolution that you won't ask anyone else to help you with problems that you can solve yourself. You feel confident and self–assured.

Method 2. Anxiety Relief

Another form of escape conditioning is called anxiety relief. This technique uses the same procedures as the previous method, except that the client seeks an escape from anxiety instead of from other types of noxious stimuli. In the escape scene the client imagines the tension rapidly subsiding as soon as the rational thought is believed.

Comment

The essential feature of all escape techniques is that the aversive state is removed only when clients think the realistic thought, thus making the thought a negative reinforcement. Whichever escape techniques are used, the therapist should record the procedure and urge clients to listen to the tape at least three times a week. Clients feel a great deal better about escape conditioning than they do about aversive conditioning. The association bonds are stronger, and clients are more motivated to practice the techniques.

Further Information

Cautela has probably done the greatest amount of work on image escape conditioning (see Ascher & Cautela, 1974; Brownell, Hayes, & Barlow, 1977; Cautela, 1966, 1967, 1971b; Hayes et al., 1978; Kazdin & Smith, 1979). There are recent discussions about whether such concepts can best be explained by behavioral or cognitive theory. See Wilson, Hayes, and Gifford (1997) and refer to the references listed in the aversive and avoidance sections.

COVERT AVOIDANCE
Principles

Avoidance conditioning is similar to escape conditioning, except that the emphasis is placed upon preventing the aversive stimulus from occurring rather than first experiencing the aversion stimulus. Under this technique, any behavior that avoids an aversive emotion is reinforced, making that behavior likely to increase in frequency. This is as true for thoughts as it is for behaviors. Clients are likely to strongly believe any thought that keeps anxiety away. Classic examples of avoidance thoughts are:

- I shouldn't think about my problems.
- I shouldn't change; change is dangerous.
- It's my parents' (spouse's, boss's, therapist's) fault.
- I am not responsible for what has happened to my life.

Covert avoidance uses this same principle by having clients switch their thoughts so that they can cope more successfully. (As with all the techniques discussed in this book, extremes are to be avoided. The goal here is to avoid pain, not to teach clients how to "cop out" of their responsibilities at every opportunity.) The rational belief substitutes for the irrational one; if it works, the rational belief will become stronger.

If the client thinks a rational thought while imagining the beginnings of a negative scene, then the aversive stimulus (whether an image of vomiting, shock, or the worst possible consequences) is avoided. If the client doesn't think the rational thought, then the aversive stimulus is presented in full and continues until the client finally thinks of the rational belief. Clients quickly learn that rational thinking postpones or eliminates punishment.

Method

1. Make a hierarchy of problem situations and their accompanying irrational thoughts.
2. Pick the lowest item on the hierarchy and have the client imagine that situation and the thoughts associated with it. Pair the thoughts with a negative emotion, image, or external aversive stimulus. Repeat several times until the client pairs the negative feeling with the irrational thought. The negative emotion should be strong and quite aversive.
3. Have the client imagine the same situations, but this time have him substitute a rational thought in place of the irrational thought immediately before the negative emotion occurs. If the rational thought is strongly believed the aversive stimulus is not presented; if it is not believed then the negative stimulus occurs.
4. Keep alternating the second and third steps, moving up the hierarchy as you do, so that the client learns that rational thinking will help him or her to avoid negative consequences.

Example

A number of rational thoughts can help clients avoid negative emotions. Here are some:

1. I can be happy even though everything isn't going perfectly.
2. I can enjoy my life even though I had a bad childhood.
3. I can always forgive myself for past mistakes.

4. Real dangers are almost always external. No thought or emotion can really hurt me.

5. I am not to blame for things I cannot control.

6. I accept that there are times in my life when I will get anxious or depressed, and I don't have to push these emotions out of my life forever to be generally happy.

7. Embarrassing myself may be amusing for me as well as for others. I can afford to laugh at myself.

8. My life is not so important to humanity that I have to live in dread of all possible misfortunes that may befall me.

9. I am not in the center of everyone else's universe. People are not spending their lives concentrating on how many mistakes I make.

10. The world was created by nature, not by me. It doesn't have to follow my rules of fairness, justice, or equality.

11. It is not possible for me to be better in everything than everybody else.

12. Nobody will care about my petty mistakes after I am gone.

13. Looking back at my life I can see that most of the things I worried about in the past proved to be unimportant and insignificant.

14. The more I achieve, the more some people will resent me. I should remember Mark Twain's epigram, "Few of us can stand prosperity—another man's I mean."

15. The progression of the human species will not be permanently impeded if I don't reach my personal search for glory. In fact, most people won't even notice. They are too busy with their own searches.

16. Nature hasn't given me the power to control everything around me. Besides, it's not a whole lot of fun being responsible for the world.

17. I am not the only one losing out on the good life. Nobody has it. The guy who appears to have it—doesn't! It's just an illusion because we don't know him well enough. The millionaire sits on top of a pile of broken relationships; the movie star loses the freedom to walk down a public street without being attacked by the paparazzi. The single person is lonely; the married person is bored. We all have our shining moments, those few fleeting moments when we and the world around us seem to glitter (the birth of a child, making love to someone we love, winning the big

game, getting the degree, etc.), but such times are few and mightily short. The only real profanity is when we pulverize these shining moments with thoughts such as, "It's not shiny enough. Is this all there is? It's not as much as I was promised. Is it going to end soon? I wonder if I am handling the moment correctly. Others have shinier moments."

Comment

With most of our clients, avoidance conditioning occurred naturally after they had practiced aversive–escape conditioning, when they started to think the realistic thought earlier in the conditioning sequence in order to avoid the negative stimulus.

Further Information

The fundamental principles of avoidance conditioning have been established for many years. See Seligman and Johnson (1973) for an emphasis of the cognitive components. For noncognitive, see Azrin, Huchinson, and Hake (1967), de Villiers (1974), Foree and Lo Lordo (1975), Garcia and Koelling (1966), Herrnstein (1969), Hineline and Rachlin (1969), Kamin (1956), Kamin, Brimer, and Black (1963), Mowrer and Lamoreaux (1946), Richie (1951), Sidman (1953, 1966), Solomon (1964), Solomon and Wynne (1954, 1956), Turner and Solomon (1962).

Recently, behavior analysts suggest that teaching cognitive avoidance may have negative effects on clients. Suppression may cause a rebound effect (see Hayes, 1995; Hayes, Strosahl, & Wilson, 1996; Hayes & Wilson, 1994; and Hayes, Wilson, Gifford, Follette, & Strosahl, 1996).

FIVE

Countering Techniques: Soft

In the previous chapter, we discussed countering techniques that try to increase clients' levels of arousal. High emotional countering can be effective for certain types of beliefs, particularly when it pulls in the client's anger against irrational cognitions. An aggressive or assertive attack against a depressive or passive thought helps clients change not only their thoughts, but also the emotions that accompany them. But there are times when soft emotions are more helpful in parrying clients' beliefs. Soft emotional techniques, such as calm, relaxed countering, can defuse high emotional arousal and make it easier for clients to more gently change their beliefs.

For anxiety–producing beliefs, it is often far better to counter in a more relaxed manner. It has been theorized that soft countering reduces the client's state of anxiety, while aggressive countering increases it. In a relaxed state the irrational belief is challenged by both the counter thought and the counter emotion, providing two active treatment elements.

This chapter describes how to teach clients to use soft emotions to counter their beliefs.

RELAXED COUNTERING
Principles

The most common type of soft countering uses relaxation training. Clients are first instructed in any one of the many types of relaxation, and then countering techniques are employed. The most crucial element in using this technique is to be sure that clients remain calm throughout the procedure.

The technique pairs relaxation with anxiety–provoking stimuli to inhibit conditioned anxiety responses. This is similar to counter conditioning—a procedure that pairs a positive to a negative stimulus so that the positive replaces the negative. In order for the procedure to work, the positive stimulus must be stronger than the negative. This is achieved by exposing the subject gradually to the feared event. Schematically, negative and positive conditioned responses look like this:

$$CS- \longrightarrow CR-$$
$$CS+ \longrightarrow CR+$$

After pairing a strong CS+ with a weaker CS–, we have:

$$CS \longrightarrow CR+$$

In the traditional counter–conditioning approach, the CS– consists of a series of anxiety–producing images that are arranged in a graduated hierarchy. These images are paired with relaxation until the relaxed response substitutes for the anxious one.

Cognitive restructuring modifies this procedure by desensitizing client beliefs instead of their images, thus reducing or eliminating any negative emotion connected to those beliefs. Images are used only to provide a context or background for visualizing different beliefs.

Method 1

1. Initially the client is trained in one of the several available methods of relaxation. These include standard relaxation, applied relaxation, EMG, GSR, pulse rate reduction, white or pink noise, alpha–theta relaxing scripts, nature sounds, and self–hypnosis (see Further Information).
2. Develop a hierarchy of irrational beliefs that are causing anxiety. Order the hierarchy by degrees of fear the thoughts elicit or how strongly the thoughts are believed.
3. Instruct the client to imagine the least provocative thought on the hierarchy. When this thought is clearly in mind, begin deep muscle relaxation. Continue with this procedure until the client's tension level returns to zero, indicating that the thought no longer produces anxiety. For example:

Now I would like you to think of the next thought on your hierarchy. Picture this thought as clearly as you can. If you wish, you can imagine a particular situation in the past when you have often had the thought. Continue thinking the thought until it is clearly in mind. Tell me when you have it by signaling with your right hand. . . . Okay, stop! Now relax yourself just as you have been taught, and keep relaxing until you feel comfortable again. Tell me when you are ready. (Biofeedback measures or a verbal report can be used instead of a hand signal.) Now I would like you to do it again. Think the thought, get it clearly in mind, and then relax yourself. You can imagine a scene where you are likely to have the thought if it helps you, but make sure it's different from the one you used before.

4. Continue through the client's hierarchy of thoughts until the anxiety for all items is zero.
5. Tape the procedure so the client can practice at home.

Method 2

You can vary your technique by substituting responses other than relaxation. You can use positive physical responses, assertive responses, nature tapes, positive images that a client finds personally reinforcing, or low heartbeat, GSR, or EMG readings.

Method 3

General images can also be associated with irrational thoughts as a substitute for relaxation. In most cases the therapist should help the clients interweave these images with the irrational thoughts in such a way that the emotional valence of the image transfers to the beliefs. The following images have proven useful: Superman, Power Rangers, favorite heroes and heroines, favorite objects, sunflowers, lotus blossoms, sun, stars, moon, religious figures (Christ, Buddha, Mohammed), a wise guru, natural life forces (rivers, mountains, oceans), watching oneself in a movie, visualizing oneself as a parent, adult, or child, or imagining oneself as an animal.

Ideally, one or more of these positive images are interwoven with the negative belief. For instance, interweaving the thought, "I need to be better than everyone else," with the feeling that a client has toward children may bring home the idea that a child is worthwhile even though an adult may be stronger and wiser and may have achieved more. Therefore, being superior is not a prerequisite for being worth-while. Similarly, the Power Ranger image could be interwoven with the thought, "I am inferior to other girls because I can't ride a bike." Many eastern religions, including Zen and Yoga, have used image desensitization for centuries.

Example

Employ this countering technique after a relaxed state has been induced.

> I'd like you to imagine the next scene on your list as clearly as you can, using all your senses. While imagining this scene, listen to the irrational things you tell yourself about it. Continue until you have both the scene and one key thought clearly in mind. Indicate when you are ready.

(Client gives the signal.)

> Now relax completely. Let your muscles become loose and limp to the point where they feel warm and heavy.

(Repeat parts of the relaxation technique used in the beginning of the session.)

> Indicate when you are fully relaxed.
> Now, I'd like you to stay in this relaxed state. If at any time you start to feel tense, stop what you're doing and relax yourself. While you relax, I would like you to talk to yourself silently, in a soft and caring manner. Convince yourself that your thinking is not true. Imagine that you are talking to yourself in the way that a loving parent talks to a child afraid of imaginary monsters in the bedroom—you need to be patient but firm. Gently persuade this child that her fears are not useful.
> Keep persuading the child until you feel a distinct weakening of your old useless thinking and a distinct lessening of the unpleasant emotion. Take as much time as you need. Indicate when you are done.

This technique is repeated twice more, after which the client again imagines the test scene while the therapist monitors the client's state of relaxation. If the client remains relaxed while imagining the scene, the next item in the list is presented, and so on, until the client can visualize each scene with a minimum of anxiety.

Comment

If the client becomes aroused at any time during the procedure, stop the process and return to the relaxation procedure.

We have found that the first method, which pairs relaxation with anxiety–producing thoughts, is not as effective as other desensitization techniques. Some clients, particularly agoraphobics, get anxious when trying to relax ("I may lose control"). In addition, relaxation is a phys-iological sensory response, while thoughts are cognitive. Thus, this method mixes two very different perceptual modes, which seems to dilute the effectiveness of the technique. The best substitute response is in the same mode as the original negative conditioned stimulus (visual, auditory, kinesthetic, sensory, or emotional). For this reason, the third method, which counters negative thoughts with positive thoughts, is usually the most effective.

Further Information

This technique is similar to some of Wolpe's desensitization proce-dures, but with a dose of cognition (Wolpe 1958, 1969, 1973; Wolpe & Lazarus, 1967; Wolpe, Salter, & Reyna, 1964). His later work (Wolpe, 1978, 1981a, 1981b; Wolpe, Lande, McNally, & Schotte, 1985) shows that he recognizes the importance of cognitions in some conditioning processes.

Therapists can use any form of relaxation. There are mountains of books, manuals, and tapes on the subject. Tapes can be found from Davidson (1997) and CDs from Relaxation Company (1996). Relaxation with a cognitive–behavioral spin can be obtained from Smith (1990) and you can find a complete listing from Sutcliffe (1994). Please don't forget the work of the originator of the relaxation technique, Jacobson (1974), and the shorter version of his work by Wolpe (1973). Ost has created applied relaxation and has compared its effects to cognitive therapy (Ost & Westling, 1995).

ANTICATASTROPHIC PRACTICE
Principles

Because most people are consistent in their thinking, in different situations and at different times a client may distort reality in the same way. The most common type of distortion is catastrophizing, the extreme exaggeration of impending doom. Many clients observe a minor threat in the environment and believe the worst conceivable danger is imminent. After years of practice, their exaggerations become habitual, causing chronic anxiety and a constant dread of the environment.

What these clients fail to recognize is that the word catastrophe implies a *great* calamity, misfortune, or disaster. Although clients may accurately perceive some danger in a given situation, in catastrophizing they grossly exaggerate the degree of danger, along with its potential for damage. Their brains expand pain into torture, embarrassment into disgrace, an unpleasant experience into an intolerable one.

The best counters to catastrophic beliefs employ soft countering, in which clients undercut the high emotional energy invested in irrational thoughts by relaxing and calmly thinking of the best conceivable outcome they can imagine. The new interpretation overcorrects the negative emotion caused by the catastrophizing, improving the probability that the final affective response will approximate reality.

Method

1. List the situations the client catastrophizes.
2. Record the damage the client anticipates for each situation.
3. On a continuum from 1 to 10, record the extent of damage that the client anticipates (1 equals no damage and 10 equals horrific damage).
4. After discussing countercatastrophizing, ask the client to imagine the best possible outcome that could happen in each of the situations. Record this outcome on the same 1 to 10 continuum.
5. Have the client decide, based on past experience, whether the catastrophe or best possible outcome is most likely to occur.
6. Where appropriate, have the client use the continuum to predict danger in upcoming situations that are feared. After the event actually occurs, have the client check the scale to see whether the anticipated level of damage occurred.
7. Clients should practice countercatastrophizing regularly until they can more realistically assess anticipated damage.

Example: The Story of Dean

Dean, a top businessman, was referred to me by his private physician. He was unusually successful, having expertly advised major corporations worldwide for many years. Despite this, he suffered from chronic anxiety and had panic attacks before each presentation. A year and a half of chlordiazepoxide treatment had not reduced his anxiety.

As is typical with this type of anxiety, Dean thought the same core belief before each presentation. He imagined that his head would start shaking because he was nervous, and all the corporate executives would discover that he wasn't the cool, calm professional he pretended to be. He imagined this tic would destroy his facade, and that everyone in the audience would see his "cowardice."

This man's deeply rooted core belief was that he was basically inferior and needed to hide behind a competent facade. Letting others see behind the facade would mean complete and instantaneous rejection. The damage would be irreparable; it would be the worst possible thing that could ever happen to him.

Dean's core attitude can be broken down into specific sub–beliefs, as follows:

1. Everyone in the audience will ignore what I am saying the minute they see my head shake.
2. They will know that I am a total fake and will never believe me again.
3. Because they will see me as a sissy and not a real man, they will never associate with me again.
4. Since these top–level executives wouldn't want to be around such a wimp, I will never be able to give my lectures again. I will lose all my male friends, women will hate my weakness, and I will become poor, alone, and destitute.

For each one of Dean's thoughts we made a catastrophe scale as shown below. The X on each scale indicates the extent of the predicted damage, were the event to occur.

How catastrophic would it be if . . .

everyone saw my tic?

|————————————————————————————————X——|
1   2   3   4   5 ·   6   7   8   9   10

the audience concentrated on it?

|————————————————————————————X————————|
1   2   3   4   5   6   7   8   9   10

the audience thought I was a total fake?

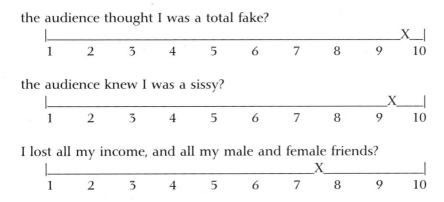

the audience knew I was a sissy?

I lost all my income, and all my male and female friends?

Next we listed the best possible things that could happen and marked anticipated damage from these outcomes on the same scale. The outcome was that few people would see his tic, and those who did wouldn't concentrate on it. No one would think him a fake or sissy, and he would lose neither income nor friends. The client rated all of these outcomes at about a zero damage level.

By comparing the ratings for the worst and best possible outcomes it became apparent that the client was catastrophizing by a factor of eight.

We then assembled a series of other continua taken from Dean's past predictions. By comparing what had happened in prior situations to what the client had predicted would happen, we found that very little damage had actually occurred, and that the best possible outcomes were consistently closer to reality than the worst. The client could not think of a single time out of hundreds of situations when anything remotely similar to his worst predictions had occurred.

For the next 6 weeks, this man predicted the best and worst possible outcomes of each presentation he was about to make, along with the estimated damage. The next day he went back to his scale and determined which prediction was most accurate. Without exception, the "best possible outcome" occurred every time.

Comment

The use of the continuum isn't essential to this method, but it generally helps clarify the client's level of catastrophizing.

Clients often ask, "What if the worst thing imaginable *does* happen, even though it's highly unlikely? Shouldn't I worry about that?" In this situation, you can point out that if they feared all low probabilities that could occur, they would have to hide in caves to avoid meteors, avoid crossing streets to keep from getting hit by trucks, and stop eating food to keep from being poisoned. Even though these things can and do happen, people can still be happy. Our job in life is to avoid high probability dangers, not to avoid every conceivable catastrophe.

Further Information

Beck (Beck, 1993; Beck, Emery, & Greenberg, 1985; Beck & Zebb, 1994) states that catastrophic misinterpretation is one of the key cognitive components for panic disorders. It is a central element in treating social phobias in individual and group cognitive therapy (Heimberg & Juster, 1995; Stein, 1995) and important in obsessive-compulsive disorders (Salkovskis, 1996; Salkovskis, Richards, & Forrester, 1995).

Catastrophic thinking is discussed in detail by the rational emotive behavioral therapists. See Ellis (1973, 1995, 1996), Ellis and Grieger (1977), and Maultsby (1984, 1990).

COPING STATEMENTS
Principles

Many clients expect to fail miserably in everything they do. Bandura (1997) and others have described this expectation as "low self-efficacy," the belief that one cannot execute the behaviors required to produce positive outcomes. Clients exhibiting this expectation consistently underestimate their ability to cope with various situations. They believe they will fail at their jobs, be rejected by their lovers, or flunk out of school, and after a while these types of expectations tend to become self-fulfilling. Coping imagery can avert this pattern, helping improve client self-efficacy.

Coping imagery is best done as a soft countering procedure, executed in a relaxed, calm manner. It can be distinguished from mastery imagery done in an aroused emotional state because in mastery, the clients imagine doing a task perfectly; in coping, they anticipate various problems with the task, but also picture dealing with these problems. Coping statements are superior to mastery imagery because they sensitize the clients to possible mistakes and prepare them to recover from errors they may make in real situations.

Method

1. Create a hierarchy of situations in which the client is depressed or anxious.
2. With the client's help, prepare a self-talk dialogue to be used during the stressful situation. The dialogue should realistically anticipate mistakes, errors, and negative emotions, and include step-by-step instructions on how to overcome these problems. It should cover the time before, during, and after the anxious situation.
3. Rehearse the dialogue out loud with the client for each item on the hierarchy. For best results, use a modeling procedure (Meichenbaum, 1993, 1994) in which the therapist says the dialogue and the client first repeats it, then imagines it. Monitor the client throughout the rehearsal and correct any mistakes.
4. Encourage clients to practice their coping techniques, using the method that seems most effective. For instance, some clients find it beneficial to listen passively to a cassette tape of the therapist reading the dialogue, while others prefer a tape that describes each situation on the hierarchy in detail, thus allowing them to practice the dialogues covertly. Still others carry the dialogues on index cards and read them when faced with a real situation. In most cases, clients need to practice their scripts for at least six weeks.

Example: The Story of Paula

Paula, who was referred to me by another psychologist, had been agoraphobic for two years. One of the highest fears on her hierarchy was shopping alone in a large supermarket; whenever she tried to shop, her anxiety would overwhelm her and she would have to leave. By the time I first saw her she hadn't been to a large store for a year and a half.

We practiced the following dialogue for several sessions. Initially we recorded it and she listened to the recording three times a week for five weeks. She then practiced the script in vivo six times, during actual agoraphobic situations. This technique finally reduced her phobia sufficiently so that she could shop comfortably in large supermarkets.

Her coping dialogue follows:

This morning I'm going to the supermarket. I'll probably be tense in the beginning, but only because I have stayed away from the store some time—not because stores are really something to fear. Stores are *NOT* dangerous. Even little children and very old people go to grocery stores. If stores were dangerous, they'd have a big warning sign in front reading WARNING, THE SURGEON GENERAL HAS DETERMINED THAT SUPERMARKETS ARE DANGEROUS TO YOUR HEALTH.

(*Paula imagines entering store.*) Here I am, looking around! It's like every other store. There's a lot of produce and canned goods and meats. No one in the history of the world has ever been attacked by a can of peas. Still, I feel a little nervous inside. Since stores don't have the power to create fear, it must be something I am telling myself. Let's see what superstitious notion I am buying into. Ah, yes! It's that same old idiotic thought—that I'm going to lose control and embarrass myself in front of all these people. Golden oldie bullshit! I have been saying this nonsense to myself for two years, I have never lost control and I never will. It's just a stupid game I play with myself, like pretending if I put my finger in my ear, my nose will fall off. These people have more things to do in this store than to watch me to see if I show the tiniest sign of tension. They are more interested in finding a ripe tomato. Besides, I don't have to control this tension. All I have to do is buy my can of succotash and leave—big deal! It doesn't matter how tense I get. My job isn't to shop without tension; it's only to shop. And I'm going to shop no matter how I feel. Even if I have to crawl through the checkout line on my hands and knees, I'm going to stay. My life has been ruled by a silly superstition long enough.

(*Paula completes shopping, leaves store.*) There, I did it! That's the only thing that counts. What I do in life is far more important than how I feel when doing it. I'll keep doing this until I get rid of my superstitions and the fear they produce.

Comment

While most clients benefit a great deal from practicing coping statements through imagery, these statements ultimately must be practiced in vivo. Otherwise, the client can sabotage the technique, saying, for example, "It's very nice to think this way, but I still haven't gone to the store."

We don't believe that you should pressure clients to practice their scripts in the environment until they have rehearsed them extensively and covertly. To do so would only create more anxiety, increasing the probability of failure.

Further Information

For early information on coping statements see Cautela (1971b), Goldfried (1971), and Suinn and Richardson (1971). A more thorough investigation of the theory behind this technique is provided by Lazarus, Kanner, and Folkman (1980), Mahoney (1993b), Mahoney and Thoresen (1974), and Meichenbaum (1975, 1977, 1985, 1993).

Cannon (1998) has developed a form of coping based on cognitive rehearsal using hypnosis.

There is also an extensive body of literature on self–efficacy (see Bandura 1977a, 1977b, 1978, 1982, 1984, 1995, 1997; Bandura, Adams, Hardy, & Howells, 1980; Bandura, Reese, & Adams, 1982; Bandura & Schunk 1981; and Teasdale, 1978).

More information about coping vs. mastery imagery can be found in Mahoney and Arnkoff (1978), Richardson (1969), and Singer (1974, 1976, 1995).

COVERT EXTINCTION
Principles

In a classical conditioning paradigm, a client can develop a phobia as a result of having been exposed to a terrifying event. Any stimulus present at the same time as the fear can get conditioned, so that the stimulus develops the ability to produce the anxiety. For example, a client once had difficulty breathing when he drove his car on a long trip because carbon monoxide was leaking from the exhaust system into the car. His respiratory difficulties produced a strong anxiety (UCR). After discovering the leak he repaired the car, but developed anxiety (CR) whenever he drove again and finally stopped driving altogether. Schematically his phobia is:

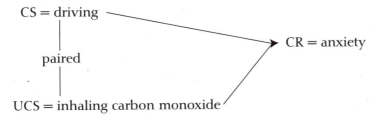

How can this conditioned reflex be eliminated? Even though the client stopped driving for several months, it did not remove the anxiety, for when he was forced to be a passenger in someone else's car, he became anxious again. His conditioned anxiety was not easily removed. Theoretically, had he continued driving, he would have been exposed to the CS without the UCS, and his anxiety would have gradually disappeared. This experience is called extinction. But because he avoided driving, the CS–UCS association never had the opportunity to be eliminated.

To help this client we used covert extinction. The client imagined driving without breathing problems until he could picture the scene without anxiety. After practicing this image for several weeks, he was able to drive again, so that in vivo extinction could eliminate his phobia. Having the client imagine the CS without the UCS is the key to covert extinction. Extinction may erase the previous association, or new learning may replace the old; whatever the correct explanation, the procedure can help clients remove phobias.

Beliefs as well as external stimuli can become conditioned to traumatic events. Thus, any thought that occurs at the time of a strong anxiety response can become a CS that alone will later elicit fear. Therefore covert extinction can be used to disconnect thoughts from their emotional components.

Method 1. Behavioral in Vivo

Have clients practice the feared event until extinction takes place. The therapist must be sure that the UCS will not recur.

Method 2. Covert

Have the client imagine doing the feared activity without aversive consequences.

Method 3. Belief Extinction

1. Make a list of the thoughts that have become associated with the client's sources of anxiety.
2. Have the client imagine thinking the thoughts in various situations, but without any negative emotional response.
3. The client can practice several hundred repetitions at home until the thoughts no longer produce the CRs.

Method 4. Time Extinction

Instruct your clients to wait until they feel happy and confident; then have them read or think the irrational thoughts. Tell them to stop thinking or reading immediately if they begin to feel upset. Instruct clients not to do the exercise when they feel unhappy.

Method 5. Neutral Images

1. Make a list of the client's irrational thoughts and the situations in which they frequently occur.
2. Develop a list of neutral images to which the client attaches little emotion, such as looking at a newspaper, eating a meal, or reading a psychological dissertation. Ask the client to confirm that these activities produce only neutral emotions.
3. Pair the irrational thoughts with the neutral scenes. You will probably need over a hundred repetitions.

Method 6. Shaped Covert Extinction

Have your client imagine a subcomponent of the CS, so that the CR is not elicited. In the earlier example, the upset driver would imagine sitting in the driver's seat, or holding the steering wheel in his hands. Since the CS is not at full strength, the CR never occurs above threshold. Gradually, more and more of the CS is presented, always below threshold, until the full CS causes no response. Specifically:

1. Make a list of the client's irrational thoughts.
2. Logically dissect the thoughts into subcomponents. For example, if the client's thought is "I am worthless if I keep failing at things." You can subdivide "things" into a variety of different failings, like breaking your pencil, forgetting to put out the cat, dropping a stitch, etc.
3. Have the client image the subparts of the thoughts for many repetitions. Make sure that this focus on the subparts causes no discomfort. You can use a biofeedback measure or client self–report to determine whether the client is feeling the CR. If a CR occurs, subdivide the thought further.
4. Provided that there is no emotional response, keep building the thought closer to its original form. Continue until the entire original thought produces no negative emotions.
5. Another form of shaped covert extinction varies the fear–producing image rather than the thought. For example, fear of riding in an elevator can be subdivided by imagining a big elevator, a glass one, an

empty elevator, one that goes up only one floor or one that travels 40 floors. The image can also be varied by changing clients' perspectives of themselves in the phobic situation. Clients can picture themselves in the elevator on TV, looking back from the future, in an audience with friends watching a play of themselves in the elevator, etc. In all cases, the subcomponents of the image are presented so that clients' emotional responses remain below threshold.

Method 7. Morita Therapy

Morita therapy, created at the beginning of this century, is a Japanese therapeutic technique based on extinction procedures. Clients suffering from dysthymic disorders are isolated in a room for the first week. During this time they have anxiety and depression, but they cannot escape or avoid their discomfort. Their CRs are not intentionally exacerbated as in flooding; instead, clients simply experience their thoughts and images and let the consequences occur. Since the imagined consequences (e.g., death, insanity, total loss of control) do not occur, extinction takes place. A cognitive component that helps the extinction process is the instruction: "What one thinks, imagines, or feels is less important than what one does in life. A person can carry on an active, purposeful life, despite the burden of symptoms." This philosophy helps clients realize that there are no ultimate UCSs to thinking and feeling and, therefore, there is no reason to avoid thoughts or emotions.

Example: The Story of Kevin

Some years ago, Kevin came to me because of severe panic attacks. The only environmental trigger we could find was that his college roommate had quit school, leaving him alone in the apartment they had previously shared. After some exploration, we found the possible cause of his severe reaction to this common experience. Kevin described an experience in which he almost drowned when he was 11 years old.

He and his parents had been swimming in the Gulf of Mexico, in a spot where underwater canyons produced back currents that could pull a swimmer out to sea. Kevin remembered standing in water up to his neck, trying to see where his parents were. Suddenly a large wave hit him and dragged him into one of the underwater canyons. The current was strong and he couldn't swim against it—he was being

pulled out to sea. Fortunately, a lifeguard on shore saw what was hap‐
pening and rescued him.

After the experience, Kevin had become very afraid of the ocean,
and his fear had generalized to lakes, rivers, and large swimming
pools; he avoided them all. This was a rather typical incident creating
aquaphobia. Schematically:

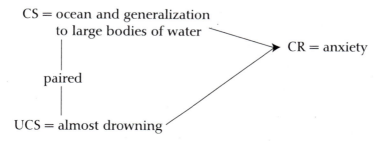

What Kevin was not aware of was that another association had also
occurred. Not only had he been in water when the panic appeared,
but he had also been thinking that he was all alone. He had noticed
that he couldn't see his parents and that there was no one else around.
Ever since that incident he not only feared water but he also feared
being alone. He recalled begging his parents not to go out without
him and demanded that he not be left in the house by himself. When
his roommate had left, he'd found himself alone for an extended time.
Schematically:

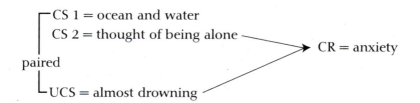

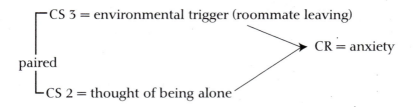

We used several covert extinction methods to remove the anxiety. Kevin listened to a series of tapes in which he imagined thinking he was alone. The scenes ranged from imagining himself alone in the bathroom to being alone on a South Pacific island with no one within a thousand miles. With each image he was told to think the thought for as long as he could without any negative consequences. If he became upset or he imagined some negative consequence to being alone, he was told to stop the scene immediately and do it again until he could think the thought in the scene without getting anxious (shaped covert extinction).

He was also instructed that outside of the above exercise he was to only think about being alone when he was feeling good and self–confident (time extinction).

After the covert treatments he was told to spend more time alone. He gave himself points for each hour he spent by himself without getting anxious, and tried to increase his points each week. He was told to stop if he became anxious (in vivo extinction).

Comment

One of the difficulties with covert extinction in clinical practice is that it is often very difficult to keep the UCS from entering the client's thoughts. It's hard for clients to image a negative scene with only neutral consequences. In most cases covert extinction is used in conjunction with a countering or perceptual shift technique.

Further Information

Cautela was one of the originators of covert extinction procedures (see Ascher & Cautela, 1972; Cautela, 1971a; Gotestam & Melin, 1974; and Weiss, Glazer, Pohorecky, Brick, & Miller, 1975.) A related concept is Beck's (1967) neutralization and habituation technique (Sokolov, 1963).

Eye movement desensitization may have an extinction component. When the old image (the pivotal picture) is brought into awareness and associated with sciatica eye movements, the emotional component may be reduced because the original CS is only partially presented, thus yielding only a partial and much diminished CR. However, there are many other possible explanations for the active element of EMDR (see Shapiro, 1995, 1998).

A subpart of shaped covert extinction is the major phobic treatment of neurolinguistic programming practitioners. Clients imagine seeing a motion picture of themselves in the phobic scene. The scene is varied by imagining it in black and white, as a still picture, run in fast forward, backwards, viewed behind a projection booth, etc. (see Bandler, 1992, 1996; Bandler & Grinder, 1979, 1996; Milliner & Grinder, 1990).

Morita therapy has been discussed in a number of publications (see Fujita, 1986; Morita & Kondo, 1998; Reynolds, 1976, 1981).

NONPATHOLOGICAL THINKING
Principles

Cognitive restructuring therapy, like cognitive behavioral therapy in general, bases its techniques on the experiments and assumptions of learning theory. In all of its many variations, learning theory avoids the use of the medical model to describe clients' problems. Many clients, however, subscribe wholeheartedly to the illness model.

These clients view strong emotions as signs of an unpleasant, if nebulous, condition they call "sick." Because they use this word, they are more likely to display the emotions and behaviors that the "sick" label elicits. Initially, they simply think themselves emotionally crippled, unbalanced, diseased, or in some way deranged for feeling strong emotions. But then they start to play the part, acting out the role of the patient with all the accompanying behavioral and cognitive manifestations such as passivity, helplessness, and expecting the doctor to cure them.

Because of the damaging effects of the "sick" label where it doesn't belong, this thought should be one of the first ones the client attacks. Soft countering is often the best vehicle for changing pathological labeling.

Method

1. Develop a master list of core beliefs connected to the client's negative emotions.
2. Go over each belief with the client and identify any sign that the client is implying a psychological sickness.
3. Explain in detail the inappropriateness of the disease label, and substitute components of the learning theory model for each belief.
4. Throughout all of your therapy sessions, help the client change any

thought or word that implies sickness. Listen for words like "deranged," "mentally unsound," "crazy," "unbalanced," "falling to pieces," "nervous breakdown," "freaking out," "ill," "sick," "unhealthy," "disturbed," etc.

5. Substitute a social learning model for a medical model. Treat clients as students under your tutelage, not as patients under your care. Expect clients to do the homework you assign, to study your principles, and to challenge you if they disagree. Make it clear that you consider counseling to be a joint project, 50/50. You instruct; they study.

Before neurotic clients enter into therapy with me, I give them a sheet that describes the kind of therapy I do, what I expect from them, and what they can expect from me. Here are some excerpts:

My Services

As you know, I practice a particular type of counseling. You and I must decide whether my therapy is the best type for you. If not, I will help you get the right kind. Remember, a recent survey found that there are over 250 different types of therapy (Corsini, 1981, 1994).

My Philosophy

I don't view our relationship as doctor–patient, friend–confidant, leader–follower, or guru–novitiate; I view it as teacher–student. It is my job to give you, as clearly as I can, the tools to solve your own problems. It is your job to use the tools. We are equal partners in your growth.

Openness

Since we are partners in your growth, you have a right to know what I am doing, why I am doing it, how long it will take and what I think are the causes and solutions to your problems. I am not a witch doctor who uses secret, mystical methods to cure people. I want you to know what I think, so always feel free to ask me about what I am doing and why.

General

I will do everything I can to help you by using standard techniques and developing new ones if the old ones haven't worked. If, despite our mutual effort, the counseling doesn't help you, I'll do my best to refer you to someone else who can help you more.

Example: The Story of Beth

For two years, Beth had severe generalized anxiety attacks, during which she was completely immobilized. By the time she came to me for treatment she had been in analysis for six years, three times per week. Originally she had entered analysis to work out her grief and anger over the early loss of her parents. After their deaths she had been sent as an adolescent to live with her aunt and uncle, whom she described as rigid and rejecting. She believed that the analysis had helped her to cope with her grief and anger, and was puzzled when after four years of therapy, her anxiety attacks began. During her last two years of analysis they had become progressively worse.

The first step in Beth's therapy was to persuade her that a more directive, cognitive approach to therapy would reduce her anxiety, though the style would differ significantly from the analysis she had undergone. Second, we explored the cognitive triggers for her anxiety, which seemed to be an offshoot of her analytic therapy. During one session with her analyst, she had misunderstood what he had said about the id, which in turn caused her to believe that deep down inside her unconscious she was a very sick and potentially crazy person. As she said, "It's like an evil force inside of me could take me over at any time. I have to constantly guard against these unconscious impulses so that they don't take me over."

This thought would occur whenever she felt emotions like anger, fear, or sadness. She would immediately label these feelings as sick, unconscious, and dangerous, then have an anxiety attack because she feared losing control. In most cases, her emotions were perfectly normal and could be understood in the context in which they had occurred. However, she had a great deal of difficulty seeing this, insisting instead that her feelings were a sign that her unconscious was about to erupt.

Beth's anxiety was eliminated after nine weeks of practice using counter index cards, listening to audiotapes, and mentally rehearsing beliefs that didn't make her seem as sick. Following are some of the situations she initially misread and later reinterpreted.

Situation 1
She got anxious during piano recitals in front of many people.
Pathological Thought
I am anxious and scared because of something sick going on in my unconscious.

Rational Belief
I am anxious about messing up in front of my friends.

Situation 2

She got angry after her boyfriend canceled his date for the third week-end in a row.

Pathological Thought
I must guard against my unconscious anger because it may erupt and make me go crazy.

Rational Belief
I am angry because he isn't considering my feelings, and I haven't been assertive enough to tell him.

Situation 3

She had an anxiety attack after reading a novel about someone having a nervous breakdown.

Pathological Belief
Deep down inside I am sick and unstable, possessed by overpowering forces.

Rational Belief
I am afraid because I think I may be unstable—not because I am. There is nothing deep down inside me, other than blood, bones, and tissues, just like everyone else. These masses of cells don't have the quality of psychological sickness and they have no mystical power of possessing the rest of me. Reading the book reminded me of my superstitious fears—fears that have nothing to do with an abstraction called the unconscious. I have created this abstraction in my mind, called it sick and abnormal, then told myself it's going to take over the rest of me. My fear comes directly from what I say to myself, not from some mystical part of me that my imagination has created.

Comment

This is an excellent technique for clients who have a neurotic disorder based on conditioned anxiety, negative reinforcement histories, or maladaptive cognitions. However, it is a terrible technique for clients who have a biochemical condition that may be generating their problem. Psychotic patients, alcohol and drug dependent clients, and those with medically based brain disorders need to learn to accept and cope with their problems—not deny them. It is antitherapeutic and damaging to tell a manic, mood disorder patient whose problem is caused by hypothyroidism that he can talk, relax, or think his problems away. See the sections on treating seriously mentally ill patients and cognitive restructuring therapy with addicted patients in chapter 12 for more information.

In the last 15 years there has been general support for a reciprocal interaction between cognitive factors and biological functioning. It is important that the therapist differentiates between the part of a client's problem that is learned and the part that is physiologic.

Further Information

Many authors argue against the use of the term "sickness" for learned psychological problems (see Korchin, 1976; Rabhn, 1974; Skinner, 1953, 1974, 1991; Szasz, 1960, 1970a, 1970b, 1978, and Ullmann & Krasner, 1965, 1969). The differences between the two views for psychopathology can be found by reviewing the empirical research of Haaga, Dyck, and Ernst (1991, and the summary of research by Fowles (1993).

COVERT REINFORCEMENT
Principles

Soft countering often uses reinforcing beliefs. Cognitions have many functions in a reinforcement paradigm; they can serve as reinforcers (e.g., "I did a good job"), as a response ("I got a pay raise because I am a good worker"), or as a discriminating stimulus ("When I am self-confident, I do better work and my boss compliments me"). If a rational belief is reinforced in the presence of a specific environmental stimulus (such as getting a pay raise) and an irrational belief is not, then the rational belief will be more likely to recur in the future, and the irrational belief less likely to do so. Covert reinforcement rewards the client's rational beliefs. Schematically, this idea can be illustrated as follows:

Sd —————————— Realistic Belief ——————— Reinforcement
S ——————————— Irrational Thought ——————— No Reinforcement

The following therapeutic techniques are available for helping clients to positively reinforce their own rational beliefs.

Method 1. Best Possible Belief

1. Create a hierarchy of problem situations and their accompanying thoughts—about 10 or 15 items.
2. Develop a list of rational beliefs for each situation.
3. Have clients imagine the ideal way of handling each situation in a relaxed emotional state. Have them picture themselves thinking the most rational, realistic beliefs possible while in the situation, and have them envision the resulting emotions and behavior as out-growths of the new thinking. The therapist might say:

> Imagine the scene, but this time picture yourself thinking the realistic thought. Picture it as clearly as you can. . . . Now imagine that you are feeling realistic emotions and are acting appropriately. Keep imagining this until you complete the whole scene thinking the correct thought and feeling and act-ing in the way that you would like. . . . Keep doing it until you can picture the whole scene easily.

4. After the above image is clearly in mind, have clients imagine the best possible consequences of thinking this new thought, not only in the situation but in all situations like it.

> Okay. Now create a picture of the best possible conse-quences of thinking this way. Imagine that you thought real-istically in all situations like this. What really good things would happen to you? How would your life be better? Don't just think of what would happen, but try to picture it hap-pening. . . . Keep doing it until it is clearly in mind.

5. Repeat the exercise a minimum of three times at each sitting. Con-tinue until clients report no negative emotional reaction when imag-ining the original scene. Self-report or biofeedback can be used to assess clients' response levels.
6. Continue the exercise, moving upward through the hierarchy that was established in step 1.
7. This exercise is usually taped, and clients are told to practice at least three times a week.

Method 2. Standard Reinforcing Images

This technique uses the same steps as the above procedure except for step 4. Instead of having clients develop their own images of the best possible consequences of rational thinking, the therapist does that task. This modification is helpful for clients who might have difficulty constructing positive images with sufficient intensity to be self–reinforcing

Imagine as you think more and more realistically that you start gaining confidence in yourself. Difficulties that used to be problems you now resolve with relative ease. Career, finances, and relationships all start improving. When problems occur, you rationally handle them and move on to new goals. You start reaching and achieving all those goals and objectives that you have set for yourself.

Method 3. External Rewards

Clients' rational beliefs can be reinforced using external rewards. Using the Premack (1965) principle, any behavior that has a high probability of being chosen (eating a candy bar) may serve as a positive reinforcer for low–probability behavior (thinking rational thoughts). Hence, a client might choose to reward himself whenever he replaces an irrational thought with a rational one.

Clients can intentionally pair positive reinforcers with desired thoughts and behaviors whenever they wish, and should be encouraged to practice doing so. In their practice, they should be encouraged to allow small rewards to accumulate to bigger rewards, depending upon the magnitude of the perceptual and behavioral hurdles that they are attempting to leap. Hence, a candy bar might be sufficient for a small hurdle, but the client might need to set the goal of taking a major vacation as a reward for overcoming a truly major hurdle.

Comment

In many cases, clients find it difficult to reinforce themselves. They may be more inclined toward self–depreciation than self–reinforcement, making it necessary for therapists to help them discover the reasons behind this inclination. Therapists often have to give clients permission to be nice to themselves.

Further Information

This technique is called self–reward in previous publications (Casey & Mullin, 1976, 1985; Mc Mullin, Assafi, & Chapman, 1978; Mc

Mullin & Casey, 1975; Mc Mullin & Giles, 1981).

Many researchers have examined the effects of covert reinforcement: Aubut and Ladouceur (1978), Bajtelsmit & Gershman (1976), Bistline, Jaremko, and Sobleman (1980), Brunn and Hedberg (1974), Cautela (1970, 1971b), Engum, Miller, and Meredith (1980), Flannery (1972), Homme (1965), Krop, Calhoon, and Verrier (1971) Ladouceur (1974, 1977), Mahoney (1991, 1993a, 1993b), Mahoney, Thoresen, and Danaher (1972), Scott and Leonard (1978), Scott and Rosenstiel (1975), Turkat and Adams (1982).

The Becks' theories (A. Beck, 1993; J. Beck, 1996) emphasize the principle that positive emotions reinforce adaptive behavior.

USE OF ALTERED STATES
Principles

Basic physiology has a lot to do with how well clients understand and respond to various soft countering techniques. Some research has shown that clients who are physically taut, with tense muscles and high levels of brain activity as a result of their processing a variety of stimuli simultaneously, are less responsive to this type of therapy. Relaxation, hypnosis, and meditation can ease muscle tensions and diminish brain activity levels, enabling these clients to narrow their focus to the task at hand.

There is some inconclusive evidence that Alpha states (8–12 Hz) and Theta states (4–7 Hz) improve clients' capacity to absorb information because clients are able to receive inputs uncritically and with fewer competing stimuli (Goleman, 1977; Grof, 1975, 1980). Our own experience suggests that invoking altered mental states is merely an adjunct technique; permanent or lasting changes are seldom effected solely by this method. This particular adjunct works best in supplementing conditioning and perceptual shifting techniques, but is less effective with other procedures.

Soft countering uses the following methods to produce relaxed states.

1. Biofeedback (Carlson & Seifert, 1994).
2. The client breathes from the diaphragm and inhales slowly through the nose, holds his or her breath, and then exhales a little air at a time. Yawning and stretching accompanying slow rhythmic breathing generate additional results.

3. The counselor may play nature tapes to induce relaxation. These tapes are recordings of the natural sounds of an ocean, a country stream, meadows, and other environmental sonances. (Many record stores carry these tapes.)
4. Separately, or along with the nature tapes, therapists can read environmental scripts that describe the sensations of being in a natural setting such as at a beach or in a mountain cabin. (Kroger and Fezler [1976] have some excellent scripts.)
5. Relaxation can be heightened if the therapist repeats phrases like, "My legs are getting heavy and warm. I am calm and relaxed. All my muscles are loose, limp, and slack." These comments will produce a meditative state if they are repeated for 20 minutes.
6. Standard relaxation instructions (Jacobson, 1974; Sutcliffe, 1994).
7. Standard hypnotic inductions (Clark & Jackson, 1983; Udolf, 1992).
8. White Noise.
9. Acoustic wave sounds.

Use of Reduced Brain–wave States

Relaxed states can be used with all CRT techniques. They are most effective with the following:

1. Unmasking the core irrational beliefs connected to emotional problems. In a relaxed state clients often focus better on their automatic thoughts.
2. Reinforcing clients' positive, cognitive changes.
3. Giving clients the necessary distance to gauge their beliefs objectively.
4. Through memory regression, enabling clients to identify the historical roots of core beliefs.
5. Improving the effectiveness of many of the techniques presented in this book, specifically, all soft countering techniques—relaxed countering, anticatastrophic practice, coping statements, extinction; perceptual shifting techniques—cognitive focusing, transposing, images, bridging; and historical and cultural resynthesizing.

Comments

Our use of Theta or Alpha states shows contradictory results. We have found the learning of cognitive methods to be state–dependent. If client's problems occur in one state, then accessing that state to change cognitions seems practical. The creation of Alpha or Theta

states has diminished efficiency. With certain clients they can be helpful, but we do not clinically support the hoopla and exaggerated
claims for the curative effects of these states. The reader should be
aware of the distinction between relaxation, which has been positively
demonstrated to help clients, and Alpha and Theta altered states,
which have not. They are correlated but not necessarily causally
related (see Beyerstein, 1985).

Further Information

Good practical books on biofeedback use are by Schwartz (1973,
1995) as well as Carlson and Seifert (1994). For critiques see Steiner and
Dince (1981).

The battle between the proponents and opponents of altered states
rages on. On the pro side are books written mostly for the lay public
(see Brown, 1974; Steam, 1976; Zaffuto, 1974). Against are more technical works (see Beatty & Legewie, 1977; Beyerstein, 1985; Orne & Paskewitz, 1973; Plotkin, 1979; Simkins, 1982).

The most famous therapist using altered states is Milton Erickson
(see Erickson & Rossi, 1981; Havens, 1985; Lankton, 1990; Lankton &
Lankton, 1983; Rossi, 1980; Rossi & Ryan, 1985).

Other good books on clinical hypnosis are Rhue (1993), Bandler and
Grinder (1996), Lynn and Kirsch (1996), and Udolf (1992).

SIX

Countering Techniques: Objective

Many countering techniques employ hard or soft levels of emotional arousal in order to shift irrational beliefs, but sometimes a cool, nonemotional style is more effective in changing thoughts. This is because an objective, impersonal consideration of the client's beliefs can defuse biased emotions, while soft or hard countering may sometimes help contribute to the bias.

The objective countering technique requires the therapist to present a logical, nonemotional argument, then persuade the client to model the therapist's style. Both client and counselor analyze the client's beliefs coldly and impersonally, as if they were using a mathematical formula.

Objective countering states that the client's beliefs can be changed if the therapist helps accumulate more logic against a thought than the client has in support of it; when the logical evidence tips the scales, the belief will shift. This view contrasts with the opinion that the emotional intensity or habitual strength of a counter is more essential than the logic behind it. Through experience the therapists will learn which beliefs can be best modified with soft counters, which with hard counters, and which with objective counters.

We have found that an objective counter is most helpful for the very resistant, defensive client, as this approach is unlikely to trigger strong emotional reactions, though some clients do benefit from the warmth, empathy, and positive caring of the therapist (Rogers, 1951, 1959). Depressed clients in particular may need a soft emotional approach to grow their counters, while panic attack patients often benefit from the attacking approach of hard countering.

An objective analysis of clients' beliefs is a clean and elegant approach to therapy. Our experience, however, shows that many clients do not honor logic as much as their therapists do. For these clients, other approaches are needed to replace or supplement objective countering.

The following are some key principles underlying various types of objective countering.

1. Have the client identify the major core beliefs underlying negative emotions.
2. Help the client dissect each belief into its basic logical components. Scrupulously avoid subjective judgments about the belief and its component parts.
3. With the client's help, examine each belief in terms of the principles of inductive and deductive logic. Decide with the client whether or not the belief is logical.
4. If the client judges a belief to be false, have them write down all the logical reasons for the rejection.
5. Tell the client to recall these reasons for rejection whenever the false belief recurs until it no longer reappears.

We use the instructions on the handout to introduce clients to objective countering.

Example of Analysis

The idea that there are intrinsically different classes of people is one core belief that is not founded in the factual and can therefore be weakened by objective discussion. Class-consciousness causes some clients to feel depressed and anxious if they believe their parents were low-class. Despite their own achievements (many are highly successful), these clients still believe, almost existentially, that at their core they lack a basic worth because they come from a poor background. These clients constantly fear being exposed. They judge their obvious talents and successes as part of a facade they hold up to fool society, and they guard against situations where others will "see though" their masks and discover who they "really" are.

Other clients worry about their class in a different way. These clients come from upper-class families but believe they lack certain admired characteristics evident among lower-class individuals. They may believe that lower-class people have an energy or life force that makes them strong and better able to handle the pragmatic problems of liv-

HANDOUT: OBJECTIVE COUNTERING

We are surrounded by an outside reality. It impinges on all of our senses, our bodies, and our brains. We are born in it, live in it, and die in it. We don't see this outside reality directly; we interpret it through our brains. Many times our interpretations are clean and clear and therefore we feel real pain, real sadness, and real fear, but these are offset because we can also feel real joy, happiness, and contentment.

Many of us had a less convoluted perception of the reality around us when we were very young, when things seemed more clear and sharp. But as we got older we started to lose the clarity of our experiences, and the outside world started looking murky. We grew more and more distant from the external reality as our brains started developing imaginary systems that blocked our views and distorted our more natural feelings. Others' views, such as those of our parents or our culture, started to impinge and distort our view of this world. Some of us lost the view altogether.

Where once only real pain could cause us unhappiness, now abstractions and cognitive fantasies cause pain. Where once a stubbed toe could cause us to cry, now hurt feelings can bring tears. Where once the pain was removed the minute the stimulus was taken away, now the pain continues for weeks, months, or even years after the stimulus has disappeared. Where once we would seek our greatest joy in clean and clear feelings, now we throw away tangible joy and pleasure for metaphysical abstractions. The abstractions give us no substance, no warmth, and no closeness because they are empty illusions, counterfeit pleasures. We often ignore the priceless wealth of our more direct experience for twisted notions we learned to develop of the world.

Our best chance for true happiness is to return again to this outside reality, and the best way we can do this is by evaporating as many illusions as we can and seeing the world more clearly again. So let's take a look at your thoughts and see what is factual and what is make-believe.

ing. Male clients often feel that they lack the masculine power and courage of their lower–class counterparts and think of themselves as wimps or dandies.

After the client is shown how to view thoughts more objectively, the abstraction causing the particular problem is identified and analyzed. In the following schema, the abstraction of class is dissected.

Definitions of Class
Synonyms: breed, blood, character, genus, level, stratum, position, rank ancestry, lineage, stock, pedigree, descent, birth, aristocracy/commoner, royalty.

Assumptions That Logically Underlie the Client's Concept
1. Each individual possesses a nonphysical class imprint.
2. This imprint is somehow passed on through genes.
3. It is immutable.
4. Different qualities of worth (high, medium, or low) intrinsically bind themselves to this nonphysical hereditary aspect called class.
5. This quality of worth is also immutable.
6. People know their class and their quality intuitively.
7. Everyone is of the same class as their parents, grandparents, and great–grandparents, ad infinitum.
8. People's children, grandchildren, etc., are of the same class and quality as they are.
9. If people appear to be of a different class or quality than their lineage, this is a facade. They are fakes, fooling society, and others will find them out sooner or later. When they are put to the test, they will always show their true class.

Evaluation of Concept
As a sociological concept class can be a useful abstraction (Davis & Moore, 1945; Warner & Lunt, 1973), but the term is bankrupt when people apply it to their own worthiness. It assumes a quality that doesn't exist: intrinsic classness. It is the concept that each person has a basic inherited ranking of worth that is independent of accomplishments and can never be changed. It assumes an almost spiritual ranking of one's social soul.

Logical Counters
1. There is no evidence—and no method of finding evidence—for the existence of a nonphysical aspect of a person called class.

2. How can a nonphysical element be inherited?
3. Even if we supposed that such an element exists there is no method through which an immutable quality of worth could be attached to it. Worth is a purely subjective judgment in the eyes of the beholder, and not intrinsic to what is being observed.
4. What particular physical, mental, psychological, spiritual, or meteorological element inside of people allows them to intuitively know their class?
5. Except when used in sociological theory, the concept of class is just an arbitrary abstraction. It is imposed on some people by others and has no meaning except insofar as it reveals the feelings of one person for another.

Comment

We do not get involved in a metaphysical debate with our clients about the virtues of Kant's, Berkeley's, or Locke's views of ontology or objective reality. We recognize the subjectivity of all views. But we do accept that all clients' beliefs of themselves or the outside world are not of equal utility.

Further Information

The importance of objective self-appraisal is mentioned by Nisbett and Ross (1980). Objectivity is also one of the major methods used in Abraham Low's will therapy and the lay organization he started for ex-hospitalized patients—Recovery Inc. (Low, 1952).

Virtually all cognitive approaches teach clients to observe themselves and their environments more objectively (Bandura, 1997; A. Beck, 1993; J. Beck, 1996; Ellis, 1988a, 1995, 1996; Lazarus, 1995; Meichenbaum, 1994). Constructivist therapists emphasize that the adaptability or usefulness of a belief is more important than its correspondence to some supposed objective reality (Mahoney, 1979, 1988, 1991, 1993a, 1993b, 1994).

ALTERNATIVE INTERPRETATION
Principles

The rule of primacy is an important principle in all of psychology. It means that people pay more attention to their first impressions of events than to later ones. These primal impressions can be of anything: our first plane ride, the first time we left home, our first romantic kiss.

But people's first interpretations of events are usually not the best. Many clients impulsively intuit the meaning of a given event and then stick to this initial interpretation, assuming that it must be correct. Later judgments, though often more objective, only rarely seem to implant themselves as solidly as the first ones. For example, some people continue to believe that anxiety causes psychosis or that tension in the pectoral muscles indicates a heart attack simply because they had these thoughts first. Once implanted, these ideas can be very difficult to change.

It is an unfortunate truth that the earliest interpretation of an event is often the worst, so clients with misguided ideas need to be taught this concept. They must learn to suspend their initial judgment until they can obtain more information and perceive situations more accurately.

Method

1. Have the client keep a written record of the worst emotions they experience during a one-week period, noting in a sentence or two the activating event (situation) and the first interpretation of this event (belief).
2. For the next week have the client continue with the same exercise but have him create at least four more interpretations for each event. Each interpretation should be different from the first, but equally plausible.
3. At the next session help the client decide which of the four interpretations has the most evidence objectively supporting it. Be sure to use logic rather than subjective impressions.
4. Instruct the client to continue to find alternative interpretations, to put first judgments in abeyance and to make a decision about the correct interpretation only when time and distance lend the necessary objectivity. Continue this procedure for at least a month until the client can do it automatically.

Examples

Situation 1
A single, 25-year-old woman just broke up with her boyfriend.

First Interpretation
There is something wrong with me. I am inadequate, and I'll probably never develop a lasting relationship with a man.

Alternative Interpretations
1. I haven't met the right man.
2. I don't want to give up my freedom right now.
3. My boyfriend and I didn't have the right chemistry together.
4. My boyfriend was afraid to commit to me or to the relationship.

Situation 2
After a year of taking tranquilizers the client discontinues them. The next day he feels a little anxious.

First Interpretation
See, I knew it. I needed the pills to keep me from getting anxious; without them I'll crack up.

Alternative Interpretations
1. I'm anxious because I don't have my crutch anymore. My rabbit's foot has been taken away.
2. I was anxious before I stopped taking the pills, so something else is probably causing the tension.
3. I have been anxious a thousand times with or without the pills. It only lasts for an hour or so, then goes away. So will this.
4. Not having the chemicals in my body makes me feel different—not worse or better, but different. I have been calling this different feeling "anxiety," because I interpret all different feelings as something scary, but I could just as well call this feeling "unfamiliar." It is not really dangerous.

Situation 3
The client's husband said she had fat legs.

First Interpretation
My legs are grotesque. I'm deformed. I feel like I shouldn't wear short pants because everyone will see them. Nature gave me a raw deal.

Alternative Interpretations
1. He's an idiot!
2. He was angry with me for not having dinner ready. He knows I'm

sensitive about my weight and was trying to hurt me.
3. He is going through his midlife crisis and wants me to look like 18–year–old so that he'll feel younger.
4. He has fat legs and he's projecting.

Situation 4
The client developed agoraphobia 6 years ago. She still has panic attacks despite four months of counseling with two therapists.

First Interpretation
I'm crazy! I'll always be afraid to go out, and if two professional therapists can't help me then no one can.

Alternative Interpretations
1. My therapists were no good.
2. The techniques they used weren't appropriate for my problem.
3. I didn't give the therapy enough time.
4. It takes more than four months to get over agoraphobia.
5. I didn't work at it.

Comment

For this technique to be effective, the accuracy of the alternative interpretations is not crucial. What is essential is for the client to realize that alternative interpretations are possible and that first explanations are not magically true simply because they're first. Having alternative ways of analyzing events helps clients to weaken the certainty of the first interpretation and makes it likely that they will consider others and ultimately arrive at one that is less damaging.

Further Information

Numerous studies in social psychology support the importance of primacy of subjects' beliefs (see Fishbein & Ajzen, 1975; Hovland & Janis, 1959; Miller & Campbell, 1959; and Petty & Cacioppo, 1981). A related concept is the "primacy hypothesis," which means that a client's primal cognitions may be so powerful that they take over other processes—emotional, cognitive, and behavioral (Haaga, Dyck, & Ernst, 1991; Beck, 1996).

Rational Beliefs
Principles

Like many therapeutic methods, countering irrational beliefs creates one problem while solving another. Successful countering weakens an irrational thought, but it also forces the client to focus on it. Focusing on the irrational thought produces the negative emotion, so countering, in effect, works backward to remove the negative emotion that the process of countering has just created. Countering must work against both the thought and the emotion it elicits. This requires an especially strong counter because negative emotions tend to strengthen irrational beliefs.

A more useful type of countering is to have the client avoid thinking the irrational thought, thus avoiding the need to work against the negative emotion that it elicits. The rational–belief technique does just this. The client imagines the realistic belief immediately after being exposed to the environmental triggers. With this approach the client doesn't argue against an irrational thought but instead concentrates on thinking rationally.

Method

1. Make a list of the situations in which the client has gotten upset. They can be specific situations from the past or present, or general life situations the client is likely to face.
2. Prepare rational beliefs or self–statements that the client can use in these situations. These beliefs should exaggerate neither the positive nor negative features of the situations but should be founded on an objective view of what is occurring. Spend some time finding the most sensible interpretation of the situation.
3. Record the trigger to each situation on one side of a 5"-by-7" index card. On the other side write a complete description of the rational perception the client is trying to achieve.
4. Several times a day for at least 6 weeks, the client should imagine being in the situation until it is clearly in mind.
5. When this visualization becomes clear the client should picture thinking the rational belief until it too becomes clear.
6. Clients should practice the exercise until they reflexively perceive the rational belief whenever they picture the event.
7. If intervening irrational thoughts enter the clients' thinking they

should immediately use "thought stopping" (Wolpe, 1969) and try once again to use the rational belief.

Example

Following are some examples of common situations and the rational beliefs that may be used in them.

Situation: afraid of meeting strangers
Rational Belief: I have an opportunity to meet new and interesting people.

Situation: guilty about sexual dreams
Rational Belief: Sexual dreams can be fun.

Situation: makes a mistake
Rational Belief: Now I have a chance to learn something new.

Situation: rejected by a friend
Rational Belief: That's unfortunate but not catastrophic.

Situation: treated unfairly
Rational Belief: I could insist on fair treatment.

Situation: fear of public speaking
Rational Belief: I have an opportunity to show off and tell others what I think.

Situation: anxious
Rational Belief: Anxiety is unpleasant, but not dangerous.

Situation: feels inferior
Rational Belief: In some things, I am. In others, I'm not.

Situation: scared
Rational Belief: Fear is just chemicals my body creates.

Situation: criticized by others
Rational Belief: If they are right, I have learned something; if wrong, I can ignore it.

Comment

Rational beliefs are not necessarily the most positive perceptions of situations—they are the most realistic. In most cases the therapist needs to investigate the situations meticulously to determine the most rational point of view.

Further Information

Many social psychological research studies support the view that attitude change is more likely to occur if subjects haven't committed themselves to a prior belief. See Brehm, 1966; Brehm, Snres, Sensenig, & Shaban, 1966.

Nowadays, "rational" is a loaded word. For some theorists it implies an abstract assumption that there is an objective reality existing independently and outside of the human frame of reference (Mahoney, 1994; Neimeyer, Mahoney, & Murphy, 1996). Such an assumption is metaphysical; its truth or falseness is not amenable to empirical means (Ayer, 1952). Even Ellis presently views rational emotive therapy (newly named rational emotive behavior therapy since 1993) in a more relativistic, constructionistic fashion (Ellis, 1988b; McGinn, 1997). But there is a lesser meaning for "rational." It is the rational of everyday experience and can be determined by the usual means we all employ (see the logical analysis section in this chapter).

UTILITARIAN COUNTERS
Principles

While some types of objective counters argue against the rationality of a client's belief and aim at correcting the logical fallacies the client may be employing, there is a totally different type of objective counter in which the therapist doesn't examine the thought's truthfulness but rather whether it is useful or not useful. While there is nothing so useful to a client as the truth, it is quite possible for a client to focus on something that is true but not particularly useful. For example, it is logically true that we will all die someday, but it is not useful for clients to concentrate on this thought every waking moment of their lives.

This pragmatic approach to countering can significantly help the client who thinks rational but useless thoughts. Utilitarian counters help clients to examine the pragmatism of beliefs rather than simply their validity.

Method

1. Prepare a list of the client's irrational thoughts.
2. Prepare a list of situations where the thoughts typically occur.
3. Help the client select a specific behavioral goal to achieve in each situation. Have them ask themselves, "What do I want to accom-

plish now?" For example, you might develop goals for the client to respond assertively to unfair criticism, or to admit openly to mistakes, etc.

4. Have the client ask for each thought, "Does this thought help me reach my goal or not?"

5. Ignoring whether the thought is true or not, help clients find self-statements that will be more useful in helping them reach their goals.

6. Tell the client to substitute the pragmatic belief for the impractical one each time the opportunity arises.

7. Help the client work through an entire hierarchy of situations, substituting useful thoughts for impractical ones.

Example

Impractical Belief: She rejected me because I am basically an inferior male.

Goal: To be less likely to be rejected in the future.

Useful Belief: She rejected me because I acted in ways she didn't like (not calling her often, not committing to her). Since other women have also rejected these behaviors, I'll need to change them if I want to stop being rejected.

Impractical Belief: I must control all my feelings to be happy.

Goal: To be happy.

Useful Belief: Trying to overcontrol causes unhappiness. When I do feel bad I'll try to understand the causes of the emotion and change these causes if I can, but I don't have to control my emotional responses.

Impractical Belief: I should be constantly on guard about any potential danger that may occur.

Goal: To protect myself.

Useful Belief: Worrying does nothing to protect me. When faced with a situation I will first determine whether it is truly dangerous. If it is, I will do something practical to reduce the danger, and if there's nothing I can do, I'll try to accept it. Once I make these decisions, I'll go on with other aspects of my life since further thinking about it would be useless (Ellis & Harper, 1998).

Impractical Belief: I must be the best in everything I try.

Goal: Achieve excellence.

Useful Belief: The best way to achieve excellence is to concentrate my time and energy on the tasks that I consider important and to spend little effort on less–useful activities. Trying to be the best in everything wastes my energy on low–priority tasks and significantly reduces my chances of reaching any goals.

Comment

A word of warning is needed on utilitarian counters. Attacking the utility of a statement does nothing to counter an irrational belief and may in fact reinforce it. For example, it may be better to directly argue against the belief, "I am inferior to most other people," rather than to suggest that there are useful ways to improve yourself.

Further Information

Pragmatists take the philosophical position that meaning, knowledge, and truth can be better defined in terms of how they function in our experience—how useful they are in adjusting or resolving problems. John Dewey is the most influential thinker and leading spokesman for the philosophy of pragmatism (Dewey, 1886, 1920). John Stuart Mill provides an earlier version of this viewpoint in ethics (Mill, 1950, 1988).

DEPERSONALIZING SELF

Principles

Depersonalization—disassociating oneself from one's own self-image—is sometimes considered to be a neurotic and even a psychotic symptom. It is a condition in which the self becomes unfamiliar, detached, or unreal (Cameron, 1963). This condition is viewed as so damaging that most mental health professionals wouldn't advocate any technique that might possibly contribute to its emergence, but our experience suggests that there are often advantages to encouraging a limited degree of depersonalization.

Depersonalization exists on one extreme end of a continuum. On the other extreme of that continuum is an equally damaging condition—hyperpersonalization. Individuals who hyperpersonalize subjectify everything to an excessive extent, seeing themselves as being the cause of everything that happens around them. Too much of this kind of self-focus can lead to serious dysthymic disorders and to obsessive introspection. The pattern of realistic beliefs and behaviors that we characterize as "normal" falls midway between these two extremes, though there are times when "normal" people experience swings either way. Our continuum can be illustrated as follows:

hyperpersonalization —————— normal —————— depersonalization

Hyperpersonalized clients consistently misattribute the causes of events. They judge all causes as proprioceptive. When they have problems in their lives, they try to change some hypothesized deficiencies in themselves rather than attempting to modify their environments. For example, agoraphobics try to solve anxiety by gaining more control over themselves rather than by trying to find the environmental triggers. Obsessive clients attribute great significance and importance to their own internal processing.

Therapists who find themselves confronted by hyperpersonalizing clients can work to consciously shift their clients' perspectives from that extreme on the continuum back toward the depersonalization extreme. The goal is not to move them all the way, but it might be necessary (depending upon the intensity of the client's tendencies toward self-blame) to move them even a little right of the "normal" zone. This would be done on the assumption that they will probably experience a certain degree of posttherapeutic slippage in the direction of their prior preoccupation.

The first step in depersonalization is to change the overpersonalized cause attribution. The therapist must help clients look at themselves from the outside as others look at them, as subject to environmental forces and not just as self-generating entities. The client needs to focus on observable data to find cause and to avoid excessive internal attribution.

Method

1. Make a list of 20 negative events your clients have recently experienced.
2. Record the hypothesized internal self-deficiencies (beliefs causing hyperpersonalization) that the clients think caused the events.
3. Teach clients to look for the causes of these events outside of them-

selves. Use the scientific method: look for stimuli, reinforcements, operants, or environmental contingencies that served as triggers for the negative events. Rewrite all proprioceptive causes as external.

4. When there are multiple causes, use the law of parsimony—the simplest explanation should be used first—to determine the most likely one.

5. Have clients practice keeping a daily log of events, supposed internal causes, and external causes. Teach them to see themselves and others as objects subject to environmental influences.

6. Once the clients have learned not to take responsibility for these influences, teach them the kinds of problem–solving methods that can be used to modify the environment.

Example

One of the best examples of hyperpersonalization is the way that some clients honor their intuitive feelings. They think that they have a deeply felt sense of truth and falseness that flows in a cavern somewhere inside their minds. They honor this sense as the key to all knowledge, as an almost spiritual vision of the truth. For many clients this intuition tells them that they are bad, evil, or to blame for everything. It is the ultimate in hyperpersonalization. It places the judgment of truth and falseness inside of them and out of reach of objective consideration.

But is there such a thing? The *"in-my-heart-I-know-I'm-right"* clients claim that there is, and that their gut feelings are never wrong, as negative as they may be. Is there a sixth sense or an intuition for truth that needs no research or logic?

I decided to informally test the whole theory with some of my clients. I told a sampling of them to focus their intuition on the next 10 people they met. They were told to save their opinions by recording all their feelings. The results showed that later, after they got to know these people, they were wrong 60% of the time.

When we examined why the clients' intuitions were wrong most of the time, we found one major reason—personal bias. Though most of the clients weren't even aware of it, it poisoned their judgments, lurking as a conditioned response activated by certain types of people.

This was the secret about clients' intuitions. The marvelous thing they called intuition and described as a beautiful sense inside them that saw things so clearly, consisted of just one thing—*prejudice.* Many had been fed these generalizations since they were infants. Their intuition felt spontaneous and certain because at its base was a conditioned response that their reasoning had little access to, that popped up whenever they met someone of a certain type who triggered it.

Clients' judgments were often wrong because their intuition only dug up their prejudices about how people looked or sounded, or what type of work they did, or where they came from, or what their nationality was.

Comment

The above is a very unromantic view of intuition, but it is the romantic view that causes hyperpersonalization. Clients are initially reluctant to give up honoring their intuition, but gradually they obtain the necessary motivation to shift their perceptions.

It is important for the therapist to be discriminating as to when to use this technique. Dysthemic clients often hyperpersonalize. Their infallible intuition tells them that they are to blame for everything that is going on around them. Other clients could use a heavy dose of personalization. The addict, the spouse abuser, the thief, the delinquent, and the violent client all disassociate themselves from their behavior. They blame others for their acts and deny their own responsibility. These clients would get worse if the therapist used the above technique. They need the opposite approach.

Further Information

Although the term hyperpersonalization is not used, Rachman (1997) found that obsessive clients attach great personal significance to their own thoughts. They believe that their thoughts are crucially important, extremely meaningful, and very powerful.

Depersonalization and dissociation are discussed in the context of multiple personality by Watkins (1976, 1978) and Watkins and Watkins (1980, 1981). Causality, both overly personalized and depersonalized, is examined by Sober-Ain and Kidd (1984) and Taylor and Fiske (1975). McGinn and Young (1996) use depersonalization and disconnection to teach patients to distance themselves from their damaging schemas in schema-focused therapy (Young, 1992, 1994; Young & Rygh, 1994).

PUBLIC MEANINGS
Principles

In the previous section we introduced the concepts of hyperpersonalization and depersonalization. A parallel concept pertains to the ways in which clients view events in their lives. Any event can be said to have both a "private" and a "public" meaning.

Private meanings are associated with the emotional intensity that people experience when an event is happening to them; they are subjective. Public meaning is the way an event is experienced externally, from the onlooker's viewpoint. The difference between the two is the same as the difference between our reaction when we accidentally strike our thumb with a hammer and our reaction when we see someone else succumb to the same misfortune.

Helping clients learn to depersonalize their beliefs is one way to remove their beliefs from the strong, emotional components that bias their perceptions. The success of the technique requires a great deal of practice over an extended period of time. An alternative technique involves teaching clients to shift from a private to a public perspective on any event that causes them pain.

Method

1. Teach clients to distinguish between events they perceive and their thoughts about those events.
2. Help clients observe events in terms of public and private meanings. Public meanings can be perceived by having clients practice observing the situations from another person's frame of reference. Events must be objectified. Remind clients that they already have a public view, since they have been observing others in thousands of situations all of their lives. The therapist helps clients transfer the perceptions they have of others to themselves.
3. To change meanings from private to public, clients must learn to remove from their perceptions the following: emotional variables, intense self–introspection, and certain metaphysical assumptions. Obviously this cannot be done completely, but to the extent that clients can approximate their removal they can more objectively view events.
4. After the concept of public meaning has been explained, help them make a list of all the major situations they have encountered; for

each event have them list the public and private meaning.

5. Initially clients will have to interpret events publicly after they have first automatically perceived them privately. Through a gradual shaping process, clients will be able to bring the objective view closer and closer to the time of the event itself, ultimately replacing the personal with the public view during the event itself.

Example 1

Event: anxiety attack
Private meaning: I'm going to die.
Public meaning: Adrenaline and other chemicals are pumping into my blood stream.

Event: criticized by another
Private meaning: I must have done something wrong. I am inferior.
Public meaning: Someone disagrees with something I may have done. The cause of this disagreement is not known.

Event: failed in a business project
Private meaning: I'm incompetent, I'm a failure, and I'm climbing down the ladder of success.
Public meaning: My planning and preparation were ineffective.

Event: lost an argument
Private meaning: I am a weak, wishy–washy wimp.
Public meaning: He knew more about the subject than I, and may even have had more debating experience.

Event: have few friends
Private meaning: Deep down inside I am basically unlovable.
Public meaning: I don't try to get friends and I don't treat people very nicely.

Event: not good at sports
Private meaning: I am a rotten male.
Public meaning: I don't have the reflexes, training, or practice.

Event: 15 pounds heavier than when I was 17.
Private meaning: I have lost my self–discipline.
Public meaning: A 37–year–old woman does not have the same body metabolism as a teenager.

Example 2

The private meaning of fear is the perception that something terrible is about to happen and must be avoided at all costs. The public, more objective meaning is that there may or may not be some real danger present, and that it is necessary to look at the situation to determine whether danger actually exists. Clients who need guidance in order to view danger from a public rather than subjective perspective will find the following five principles helpful. In general, fear is objective if:

1. There is a real danger to the person and real damage could occur. It is irrational to be afraid of monsters under the bed since they do not exist and something that does not exist can not hurt us. Some clients are afraid of sorcerers and witches.
2. The level of the fear is equal to the level of damage possible. It is inappropriate to feel terrified about getting a small splinter in your foot, since the fear would be far greater than the potential damage. Some clients are terrified of making a minor social indiscretion in public.
3. The fear is appropriate to the probability of the danger occurring. If a person is afraid of being hit by a meteor the fear would be irrational because of its low probability. Some clients are remarkably fearful about low-probability dangers such as plane crashes, while totally oblivious to much higher probability events such as automobile accidents.
4. The danger can be controlled. Fear of the sun turning into a supernova would not be useful since the event is beyond human control. Many clients are afraid of having some kind of hidden hereditary disease.
5. The fear is useful, as it would be in a situation where the fear keeps an individual more alert to an avoidable danger. Being alert about having a "nervous breakdown" doesn't in any way reduce the probability of having one.

Comment

Few clients are able to master this technique. We are all prone to getting stuck in our private views of events with our emotions bubbling away. But clients who are able have an excellent tool that they can use to evaporate panic attacks, neutralize grief, or extinguish rage.

Further Information

Aaron Beck uses a related concept called "distancing" (Beck, 1967, 1975, 1993; Beck, Emery, & Greenberg, 1985), which produces a similar reduction in emotional intensity.

DISPUTING IRRATIONAL BELIEFS (DIB)
Principles

Disputing irrational beliefs (DIB) is a simple but powerful technique that is often helpful to clients who have difficulty gauging the truth or falseness of their own beliefs. With this technique, which was developed by Ellis, clients are asked to articulate the thought in analyzable form and then to answer a series of open–ended questions about that belief.

Certain clients will need to bolster their objective–thinking skills and to cling tightly to their rules of evidence during this exercise if it is to be useful. Analysis requires precise thinking and a scrupulous avoidance of sidetracking, both of which are difficult to master. DIB can be useful for clients who get entangled with higher–level abstractions.

Method

1. Instruct your clients to answer the following questions in the order given when testing their beliefs.

   a. What belief bothers you?
   b. Can you rationally support this belief?
   c. What evidence exists for its falseness?
   d. Does any evidence exist for its truth?
   e. Realistically and objectively, what is likely to happen if you think this way?
   f. What could continue to happen if you don't think this way?

2. Have your clients practice applying this series of questions to each of their beliefs. They can do this at home but they must come to subsequent sessions prepared to report on the results of their analyses. Employ other cognitive techniques in addressing and problems that persist.

Example: The Story of Richard

Richard came to see me because of depression and grief over the breakup of his relationship with his girlfriend. They had been lovers for about two years. The relationship had never gone well, but they had clung to each other simply because they were both lonely. They fought with each other all the time about their differences, each claiming that the other was wrong and should change. Finally they inflicted so much pain on each other that the relationship became far more aversive than reinforcing. At this point the relationship ended.

With this type of depression, the client usually believes that he wasn't good enough for his girlfriend, and that's why she left. On my advice, he used analysis to look at his belief.

1. *What belief bothers me?* I think I am not worthy of her.
2. *Can you rationally support this belief? And what evidence exists for it falseness?* No. I can't support it. My goodness or badness is a multidimensional thing. It is a totally subjective view on my part. My conclusion would be totally dependent on what aspect of her I compared with what aspect of me. In addition, there would be no way my "basic" worthwhileness could be rated or compared.
3. *Does any evidence exist for its truth?* There is no evidence that I am not worthy of her. She does have some traits that are superior to mine—she is more sociable and more popular—but I think more clearly and act more responsibly. We are both equally worthy.
4. *Realistically and objectively, what is likely to happen?* I will probably sooner or later forget her and meet someone more compatible.
5. *What could continue to happen if I continue to think in the old way?* I'll continue to feel unworthy. I'll go out with other women feeling unworthy and I'll continue to act without confidence so that they will be more likely to reject me more frequently. When I get rejected again I'll feel more and more unworthy.

Further Information

This technique is a variation of Ellis's procedure. The original can be studied by examining Ellis (1974, 1996) and Ellis and Whiteley (1979).

LOGICAL ANALYSIS
Principles

Objective countering uses methods from fields other than psychology. A number of different disciplines are employed, but one of the major ones is logical analysis. The method is based on the disciplines of epistemology, inductive and deductive logic, and linguistical analysis.

Certain components of logical analysis can be used in counseling as a method of fighting damaging imagination. Since a client's discomfort begins with a thought, the therapist uses a cognitive process to assess the validity of that thought and to rectify any emotional problems sparked by it.

Generally, the process involves analyzing clients' thoughts in terms of: (a) what exactly clients mean by their thought; (b) whether they know the right way to verify it; and (c) if they have good evidence for believing it (Wilson, 1967).

Specifically, the process of logical analysis includes 5 steps, with a variety of techniques associated with each. These steps might best be understood if they are presented in the form of an analogy. Have your clients imagine that their thoughts have been put on trial in a courtroom. The client is both judge and jury and his or her goal is to determine the guilt or innocence, truth or falseness, rationality or irrationality of each belief. As in any other courtroom, the cognitive courtroom has established procedures for clarifying claims and counterclaims, evaluating evidence that is both pro and con, and arriving at a carefully considered final verdict regarding the validity of each thought. The process is as follows.

Step 1. Turning Feelings into Belief Assertions (Present the Charges)

Principles
The first thing that happens in a court of law is that the defendant is charged with a specific crime. The charge is not general. The prosecutor doesn't announce, "Your honor, this defendant is charged with not being a very nice person." It is a detailed report, such as, "Mr. Smith is charged with leaving the site of an auto accident on July 10th, at 10:30 P.M. on the corner of 5th and Main Street."

Clients are rarely so specific in their cognitive charges against themselves or against the world. They usually seek a therapist for emotional discomfort and are likely to express this discomfort in vague terms that describe their feelings rather than the precise thoughts that provoked them. Most clients are unaware that underneath many expressions of feelings is a latent claim or assertion about the way the world is or the way they think it should be.

While the expression of an emotion is not true or false in the usual sense, the belief underlying the claim is. Therefore, the first task in logical analysis is to discover the latent meanings beneath clients' emotional expressions.

Method

1. Have your clients present a list of their problem feelings and ask them to state those feelings as completely as possible.
2. Look for the claim or assertion underlying each expression, and recast imperatives and value statements into empirical and analytical statements (statements whose truth or falseness can be ascertained).

Example

Client's statement: "I am scared."
Underlying assertion: "There is something out there that is dangerous and it is useful for me to fear it."

Client statement: "I hate men."
Underlying assertion: "The male gender deserves to be despised."

Client statement: "It's awful to feel unhappy."
Underlying assertion: "One of the worst things that can happen to a human being is having an unpleasant feeling state."

Client statement: "I am no good because I am not rich."
Underlying assertion: "Worth as a human being is based upon how much money a person has."

Client statement: "It shouldn't have happened to me."
Underlying assertion: "There is a universal order that the world is supposed to follow. I can make a legitimate claim against the world when I perceive that this natural order is violated."

Step 2. Defining Beliefs
(What Law Has Been Violated?)

Principles

Once the charges have been presented in a courtroom, the prose-cutor states which particular law has been violated. This is not a vague citation such as, "Your Honor, we don't like what he did," but rather, "Leaving the scene of an accident is a violation of municipal code 5039."

Once their emotions have been stated in an analyzable form, the therapist helps clients to define each claim or assertion as something specific. The language in the claim is inherently an imperfect commu-nication. Human beings tend to complicate the communication process by resorting to vague abstractions, emotional outbursts, or sugar–coated platitudes in order to express their feelings and the cog-nitions that gave rise to those feelings. It is the therapist's job to help clients define their claims in as concrete and specific a manner as pos-sible.

Method

1. *List the core beliefs.* Have your clients write a list of their core beliefs, expressed in the form of analyzable assertions.
2. *Specify.* Taking one assertion at a time, go through each important word carefully. Ask the client to make each word as specific and concrete as possible. You may wish to use the following instruc-tions.

> Words have different levels of abstraction. To analyze thoughts effectively we should use the most concrete level. For instance, "this table" (pointing to a table nearby me) is a specific thing. Only one table in the universe is "this table." But we could say more abstractly "table in the room"—there are several—or "furniture," or be even more abstract and say "object in this room." In each case we are moving from the concrete to the abstract. Notice what happens when we reach the "object in this room" level of abstraction—it doesn't mean much. For instance, if we asked, "True or false? Is the object in this room brown?" we would be unable to answer because "object" is too general. To know the color, we must know what specific "object" we are talking about.

Our thoughts are like this too. In order to understand the phrase "I need to be rich to be happy," we have to know specifically what you mean by "need," "rich," and "happy." If you mean "rich is being a millionaire," we could judge whether all millionaires are happy, and whether the more millions that people possess, the happier they are. But if you mean "rich equals not poor" or "having the basic necessities of life," our judgment may be considerably different.

3. *Pin down the concepts.* Develop a series of questions that will help clients pin down their concepts. For example, the therapist can question the belief "I am inferior" by asking, "What part of you is inferior? Have you always been? How do you know that you will always remain inferior? Inferior compared to whom? When? All the time or just some of the time? In every way or in just a few ways? What does 'I am', in your sentence mean? What level of 'inferior' are you talking about? Are you at the absolute bottom or just a little bit inferior? What scale do you use to judge your inferiority? Is the scale valid or did you just make it up because you were feeling bad?"

4. *Rewrite the beliefs.* After you and your clients have made each word in the sentence as specific as possible, rewrite the sentence incorporating the new definitions. For instance, one male client believed he was generally inferior to other males. Although the initial belief was abstract and vague, we found the source, and we were able to define his terms. We rewrote his sentence as:

> I am less worthwhile as a male because my erect penis length is 1$\frac{1}{2}$ centimeters shorter than the average penile length that was cited in a book I read somewhere, some time ago.
>
> After looking at the rewritten sentence he said, "Well, that's really stupid, isn't it?"

5. *Practice.* Have your clients practice defining their sentences until they understand the need for concrete definitions.

Step 3. Finding the Meaning of Concepts (What Exactly Does the Law Mean?)

Principles

In a courtroom the prosecutor will do considerably more than just read the statute that the defendant has been charged with. He will take great care to explain the key components of the law in order to show how it has been violated. For instance, he might explain "malice with forethought" means or the difference between "voluntary" and "involuntary" actions.

The defining–beliefs technique discussed above might be misleading to the extent that it suggests that defining clients' thoughts is simply a matter of relying upon what clients *believe* the definition should be or of looking up a particular term or phrase in a dictionary. The defining process is usually much harder than that. What clients *want* a definition to be is often at odds with prevailing opinion, and even lexicographers who write dictionaries are usually years behind popular usage in their definitions of certain terms.

A "real man," for example, could mean "of or belonging to the sex that produces sperm and is capable of fertilizing ova" (one dictionary's definition). Or it could mean, "a cool, tall, muscular, big–penised, hairy, beer–drinking, football–watching creature who can beat the hell out of everyone" (the client's definition). When defining clients' beliefs, we want to know how they are using words and what meaning they give to phrases, not what dictionaries say.

There is a good method for finding the meaning behind a client's phrases. The British philosopher James Wilson (1963) has developed a technique called the "analysis of concepts," which therapists can use to ferret out client meanings. It is one of the most useful techniques therapists have in their arsenal. It consists of imagining a model case and comparing it to a contrary case.

Method

1. *Model Case.* You and your client select an example of the correct use of a key concept taken directly from an analyzable assertion. The example should be an ideal that virtually anyone would think is a valid example of the concept.

   Example. Daphnia came to see me because she was suffering from a powerful guilt. She felt that she was bad, immoral, and evil and believed that she should be punished because she had hurt the feelings of a loved one on a series of occasions.

   To determine whether her behavior could correctly be judged as "bad," I asked her to search her mind for a model case that virtually everyone would agree was an example of a bad act. She recalled a newspaper article she had read. Several years earlier three men had been hunting for deer. They'd had no luck and were sitting on a hilltop feeling bored. They noticed another man walking down a road in the valley below. They had never seen him before, and for the sport of it they started shooting at him. He tried to run away but after several tries they hit and killed him. The men then left the dead man on the road and went home for dinner. I agreed with Daphnia that this was an excellent example of what everybody would agree is "bad" behavior.

2. *Contrary Model.* Select an example of a contrary case. Pick an ideal situation as similar as possible to the first, but in which the concept would clearly (in the judgment of most people) not apply. (For example, whatever "bad" means, this case is clearly *not* an example of it.)

Example. (My client and I selected the following case.) A man was driving his car along a narrow street lined with large trees and foliage. It was late at night and he was driving carefully, below the speed limit; he was a nondrinker. Suddenly a boy dashed in front of his car from behind a large bush. The man slammed on his brakes but couldn't stop. He hit the boy and killed him. He tried to help the boy but saw that it was too late. He called the police and waited for them to arrive.

3. *Compare the Model Case to the Contrary Case.* Determine what key principles were present in the model that were not present in the contrary case. What are the similarities and differences between the two? List them.

Example. When we examined the components of the model case to determine why the men's behavior could correctly be called bad, we concluded:

a. The unknown man was killed (bad event occurred).
b. The three men killed him (they caused it).
c. They had no reason to kill him (unjustified).
d. They chose to kill him (intended it).
e. They could have avoided killing him (had free choice).
f. They knew what they were doing (were aware).

When we examined the contrary case we determined the only similarities present were:

a. The boy was killed (bad event occurred).
b. The driver killed him (he caused it).
c. The driver had no reason to kill him (unjustified).

4. To determine which principles or combination of principles are
   essential to the concept, take each rule one at a time and think of
   situations that included all the other rules except this one. If the
   concept no longer applies, then the rule is essential.

   a. For example, could we judge the hunters' behavior as bad if
      nothing bad had happened—if they had been shooting at tin
      cans instead of people? No. If no one was killed, injured, hurt, or
      threatened in some way, we couldn't call an act bad.
   b. Is the act bad if someone wasn't the cause of the other's death?
      If the man were struck by lightning, we wouldn't blame the
      hunters.
   c. Is the act bad if the hunters had a good reason for shooting him?
      No. A policeman has a right to shoot an attacking felon.
   d. Is the act bad if the hunters hadn't intended it? No. As in our
      driving example, one reason the driver was not guilty of mur-
      dering the boy was that he did not intend to do so.
   e. Is the act bad if it couldn't have been avoided? No. Imagine an
      adult grabbing a child's hand and making him hit his sister. The
      child is not to blame for hitting his sister.
   f. Is the act bad if the person isn't aware of what he is doing? No.
      If a psychotic veteran shoots a man while hallucinating that he
      is being attacked by his ancient enemy, he is not to blame.

   In our example, *all* rules were necessary to call the act "bad." The
   way that Daphnia used the concept, a behavior is bad if something
   bad happens, if it is caused by another person, if there was no good
   reason for the act, if it was intentional, if a person has the freedom
   not to do it, and if a person was aware. If just one rule is missing,
   then the behavior cannot be called bad.
   The driver who hit the boy cannot be responsible because three
   rules were not present in his case that were present in the hunters'
   case: intention, freedom, and awareness. Clearly, people can't accurately call themselves bad simply because they have hurt another
   person without reason. If they do and they feel guilty about it, their
   thinking is false. And their irrationality is not just play for the academic linguist; it is a life-threatening, crucial distinction. Because of
   rules d, e, and f, the hunters should be convicted of murder; without the rules the driver is guilty of nothing but an unfortunate accident.

5. Once your analysis uncovers the crucial rules, apply them to the
   client's own beliefs.

Example. My guilty client found she could not accurately call any of her previous behavior bad, since at least one rule was always missing. In some of the "bad" acts she described, none of the rules applied!

Daphnia's insight into the illogical nature of her thinking enabled her to use other cognitive restructuring techniques later in our counseling.

Step 4. Judging Evidence (the Jury Examines the Evidence)

Principles

In the courtroom, the attorneys present the evidence for and against the defendant, and the jury retires to examine the evidence. In counseling, the client and therapist use inductive reasoning to examine the evidence for and against a belief.

A great many clients have difficulty reasoning inductively—i.e., forming general hypotheses and conclusions from specific facts. They make their judgments based on intuitive guesses rather than on evidence, and often these guesses lead to an erroneous interpretation of events, and this in turn creates more emotional turmoil. If these clients are taught some basic principles, they can learn to stop making random assumptions, thus short–circuiting the emotional pain that these assumptions so often produce.

There are many methods to teach inductive reasoning and some are quite complicated, requiring a good background in the philosophy of the scientific method (I have reviewed some of these in my earlier book, Mc Mullin, 1986, pp. 225–266). But in clinical practice I have found an easier method that provides the same kind of information. It is called graph analysis.

To understand graph analysis, consider what the word "evidence" means. In the context of logical procedures, evidence shows the association between two or more things. Or to put it in scientific terms, evidence shows the correlation between two or more variables. In a courtroom the variables may be the commission of a crime (such as stealing a car), and its correlation with a particular defendant (a witnesses saw the defendant break into the car, and the police arrested the defendant while driving the car).

In counseling the same principle applies. The therapist and client look for correlations between two or more variables that may be related to the client's symptoms. For example, the therapist may look for the association between medications and manic symptoms, alcohol use and spouse abuse, self–concept and achievement, or between a client's depression and her marriage.

To collect evidence, therefore, the client and therapist need to look for correlations that show a relationship among certain variables and a client's symptoms. But the process is difficult. There can be an enormous number of factors that could be related to any symptom. How can one determine which variables are correlated and which are irrelevant? Graphs analysis provides a way to only analyze those variable that show promise.

Nowadays I use graph analysis with almost all my clients, usually with good results. This is also a valuable technique to teach clients, who can prepare and plot their own variables.

Method

1. On graph paper plot any two or more variables that may be important to you and your client. (For example, maybe you wish to know what causes Fred's panic attacks. You think they could be caused by something in his marriage or his job.)

2. On the Y axis, chart the intensity of the targeted symptom, emotion, or behavior. (In our example you would plot the frequency of Fred's panic attacks. See figure 6.1.)

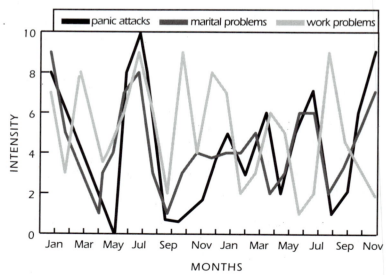

FIGURE 6.1 Fred's graph. The higher the line, the greater the intensity of the panic attacks, marital or job problems.

3. On the X axis, record the time period when these symptoms or behaviors occurred. You can use any time duration: hours, weeks, months, years, throughout the life of a client (these are called life-time graphs), or the time before and after some major traumatic event. (If Fred started his attacks 2 years ago, you would list every month for the last 2 years.)

4. Plot on the same graph any variables that you believe may be related to the symptom, emotion, or behavior you are tracking. (You would plot the intensity of Fred's problems with his marriage and job on the Y axis.)

Discuss with your client the relationships among the lines. (We would show Fred that the difficulties with his job seem unrelated to his panic attacks. However, his marital problems and panic attacks do seem cor-related. From the graph alone we can not know which causes which, but further inquiry would probably reveal the connection.)

Any client variables can be charted on the graph. The following examples come from different clients and show the variety of factors that can be plotted.

Examples

Figure 6.2 suggests a negative correlation between Karen's happi-ness and dependency. The more dependent Karen was on others, the less happy she was. Karen was sexually abused as a child and physi-cally abused by her two husbands. Only when she was free of them and in control of her own life was she happy.

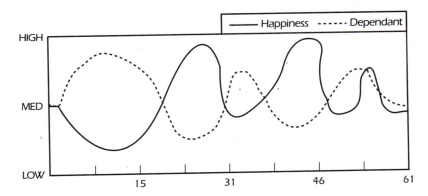

FIGURE 6.2 Karen's lifeline graph: correlation between Karen's happiness and dependency. The higher the line the more she rated her life as happy or judged her relationships as dependent.

Not only can graphs be plotted for individual clients, but they can also be created for groups of clients with certain symptoms. Figure 6.3 is a combined graph correlating alcohol use and happiness for 244 clients from four different treatment facilities in three countries. The chart shows that the average alcoholic client in the sample did not have noticeably bad childhoods. These are averages, so some clients had positive childhoods (40%), some had neutral (19%) and some had negative (41%). When these clients started to drink alcohol (at the mean age of 13.9), their happiness sharply declined. The graph shows an arbitrary item at age 35 to represent those clients who stopped drinking but then started again. In general, the graph shows clients' overall happiness was inversely related to their alcohol use.

Graphs can be used for finding the effectiveness of certain treatment as well as the causes of certain symptoms. Figure 6.4 demonstrates that lithium was an effective treatment for Alan's manic symptoms. After seven days of receiving a full dosage, the medication took effect.

Graphs can also be used to track the correlation between cognitions and behaviors. Figure 6.5 tracks five beliefs that affect whether psychotic patients are able to live successfully in the community or whether they keep returning to hospitals. The higher the line the more the patients accepted the various cognitions. A score of five means that they strongly believe a thought, and a score of one means they strongly reject the thought. As the graph shows, patients who were able to live in the community were more likely to accept that they had

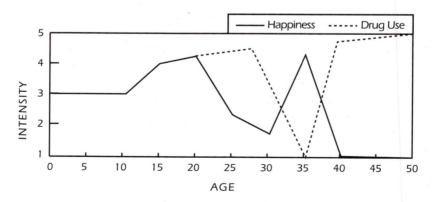

FIGURE 6.3 Combined lifeline graph: group correlation between alcohol use and overall happiness. The higher the line, the greater either happiness or alcohol use.

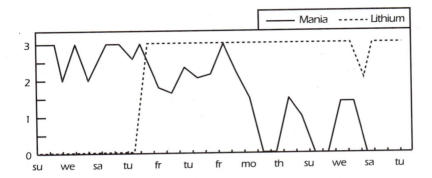

FIGURE 6.4 Effects of lithium on Alan's manic symptoms. A high line indicated either high levels of lithium or high manic behavior..

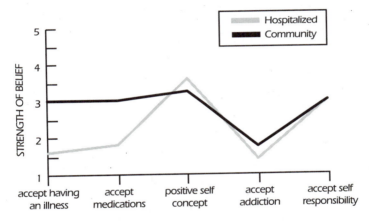

FIGURE 6.5 Comparison of the beliefs of seriously mentally ill patients who
are rehospitalized and those who are able to live in the community.

a mental illness and needed to take their medications, while the hospitalized group was more likely to believe that they didn't have a
mental health problem and that they didn't need their medications
(see the section on treating seriously mentally ill patients for more
information about this study).

Comment

My ex-father in law—Harry Jessup Dunham (1913–1993)—showed
me the importance of using graphs. He was an engineer for the Apollo
program for NASA, which sent men to the moon in the late sixties and

early seventies. One day I was running correlational analyses on many variables in order to find what might be causing a client's panic attacks. He watched me for a while, then walked over and suggested that it would be a lot easier and save a lot of valuable calculating time if I would get at least a rough idea of whether the variables were related before I tried to correlate them. He reminded me that I could do that by using graphs.

Graph analysis had been one of the basic topics covered in my statistics courses, but I never used it in my therapeutic practice. But NASA engineers working on Apollo used graphs all the time. Mr. Dunham told me that it would have taken months to calculate all of the possible relations of all the possible variable involved in sending a rocket to the moon, so instead the engineers draw a graph and only analyze those variables that show promise.

He said that all I had to do was to get some graph paper and plot the intensity of each variable on the vertical Y axis (ordinate) and its occurrence over time on the horizontal X axis (abscissa). Each variable, in turn, could be plotted on the same graph. Those lines that had similar or exact opposite curves were probably related and worth correlational analysis, while the others could be discarded. The total number of likely variables was thus reduced to a far more manageable quantity.

Step 5. Decision and Commitment (the Jury Gives the Verdict)

Principles

The whole purpose of a trial is for the jury to come to a decision about the guilt or innocence of the defendant. Similarly, the whole purpose of logical analysis is for the client to make a decision about the truth or falseness of his assertion.

Clients often avoid the final step because they are reluctant to make a commitment to change a thought. It is easier to stay on the fence and continue equivocating. For cognitive change to take place it is essential that a commitment be made.

Method

1. Tell clients that they must make a decision here and now as to whether the B is true or false.
2. If the B is true the clients should do something to change the situation, or, if it can't be changed, they must learn to accept it.

3. If the B is false have clients commit to working against the B in thought and action no matter how long it takes.
4. Have clients write a decision and a contract about what they are going to do to change the thought. The proof of a commitment is the action taken.
5. The therapist is sometimes in a situation where a client believes a thought is true even though the counselor doesn't think so. If the client has gone through the logical analysis process it is important that the therapist support even unpopular decisions. The client has the right to not work on a cognition or to believe in a thought that you may think is irrational. You can point out the results of the thinking, the ultimate consequences, but it is up to the client to make the decision. Even the act of making a decision is therapeutic, and I have found that clients will often change irrational ones later on.

Further Information

Philosophy, not psychology, has the most useful references for log-ical analysis. The best references for taking feelings and turning them into cognitive assertions lie in Linguistic Analysis (see Klemke, 1983; Langacker, 1972; and especially Wilson, 1967). Excellent examples of defining concepts and words can be found in Ayer (1952, 1984, 1988), Munitz (1981), Quine (1987), Ryle (1949, 1957, 1960), Urmson (1950), Wilson (1967).

The defining–concept approach is a modification of Wilson's (1963) method of analysis. The reader should go directly to this work for a more comprehensive explanation of the procedure.

Descriptions of the theoretical conditions necessary to find causes are included in the general works of Brown and Ghiselli (1955), Ray and Ravizza (1981), and Simon (1978). The method of agreement and difference is completely explained in Mill's classic work (Nagel, 1950).

Judging evidence and using inductive reasoning is explained in the classic works of Bertrand Russell (1945, 1957, 1961), Alfred North Whitehead (1967), Ackermann (1965), and Taylor (1963). Similar discus-sions in cognitive psychology can be found in the works of Bruner, Goodnow, and Austin (1956), Haygood and Bourne (1965), Johnson (1972), Popper (1959), Trabasso and Bower (1968), Watson and Johnson–Laird (1972). More complex examples are can be found in the work of Anderson (1980); Teasdale discusses the influence of schematic modes on logical reasoning (Teasdale 1993, 1996; Teasdale & Barnard, 1993).

Graph theory is a major and intricate component of mathematics, computer science, chemistry, and many other disciplines. But for our purposes we are proposing nothing so involved. The type of graphing used in therapy can be found in any beginning statistic book. Victoria Coleman (1998) has developed a more involved lifeline graphing procedure.

Decision and commitment are the key features of acceptance and commitment therapy (ACT) (Hayes, Strosahl, & Wilson, 1996; Hayes & Wilson, 1994).

LOGICAL FALLACIES
Principles

Logical fallacies are unsubstantiated assertions that are often delivered with a conviction that makes them *sound* as though they are proven facts. Some of these fallacies derive from clients' perceptual distortions (e.g., overgeneralizations), others from psychological errors (e.g., catastrophizing), while still others are logical distortions (e.g., a priori thinking). Sometimes fallacies result when people mistake correlation for causalities.

Whatever their origins, fallacies can take on a special life of their own when they are popularized in the media and become part of a national credo. Once they have achieved this stature they hold a special appeal for those who seek the approval of others by resorting to these commonly held misperceptions.

Fallacies are most likely to creep into the interactions between client and therapist during the logical analysis process, when the client is manipulating the evidence that has been amassed for or against a damaging belief. "Better safe than sorry," our client might say, quoting a popular platitude, without recognizing that the platitude has nothing to do with the rules of evidence that he has established, and therefore cannot be advanced as proof of an assertion.

The best way to teach clients about logical fallacies is by calling their attention to such utterances the moment that they are expressed and by immediately pointing out how they contribute *nothing* to our evaluation of whether a belief is true or false. More often than not they are merely diversions that help clients avoid coming to grips with a lifetime's accumulation of mistaken perceptions. Put all of the logical fallacies you can assemble on one side of a scale and one piece of solid evidence on the other, and the scale will instantly tip in favor of the evidence.

Method

Once clients recognize how essentially vacuous logical fallacies are, they can be taught to avoid resorting to these linguistic diversions. The best way to teach them this is by presenting them with examples and encouraging them to counter every fallacy they utter or hear until they become satiated with the pointlessness of these assertions.

Example

Following is a list of common types of logical fallacies with their definitions and some examples of each.

Sensationalism

Simple, innocent emotions that happen to almost everyone are built up into terrible, overwhelming, psychiatric emergencies.

- "I must be depressed because I feel sad after my vacation."
- "It's dangerous to get nervous."

Overgeneralization

A few instances of a category are taken to represent the total category.

- "I am inferior to Mike because he always beats me in racquetball."
- "Anybody who can't spell is stupid."

Personalizing

Viewing random events as a personal attack on oneself.

- "I broke my leg because God is punishing me for my past sins."
- "There is a good reason for everything that happens to a person."

Anthropomorphism

Attributing human characteristics to inanimate objects.

- "The car refused to budge."
- "The thunder boomed angrily."
- "Lady luck was against me."

Permatizing

Making something temporary into something permanent.

- "I am going to be scared forever."
- "I'll never be happy."

Fault–finding

Looking for someone (others or self) to blame when something goes wrong.

- "It's my (or my spouse's) fault that the marriage didn't last."
- "All criminals are produced by bad parents."

Pathologizing

Calling a learned reaction a disease.

- "Anybody who is anxious all the time is really sick.
- "Overaggressiveness is a disease."

Perfectionism

Picking the highest theoretically conceivable standard for oneself and others, even though practically no one has ever been able to achieve it, and then using it as the common measure for a person's worth.

- "I should never make mistakes."
- "I have to be better than everybody else, in everything."

Dichotomous Thinking

Judging a concept that is actually on a continuum as two mutually exclusive parts (also called all–or–nothing, or good–and–bad thinking).

- "Abortion is either right or wrong."
- "If it's worth doing, it's worth doing well."
- "In this world you are either a winner or loser."
- "Some men have it and some men don't."

"Awfulizing"

Looking for the worst possible outcome of any event.

- "This pain in my leg means I have cancer."
- "My husband is late; he must be having an affair."
- "If I don't get an A in this class, I'll never get into medical school."

"Musturbation"

Making "wants" into "musts," "oughts," and "shoulds."

- "I have to get her back."
- "I need to become a great actress to ever be happy."
- "I must be sure to decide."

Entitlement

Claiming an exceptional privilege that doesn't exist (the prince–in–disguise syndrome).

- "I shouldn't have to put up with all the petty things they make me do at work."
- "It's unfair that I have to show my driver's license to cash a check."
- "Why do I have to wait in line at the airport like everyone else?"

Psychologizing

Finding psychological causes for events, while ignoring other causes.

- "I bumped into the table because I was trying to hurt myself."
- "My sore shoulder must be caused by unconscious anxiety."
- "You forgot my name because you're blocking it."
- "You're single because you're afraid of getting married."
- "You didn't succeed because you have a fear of success."
- "You failed because you were trying to fail."

Nonparsimonious Reasoning

Choosing the more complex explanation over the simplest.

- "You don't like it when I criticize you because you had a love–hate relationship with your father, and all men represent father figures to you."
- "You are just transferring your infantile repressed hostility onto me."
- "People become psychotic because they regress to a more primitive stage in their psychosexual development."

Reification

Assuming that an abstraction (e.g., personality traits, IQ, schizophrenia) stands for a real, concrete entity.

- "He lacks courage."
- "He is basically lazy."
- "Justice, beauty, and virtue are the ultimate form of reality" (Greek philosophers).
- "She has less willpower than others."
- "I'm having a nervous breakdown."

Homocentric Error
Assuming that the human race is God's pet.

- "God made this planet for human beings."
- "The sun revolves around the earth."

Egocentric Error
Concluding that since you are the center of your world, you are the center of everyone else's world.

- "Everybody should treat me nicely."
- "I should get what I want in life."
- "The world ought to be fair."

Subjective Error
Believing that you cause other people's behavior and emotions.

- "I am sorry that I made you feel depressed."
- "I am making my husband unhappy."

Slippery Slope
Assuming that what is true in a singular instance is true in all following instances.

- "If we allow them to ban our assault weapons, they'll soon be banning our target rifles."

Apriorisms
Deducing facts from principles instead of inducing principles from facts.

- "Women have fewer teeth than men because they have smaller jaws." (Aristotle)
- "Melting snow could not cause the Nile to rise, because the equatorial regions are too warm for snow." (Plato)
- "When people are nice to you they are just trying to get something."

Overpowering
Attempting to solve all problems by bulldozing over them.

- "When the going gets tough, the tough get going."
- "Alcoholism can be solved by willpower alone."
- "All you need is heart."

Possibilities Equal Probabilities
If it is possible for an event to occur, then it is probable.

- "If something can go wrong, it will."
- "I should worry about getting diseases from plants."
- "Flying in planes is dangerous."

Anecdotal Evidence
Considering one uncontrolled case as proof of a larger principle.

- "I know someone who . . . "

Arguing Ad Hominem
Attacking the opponent instead of the opponent's argument; also "damning the source" or "pointing to another's wrong."

- "You had to have been there and done that to advise me."
- "You can't know what you are talking about because you don't have a college degree."
- "You need to be a drug addict to help a drug addict."

Ipse Dixit
Asserting that something is true because an authority says so; appealing to authority. "Freud said . . . , Skinner said . . . , Ellis says . . . , Beck says . . . , Mc Mullin says . . . "

- "A famous professor at an Ivy League college believes . . . "
- "Four out of five doctors believe . . . "

Competition
Judging one's worth by always comparing oneself to another.

- "I am not skilled because there are many people who can do better."
- "Winning is everything."

Mystification
Explaining physical events by metaphysical or esoteric interpretations.

- "Memories of past lives obtained by age regression hypnosis are evidence for a former life."
- "Many of the activities chronicled in the Old Testament about the

Exodus were caused by a comet that later became the planet Venus."
- "Out-of-body experiences prove life continues after death."
- "The metal alloy Nitinol can be bent by psychic energy."
- "People can view objects from a distance even though they do not have direct physical sight of the object (remote viewing)."
- "The Nazca lines in Peru were landing fields for spaceships bearing ancient astronauts."
- "The blue sky, the flickering of stars, the Northern Lights, and sun-spot activity are caused by orgone energy, the basic élan of life."
- "A mother's experiences a day after conception will leave an imprint on the unconscious mind of the fetus."

Correlation Equals Causation
Assuming that if two variables are associated then one causes the other.

- "Unconscious anger at yourself causes all depression."
- "Planes cause fear since I only have fear in planes."
- "Thunder causes lightning."

Ignoring Counter Evidence
Assuming that all a theory needs is some evidence that supports it. (This is not enough; one must also show that the evidence for a theory is stronger than the evidence against it.)

- "Since some subjects have obtained a high hit rate in psi research, extrasensory perception has been proven."
- "Since monoamine oxidase inhibitors, tricyclics, and alprazolam have reduced some clients' panic reactions, all panics are totally biologically based and psychological therapy of any sort is unnecessary."

Oversocialized Thinking
Overculturated people are those who uncritically subscribe to the prevailing social attitudes and uncritically accept the general cultural belief. A form of this fallacy called "arguing ad populum" makes statements that appeal to the common prejudices of the masses.

- "A woman's place is in the home."
- "My country right or wrong."
- "Marriage should be 'til death do us part."
- "You can't trust anyone over 30."

- "Spare the rod and spoil the child."
- "Poor self–esteem is at the bottom of all psychological problems."

Self–Righteousness
Believing that good intentions are more important than outcomes.

- "But I was only trying to help you."
- "Extremism in the defense of liberty is no vice."
- "Violence is virtuous if its purpose is to remove injustice."
- "It's true because I meant well."

Sidetracking
Changing the subject of a discussion to a nongermane, irrelevant issue in order to hide the weakness of one's positions. These strategies are commonly referred to as "red herrings."

1. *Dishonest questions.* Rapidly asking a series of questions so that the opponent must stop the argument to answer them.
   - "Why are you criticizing me for being late? Did you have a bad day? Why is this so important to you? Are you having that PMS problem again? Have you gone to the doctor about it? Is there something else that you're *really* angry about?"
2. *Pointing to another's wrong.*
   - "Since you've accused me of being fat, what's that spare tire doing around your waist?"
3. *Archeological blaming.* Dredging up a past wrong.
   - "You say I was rude at the party. What about last year's party where you embarrassed the hell out of me?"
4. *Emotive language.* Trying to get the other person upset by using emo–tionally loaded phrases.
   - "You are so stupid, ugly, and dumb that you can't possibly know a goddamn thing! "
5. *Judo approach.* Overagreeing with a complaint so that the other per–son withdraws it.
   - "You're right! I've been cruel and unkind to you. You have a per–fect right to be so upset. I am really a hard person to live with. I don't see how you do it."
6. *Anger attack.* Trying to sidetrack people by getting angry at them. Most people will respond to the anger and drop their position.
   - "How dare you criticize me! You have no damn right to do so."
7. *Invincible ignorance.* Totally denying that there is any problem whatsoever.

- "I have absolutely no idea what you are talking about. I didn't have anything to drink at the party."

Forestalling Disagreement
Phrasing one's point of view so that it would be difficult or embarrassing to disagree with it.

- "Everyone should know that. . ."
- "As any fool can see. . ."
- "It is obvious to anyone with brains that. . ."
- "Unless you don't know anything about the subject, it's clear that. . ."

Tried and True
Suggesting that a belief is true simply because it represents the traditional view (similar to oversocialized thinking except that the appeal is to tradition rather than to what is presently popular).

- "What was good enough for my father is good enough for me."
- "Don't change horses in midstream."
- "That's our policy."
- "It's always been done this way."

Impressing with Large Numbers
Assuming that a thought is true if many people believe it.

- "Fifty million Americans can't be wrong."
- "Counseling isn't helpful because I can name 10 people who went for therapy and none of them got better."
- "In a recent survey, hundreds of doctors recommended that. . ."
- "Get with it! Everybody who's anybody believes this."

Begging the Question
Making a statement that sounds as if it is asserting a cause-and-effect relationship, but is really just restating the same assertion in another form (a type of tautology that takes for granted the very thing in dispute).

- "I avoid flying because I am a coward" (part of the definition of "coward" is to avoid things unnecessarily).
- "Anybody with this much anxiety must be crazy" (the client's definition of crazy is anybody with strong uncontrolled emotions).
- "Narcissistic personality is caused by egocentric focusing."

Appeal to Ignorance
Assuming that if you don't understand something, then no one can.

* "I can't figure out why I get depressed. It must be random bad luck."
* "This conditioning crap is just so much bullshit. All you have to do is take the bull by the horns and get some willpower and courage to overcome your fears."

Further Information

The fallacies come from a variety of sources. Some are malapropisms, two come from Albert Ellis (Ellis, 1985), but most can be found in a variety of books on logic (see Fearnside & Holther, 1959). Some of the examples come from Gardner (1957, 1981, 1991), Randi (1989, 1995), Carl Sagan (1995), Sprague de Camp (1983), and Taylor (1963).

FINDING THE GOOD REASON
Principle

There is one type of fallacy that is so universal and so pernicious that it deserves to be treated separately from the others.

Most clients believe in a cognitive fallacy, a fallacy that pollutes the clarity of their thinking. It's called *"finding the good reason."* It is based on the fact that clients have the habit of making things up just to make themselves feel good. It doesn't matter that a thought is false or that the client lacks good evidence for believing it. Many clients accept it for the very basic, simple reason that it feels good to believe it.

The fallacy may be defined as: "Defending a position by picking the most favorable sounding argument, rather than choosing the most logical or rational one." More simply it means that *clients feel first and reason second*. Many clients first have an emotion and then search around for the best–sounding argument or the most rational explanation for their feeling. They then offer their chosen rationalization as the sole reason for their belief.

The explanations have nothing to do with why clients believe as they do. They simply make up the logic to support their emotions. Their feelings do the driving; their logic hitchhikes along for the ride.

Finding the good reason is a very damaging fallacy. It destroys perception of the truth and implies that one side is correct while the other side is worthless. But the most damaging thing about this fallacy is that clients stop looking for the truth at all. Instead, they spend their time searching for the most convincing way to show that they are right. This leaves little time and less energy to find out whether they were right in the first place.

The fallacy can be fatal to some clients. Using this fallacy can create a personal holocaust that permanently destroys the client's life. Finding the best reasons for symptoms protects those symptoms from changing. It's like building a wall around the pathology so that nothing can reach it. An addict who has an excuse to snort cocaine will keep on using, a suicidal person who feels justified in hating the world may succeed in an attempt, a married partner who keeps blaming his or her spouse will end up with a broken marriage. Finding the good reason locks problems in place and keeps people from solving them.

Example

Clients who are addicted employ the fallacy perfectly. Whenever they drink or use they search for the best explanation for why. Out of all the possible reasons they pick the justification that makes them feel the best and puts them in the best light. Some addicts say they've earned their binges because they worked hard all week. Others say that their spouses drive them to drink. Some suggest they need to drink to calm themselves down, and so on, ad nauseam. The excuses are always the most flattering reasons they can think of for drinking or drugging.

Other clients use the fallacy. Anxious clients explain their fears by saying that they aren't responsible for being scared. "It must be because something terrible happened when I was young." Their "good reason" makes them feel like noble victims heroically struggling against an insurmountable past. What causes clients to be afraid today is what they tell themselves in the *present*, not the occurrence of some ancient event.

Angry clients insist that they are justified in feeling bitter. "The world is such an unjust, unfair place that I have the right to be angry." Their explanation implies that they are superior to others because they have a higher sense of justice and fairness than the rest of humanity.

Almost all clients with marital problems blame their spouses. "The relationship would work if he (or she) weren't so selfish." The implication is that since they are perfect spouses they must have had the misfortune of being stuck with an inferior partner.

Method

Possibly the best method of undercutting this fallacy is to tell clients to recognize their tendency as human beings to try to find the good reason and to offset this by actively searching for the worst reason. I often tell clients, to "Go out and find the worst reason for believing something and put this next to your best reason. Then, by having both the best and worst sitting together in your brain, you can more easily find the real reason."

Example

Here are some of the best and worst reasons my clients have developed for various positions.

Position: Being an alcoholic.
Best Reason: "I have had a poor unfortunate childhood."
Worst Reason: "I am a drunk who won't admit it."

Position: Having a phobia.
Best Reason: "I am an emotionally sensitive person who can perceive dangers that others miss."
Worst Reason: "I'm a coward who doesn't have enough guts to face my fears."

Position: Problems in a marriage
Best Reason: "My spouse is insensitive to my needs."
Worst Reason: "I am a spoiled brat who is not willing to pull my own weight in the relationship."

Comment 1

It is obvious that not only clients use this fallacy. We all share it. For example:

Position: Ticketed for speeding.
Best Reason: "These cops have nothing to do but harass poor honest citizens."
Worst Reason: "I am an arrogant son–of–a–bitch who thinks the law shouldn't apply to me."

Position: Politically conservative.

Best Reason: "I am a patriot who wishes to maintain the best policies that my country has taken decades to develop."
Worst Reason: "I want to hold onto all the money I made under the old system, and I don't want anybody else to get any of it."

Position: Politically liberal.
Best Reason: "I want to improve society in every way possible so that it becomes more equitable and beneficial to all people."
Worst Reason: "I don't have the skill, industry, or guts to make it in a competitive world, so we should change everything to give me a better chance in a new system."

Position: Being a Freudian therapist.
Best Reason: "This is the only system for working on the underlying causes of emotional problems; all of the others just work on the surface symptoms."
Worst Reason: "It takes clients years to complete this therapy. Think of all the money I can rack up."

Position: Being a cognitive–behavioral therapist
Best Reason: "It's the most scientifically precise and carefully researched method."
Worst Reason: "I can't stand ambiguity. Feelings and emotions are sloppy and disconcerting; I need things to be clean and orderly."

Position: Being a New Age therapist.
Best Reason: "I believe that we need to treat the total person—spiritual, emotional, behavioral—not to dissect them into minute little parts."
Worst Reason: "I could never pass a graduate program of scientifically based therapies. My theory is so fuzzy and ethereal that no one can judge whether I know anything or not."

Comment 2

"Finding the good reason" is similar to the concept of "rationalization," which has long been established in psychology. We use the concept here more as a self–reinforcing cognition; the person believes some thought simply because it feels good to believe it. We contrast this meaning with the older psychodynamic view of rationalization as being a defense mechanism or psychological strategy to avoid the admittance of unwanted unconscious material into consciousness.

Further Information

This fallacy is well known to the public, see Bowler's (1986) book *The True Believers.*

The best counters to this fallacy do not come from psychologists, psychiatrists, philosophers, logicians, or scientists, but from humorists. What makes some humorists so funny is their ability to suddenly shock us into seeing what underlies people's surface explanations. Readers will undoubtedly have their own list, but my favorite humorists that expose human facades are Dave Barry (1994, 1996, 1997), and of course the classic exposer—Mark Twain (see particularly: Twain, 1906, 1916, 1962, 1972a, 1972b, 1980).

SEVEN

Perceptual Shifting: Basic Procedures

THE MOST INNOVATIVE TECHNIQUES used in cognitive restructuring therapy derive from perceptual shifting theory.

These techniques focus on clients' overall perceptions. While the countering chapters in this book emphasize changing clients' internal dialogues or self–language, perceptual shifting aims more broadly at modifying the general pattern of the ways clients look at the world. This broader focus deals with perceptual patterns, gestalts, schemata, and themes.

Perceptual shifting is covered in three chapters. "Basic Procedures" discusses the fundamentals of the shifting technique. "Transposing" makes creative use of picture analogies to help clients to change their perceptions. Clients are shown ambiguous drawings and hidden pictures and asked to shift from one image to another. After they learn to shift images perceptually, they use the same techniques to shift their thoughts conceptually. "Bridging" teaches the therapist to search for anchors that can carry clients' old beliefs toward new ones. Client values, word labels, and therapist–created associations are all used as anchors.

There is much evidence in support of this perceptual shifting approach scattered throughout psychological literature. It is encompassed under such phrases as:

- Sleep and dream research
- Attitude change theory
- Ambiguous pictures
- Gestalt psychology
- Insight "Aha" experience
- Conditioned seeing
- Operant seeing
- Contextual organization in cognitive psychology
- Dramatic life changes

- Contingency vs. contiguity in classical conditioning
- Personal "meanings" and conceptual "clicks"
- Religious conversion
- "Brainwashing"
- Logotherapy
- Flooding
- Perceptual focusing
- Split brain hemisphere research
- Constructionistic vs. rationalistic
- Frontal–lobe vs. brain–stem functioning
- Visual perceptual psychology
- Cognitive developmental theory
- Cognitive neuroscience
- Neural networks
- Linguistical prototypes
- Connectionist vs. serial digital information processes

Although the various perceptual shifting techniques differ greatly in their methodologies, all reflect the following common assumptions:

1. The brain selectively screens sensory and proprioceptive data.
2. The brain forms these data into patterns.
3. The patterns that the brain forms are influenced by incoming data, but remain distinct from it.
4. In most cases, these patterns are learned in the same way that the brain learns other information. However, some patterns are instinctual, and trigger automatic emotional and behavioral responses.
5. Though there are an infinite number of possible patterns, the brain uses only a few personalized schemata.
6. Once formed, patterns have a tendency to persist unless unlearned.
7. Most patterns are taught by significant others (family, reference group, culture).
8. The more frequently a pattern is repeated, the stronger it gets and the more difficult it is to remove or replace.
9. Patterns are formed more easily and have more staying power in the younger brain.
10. Emotional and behavioral responses are triggered by the brain's patterns rather than by the individual stimuli, though individual stimuli are often mistakenly believed to be the sole sources of a client's responses.
11. Classical and operant conditioning can associate emotions and behaviors to the patterns.
12. Environmental stimuli can become conditioned to the patterns. Later, these triggers alone develop the ability to elicit the patterns.

13. Language and images are ways of describing the patterns, but these patterns arise prior to language or visual representations.
14. Changing the representational description of the patterns may loop back and change the pattern itself, but it is not a one-to-one relationship.
15. Patterns are not generally formed on a logical basis, but more usually through emotional-experiential learning.
16. If a pattern is incomplete, the brain will make an automatic closure.
17. Some patterns, once formed, may be immutable.
18. If a pattern cannot be immediately ascertained, a state of panic is produced.
19. The quickest, most complete method of modifying negative emotions and nonadaptive behaviors is to change the patterns that elicit them.

What exactly are these patterns that appear so essential to cognitive therapy? First understand that the word "pattern" is used arbitrarily. Other terms, including "schemata," "themes," "meanings," or "gestalt," could be employed, but "pattern" has a broader connotation.

A pattern is the way the brain organizes raw data, which may be anything that the brain is aware of: input from the sense organs, from memory storage, from body sensations, or from subcortical regions of the brain. The brain takes separate bits of information, which viewed alone would be meaningless, and groups it into patterns. These patterns impose order onto the world. A pattern is not simply language or images, but what clients refer to when they are searching for the right word or image to describe what they are thinking. There are many nonvisual, nonlinguistical patterns. A melody played on a piano remains the same even if played in a different key; similarly, a sentence can be written with different words but convey the same meaning. Both the melody and the meaning of the sentence are patterns—the notes and words are not. They are the ways that we communicate patterns. Even animals that have no language and blind people who have no visual imagery still use patterns.

All people have nonverbal, nonvisual patterns. An example would be a flight of stairs we have walked down a thousand times before and no longer look at while descending. We become aware of the pattern (in this case kinesthetic) only if it is mistaken. If another step is expected when there isn't one, our foot is jolted by hitting the bottom. Only then do we realize that our pattern was off.

In the pages that follow, I briefly introduce the underlying principles and assumptions for each of the pattern–change techniques. I summarize the steps the therapist should take in executing the technique, provide examples of the technique's successful use, and then end each discussion with helpful comments and a list of references with further information.

A key point deserves emphasis here. For the purposes of this presentation, the techniques are covered individually and in detail. However, the singularity of our focus on each one should not obscure the extent to which a skilled therapist may combine them into a coordinated pattern for positive change.

BASIC PERCEPTUAL SHIFT
Principles

While analyzing subjects' dreams, Hobson and McCarley (1977) of Harvard discovered some interesting facts about the human brain that not only make sense out of how the brain functions during sleep, but also give clues about how it works when awake.

According to their research, the brain does more than receive, store, and retrieve neurochemical information. It transforms information, organizing raw bits of data into schemata, patterns, and themes. The senses feed the brain most of these raw data when the organism is awake. When asleep, the brain uses more internal data from long– and short–term memory, emotions, and the organism's present physical stimulation. In both states, the forebrain organizes the data provided by the rest of the brain into coherent patterns, synthesizing the data into larger wholes. In sleep the brain's syntheses are called dreams. Awake, they are called beliefs, attitudes, and thoughts.

Many negative emotions occur because clients synthesize raw data into maladaptive themes, continually organizing information into fearful, depressing, or angry patterns. A long history of thinking distortedly—along with the strong emotional arousal this creates—makes these themes prepotent, so that the brain consistently selects the same interpretation from its repertoire, no matter how inappropriate it is to the present circumstances.

Method

1. Have your client draw four columns on a large piece of paper (see table 7.1.) In the first column, have the client list every thought or

Table 7.1
Perceptual Shift Worksheet

Thought/Belief	Useful or Not	Your Best Argument against Thought	Evidence from Your Own Experience Proving the Best Argument

belief that causes negative emotions in a particular situation (e.g., "I am afraid to fly in planes because I could get scared and all the other passengers would see it," or "Planes are dangerous because you can't escape"). Obviously, the list cannot go on indefinitely. However, even if some of the thoughts seem repetitious, it is better to include them than to leave a major theme unrecorded.

2. In the second column, help your clients decide whether each belief is useful or not useful. Look for the evidence both for and against it, and determine which is stronger. It is essential that clients make this decision based on objective data rather than subjective feelings.

3. In the third column, have the client record the best argument against each thought or belief. Ideally, this argument will be emotionally persuasive as well as rationally sound.

4. In the last column, have the client list the evidence in support of each argument. This is the key to the perceptual shift technique. With the assistance of the therapist, the client should prove that the argument is correct by searching out evidence from his or her own life experiences. For instance, remembering and stating that 20 panic attacks never caused a psychotic break effectively argues against the thought that panic attacks cause insanity, and it does so by using not only abstract logic, but the client's own experiences as well.

5. To bring about the actual perceptual shift, the client should meditate at least 30 minutes a day on those critical past incidences that disprove the irrational theme.

Example 1

In the years that I have counseled agoraphobics, I have isolated one basic false belief that produces most of their anxiety: "I could lose control over myself." Through the use of the cognitive techniques covered in this book, most clients have been able to purge these and other beliefs, and to significantly reduce or eliminate their panic attacks. They didn't shift their perception quickly; many worked for more than a year. But based on self-reports, objective tests, behavioral measures, and collateral reports, the average client was able to reduce anxiety significantly.

However, even after successfully shifting the core belief and being panic-free for a year, almost all clients still feel some residual, low-level tension; they often mention feeling slightly on guard.

Some time ago, one of my patients described this feeling. She asked,

"If the panic I used to have is called agoraphobia, what is this tension I'm having now called?" Not having an immediate answer, I made one up, and said, "Let's call it 'Harold.'" Since that time, I have told many clients of "Harold" and often use the name to describe the feeling.

What is Harold? Where does this low–level tension come from? It is my hypothesis that "Harold" is the postagoraphobic feeling of vigilance and tension that clients create to protect against the panic of agoraphobia. Harold guards against losing control. As one client described it: "I have to be on guard and feel a little twinge of anxiety because then I will be prepared for my panics. If I get too relaxed then the panic may sneak up on me."

Harold is like a sentry on guard against agoraphobic panic; he stays on duty long after the condition is gone. The agoraphobic fear may have disappeared for several years, the client may feel that he or she will never again fear losing control, but Harold continues unabated. It often seems more difficult to remove this guardian of danger than it was to remove the danger itself.

Harold is not an anthropomorphic entity. Like any other fear, it is triggered by a series of thoughts and beliefs, and like any other fear, it can be shifted using the basic perceptual shift, as the following case history demonstrates.

Example 2: The Story of Denise

Denise initially came to see me for agoraphobic anxiety. Afraid to travel far from her house, she had restricted herself to a five–mile "safe" radius (the agoraphobic's "territory"). Using cognitive techniques, she had eliminated her fears in 6 months' time, and had flown alone on several occasions to visit her relatives—some two thousand miles away—without feeling any panic. By the time she returned for additional therapy she no longer feared losing control or becoming psychotic. However, she still felt low–level tension (Harold) and wanted to do something directly to reduce it.

Her worksheet looked like this:

Column 1. Thoughts or Beliefs Related to Harold

1. If I don't constantly watch out for agoraphobia it could sneak up on me.
2. I must be prepared to escape in case agoraphobia comes back. I must make sure all my escape paths are clear.
3. A watched pot never boils—watched agoraphobia never boils. (If I keep looking for it, it is less likely to happen.)

4. I need to think about my past agoraphobia all the time, because then I will have all my tools ready when I need them. If I forget how to use my tools, then agoraphobia could get me again.
5. I must never allow myself to be too calm, too relaxed, or too happy, because my guard would be down.
6. My panics will come back unless I constantly worry about them coming back.
7. Any time I feel calm I'm just fooling myself, because agoraphobia may be lurking in the background.

Column 2. Useful or Not Useful

Denise rated all of these beliefs not useful, but was only able to do so after thinking of an analogy. She imagined a man who believed that plants could infect him with a terrible disease and who was afraid of touching them. She then pictured the same man as having erased his irrational fear and being able to touch any plant he wanted, but still feeling tension whenever he was around plants. Through this analogy she was able to see that his continuing fear around plants was as unnecessary as her continuing fear of losing control. Specific reasons behind this belief became evident in the third column of her work-sheet.

Column 3. Best Argument Against Belief

1. Since losing control doesn't cause psychosis, I don't have to guard against it.
2. Watching out for the danger will increase my fear without reducing the danger.
3. Since there is no real danger, there is no real reason to guard.
4. It is better to get anxious once a month for an hour or two than to spend the whole month worrying about getting anxious.
5. Watching for anxiety doesn't reduce the chance of getting it.
6. Letting myself forget that I was an agoraphobic will just make me feel better, and it won't make it more likely that the agoraphobia will return.

Column 4. Evidence Proving the Best Argument

1. The client remembered all the incidents when she got panicky despite watching for it, and all the times it didn't occur when she wasn't watching. She concentrated on the plant analogy and reminded herself that guarding against a terrible plant disease doesn't reduce the chance of catching one if plants are unlikely to give terrible diseases.

2. She remembered the scores of times she had feared the return of agoraphobia without it having happened. All that her fear did was to give her pain without providing any real protection.
3. She thought about childhood fears, such as monsters under the bed or tigers in the woods, and how silly it is for a child to run away from them. She related these childhood fears to the fear of going crazy or having a nervous breakdown.
4. She speculated about all the things she could have done instead of guarding against agoraphobia, such as reading books, taking courses, renewing friendships, playing with her children, smelling roses.
5. She reflected on all the pots in life that boil whether we watch them or not. Children grow up. Love dies or deepens. Our world changes.

In keeping with the last step of the process, the client rehearsed the basic perceptual shift techniques on a decelerating schedule. In the beginning, she practiced every day, then every other day, then once a week, then only as needed. She was instructed to try to shift Harold only during the practice periods. At other times she concentrated on other aspects of her life, and found that this technique worked. She has not thought of Harold for many years now.

Comment

The perceptual shift technique has a great advantage over many other techniques in that it can be effectively used in a crisis and it attacks all the relevant cognitions causing the crisis. Since it is an advanced technique, the therapist should employ it only after more preliminary cognitive approaches have been presented.

Further Information

This treatment is a variation of a technique described by Mc Mullin, Assafi, and Chapman (1978) and Mc Mullin and Giles (1981).

Baumbacher (1989) describes Harold more elegantly as "signal anxiety." He discusses how panic clients misperceive the first physiological sensations associated with anxiety, and how this misperception can lead to a full-blown panic response.

Presently most cognitive therapists are looking at Bs as nonlinear themes or schemas (see Beck, 1996; Bricker, Young, & Flanagan, 1993; Ellis, 1996; Mahoney, 1993b, 1994; McGinn & Young, 1996).

EIGHT

Perceptual Shifting: Transposing

THE COMMON FEATURE IN ALL transposing techniques is the use of ambiguous drawings to teach clients how to shift their perceptions. Once clients have mastered shifting from one image to another, they are taught to use the same techniques to change their cognitions and attitudes.

Initially, ambiguous drawings were used simply as an analogy to illustrate what perceptual shifting meant. Clients were shown one or two images and then immediately set to work on their attitudes and beliefs. But clients often asked to see the pictures again, stating that they wanted to discover how they were able to change what they saw. These requests were often expressed right in the middle of working on one of their cognitions, and were often considered a distraction or a sidetrack to the real purposes of counseling. Later we realized that the clients found having these pictures accessible very helpful in understanding what they needed to do with their cognitions. We therefore incorporated the ambiguous drawings as a major component in training clients to make perceptual shifts.

The drawings have the advantage of being both nonverbal and global—nonverbal because the images emphasize that brain patterns are more basic than clients' verbal descriptions of them, and global because the drawings illustrate that perceptual shifting requires working with the pattern of stimuli rather than with the individual stimulus. We have found transposing techniques among our most valuable procedures.

TRANSPOSING IMAGES
Principles

We have made frequent use of reversible images to teach clients about how their brains organize the same information into different patterns, and how they can learn to shift the patterns that are harmful to them.

The technique involves showing clients reversible drawings or hidden figures in which the raw material for a wide range of concrete images is hidden. The clients' minds extract one or the other image(s), depending upon the manner in which they are conditioned to processing information.

In the following pages, we will show two methods of using transposing techniques.

Look first at figure 8.1. Clients usually see either the image of a witch or the image of a young woman from this assemblage of black

FIGURE 8.1   Old woman–young woman visual analogy of transposition. Drawn by cartoonist W. W. Hill, originally published in *Puck*, November 6, 1915. Later published by E. G. Boring, 1930.

ink lines on white paper, but neither image is really in the picture. The perception is the result of their brain's effort to organize the raw material into a meaningful pattern. The raw material reflected on the retina is the same, but different clients will *interpret* different images.

If, through conditioning, clients associate pain with the image of the witch and pleasure with the image of the young woman, then the result of these perceptions will provoke either the positive or negative emotion. Remember, the raw material of the drawing doesn't create the emotions; the brain does.

Using the picture as a guideline, we hypothesize that many clients who are unhappy, anxious, or depressed have learned to see "witch-type" images in the world around them. Or more precisely, since the witch is not "in" the picture, they have learned to see witches in ambiguous data. To remove their negative emotions, therapists need to help clients to see the young woman.

Any of several strategies may be employed in helping clients to destigmatize seeing witches. Through conditioning, we can pair relaxation with perceptions of witches (see our discussion on cognitive desensitization). We can also train clients to see only the young woman, thus avoiding any discomforts that might be incited by the other image.

A key point to be emphasized here is that what is true for clients' perceptions of these drawings is also true for clients' perceptions of themselves. If clients form gestalts that screen out most positive data, they will "see" a negative world. If their brains continue organizing ambiguous stimuli into danger they will feel anxious. And if they organize their environments into being treated unjustly, they will feel chronic anger.

The transposing technique emphasizes changing clients' general patterns of thinking, their gestalten, the way their brains organize their experiences. Using the analogy of reversible or embedded figures, we have been able to help clients to restructure their gestalten into more-realistic, less-damaging conceptual wholes.

Method 1. Reversible Images

1. Assemble a useful collection of reversible images (see figures 8.1, 8.2, and 8.3, and the section on Further Information for additional references).
2. Show clients a series of reversible figures. At least four figures are used. Show the figures to them one at a time, and ask your clients to tell you what they see. Ask them to try to see an alternative fig-

Donkey/Seal   Old Man/Young Man   Man/Woman & Baby

FIGURE 8.2 Three reversible images. The donkey/seal image was created by G. H. Fisher (1968). The old–man/young–man image, originally called "husband and father–in–law," was created by Botwinick and published in the *American Journal of Psychology* in 1961. The man/woman/baby image was created by Fisher (1967).

FIGURE 8.3 *The Isle of Dogs.* An 18th–century engraving. Unknown artist.

ure embedded in the pictures. Give hints one at time until the clients are able to perceive the new figure. The hints come from the subcomponents of the picture i.e., "This part could be seen as either the old woman's nose or the young woman's chin."

While showing the pictures explain to the client that the perceptual process of transposing one figure into the other is the same as what they must do to change a negative belief to a positive one. Have them carefully monitor how they are switching what they see in the drawings. We give the exercise "How to Look at Things in New Ways" to all clients to help them use the technique.

3. Next, draw a line on a piece of paper. (Both you and your client should have paper in front of you.) On the left side write all the components of the client's negative gestalt, one at a time. Make it an exhaustive list. At the bottom of the column summarize all the details of the old perception into one major theme.

4. On the right column, transpose each detail of the old perception into a more realistic, less damaging new perception. Discuss each transposition with the client until you both agree that the new way of perceiving each detail is acceptable. At the bottom of the column, have the client summarize all the subparts of the new perceptions into one global, gestalt theme.

5. Have your client practice transposing perceptions by reading the old way of believing and trying to transpose it into the new gestalten. Continue practicing until your client can readily transpose each detail, and their total, from one view to the other.

6. Have your clients practice transposing every day until the new gestalts form automatically and they have difficulty remembering the old perceptions.

Example 1: Ambiguous-drawing shift

In the first drawing example, the old perception is of an old woman, while the new gestalt is of a young woman. The transposition of the subparts is:

Old Woman	Young Woman
tip of nose	tip of chin
eye	ear
mouth	neck band
wart on nose	nose
looking at us	looking away
chin	lower neck
hair on nose	eyelash

HOW TO LOOK AT THINGS IN NEW WAYS

The brain is an amazing living thing. It not only accepts, stores, and retrieves data, but it also dramatically transforms that data. It goes far beyond the information available and creates a whole new world. It takes raw bits of information and transforms them into intricate patterns, themes, and stories.

Our brain functions less like a computer running a program than like an artist painting pictures through which we see and feel and touch the world. Our brain gathers various materials to paint; it takes magenta memories, mixes them with cyan emotions, gathers some green from instincts, some brown, yellow, and white from our senses. It doesn't throw these colors randomly on the palette of our mind; it doesn't paint by the numbers. It composes panoramic scenes, dramas, triumphs, and tragedies with its brush strokes.

Sometimes the pictures are masterpieces of creativity and imagination. The theories of Albert Einstein, Thomas Jefferson, and John Stuart Mill are as much works of art as the paintings of Nicolas Poussin, Claude Monet, and Vincent Van Gogh. Their brains' creations can enrich and ennoble our lives, giving us new ways to perceive the world we live in.

Still other brains paint bizarre, disturbing portraits of the upsetting sides of life. The philosopher Frederick Nietzsche and the artist William Blake create feelings of horror in some people. But we need to see even these views because life has its disturbing aspects as well as its enriching ones.

We are all artists. Our paintings determine whether we feel happy, sad, enraged, broken-hearted, or enraptured. The world doesn't create our emotions—our brain does. Sometimes our paintings are so disturbing that they can overwhelm us. They can twist our lives so much that we cannot function effectively, and that is when counseling comes into play.

My job is to help you paint new pictures. It's not that you don't know how to draw or that you paint bungled and botched pictures; it's more that you may never have learned to draw your own pictures. You grew up trying to copy other people's paintings, or, worse, you learned only to paint by the numbers. As an adult you have tried to pass these paintings off as your own. My job is not to tell you what to paint, but rather to get you to paint your own themes based on your own life experiences.

Maybe the best way to explain how our brain paints is to show you rather than tell you. I will show you a reversible drawing—a picture that contains two images dependent upon how you perceive it.

It's a famous drawing that has been published many times—you may have seen it before. A British magazine called Puck originally published it in 1905 and called it "My wife and my mother-in-law."

Just as an experiment, take a look at the picture and try to see both the young women and the old women. Practice until you can see both clearly.

(Client practices with the therapist's help.)

We see one image or the other because of our brain. It isn't just a computer; it doesn't just add up the raw data in the picture; it transforms the picture. I don't think any computer could transform this picture as well, but our brain can—instantaneously and automatically. It takes the lines and shadows in the drawing and combines them with our memories of similar drawings. It finds a theme—young woman or old woman.

But the most important thing to realize is that neither the old woman nor a young woman is actually in the picture. The picture is just a series of ink spots on a piece of paper—nothing more. We may see the young women or we may see the old. Seeing one or the other does not signify that we are sick or stupid. Our brain creates the image based on the tapestry of our own visual memories. The ink spots are the canvas; our brain is the artist.

This drawing illustrates how our brain transforms all that we see. We view the universe based on these transformations, including what we think of ourselves, how we experience others, what we deem as good or bad, beautiful or ugly. What makes us laugh, cry, love, or hate—all are based on the pictures our brains create.

What brains we have!

Example 2: Karen's Conceptual Shift

Karen came to see me at the suggestion of her physician, who had heard of my treatment in helping local athletes improve their skills. She was a champion racewalker and was concerned about her deteriorating performance in racewalking events. She had first become involved in the sport about 8 years earlier and had made remarkable progress in regional and state competition. But recently she had become increasingly anxious immediately before each contest, and as a result her performance had begun to deteriorate. She had been disqualified several times for "lifting or bent knee."

An analysis of the cognitive component of her anxiety revealed a person high in need–achievement and perfectionism, and with a severe dread of failure. Her background showed that her father had constantly disapproved of her and continually pressed her to succeed. Despite early success in school, economic circumstances and an early marriage had prevented her from achieving her full potential. As an adult she felt that other areas for achievement were closed to her, and thus had taken up racewalking.

Table 8.1 depicts Karen's chart, representing her old and new gestalts.

Karen eventually transposed to the new gestalt. By concentrating on shifting the subparts, she perceived the new way of looking at herself. Initially the new gestalt was fleeting and she could only see it occasionally. Gradually, through practice, the new perception became more prominent and the old theme faded.

Method 2. Hidden Images

Another type of drawing helps clients learn a slightly different type of transposition. Instead of shifting from one image to another in a drawing, clients look for form in a picture where no form is immediately perceivable. Clinically it would be equivalent to a client trying to find the meaning in a series of life experiences that are initially puzzling but later become understandable. A wife who keeps taking back her abusing husband, or an alcoholic who keeps flunking out of treatment programs may not immediately be able to make sense of his or her behavior. It is the therapist's responsibility to help them find the hidden meanings.

1. Select a group of hidden images.
2. Show clients the images, starting with the easiest and progressing to the most difficult.

TABLE 8.1
Chart of Old and New Gestalts

Old Gestalt	New Gestalt
I must be very successful; otherwise no one will ever love me, approve of me, or accept me, and then I will be totally alone.	Success, love, respect, and acceptance are all byproducts of accepting myself. They may or may not come, and may mean little in themselves. Unless I accept that I am a good, worthwhile person just the way I am I will never be happy.

Subparts	*Subparts*
The worst thing in life is to fail.	The worst thing in life is to be motivated solely by a fear of failure.
If I don't totally win, I fail.	If I don't win I just don't win.
Success is an illusion; failure is real.	Success and failure are both illusions.
One must be in control of everything (self and environment) or one will fail.	Many times one just has to let life happen. One can't control most things in life.
If I can't do something perfectly, I shouldn't do it at all.	If something is not worth doing, it is not worth doing well.
I am running out of time to succeed.	Success is irrelevant. There is no time limit to happiness.
If I worry about failing, I'll be more likely to succeed.	Worrying doesn't change anything; it just makes me feel bad.
I must have everybody respect and approve of me.	If I didn't respect myself it wouldn't matter if everyone in the world respected me.

3. Explain what to look for and where they may find the images in the drawing. Help the clients by working with parts of the images.
4. Make sure that you give clients enough time to find the image and notice their method of searching.
5. After you have helped your clients find the hidden images in the pictures, switch to a discussion of their cognitions. Use the drawings

as a guide and help the clients find the hidden meaning in their experiences.

6. To help them ingrain the new images into their awareness, use the following procedures.

> (a) Have them tie the new belief to a strong personal memory.
>
> (b) Make sure the new cognition is a general gestalt, not a sub-part.
>
> (c) Clients should make the new theme as significant as possible, both personally and emotionally.
>
> (d) Simple repetition of seeing the new belief is not effective. The clients must mentally fill out the new image until it becomes very meaningful personally.
>
> (e) Although repetition doesn't increase the strength of the trans-position, it does help clients remember the transposition that has been made.

Comment

It is important that clients not feel rushed during the transposition exercises. Encourage them to relax and take their time. Since new per-ceptions are often fleeting, it is also important that clients practice their transpositions frequently.

FIGURE 8.4 Hidden image of Napoleon at his tomb in St. Helena, drawn by an unknown artist between 1821 and 1836, reproduced by Fernberger, 1950.

FIGURE 8.5 Hidden image of Christ, drawn by Dorothy Archbold and published by Porter, 1954.

The images are used in group cognitive therapy as much as in individual sessions and can often be more effective in the group process. In groups the images are shown most forcibly with a desktop computer. Using presentation software so that the images can be projected onto a screen or a large external monitor, the therapist can use the desktop mouse to identify and outline the images. Some action programs allow the image to emerge from its background.

The great advantage of using transposing in a group is that clients who see the image can help those who can't. Group transpositions teach clients how to give and receive aid from others—a lesson that clients need in order to learn to change their own beliefs.

Each time you use the images in group therapy, ask the group not only to help each other to see the images, but also, and far more importantly, to develop a list of rules or guidelines to use while making transpositions.

Over the years we have used the drawings with hundreds of groups in a great variety of clinical populations. Table 8.2 lists the most common rules group therapy clients have developed.

Further Information

More reversal and embedded pictures can be found in Attneave (1968), Berger (1977), Block and Yuker (1989), Boring (1930), Dallenbach (1951), W. Ellis (1939), Fernberger (1950), Fisher (1967, 1968), Gregory

TABLE 8.2
*Transformation Rules**

To change what you see	To change what you believe
Know what image you are looking for.	Know what attitude you are trying to get yourself to believe.
Accept help from someone who sees the image.	Listen to your therapist, who sees and understands the new cognition.
Take all the time you need to find the image.	Don't expect to get the therapist's meaning immediately.
Look for it!	Look for it! Don't just passively hope that one day you will wake up believing the new thought.
Keep trying and don't give up.	Keep trying. It may take months to transpose a belief.
If you can't see the whole image, try to see part of it.	If you can't accept the total belief, try to accept part of it.
When you forget what you saw, go back and try to see it again.	When your new belief shifts back to your old one, follow the techniques again until you believe it.
Keep practicing seeing the images until they become second nature, so that you spontaneously and automatically see them.	Keep practicing the new belief until it becomes habitual and you have difficulty recalling the old belief.

* See the discussion of quantum leaps in the section on difficult transpositions for more details about these rules.

(1977), Joyce (1994), Mach (1959), Martin (1914), Newhall (1952), Wever (1927). One of the best sources is the work of M. C. Escher (1971).

DIFFICULT TRANSPOSITIONS
Principles

There is one great difficulty with the previous techniques—the images are too easy for many clients. Some clients will see the images immediately while others may take five or ten minutes to find them. But helping clients to change their own beliefs is far more difficult. It may take clients months or even years to make a major cognitive shift, so even though they are quite willing to spend 10 to 15 minutes looking for a new image, they may be quite unwilling to spend several months looking for a new thought.

To approach the difficulty level of changing an attitude, more difficult drawings must be employed. These drawings require clients to spend more time and effort in finding the image, thus better approximating their effort in changing beliefs.

Method

1. Show clients one of the images in figures 8.6, 8.7, 8.8, or 8.9, or pick one of your own.
2. Explain to your clients that the drawings are like their beliefs. Trying to see the rational thought in their lives is like trying to make sense out of the drawings.
3. The most important part of the exercise is to monitor how the client handles the frustration of not being able to find the images. (particularly figure 8.6—the cow). Do they get discouraged and give up? Do they become angry with you for showing them the picture? Do they refuse to try further? Do they condemn themselves for not finding it? Do they claim that you are wrong and that there is no image to be found?
4. While clients are doing the task, instruct them to report any and all stream–of–conscious thoughts and feelings. Write down all comments and your observations of the clients' behaviors as they search for the image.
5. Tell clients that their frustrations, self–anger, or feelings of inferiority about this task are likely to be the same feelings and thoughts they will have when working on their cognitions. Discuss the relationships between the two in detail. Any problems clients have when looking for the difficult images will multiply when they try to change their beliefs. Thus, if they give up on the drawings or get angry with you, they are likely to do the same with their beliefs.
6. Help your clients solve these problems so that they successfully complete the task. If they are too tense, teach them relaxation while doing the exercise; if they are self–condemning, help them counter the beliefs; if they wish to give up, encourage them to continue. In any case, sustain your help until they can do the exercises successfully.

FIGURE 8.6 Concealed cow. Drawn by Leo Potishman and published by Dallenbach, 1951.

FIGURE 8.7 Can you trust this man? The answer is written all over his face. (See further information for answer and reference.)

FIGURE 8.8 What is this? (See further information for answer and reference.)

FIGURE 8.9 This word can be read in three languages: English, Chinese, or Japanese. It names a city. (See further information for answer and reference.)

7. Show the clients that the techniques they used in solving the drawing puzzles are the same that they can use to transpose their beliefs. List each correction and have them record them for further reference.

Example 1: The Story of the Drawings

Some readers may be interested in the story behind my use of images to teach perceptual shifting. The story may also explain why I find images so central to cognitive restructuring therapy.

Quantum Leaps

For some time I had noticed that cognitive change was difficult for almost all clients; it took a great deal of effort, and many clients found it easier to simply continue in the same old way of thinking rather than put in the effort to see something new. Still, some learned new skills, tried new experiences, shifted their attitudes.

These changes generally occurred at a very slow pace. Whether the client was learning to be assertive, working on guilt, mastering anxiety, or building a successful marriage, years of practice and work were required. Like in mountain climbing, most clients slowly worked their way from one rocky crag to another, only gradually climbing up the precipice. If they reached the top, they had a clearer view and felt stronger for having made it. Other clients gave up halfway, lacking the patience or endurance required to reach their goal.

While the overwhelming majority of clients followed this pattern, some clients made dramatic changes. In a few days time they changed a way of thinking that they had held for most of their lives. It was as if while climbing the mountain they suddenly jumped to the summit—making a quantum leap.

These leaps fascinated me. How could clients who had believed the same nonsense for 30 years suddenly stop believing in it at all? How could they have changed in a few days or hours what had taken a lifetime to build? What were the principles behind these leaps?

I first observed these quantum leaps when I was a student at a southern university. One Saturday afternoon a tent revival meeting was held out in the countryside, not too far from the campus. Having the afternoon free and being curious, I decided to go.

In an open field I found a large canvas tent sheltering four hundred folding chairs. It was as hot and steamy as a sauna, and people meandered into the seats from all sides. A long–haired preacher was in the front, ranting and raving about the horrors of hell and describing how it would feel to be burnt by flames forever—how the pain, the stench of burning flesh, and the wailing would overwhelm us.

The people in attendance appeared to be farmers; they wore overalls and looked like they had just finished plowing their fields. At first I didn't see anybody there from the university; this wasn't the kind of service students were likely to attend. But then I spotted Roy, a young freshman who had visited me at the student counseling center for one session. He was a local boy attending school on a football scholarship and majoring in P.E., and he'd been sent to see me because he had a severe drug problem. He drank heavily, and his dorm adviser worried that he'd be thrown off the team and expelled from school. It had been clear in the one session that he'd attended that he didn't really want to stop.

Roy and the others listened to the preacher describe all the horrors of hell; he harangued them for an hour, and the people were getting more and more upset. Some moaned and cried out, "Save me!" Others stood up shrieking. The preacher's description reached a crescendo, and he said, "This is the place God has prepared for liars (audience moaned), unbelievers (moan), hippies (hiss); winos and drugees (moan and hiss), fornicators (bigger moan); adulterators (biggest moan)." Then suddenly the preacher warned that in order to keep out of the eternal fires of damnation they must renounce the devil and come to Jesus now. "Walk right up to the front of the tent and stand with Jesus." A little old lady walked up first, crying and waving her arms. Then another, then the aisles were filled with people walking to the front, moaning and waving their hands and crying out, "Save me Jesus." I noticed that Roy went up with the rest.

The preacher thanked Jesus for saving these sinners, and then he described in great detail what heaven was like. He said that in heaven we would gather with all of our friends and relatives who had gone to Jesus, that all our physical infirmities would be washed away. We would be forever young, we would talk with the prophets, we would be soothed and comforted in the arms of the Jesus. He went on for a while like this, then the people sang some hymns (almost everybody sang) and the revival ended.

I saw Roy on campus a few months later and asked him how he was doing. He said he had stopped drinking and using drugs, he had made the football team and was doing fairly well in school. The several other times I saw Roy he told me the same thing. He continued to do well, stayed clear of drugs and drinking, and was still on the football team. Roy had made a quantum leap, all because of that afternoon at the tent revival meeting.

Over the years I have observed other quantum leaps. Though most clients struggled and plodded, making changes in slow, minute steps, there were still about 10 percent who had made dramatic changes.

I had never understood how some people could make these shifts until a chance experience at a university library. I was researching some articles for a book and thumbing through an old German psychology journal in which I noticed an article about hidden images. One particular drawing, captioned as a sketch of a cow, caught my attention. To me it looked like a mass of meaningless blotches, and I pushed it away. A few weeks later I returned to the same library and was looking in the same journal. I saw the cow picture again but still didn't see the cow. I thought, "Stupid picture. There is no cow!" I pushed the article to the side and worked on something else. But right before I left the library, I glanced over at the picture sitting on the side of the desk and the image emerged—the head and forequarters of a cow. The shift was not gradual; it occurred suddenly—a visual metamorphosis, a perceptual quantum leap.

I immediately thought of Roy. He had also seen something suddenly. Could it be that seeing an image pop up in a drawing is the same as having a new attitude pop up in our brains? Though one is a perception while the other is a conception, if therapists could figure out how an image suddenly leaps out in these drawings, then maybe we could discover how some clients make quantum leaps.

Over the years I have collected so many reams of these pictures for study that it has almost become embarrassing. Colleagues must think twice about having me appear on a panel or workshop—"If we invite Dr. Mc Mullin, he may show his damn pictures again." Still, these pictures are the best analogy I have found to explain a complex principle of psychology. They are my Rosetta stone to understanding cognitive change and growth. I believe they explain how clients make quantum leaps.

When clients look at the cow, what do they see? Most don't see the cow immediately. In fact very few do. If they don't, it doesn't surprise me. This is one of the most difficult pictures in my portfolio, and it takes time (often weeks) before the cow emerges. Clients see the cow when their brains are ready.

But what is more interesting than the amount of time it takes for clients to see the cow is the process the clients go through. How are they suddenly able to see something that they hadn't been able to see at all? The drawing doesn't change; it remains the same whether they see the cow or not. The image on their retinas is the same. Their optic nerve and the information reaching the occipital area of their brains are not changed. The only difference is in what their brain does after this—the way their brain organizes the raw data. The splotches on the paper remain meaningless blotches or turn into a cow. When they image a cow, it is because their brains have made a transformation. Only their brains cause the quantum leaps.

What counts about the exercise is not whether one sees the cow or not, but the set of rules we use to discern and comprehend things. How are our brains able to create the cow? What principles lie behind the transition from seeing nothing to seeing something? What methods do clients use?

When I ask my clients how they are able to see the cow, some answer quickly. They say it is easy; all you do is look at this or that part of the picture and the cow emerges. If you inspect the left you notice part of the cow's right ear; near the bottom is the nose; about in the middle is the cow's left eye.

Despite the apparent logic of this view, I do not think it is accurate. It's not where the clients look, but what their brains do with what they see. Clients can stare at just one spot in the drawing and still recognize the cow without altering their focal point.

The way clients' brains generate a cow in the drawing is the same way their brains make quantum leaps. The picture is the key. What is true for the picture is true for their attitudes. In my work with clients I have discovered five elements that seem essential both for seeing hidden images in drawings and changing long-held beliefs. These principles are at the heart of all quantum leaps: willingness, guidance, flexibility, time, and repetition.

Willingness

The first element, willingness, refers to the fact that clients must be motivated enough to look at things in a new way. If they dogmatically and rigidly hold to their old viewpoint, there is no room for new attitudes. If they look at the picture and see nothing, then rigidly insist that there is nothing to see, no other way of looking at it, they will never see the cow.

The same principle is true for beliefs. If clients are absolutely sure they are right and they allow for no possibility of being wrong, they will never change what they think. One client I encountered was absolutely sure he was a weak, passive, wimpy person. He always tried to compensate by acting tough and mean—the short man syndrome. The truth was that he wasn't what he thought. He was neither weak nor passive—in fact, he was far too aggressive and violent. But because of his perception he continued trying to make himself tougher and meaner. He forced himself to the point where he became so obnoxious that no one wanted to be around him; he was fired from jobs and lost his girlfriends.

When he was shown his mistaken self–perception, he refused to listen. He dogmatically rejected the possibility that he could be wrong, and refused to accept that there could be another way of looking at himself. He never changed, still can't hold a job, and has no friends or intimate relationships because of his hyper–aggressiveness.

Guidance

The second principle behind quantum leaps is guidance. To see something new, it helps to have someone who has already seen the new viewpoint act as a guide. The best coaches are the members in group therapy who have already made quantum leaps. They know exactly what to look for and can guide the others. It is easier to find the cow when told to look for a cow; if clients think they are looking for a meridian of longitude they will be looking forever.

Similarly, someone who believes the new attitude is better able to teach others to see it. This may explain why self–help groups like Alcoholic Anonymous, Recovery Inc., The National Alliance for the Mentally Ill, etc., are so helpful to clients. Cocaine addicts benefit from listening to recovering addicts, agoraphobics learn from people who have overcome their panics, people suffering from grief find survivors' groups helpful. All of these recovering people have already made their quantum leaps, and are able to show the beginning client the way.

Flexibility

The third principle is flexibility. Clients need to attempt different strategies in order to make a perceptual leap. To see the cow they may look at different parts of the drawing, or bring the picture close to their eyes, or move it farther away. Perhaps they need to put the picture aside for a while and then look at it later. One way or another, they need to vary their strategy rather than continuing to try the same method.

This same premise holds true for beliefs. To change an attitude, clients need to look at their beliefs in new ways until the shift takes place. Clients who keep attempting to do the same thing over and over again never change. Clients who do shift use different strategies. They make the old attitude weaker and inject strength into the new one.

Some may tie the new belief into some powerful, personal memory that is emotionally intense. Some will reinforce themselves whenever they perceive the new belief and punish themselves when they detect the old. Some divide their beliefs into parts and shift the parts before they working on their total gestalt. What is important is that they all concocted some strategy, some new system to shift their cognitions.

Time

The fourth principle is time. Changing clients' viewpoints will take time. Their brains need time to process the information until a new perception comes together. If they stop looking for the cow after only a few seconds they will never see it.

The same principle is true for changing their beliefs, philosophies, or attitudes. It may require only a few minutes to shift the image in a picture, but it takes months or years to change a philosophy. No matter how long it takes, it is important for clients to continue to work at the change. Otherwise they will never be able to make the quantum leap. The brain makes the shift when they are ready, a moment many clients have described as an "Aha" experience: "One morning I woke up to an 'aha'. I could see it. I could see what I had been working towards for all these weeks." The perception they had been searching for suddenly appeared—their brains snapped everything together in a clear, powerful, certain image. They made their quantum leap.

Repetition

The fifth and final principle is repetition. One of the unfortunate aspects about quantum leaps is that even after clients have transformed the way they look at themselves, they often leap back. The cow picture again illustrates the process. If they put the picture aside and then look at it again later, they will only see the meaningless blotches rather than the cow. Similarly, though they may feel excited and happy about having changed their attitudes, a few weeks later they may wake up thinking the same old belief again. At this point I reassure the clients that nothing terrible has happened. "After thinking in a certain way for 20 years, it is not surprising that your brain shifted back to the old way whenever it is given it half a chance."

The solution for these backward leaps is the same as for the drawings—practice! If clients want to see the cow every time they look at the drawing, they must keep on practicing. After a time they find it more and more difficult not to see the cow. Likewise, if they keep retreating to their old cognitions, they need to keep practicing seeing the new belief. Many clients have to make the same leap repeatedly until it becomes permanent.

I believe it is possible to change almost any attitude, belief, value, opinion or even any prejudice using the above principles. Like Roy, most clients are not truly stuck with any of their old attitudes, no matter how ingrained. No matter how deep the roots are or how ancient their origins, change is possible.

Example 2: The Story of Terry

Terry was referred to me by another cognitive therapist whom she had been seeing for about four months about a relationship problem. The therapy had been helpful for the relationship but had not been beneficial in reducing her constant, low–level anxiety. After our intake sessions, it was clear that she was a social phobic. She was afraid of being scrutinized by others and worried about doing things that others would consider shameful. She avoided public exposure whenever possible.

We followed the traditional cognitive restructuring approach, and she made good progress, but when we started using the transposition technique, she had difficulties. She was doing her homework (at least one half–hour of practice a day), but she reported that she wasn't able to shift her thoughts. We decided that the "difficult pictures" might give us some clues as to how she might be sabotaging her own efforts to transpose her beliefs.

The following is a transcript of part of the session where the difficult transposition approach was used.

> THERAPIST: I am going to show you some more drawings. These are similar to the ones I showed you before, but they are a little more difficult. This time, I would like you to do something special while looking for the images. Please tell me what you are feeling and what you are saying to yourself during the exercise. Most of the time people don't tell us their emotions or thoughts. They block them out. But for this exercise I want you to focus and report on these automatic thoughts and feelings just as you experience them. Do you agree? Look at this picture. Do you see anything? Take all the time you need.
>
> TERRY: This looks tough. . . . I'm not sure I can do it. I don't see it at all—are you sure it's there? . . . Is it the same size or do I have to turn it? I don't like doing this—I can't do it. . . . I almost had

it. . . . Nope, it's gone again. This is silly! I don't see why I have to do this. It's a dumb exercise. I really want to stop.

(Throughout the exercise I encouraged her to continue.)

TERRY: I'm not smart enough to do this. Maybe your other clients are brighter. . . . This isn't going to work for me. I see where it is supposed to be but I can't see it.

(The above remarks covered a period of about 10 minutes. During this time Terry became increasingly agitated. She started to push herself harder and harder to see the form.)

TERRY: It's no good. I can't do anything right. You must think I'm really stupid. Do any of your other clients take this long to see it?

(After a few more minutes during which Terry made similar remarks, I decided to intervene.)

THERAPIST: Okay. Stop for a moment and let's talk about it. Do you notice that what you are thinking and feeling while doing the exercise is similar to what you think and feel when you are at home trying to change your beliefs?
TERRY: Yes! I have trouble with that too.
THERAPIST: Well, let's analyze what you are thinking and feeling. In fact, I would appreciate it if you would write it down. First, you told yourself it was tough, and that you probably couldn't do it. Next you attacked yourself for not seeing it by calling yourself stupid. Then you worried about what I would think of you for not seeing it, and finally you got angry at me for giving you the exercise. Is my summary accurate?
TERRY: I'm not sure.

(We had recorded the session, and I had Terry listen to her remarks on the tape.)

TERRY: Yeah! I sure did attack myself!
THERAPIST: Yes you did! And did you notice that you were getting more and more anxious the harder you tried, and the more you attacked?
TERRY: Sure, I was getting pretty nervous.
THERAPIST: Okay, let's try something different this time. You noticed that the more you attacked yourself, the less you were

able to concentrate on the task. Well, let's try to change things a bit. This time I want you to look at the pictures in a very relaxed way. We will practice by going back and doing some relaxation exercises we did a few sessions ago. Whenever you start feeling tense, I want you to stop what you are doing, take a deep breath, and relax your muscles in the way I have shown you. In addition, whenever you start thinking those self–attacking thoughts, I want you to quietly say, "Stop, calm, relax," and then immediately concentrate on the task again. Whenever your mind wanders in any way from the task, stop the thinking and return again to seeing the picture. Instead of pressuring yourself to see the pictures, I want you to relax and just let the picture come. Do you understand?

(We practiced the relaxation for about 15 minutes. Then she returned to looking at the pictures. Whenever she appeared to tense up, I told her to relax. If she started to frown I told her to stop the thought and calmly return to the task without pressuring herself, to just wait and let the picture come on its own accord. After about two minutes she could see the form and showed me by drawing it with her finger. We then did two more drawings and she got them both in less than a minute.)

THERAPIST: All right, I think we learned something here. It's probably the reason you have had difficulty doing the transpositions at home. When you push yourself to see something, it just makes you more tense, you start criticizing yourself, and you are less likely to see it. What you did here is probably what you need to do at home. So I would like you to start practicing relaxing, do the "stop, calm, relax technique, and let the transpositions come instead of trying to make them appear.

Comment

If the client finds the reversible or hidden figures too easily, the therapist may need more difficult drawings than the ones presented. In these cases you may find it helpful to show your clients any one of the many 3–D illustrations available. In most cases clients only see the 2–D versions. Explain that there is a 3–D image that is visible if they will follow your instructions and practice looking for it. Use any one of the teaching methods available—Horibuchi (1994a, pp. 10, 90–94) is particularly helpful.

Be sure to tell clients that there are two techniques with which to see the images—parallel and cross-eyed—and that each method reveals a different image. Help clients practice until they can see the image, and tell them that they will need to follow the same process to find the new beliefs.

3-D images better employ the practice effect than reversible drawings. The more 3-D images your patients can find, the better able they are to see completely new images. Likewise, you can tell your clients that the more they practice, the more effectively and easily they can change their beliefs.

Further Information

Figure 8.7 You cannot trust this man! If you turn the book 65 degrees to the left, you will see his face spells out the word "liar." Picture is courtesy of Paul Agule (Blook & Yuker, 1989).

Figure 8.8 This is a map of the Mediterranean Sea (Block & Yuker, 1989).

Figure 8.9 The city is "Tokyo." It can be seen by turning the book 90 degrees to the right. Picture courtesy of David Moser (Block & Yuker, 1989).

Clients have found the following 3-D images most useful: Horibuchi (1994a, 1994b) provides an interesting history of stereogram along with some imaginative pictures. *Magic Eye* (1994a, 1994b) has the most readily available drawings. Anderson (1994) provides several series of illusions. They are inexpensive, so your clients can buy them and practice seeing the images at home. Worsick (1994) has written an interactive storybook with 3-D illustrations, and Rumor (1994) provides a video with over 100 images that will provide the client with extensive practice.

PROGRESSIVE IMAGE MODIFICATION
Principles

For many clients there is a huge gap between their old irrational belief and the new more useful belief. The gap may be so large that the clients find it almost impossible to leap from one to the other. In such cases the therapist teaches clients to make smaller, more gradual changes in the beliefs, progressing step by step so that the damaging attitudes can be successively transformed into rational ones. Figure 8.10 illustrates the process.

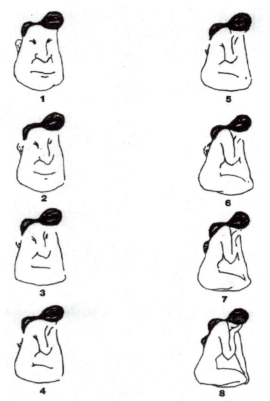

FIGURE 8.10 Progressive images: man–woman figures devised by Gerald Fisher (1968).

The drawings in this illustration are progressively modified from the face of a man in #1 to the body of a woman in #8. Let us assume that whenever the client sees picture #1 he or she becomes anxious, but the client does not get anxious upon seeing #8. When can the anxiety be reduced? At #4, #5, or later?

For therapeutic purposes, clients don't have to shift to #8 if seeing #5 removes their anxiety. Further shifting would be a waste of therapeutic time. The purpose of progressive shaping is to get clients to disrupt their patterns just enough to remove the source of the negative emotion. From that point forth, through a process of gestalt shaping and repetition, clients should be encouraged to work backwards toward the original pattern (#1) by progressively imagining no anxiety response, until the first picture is disconnected from the emotional response.

The change process reflected in this analogy accurately describes what clients experience in shifting their perceptions. With the help of a therapist, they are led gradually through a process of changing various components in their general belief structures until they can isolate the source of the discomfort that first brought them into therapy. Once this is achieved, clients are taught to practice the pattern without the problem component. Practice is the mending ingredient. Clients must rehearse seeing the pattern without the problem component until doing so becomes automatic.

Method

1. Have clients concentrate on the key general pattern connected with their problem, and ask them to describe it fully. It is ideal if clients can form the theme into a visualization.
2. After employing some relaxation to help clients concentrate, have them imagine the theme again, but to change some component of the pattern. You can change a visual component, an emotional component, or some other aspect of the pattern.
3. Continue changing aspects of the theme until clients report no emotional disturbance.
4. Once this occurs, clients concentrate on visualizing the elements in the changed pattern that have removed the emotion. These should be described in as much detail as possible.
5. After the key element has been isolated, have your clients picture the other themes again, but this time change the element so that no emotion occurs. If you have correctly isolated the key element, the clients should be able to imagine the scenes without any emotional disturbance.

Example: The Story of Chad

Chad was a 27–year–old man who sought counseling because he was deeply depressed. He was an exceptional young man—bright, creative, and empathic—but not particularly successful.

Chad's overall mistaken theme was his vision of himself as a person basically inferior in intelligence, social skills, and emotional stability. After initially teaching him relaxation, we concentrated on changing various aspects of this image. We had him visualize that he was inferior in all aspects of his life but work, then in everything but work and going to parties, then everything but work, parties, and love relationships. Still, Chad felt depressed.

We changed tactics and had him imagine another series of images, in which he progressively modified the concept of the objective trueness of his inferiority. In his first picture he imagined his belief to be 100% true, that in objective reality he was as inferior as he imagined, and he pictured himself feeling and acting inferior. In the next picture he imagined that the thought was only 75% true. We continued until the fifth image, in which he imagined that his belief in his own inferiority was totally untrue.

Throughout the practice, Chad visualized himself continuing to act, feel, and think as if he were inferior, even though in confirmable truth, he was not. This exercise led to a very important insight for him. He discovered that his behavior and feelings were totally controlled by what he thought rather than by what was confirmable—that simply thinking himself inferior caused him to act that way. He acted and felt exactly the same at the 25% level of truth as he did on the 75% level. The truth or falseness of his thought did not affect his behavior or emotions; only his belief mattered. By separating confirmable truth and falseness from the perception of truth and falseness, Chad was able to go back to the original gestalt and see his mistake. He was using acting inferior as evidence for being inferior, but the progressive modification process showed him that no matter how he acted or felt, the truth based on evidence had nothing whatsoever to do with his perception.

Comment

The therapist usually doesn't know in advance what the problem component might be in each client's schemata. He or she must therefore be flexible in modifying the pattern to find and then isolate that component.

Further Information

We conducted some informal experimentation with pictures like the one presented in the analogy. Using 15 clients, we found that they could see the alternative image only after they had gone through at least four modifications. Our clinical experience with concepts, rather than drawings, indicates a comparable response.

Progressive modification of themes and schemas may be found in the work of Bugelski (1970), Dobson and Kendall (1993), Klinger (1980), Lazarus (1971, 1977, 1981, 1982, 1989, 1995, 1997, 1998), Sheikh (1983a,

1993b), Sheikh and Shaffer (1979), Singer (1974, 1976, 1995), Singer and Pope (1978), Williams (1996a, 1996b).

RATIONAL EMOTIVE IMAGERY
Principles

Albert Ellis and other rational emotive behavior therapists have used a technique called rational emotive imagery (REI), which aims at shifting clients' overall perceptions. It is included in the transformation section rather than in the countering section because the technique addresses overall patterns of thinking rather than specific, individual cognitions.

In most of the cognitive techniques described in this book, the therapist follows a basic procedure of precisely identifying the client's damaging beliefs and then applying certain predesigned exercises and approaches in order to facilitate the changing unrealistic perceptions. In this role, the therapist directs the curative process: He or she writes a prescription and then guides the client in the use of that prescription.

With the REI technique, the client rather than the therapist writes the prescription. The therapist helps the client to identify clearly the source of discomfort and to focus deeply upon the core theme of that discomfort (e.g., fear, a feeling of rejection, a feeling of inferiority, an intense distrust of others). Once the dominant core theme has been identified, the therapist invites the client to focus his or her creative energies on defining strategies for reducing the intensity of the core theme. Hence, in responding to an intense distrust of others, a client might elect to use what is essentially a countering technique with which she assures herself that some people are more trustworthy than others. She might emphasize the need to do a better job of determining in advance who can be trusted, or of not disclosing matters on which she is most vulnerable to abuse. She might decide to adopt some combination of these approaches.

Clearly, the success of this approach depends upon three factors: (1) the extent to which the client copes effectively with a relatively unstructured therapeutic procedure; (2) the extent to which the client exercises personal creativity in defining cognitive strategies; and, most importantly; (3) the extent to which the client is able to invest him- or herself in the therapeutic process.

As the experienced reader will recognize, we have made some slight modifications in Ellis's original conceptualization of this technique (see Step #7).

Method

1. It helps to have clients relax before they begin the exercise, as it can improve their concentration.
2. Develop a hierarchy of 10 situations in which clients have gotten upset. Be sure these situations are described in enough detail that the clients can imagine them vividly. See if you can identify any common denominators among the 10 that might help you to reduce them to a few core themes. Make sure that clients agree that the final list accurately reflects the major sources of their discomfort.
3. Ask clients to imagine each of the situations, the feelings that are associated with those situations, and the core themes that best characterize those feelings. Ask them to keep these clearly in mind.
4. Have the clients begin with any one of those core themes and focus on the associated feeling, using any strategies they can devise for modifying those feelings. Have them keep working until they start feeling a change in their emotions.
5. Tell clients to focus on what they told themselves to make the feelings shift. If it helps them to concentrate and recall more clearly, have them write down the advice they give themselves. Have them become totally aware of their beliefs.
6. Clients should practice 15 minutes a day until they can consistently create the alternative emotions. Once their first choice core theme has been treated in this way, they should use the same technique with all of the remaining core themes from the list devised in step #2.
7. To help gain control over their emotions, clients can practice feeling different emotions while imagining the original situations that they recounted in step #2. They can practice feeling happy, sad, angry, confident, relaxed, or any other emotion simply by alternating their self-talk.

Example: The Story of Margo

Rational emotive behavior therapy literature gives numerous examples of this technique. We have included only one from our caseload.

Margo was a 28-year-old woman who came to me after seeing at least 6 other therapists. With each of her previous counselors she had tried one or two sessions, felt no better, and quit to move on to another therapist. This had been going on for a couple years.

After her first few visits, it was clear why she hadn't made any progress. She simply was not interested in really working at her own self-improvement. She was very resistant, answering my probes with a simple and abrupt "I don't know." She did none of the assigned readings, nor did she try to learn anything about the techniques or theory behind the therapy. Instead, she expected, and at times demanded, that I somehow solve her depression for her. She consistently reacted badly to the suggestion that she put forth any effort.

Highly structured cognitive techniques weren't affective with Margo because they allowed her to be passive in the therapeutic process. She needed less counselor involvement and more client initiative. It was decided that rational emotive imagery might prompt the necessary participation.

The key scene in Margo's hierarchy was her perception that her problems as an adult were caused by her parents. She felt that she hadn't received the nurturance necessary for her to be happy, and that depression, her broken relationships with men, poor job, and financial difficulties were all her parents' fault. She had misunderstood a comment made by a novice analytic counselor years earlier, and as a result she was certain that her parents were to blame for everything. She hadn't seen or talked to them in five years.

After listening to her tirades against her parents, I concluded that Margo's anger was extremely overblown. Her parents had made mistakes, as all parents do, but it sounded like they generally supported and tried to help their daughter in the ways that they had thought best.

When we started the imagery, she imagined living with her parents and all of the "terrible" things they had done. The emotion she recognized was intense rage. When she was told to shift it to a lesser emotion, such as anger or disappointment, she said she *couldn't*, but it became clear from her nonverbal behavior that she *wouldn't*. She asked to try something besides this technique, but I refused and persisted in using it. She became angry with me for not granting her request, but I continued the same technique. The session ended in a stalemate.

Margo canceled the next three appointments. I heard later that she went to two other therapists for sessions, looking to them to solve her depression. A month later she came back to see me, still angry but "ready to give me one last try." She expected that she had sufficiently punished me and that I would drop the rational emotive imagery, but I did not.

It should be noted, parenthetically, that this persistence is unusual in cognitive restructuring. Generally if one technique doesn't work, I freely switch to another. But nothing worked with this client. Her failures with the previous six therapists were not the fault of the therapists or their techniques. I felt it had become necessary to do something radically different, and that sticking with one technique rather than allowing Margo to escape the problem might be what was needed. If I were to attempt this with 10 different clients, I would probably fail 9 out of 10.

After talking to her frankly about what I thought the problem was, we continued the rational emotive imagery. She did not fully cooperate, but this time she did make some changes. She reduced her rage slightly but said that the only way she could accomplish this was to say to herself that she was somewhat responsible. When she said that to herself, she began to feel scared and quite guilty. I then switched the imagery work to the new perception of self–blame and fear. Using rational emotive imagery she was able to reduce these feelings somewhat. We then alternated the image work between anger toward her parents and fear and guilt about herself. Gradually, over a period of many sessions, Margo was able to reduce her guilt and anger until her depression lifted.

Comment

The flexibility of this technique is its greatest virtue and its greatest flaw. Some clients need more specific instruction on how to change their emotions. Others prefer taking more responsibility for their own perceptual shifting.

Further Information

The technique is described in several publications: Maultsby and Ellis (1974), Maultsby (1971, 1976, 1984, 1990), and Wilde (1998).

IMAGE TECHNIQUES
Principles

Images are used in transformations and other aspects of cognitive restructuring; about a third of the techniques listed in this book use some form of imagery. While countering attempts modify clients' *language* far more than their *images*, transformations are primarily based on images and visualization. Images better show what clients need to change in order to feel better because they stress the overall pattern-shifts, while purer linguistic techniques aim at changing more specific thoughts.

Still, even pure linguistic techniques can be adapted into image visualization procedures. For many clients, the best approach is to interweave linguistic and imaging techniques, as the combination produces more powerful changes than one approach alone. However, if a client is especially adept at visualization or seems especially responsive to image modification, the therapist may wish to emphasize the image work.

Method

1. In order to turn language techniques into transformation techniques, complete the first three steps of CRT: Find the client's core metaphysical beliefs (Guidano, 1991; Guidano & Liotto, 1983), objectively analyze their truths or falsehoods, and develop a series of counters or rational replacement beliefs (Mc Mullin & Giles, 1981).

   Although these three steps can use visualization successfully, we have found that language generally is a more flexible tool than visualization in the initial stages of CRT, largely because of problems clients encounter in visualizing their beliefs. It is difficult, for example, to imagine visual images to accompany a belief such as, "I feel I have no purpose in life." We recommend the use of linguistic techniques in the early stages for the sake of simplicity and efficiency.

2. Determine the imagining capacity of clients by using one of the scales developed by Lazarus (1977, 1981, 1982, 1989, 1995, 1998). These scales help to determine the client's overall visualization ability and to pinpoint areas in need of improvement. They examine

the client's ability to create images of self vs. others; past, present, and future; pleasant and unpleasant; and a range of other areas.

3. If clients score low on their visualization capacity, you may wish to employ the image-building techniques described by Lazarus (1982).

4. Select specific images to help your clients shift from irrational beliefs to rational ones. Since images do not involve language, clients can often shift their perceptions more rapidly and completely by using visual images rather than semantics. You can use many different types of images to create these perceptual shifts. Following is a list of some of the major types.

- Coping images, in which clients imagine themselves successfully handling difficult situations, are used to correct passive, avoidant thinking. ("Picture asking your boss for a raise.")

- Relaxing images, including nature scenes and sensual visualizations, are used to counter fear-producing, anxious thoughts. These are frequently used as part of cognitive desensitization.

- Mastery images, in which clients imagine themselves completing tasks perfectly, can be paired against irrational thoughts of failure and helplessness. ("Imagine having a successful, happy marriage.")

- Small-detail coping images, which focus on specifics, help clients who feel overwhelmed by complex problems. With this method, clients break major problems into a series of minor ones and imagine themselves surmounting each of these smaller difficulties. For instance, a client might break down the problem of buying a car into 20 small tasks and imagine successfully completing each consecutive task, beginning with buying *Consumer Reports New Car Guide* and ending with the successful purchase of the ideal vehicle.

- Modeling images may be used if a client has trouble envisioning the component steps in resolving a problem or mastering a skill. In this technique, the client pictures imitating a model who excels in a given task. For instance, the client might analyze and then visualize the forehand stroke of Pete Sampras or the debating skill of William F. Buckley.

- Noxious images are used in aversive, escape, and avoidant conditioning to counter negative behaviors. ("Picture your smoking causing your kids to get emphysema.")

- Idealized images are used when clients can't think of their final goal. ("Ten years from now, where do you want to be living, and with whom? What do you want to be doing?")

- Rewarding images reinforce realistic thinking. ("What good things could happen to you if you finish the project?")
- Leveling images reduce the negative effects of aversive, fearful visualizations. ("Picture your boss in a duck costume, quacking.")
- Reconceptualizing images changes the interpretation of events. ("Imagine that your wife wasn't angry at you, but had had a bad day at work.")
- Negative vs. positive images—visualizing a negative situation against a positive background, as in higher-order conditioning, can change the emotional valence of the situation. ("Imagine being criticized by an antagonist, while sitting in a tropical lagoon on a warm summer day.")
- Corrective images undo mistakes the clients have made in the past. ("Picture how you would do it if you had it to do all over again.")
- Generalized corrective images have the client correct all past incidence of a specific type. For example, a passive client might imagine having been assertive every major time he had backed away from a problem.
- Future perspective images have clients look back to the present situation from some future time, thereby clarifying key values. ("Imagine you are 85 looking back at your life. What do you consider important and unimportant now?")
- Blowup images teach clients to cope with the worst possible consequences of an event. ("What is the worst thing that could possibly happen as a result of losing your job? What would you do about it?")
- Visualization of low-probability images requires that clients picture all the terrible events that could happen to them, so that they learn to give up trying to control everything. Paradoxical techniques often employ these images. ("What terrible things could happen to you while reading the Sunday funnies? While taking a bath? While lying in your bed?")
- Assertive response images may be contrasted with images of passive, aggressive, and passive-aggressive responses, so that the client can see the consequences of each response. ("Imagine asking for your money back passively, aggressively, and assertively.")
- Ultimate consequences images have clients visualize a trouble-

some situation a week, month, or year after the event to determine the lasting consequences. ("If you kill yourself, how sad do
you imagine your girlfriend will be 8 years from now?")

- Empathy images teach clients to perceive the world from
  another's internal frame of reference. ("How does the person you
  hurt feel about you?")
- Cathartic images allow the client to imagine expressing previously unexpressed emotions like anger, love, jealousy, or sadness.
  ("Imagine yelling back at your boyfriend.")
- Zero reaction images have clients visualize receiving only neutral
  consequences in phobic situations. These images are often used
  in extinction procedures. ("Imagine getting up in front of the
  whole congregation and then walking out. Picture nobody noticing or caring.")
- Fanciful images solve problems in imagination that cannot be
  solved in reality. ("Picture your dead grandmother before you
  now. What advise would she give you? How does she feel about
  what you have done?")
- Preventive images are used to prepare clients to cope with problems they may encounter in the future, such as death, rejection,
  physical illness, poverty, etc.
- Negative reinforcing images involve the clients' imagining a fearful situation that removes them from an even more fearful situation. ("Imagine that holding a snake keeps you from being
  criticized by your peers.")
- Security images give clients a feeling of safety in a threatening
  situation ("When you are on the plane, imagine your mother is
  holding you in your warm, pink blanket.")
- Satiated images, used in covert flooding procedures, repeat the
  same visualization over and over again until the client gets tired
  of imagining it. ("Imagine, 50 times a day for the next two weeks,
  that your wife makes love to every man you see.")
- Alternative images are used when clients must decide between
  different courses of action. ("Visualize what your life would be
  like living in New York City for the next year versus what it
  would be like living in Key West, Florida.")
- Negative consequences images show the aversive results of
  something the client may see as positive. ("Imagine that after you
  become famous you are trapped in your house, unable to go
  anywhere because the paparazzi are stalking you.")

- Resisting–temptation images turn appealing objects into aversive objects ("Imagine your cigarette is dried buffalo chips.")
- Time–tripping images allow the client to detach from a distressing incident by imagining going forward in time (6 months) and then looking back on the incident (Lazarus, 1998). ("Imagine how you will feel in 6 months about your boyfriend dumping you.")

5. Have clients practice visualization until selected images become vivid.
6. After clients finish practicing their images, reintroduce the language component by asking them to summarize changes in their belief system. ("Now that you have shifted your emotions by using these images, what are your conclusions? What irrational thoughts were you thinking before? What rational beliefs do you have now?")

Example

As implied above, specific images are paired with specific irrational beliefs in order to bring about cognitive changes. Below are some of the visualizations we have used to correct various client irrationalities.

Core belief: People must always love me or I will be miserable.
Corrective images: Progressive coping images. Provide clients with coping images that show them: (a) being loved by everyone, (b) being loved by everyone in their environment except for one person, (c) being loved by most people, (d) being loved by half the people they know, (e) being loved by only a few people in their environment, (f) being loved by only one person. Describe these images in such a way that clients successfully cope with a decreasing number of people who love them.

Core belief: Making mistakes is terrible.
Corrective images: Noxious images may be used. Clients pair the aversive images with trying to be perfect all the time. ("Imagine the suicidal boredom perfection would bring.")

Core belief: It's terrible when things go wrong.
Corrective images: Leveling and zero–reaction images. Have clients picture nothing at all happening when something goes wrong.

Core belief: My emotions can't be controlled.
Corrective images: Rewarding images. Teach the client to imagine all the positive consequences of having their emotions free and spontaneous.

Core belief: Self–discipline is too hard to achieve.
Corrective images: Mastery images. Clients picture excellent self–discipline in a variety of situations.

Core belief: I must always depend on others.
Corrective images: Idealized images. Clients visualize scenes of freedom, independence, and being untethered.

Core belief: My bad childhood must make my adult life miserable.
Corrective images: Modeling images. Clients imagine a whole series of people who have been happy and successful despite having had a horrible childhood.

Core belief: I believe there is a right, correct, perfect solution for my problems and all I have to do is find it.
Corrective images: Small–detail coping images. Have clients imagine the necessary but small steps they must take to solve each specific problem.

Core belief: I am an exceptional person (a prince in disguise or Clark Kent looking for a phone booth). I require special privileges and favors; therefore, I shouldn't have to live within the limits and restrictions of ordinary mortals.
Corrective images: Empathy images. "If you were someone else, would you want to be friends with you? Would you like being around you?"

Comment

Some cognitive therapies primarily emphasize linguistic techniques, while others emphasize images. In cognitive restructuring we have found the combination far more effective than either one alone.

Further Information

The literature on imagery is extensive. The reader should refer to the major works of Kosslyn (1980), Kosslyn and Pomerantz (1977),

Lazarus (1977, 1982, 1989, 1995, 1998), Lazarus and Lazarus (1997), Richardson (1969), Sheikh (1983a, 1983b), Singer (1974, 1976, 1995), and Singer and Pope (1978). Imagery is also a major component of two other therapies that are often used along with cognitive restructuring: schema–focused therapy (McGinn & Young, 1996) and focusing–oriented psychotherapy (Gendlin, 1996a, 1996b).

NINE

Perceptual Shifting: Bridging

BRIDGING HELPS CLIENTS MOVE from old, damaging beliefs to new, more useful attitudes. It does this through the use of anchors that bridge old attitudes with new. Anchors can be thoughts, images, words, symbols, or any other type of mental association that carries the client from one thought to the other. Usually these anchors are already in the client's repertoire; it is the therapist's job to help the client associate them with new beliefs and to make the connections strong and persistent.

The first three techniques in this chapter use anchors already in use by the client: general anchors, value anchors, and word and symbolic anchors. The last technique, higher-order conditioning, creates anchors that are not already in the client's repertoire.

Although bridging may seem to be an advanced cognitive technique used only by mental health professionals, it is actually quite common and has been used for centuries by the general public. Some have even made it into an art. Two examples clarify this point.

Example 1

When I was a new psychologist working at my first job after graduation, I was driving down the main street of a small town in western Pennsylvania. Ahead of me I noticed a young boy riding his bike across a busy street. He didn't notice a car in front of him, and ran into it head first. He collapsed unconscious on the street, his bike a mangled mess, while cars pulled over and people got out to see if they could help. I was among them.

The police and an ambulance were called. The boy had only a mild concussion and, except for having a headache for a few days, he was fine. At the time, however, he didn't look fine. His mother had been contacted immediately, and she came running as fast as she could towards the accident. When she saw her son lying unconscious on the street, she started to scream. She screamed as loudly as she could and flailed her arms back and forth as she kept running toward him. Her screaming was as loud and intense as I had ever heard; her face turned bright red, and she started to pound the street with her fist. As the boy regained consciousness the onlookers started to worry more about the mother than the son.

Everybody tried to calm her down. We told her that the ambulance had been called and that it looked as if her son wasn't seriously hurt. We suggested that she might find it useful to relax her breathing. She looked as if she hadn't heard a word we said and continued screaming.

At that point an auto mechanic from a nearby gas station came running up. He looked at the boy, turned to the mother, and said in a quiet, soft voice, *"Your screaming is hurting your son. He needs your help NOW, not your yelling. Go and comfort him!"*

She looked at her son, then at the mechanic, and then back at her son. Suddenly, instantaneously, she stopped. She ceased yelling in mid–scream, with no residual whimpers or sobs, as if she had cut her emotions off with a knife. She calmly bent down and stroked her son's forehead, whispering to him until the ambulance arrived.

While the boy was not seriously injured, what is striking is the power of the mechanic's statement. He had said exactly the right thing, in exactly the right way, at exactly the right time. This is a classic example of bridging. The mother's old thought, "It's terrible, horrible, and catastrophic that my son is injured and I can't stand it" was bridged to the new attitude, "My son needs my help." The anchor that connected the two was, "Your screaming is hurting your son." Her desire to help her son had already been deeply ingrained in her reper-toire; all the mechanic had to do was to show the mother that her actions were violating her deeply ingrained belief.

Some of the best bridge builders in our society have no training or degrees. Academic education can provide helpful theoretical informa-tion, but experience with people is the best teacher for bridge building.

Example 2

In another incident, some well-known professor types were appearing on a talk show to discuss their differing theories on the causes of poverty. They were college professors, economists, political scientists, agronomists, sociologist, engineers and the like; all had a Ph.D. and were preeminent in their fields. The engineer said that poverty is caused by a lack of industrialization while the political scientist suggested that political conflicts were the culprit. The sociologists discussed class stratification, the economist talked about supply and demand. They all argued about the problem in great detail. They were well informed, lucid, and certainly seemed to know what they were talking about. The intricacies of their arguments were impressive, but the studio audience seemed to have difficulty deciding which of their complex theories was correct.

That evening a public television station presented a documentary about the late Mother Theresa. It mostly showed her helping the poor and sick in poverty-stricken areas of India, Peru, Lebanon, and other countries. In a brief scene she was shown climbing steps with her sisters into a building in Calcutta. A newspaper reporter was shouting questions at her but she didn't respond. Finally the reporter asked, "Why are there so many poor people in the world?" She kept on walking, but at the top of the stairs she turned around, looked him in the eye and said, *"Because people don't share."* She turned around and continued into the building.

The documentary didn't dwell on this moment or consider the comment a remarkable thing; it quickly moved on to other events in Mother Theresa's life. Nonetheless, her statement was shocking. It seemed a facile thing to say about such a complex problem, but the more I thought about it the more I realized that she was exactly right. Her short sentence had cut through all the erudite comments that the professors had made and captured the core of the matter. It was a powerful thing to say, and an ideal bridge. It changed the view of poverty immediately and completely.

Over the years people from diverse backgrounds have shown the ability to be excellent bridge builders. Whether statesmen or used car salesmen, poets or Army sergeants, auto mechanics or tiny old ladies dedicated to helping the poor, they all share the ability to find the key to the way people perceive something, and to make a statement that bridges to another belief and produces a dramatic, conceptual shift.

BRIDGE PERCEPTIONS

Principles

Clients learn new information more readily if some component of that new information is already stored in their memories. That common element between the old knowledge and the new constitutes a bridge across which clients can move more easily from mistaken beliefs to more rational, functional thoughts. This type of transition is illustrated in the following example.

Example 1

Old belief: People are no good. They are mean and spiteful.
New Belief: People are people. They act the way nature planned. Sometimes we like what they do, sometimes we don't.

The therapist might attempt to move the client from the old belief to the new belief by employing countering techniques, but there is a strong probability that it will neither be as efficient nor as long–lasting as the results that could be derived from the bridging technique.

Upon careful analysis of the old belief, the reader should note that there are two components that serve as a bridge to the new belief: the subject "people" and the assessment that "they are mean and spiteful." The new belief is also concerned with "people," and it too acknowledges that human behavior can be disappointing, but it interprets that reality as a fact of "nature."

For example, one of my clients hated adults for being mean and spiteful but revealed during our sessions that she *loved* babies. Why, I asked, didn't she dislike babies, whom some people might consider "mean and spiteful" for throwing tantrums, wetting their pants, or spitting up food? "That's silly," argued the client. "They're just doing those things naturally."

We pointed out that people who yell at us because they have a cold or who withdraw when they are scared are acting out of much the same motivation as babies—naturally. If she could accept and even like babies, perhaps she could accept such adults as well. "Babies" is the anchor that carries the emotion from one attitude to another.

The client practiced changing her image of adults. Every time people did something she didn't like, she concentrated on picturing them not as adults, but as big babies dressed in adult clothes, speaking in adult words but with the underlying motivation of a baby. After picturing 43 situations with this image, she was able to adopt a new and more rational attitude toward adult misbehavior.

Method

1. Use clients' master list of beliefs.
2. Make a companion list of possible replacement beliefs, making cer-

tain that your clients agree that these would be more useful perceptions if their validity could be demonstrated.

3. During counseling, search for an attitude already accepted by
   clients that could bridge the old perception to the new. In some
   cases you will need a series of themes and it may take you and your
   clients some time to find them. Pick bridges that have the most personal meaning for clients so that they can be tied most directly with
   their concept of self.

4. Once the bridges have been identified, have clients practice shifting
   their beliefs from the old to the new. The practice should continue
   until the new attitude replaces the old. If enough real situations do
   not exist, encourage your clients to imagine as many such situations as possible.

Example 2

Old belief: The client is afraid of riding a ski chairlift. "If I get anxious on
the chair I won't be able to escape for 10 minutes, and I could lose
control and embarrass myself."
New belief: A chairlift is an opportunity to relax, look at the beautiful
winter scenery, anticipate the downhill run, and talk with a friend.
Bridge belief: The following exchange illustrates how a bridge can be
established.

THERAPIST: Skiing is a risky sport, wouldn't you agree?
CLIENT: Sure, but I enjoy it.
THERAPIST: Then you enjoy taking risks?
CLIENT: It's the only way to really enjoy life to the fullest.
THERAPIST: Aren't there riskier aspects to skiing than in riding the
   chairlifts?
CLIENT: Well . . . yes. I guess so.
THERAPIST: Why, then, are you unnerved by the lesser risk?
CLIENT: Gee. I don't know. I guess, now that I think about it, it
   doesn't make a lot of sense, does it?

The client and I wrote the following bridge belief in this example
into a more general philosophy for the client to read each week.

You can look at all the enjoyable, pleasurable, or beautiful
things in life negatively. While you relax on an ocean beach a
tidal wave could engulf you or a great white shark could gobble
you up. You could be bitten by a black mamba snake while lying

on soft grass next to a gentle country stream. While sailing under a silver moon on a Caribbean lagoon, you could hit a coral reef and drown. A sparrow in an English meadow could suddenly attack you à la Hitchcock. You could break your eardrums while listening to Mozart's Jupiter symphony, or your stereo system could electrocute you. While making love you could have a heart attack or catch a disease. Even if you watch one of your favorite plays by George Bernard Shaw, the theater could catch on fire. You could also worry about playing with young children because some adult could accuse you of molesting them, or you could choke to death eating a tender, juicy drumstick from your mother's Thanksgiving turkey.

You could try to protect yourself by avoiding all the enjoyable and pleasurable things of life. You could retreat to your room and worry about being trapped in an earthquake or the room catching on fire. But once you throw away the bright and beautiful, what worthwhile aspect of life do you have left to protect?

Example 3

Old belief: From a teenage boy: "My parents prefer my older brother. They give him everything, and I get what is left over."

New belief: "Our parents love us both, but they treat us differently because we are different people. They celebrate my individuality and wouldn't want me to be a clone of my brother. They give me what they think I need, and my brother what he needs."

Bridge belief: The therapist gleaned the following example from the client's personal history. "Remember the two kittens your parents asked you to take care of when you were young? One was warm and fuzzy and always wanted to be petted; he loved to cuddle next to you while you slept. The other was frisky and adventuresome; he was always chasing mice, climbing trees, and getting into your potted plants. If the kittens could speak, one could have accused you of giving more freedom to his brother, the other of not giving him enough love. But you loved them both and didn't prefer one over the other. You gave both what they needed. Maybe your parents are treating you the same way."

Comment

If you can find exactly the right bridge, your client's perceptions will change dramatically, and your client won't have to invest a great deal of time and effort in practicing the new perception. But you must search patiently with your client in order to find the bridge that has the strongest and most personal meaning.

Further Information

Finding the key bridge perception may be the core element underlying rapid religious or other types of conversion (Sargant, 1996). Symons and Johnson (1997) reviewed a variety of studies and confirmed the importance of making bridges personally relevant. They determined that subjects best remembered those concepts that had the most self–references.

Other therapists use metaphors as bridges (see Gordon, 1978; Martin, Cummings, & Hallberg 1992; and Neukrug, 1998; Shorr, 1972, 1974).

HIERARCHY OF VALUES BRIDGES
Principles

One of the most effective types of bridges, and one of the therapist's most important tools, uses the client's value system as an anchor. Our experience shows that an appeal to personal values is a highly effective bridging technique. Values offer the advantage of being proprioceptive and deeply rooted within clients' concepts of reality. Clients frequently will not accept a rational judgment that their attitudes or behaviors are incorrect, but they will rarely refute a proven discrepancy between their attitudes or behaviors and their actual values.

Through careful management of the therapeutic process, the counselor can help clients get in touch with their personal hierarchy of values. Old, mistaken beliefs are also associated with that hierarchy, but if the therapist can demonstrate that new, preferred beliefs enjoy a *higher* value on that hierarchy, he or she can facilitate clients' movement toward a more effective attitude.

Method

1. Discover the client's personal hierarchy of values. This can be done by using a standardized value test, or a better method is to find the values through selective questioning. Distinguish between questions that merely elicit value judgments ("How do you feel about marriage?") and questions that force clients to *rank* their values in

an hierarchical fashion ("Which would you rather have—the security that comes from having someone else around who cares for you or the freedom of being single but perhaps somewhat lonely?") The latter type of question, repeated over a wide range of topics, eventually leads to the construction of a personal hierarchy. For example, through the following series of questions and answers, it becomes clear that the client values freedom more than wealth, and wealth more than personal relationships:

Questions	Answers
Which do you prefer:	
• Wealth or popularity?	Wealth
• Security or independence?	Independence
• Wealth or independence?	Independence
• Lots of friends or wealth?	Wealth
• Health or lots of friends?	Friends
• Friends or your independence?	Independence
• Being paid well or being the boss?	Being the boss

The therapist should be mindful that though this questioning technique can be useful, it does have its limitations. Clients will be tempted to provide an answer that they think the therapist wants to hear. After using the questions in developing a basic hierarchy, elicit information from your clients about their past and present attitudes and experiences, what they have actually done and thus actually believe. See if these confirm their reported value preferences. A hierarchy can also be developed by using a Q-sort technique or fantasy analogies similar to such games as "Genie in a Bottle" or "Three Wishes."

2. Make a list of old, damaging beliefs and have your clients associate each of these with a particular value on their personal hierarchies. (Any beliefs that don't fit on the hierarchy are immediately highlighted as being incongruous with clients' realities.)

3. Make a list of the new, preferred beliefs and challenge your clients to associate each of these with a particular value on their personal hierarchies. Those new beliefs that can clearly be juxtaposed to higher values than the contrary, older beliefs are highlighted. The clients should then practice perceiving the higher value whenever they think of the new belief.

4. For repetition, have clients practice seeing the higher value in a

variety of situations. This can be done by using images in the counseling room or by waiting until an environmental stimulus triggers the thought.

Examples

Old belief: It would be very bad if my husband's colleagues did not approve of me.
Higher client value: Christian religious beliefs.
New belief: To truly follow Christ's teachings, don't strive to be popular and appeal to what people think. More importantly, Christians should use their God–given inner conscience and be true to His principles.

Old belief: Everything I try to do ends up in failure.
Higher client value: Endurance, "When the going gets tough, the tough get going!"
New belief: I am not in control of whether I succeed or not. I am only in control of my trying. I will always strive and try to learn from my failures so that I can be more successful in future attempts.

Old belief: I am to blame for my father sexually abusing me.
Higher client value: Dominance, control, and competition.
New belief: If I keep eating myself up with this irrational guilt, I lose and let the bastard win again.

Old belief: She left me for a younger, more successful man.
Higher client value: What is objectively true.
New belief: I'm good, but I am not better than all the other men in the world.

Old belief: I must have a man in order to be happy.
Higher client value: Self–respect.
New belief: I would rather like myself alone than hate myself living as a slave to a man I disliked.

Old belief: If I take this job abroad, I'll leave all my friends.
Higher client value: Stimulation and variety.
New belief: I would die of boredom here sooner than I'd die of loneliness there.

Comment

As the examples illustrate, it is crucial that therapists remember that they are bridging on the client's value system, not the therapists'. It doesn't matter what the therapist thinks of the client's values, it's what the client thinks that counts.

In many cases it is difficult to find the client's true values. The therapist must take particular care to look for values that the client rejects in the therapist's presence because they are socially unpopular, i.e., hedonism, power, etc. Differences between stated values and actual ones can be discovered by examining clients' histories.

As an aid in helping clients visualize the superiority of the new belief over the old, I have devised a three–column worksheet on which clients are asked to record their values in hierarchical order (column #1), their old beliefs (column #2), and the proposed new beliefs (column #3), with each belief juxtaposed to the value from which it derives (see table 9.1). Applying this worksheet to our earlier example, the client might see that an all–consuming quest for wealth that deprives him of certain freedoms in life is clearly contradictory to his hierarchy of values.

Therapists may ask their clients to construct their own worksheets to periodically confirm, on the basis of their own self-analysis, that they are operating according to their highest values. Such periodic reassessments can be useful, since values can change abruptly or over a period of time. The client who suffers a near–fatal heart attack may suddenly find himself re-ranking his values in preference for those that place greater emphasis upon the quality of his life.

TABLE 9.1
Heirarchy of Values Worksheet

Rank Order of Values	Value of Old Belief	Value of New Belief
1. _____	_____	_____
2. _____	_____	_____
3. _____	_____	_____
4. _____	_____	_____
5. _____	_____	_____
6. _____	_____	_____
7. _____	_____	_____
8. _____	_____	_____
9. _____	_____	_____
10. _____	_____	_____

Further Information

Research on attitude change has demonstrated the importance of the value component of people's beliefs (see Flemming, 1967; Petty & Cacioppo, 1981; Rokeach, 1964, 1968, 1973, 1979; and Smith, Bruner, & White, 1956). Theoretically, value shifting can be viewed as another instance of Premack's principle (Premack, 1965).

Personal values have some of the strongest self–reference effects (SRE) (see Banaji & Prentice, 1994; Bellezza & Holt, 1992; Keenan, Golding, & Brown, 1992; and Rogers, Kuiper, & Kirker, 1977).

LABEL BRIDGES
Principles

A single word or symbol may serve as a bridge. Each word and symbol has a connotative as well as denotative meaning; each collects emotional responses through operant, classical, or cognitive conditioning. Once a symbol and affective response have been paired, the symbol has the capacity to elicit the emotion directly.

Symbols are by definition arbitrary, indicating only a consensus about what something means; usually one symbol can substitute for another quite easily. The exception to this generalization is found in certain words. Though words may easily enough be substituted for other words, different words often carry totally divergent emotional connotations. Many clients consistently choose words with negative connotations when they could just as easily select neutral or positive labels.

Label bridging helps clients identify their negative labels and shift them to more objective, positive, emotional associations. They learn in this process that the only difference between some words and others is their emotional valence.

Method 1. Word Labels

1. Make a list of the specific events or situations (referents) that the client associates with negative words. For instance, what referents does the client visualize when using the words "inferior," "sick," and "weak"?
2. Describe these referents in objective, nonevaluative terms. What would a motion–picture camera record of the event or situation?

What would an objective third party overhear?

3. List the major negative labels the client uses to describe the situations.

4. Help the client list the neutral and positive labels that could be used to interpret the referents. Explain how these new labels are just as valid as previous labels, but can bridge to more positive emotions.

5. Have the client practice using new labels every day, recording the situation, finding the negative label for it, and bridging to a more positive word.

Example

A person who . . .	*Could be called . . .*	*Or could be called . . .*
changes one's mind a lot	wishy–washy	flexible
expresses one's opinion	egotistical	genuine, assertive
is emotionally sensitive	hysterical, fragile	alive, caring, open
is selective in choosing a mate	afraid to commit	discriminating
gets depressed sometimes	neurotic	human
isn't good at a game	klutz, inferior	hasn't practiced
isn't orderly	sloppy, piggish	spontaneous, carefree
pleases others	social phobic	friendly
believes what others say	gullible	trusting
loves another strongly	dependent	loving
gets anxious	weak, cowardly	aware
is nontraditional	anarchist, heretical, immoral	free–spirited, self–reliant
is helped by another	manipulated	cared for
is not working hard on a task	lazy	relaxed
is sure of something	conceited	self-confident
looks at things positively	Pollyanna	optimist
talks a lot	motor–mouth	expressive
thinks before making decision	indecisive	prudent
takes risks	foolhardy	brave
sticks to projects	bullheaded	resolute
gets excited	hysterical	exuberant

Method 2. Symbolic Labels

A symbolic label can be especially effective for certain clients, particularly those who have a strong religious orientation. Richard Cox has developed a procedure using symbols and rituals to bridge from old to new beliefs (Cox, 1998). We have modified the procedure to emphasize the cognitive elements involved.

1. Identify the belief causing the problem. (Cox calls it the "demon.")
2. Help your clients to find a personal symbol that represents the problem area. The symbol needs to be deeply, emotionally rooted in the client's history. (For example, a woman who believed herself trapped in an abusive marriage immediately thought of the symbol of the crucifix. She felt it represented her sacrificing herself in order to keep her husband.)
3. Help clients identify the positive or promotive belief. ("I need to leave.")
4. Assist clients in finding a specific symbol that will bridge the damaging belief to the promotive. No symbol is too extreme and the therapist doesn't need to understand why it is important as long as the client understands it. (In our example, the client thought of her own resurrection; she pictured her tomb being opened up and her walking out into the bright shimmering sunlight, away from the marriage.)
5. Have clients practice associating the two symbols. Start with the symbol of the problem area and have clients shift to the symbol for the promotive belief. (Every time our client thought of her marriage being like a crucifixion she practiced shifting to the symbol of a resurrection. It was not long before she saw that she was not trapped, that she didn't have to sacrifice herself on the cross of her husband's abuse, and that she was free to "walk into the sunlight" whenever she wished.)

Comment

Some clients may argue that a negative word is more logically correct than a positive word; for example, one client suggested that wishy–washy people change their minds more often than flexible people; therefore, wishy–washy is a more accurate descriptor. Although there may be some concrete differences between synonyms, many differences are purely reflective of our value systems. We refer to people as wishy–washy because we think they change their minds more than we think they should—not because there is some objective standard of how often people are permitted to switch their opinions and still be called flexible. Likewise, when we call someone "lazy" we may think they are unnecessarily idle. But since everyone is doing something (sleeping, resting, thinking, playing, etc.) what we really mean is that they aren't doing what *we* think they ought to be doing.

If clients pick the right symbols, symbolic bridging can produce instantaneous and dramatic shifts that make permanent changes. However, both symbolic and word bridging are rarely used alone. Most frequently they are an adjunct to other cognitive restructuring approaches.

Further Information

Frijda, Markam, Sato, and Wiers (1995) discuss the importance of word labels and their ability to elicit emotional reactions. The "Rumplestiltskin effect" describes the dramatic changes that can take place by switching the words clients use to describe their problems (see Torrey, 1972). Symbolic bridging can be best understood by reading Cox directly (see Cox, 1973, 1998).

HIGHER-ORDER BRIDGING
Principles

Some clients do not have a sufficient number of anchors in their own repertoire to serve as bridges from the old belief to the new. For such clients the therapists can create bridges using the principles of higher-order covert conditioning.

In classical learning theory, higher-order conditioning pairs neutral stimuli with another element that is already conditioned. For example, a flashing red light (CS-1) can be paired with relaxation (US), producing a calm response (CR). If the experimenter then associates a bell with the red light, the bell (CS-2) alone can elicit the CR.

Schematically it can be represented as:

Original Conditioning

CS-1 (red light) ⟍
paired   ⟶ UR (calmness)
US (relaxation) ⟋

Higher-order Conditioning

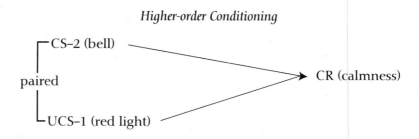

With sufficient pairing, any variable perceptible to clients can be a CS–2 and serve as an anchor for later bridges. Cognitive restructuring generally uses two types of variables—perceptions and conceptions. Perceptions are made up of visual, auditory, olfactory, and kinesthetic representations. Conceptions are beliefs, thoughts, and attitudes. Higher–order bridging involves taking the perceptual and conceptual CS–2s associated with the new belief and pairing these with the old belief. After a series of repetitions, the old belief begins to bridge toward the new.

Method

1. Have the client focus on the old belief and create a model or typical scene where this old belief occurs strongly. The scene should be imagined in vivid detail, using all the senses.
2. Record in writing all the perceptual and conceptual variables (CS–2) connected with the image.

Perceptual

a. *Visualization.* What the client pictures in the scene is dissected in great detail. For example, is the scene in color? Is it a still or motion picture? clear or fuzzy? two– or three–dimensional? Is the client seeing herself in the scene? What is the focal point (the major element in the scene that draws the client's attention)? Is the scene bright or dim? What is the angle of view? What is the size of the client in relation to objects that form the background of this scene? Are the people moving?

b. *Other senses.* Auditory—can the client clearly hear the sounds? What is their duration? How loud are they? Olfactory—what does the client smell? Kinesthetic—what is the temperature? etc.

Conceptual

a. Every major thought that the client has before, during, and after the imagined event is recorded. The therapist helps the client to state these thoughts explicitly. The types of thoughts to look for are:

    i. Expectancy—what the client anticipates will happen in the situation.

    ii. Evaluation—the assessment that the client makes of herself during the scene.

    iii. Self–efficacy—the client's judgment of his ability to complete the task effectively.

    iv. Payoffs—the anticipated reward or payoff the client thinks he will get in the situation.

    v. Punishments—the aversive things the client anticipates.

    vi. Self–concept—the client's attitudes about his or her worth as a human being.

    vii. Attributions—the attitudes and motivations the client attributes to others in the scene.

    viii. Purpose—why the client is in the scene in the first place.

b. The therapist also searches, along with the client, for logical fallacies that might surface in the client's interpretations of these scenes. Each fallacy is written down. The most common fallacies are: dichotomous thinking, overgeneralization, nonparsimonious reasoning, perfectionism, reification, subjective error, arguing ad homineum, ipse dixit, a priori thinking, finding the good reason, egocentric error, self–fulfilling prophesy, mistaking probability for possibility, etc. (see section on logical fallacies in chapter 6).

3. After recording all of the perceptual and conceptual information connected to the old belief, the therapist asks the client to picture a scene connected with the new belief—the one that we wish to bridge to. It should be a model scene, one that represents the new belief ideally. The closer the content of the new scene is to that of the old scene, the better. Like the first scene, this image should be pictured in great detail, until it is vivid.

4. As in step #2, record all of the perceptions the client has of the new scene—visual, auditory, and kinesthetic. Point out to the client the contrast between the two ways of viewing the image as the list is developed.

5. The conceptions of the new scene are likewise recorded. The therapist should pay careful attention to finding the attributions, expec-

tations, self-concept, and evaluations the client makes in the new scene. The therapist writes down the correct reasoning the client has in the visualization.

6. There is a pause in the imagery work. Therapist and client discuss the differences between the perceptual and conceptual representations of the two scenes.

7. Now the therapist is ready to do the actual higher order conditioning. The client imagines the original scene for two minutes. Gradually, the therapist introduces the perceptual and conceptual representations of the new scene, one at a time, with the client imagining the changes until they are vivid. The process continues until all the elements from the new scene are incorporated. When this is successfully done, the client is able to imagine the old scene, but with all the perceptual and conceptual components bridged to the new scene.

8. Often the whole procedure is recorded on tape so that the client can practice the conditioning two to three times a week. With enough pairings the emotional valences of the scenes switch and the client is far more likely to believe in the new thought.

Example: The Story of Alex

Alex, an attractive young man in his late twenties, had difficulty meeting women. Although he'd had several long-term successful relationships, they had all been initiated by the women. He couldn't introduce himself to eligible, attractive women, despite having memorized books on how to meet women and taken classes on the art of conversation.

His old, negative visualization revealed his problem. He described himself in a singles' bar, standing close to a very attractive woman. He visualized himself as appearing very small while all the other men towered over him (he was 6'1"). The woman was the focus of the scene; she was very colorful while he was dull and muted. He pictured a spotlight illuminating her while he stood in the shadows. She was moving in his scene while he was as rigid and still as a figure in a snapshot. Kinesthetically she seemed cool and icy while he felt hot and itchy.

His cognitions revealed even more:

Purpose: to impress her.
Expectancy: "I will fail miserably."

Self-concept: "I am an inferior male."
Efficacy: "I will fail when I try to talk to her."
Attribution: "She will despise me and think me a creep."

Logical fallacies were numerous:

Catastrophizing: "It would be terrible if she rejected me."
Overgeneralizing: "If she rejects me, all women will."
Perfectionism: "I must look like the perfect male."
Pathology: "I must be really sick to have this problem."
Traitism: "I have the 'wrong stuff.'"
Musturbation: "I must get her to like me."
Egocentric error: "If I talk to her, she will focus all of her attention on me and will inspect me for any flaws."

He easily developed a visualization of a new scene representing a new belief. He pictured himself in the same bar talking to a group of men. It had recently happened. He was the center of attention and enjoyed telling jokes and stories. There were no women around.

In his visualization he was the same size as the others. Everybody was in focus, colorful and in motion. Kinesthetically, he felt warm and pleasant.

He also thought quite differently in his new scene:

Purpose: to have fun talking to the men.
Expectancy: none, "I'll enjoy this as much as I can."
Attribution: "Who cares what they think of me. It doesn't really matter."
Self-concept: "My worth as a human being is not involved in this in any way."
Evaluation: "I'm more interested in talking to them and finding out what they think than in how I come across."
Efficacy: "I can talk to men without any problem. If the conversation doesn't work it's more likely to be their difficulty than mine."

Instead of thinking in terms of logical fallacies, he was very realistic:

Commonplace expectations vs. catastrophizing: "No big deal, I don't need them to like me."
Discriminating vs. overgeneralizing: "Even if they don't like me, many other men will and do."
Realism vs. perfectionism: "There is no reason for me to try to do anything perfectly in this situation. I'll just act normally and they can

take it or leave it."

Health vs. pathology and traitism: "What I am deep down inside is totally irrelevant while talking to these men. I'm just trying to have a pleasant conversation."

Nonchalance vs. musturbation: "I either will like the conversation or I won't. There are no musts, oughts, or shoulds."

We now had two lists of CS–2s: those connected to the old scene in which Alex was unable to approach the attractive woman, and those connected to the new scene in which he was talking with men. To use higher–order conditioning, we had Alex picture the old scene with the perceptions and conceptions previously associated with the new scene. This would enable Alex to bridge from the old to the new. The following was the beginning instruction.

> Okay, Alex. Now I would like you to relax again. Narrow your attention and focus on your muscles. Make them loose, limp, and slack. (2 minutes)
>
> That's fine. Now please recreate that first scene where you felt so tense. Imagine right now that you are in the bar and the same attractive woman is standing close by. Picture it as vividly and clearly as you can in the same way you did before. Don't change anything. See it in the same way. When it's clearly in mind, indicate by raising your finger. (2 minutes)
>
> Keep imagining the image, but I would like you to gradually, at my direction, make changes in what you see and think. First, picture that you are of the same size as the other men in the bar. Imagine that until it is clearly in mind, and indicate when you are ready. (1 minute) Now keep visualizing your larger size but add motion and color to yourself. Picture that you are moving just like the attractive woman, and that you are equally colorful. (We continued switching all the other perceptions from the new scene to the old scene.)
>
> That's good. Keep visualizing and feeling the scene in the new way that you have just practiced, but now I would like you to imagine saying different things to yourself in the scene.
>
> First picture yourself looking at her, but instead of thinking that your purpose is to try and impress her, imagine that you are thinking of her in the same way you thought about talking to the men. Imagine thinking that your purpose is to have fun talking to her rather than impressing her. Visualize this until it's clearly in mind. Indicate when you are finished (1 minute). Now, picture

thinking that there are many other women you can talk to if this conversation doesn't work out. (We continued switching all the other conceptual CS–2s from the mastery scene to the negative scene.)

The session was taped and the client listened to the tape three times a week for about six weeks. He reported that with each succeeding week he found it easier and easier to approach attractive women.

Comment

For bridging to take place the perceptual and conceptual aspects of the new scene have to be stronger than those of the old, otherwise the opposite conditioning could occur. In addition, there may be other problems with higher–order conditioning. Pavlov's work indicates that the farther away the CS is from the US, the smaller the amplitude, the longer the latency, and the less permanent the CR response. The CRs have a tendency to extinguish quickly. However, the cognitive element may be a crucial addition to the conditioning. Conceptual change may help clients maintain what would otherwise be weak, higher order associations.

Further Information

Skinner (1953, 1974) and Pavlov (1928, 1960) did the germinal work on higher–order conditioning.

EMDR and NLP practitioners use higher–order conditioning in many of their techniques. Eye-movement training and "restructuring" may be based on higher–order conditioning. Both approaches use cognitive modification, but they are not as central to their methods as they are to cognitive therapists. See Shapiro (1995, 1998) for the original EMDR, and Lohr, Kleinknecht, Tolin, and Barrett (1995) for a criticism. For NLP see Bandler (1992, 1996), Bandler and Grinder (1979, 1996), Dilts, Grinder, Bandler, DeLozier, and Cameron–Bandler (1979), Grinder and Bandler (1975, 1982).

Some basic research on higher–order conditioning may be found in Kelleher (1966), Rizley and Rescorla (1972), and Stubbs and Cohen (1972).

TEN

Historical Resynthesis

Beliefs and attitudes have a long history; they do not simply appear overnight. The cognitions that clients have today are only the most recent reincarnation of beliefs that may have originated many years before. Almost all beliefs have a developmental history that stretches into the distant past. Often the roots of a present cognition are more informative than the content. Many times an attitude may have been once useful and accurate when it was first formed but has long since become anachronistic. Consider the Figure 10.1, which represents the historical development of clients' beliefs. The dots stand for raw sensory data entering the brain; the data may come from a client's senses (seeing, hearing, tasting, touching, smelling), they may be somatic (a physical sensation from the body, such as a hurt elbow or a stuffy nose), or they may come from emotions (sadness, anger, or fear). The

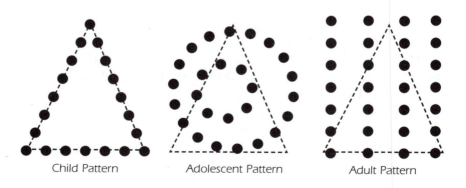

Child Pattern   Adolescent Pattern   Adult Pattern

Figure 10.1 Distorted life themes

data are disorganized, and don't have meaning until the brain groups them into an organized pattern.

If clients' brains were computers, everybody's data would be grouped into the same patterns: a triangle for the first pattern, a circle for the second, and a square for the third. But human brains don't simply scan data—they transform it. They create patterns based on habit and emotions and what other brains have taught them. As children clients may perceive triangles; as they grow, they may continue to see triangles even though circles or squares provide a better fit. Clients can spend their entire lives seeing triangles simply because they first saw them when they were young.

Computers don't make this type of mistake, but humans do all the time. For example, as children, clients may look at the raw data of themselves and the world and form the pattern that they are weak and small (the triangle)—this pattern is accurate at that stage in their development. As they get older the raw data change; they are less weak and powerless (the circle and square), but many clients continue to see the triangle and continue to think of themselves as weak and powerless.

Early traumatic learning, bad teaching, or emotional disturbance may preclude some clients' progression to new ways of transforming data. These clients consistently organize their experiences into two different types of themes: damaging ones that once reflected the world accurately but which became irrelevant as the world changed, or themes that were always false and distorted. In either case, these earlier themes cause clients much distress and therefore need to be removed. In these cases, clients' problems are not treated simply by changing their present damaging beliefs. The therapist also needs to remove the historical misinterpretation that originally generated the distortion.

RESYNTHESIZING CRITICAL LIFE EVENTS

Principles

Removing the historical roots of clients' misperceptions has proven to be a successful remedial strategy for most clients. Hence, today's cognitive therapists are much more likely to incorporate techniques that accomplish this as a standard part of their therapeutic repertoire. Past critical life events often forge misperceptions. Because clients have stored these events in their memories, they often need to correct the cognitive mistakes made during the earlier critical event in order to shift their present thinking.

Method

1. Relax the client.
2. Use the lists of critical events you have compiled (see chapter 3).
3. At times you will find it more appropriate to substitute more specific lists for general ones. The specific lists recount the key events linked to the client's symptoms. For example, if clients are anxious, then have them write three lists of the key anxiety attacks they have had—one for childhood, one for adolescence, and one for adulthood. Or, when working with delayed stress syndrome, employ three other lists: pre-traumatic event, during traumatic event, and post-traumatic event.
4. Suggest that your client describe these critical events in detail.
5. After discussion with your client, ascertain whether any of the beliefs that were created by the critical events still cause problems in the present.
6. Also discuss how the client's emotions and behaviors altered because of the beliefs formed at the time of the critical events.
7. Help your clients to reinterpret the old events with new, more useful beliefs. Have them scrutinize the events with the advantage of distance and time so that they can rectify earlier mistaken perceptions with adult reasoning.
8. Use corrective coping imagery so that your clients can revise the event by imagining that they had thought and acted reasonably.
9. Review all major critical events; detect the belief and have the client imagine correcting the situation.

Example 1: The Story of Mark

Mark was sent to me by another cognitive therapist. He was suffering from agoraphobia, had seen several different therapists over five years, and had made some progress. He was capable of traveling most places and performing most activities without undue fear, but in one area he hadn't mastered his fear—he still couldn't fly. He'd had several *in vivo* practice sessions from a psychiatrist who owned his own plane with no success. He still hadn't flown.

We did a complete analysis of the thoughts he had about flying and found them to be typical for an agoraphobic. Mark didn't fear the plane crashing; he was afraid of getting panicky while airborne. He feared being trapped on a plane while having an anxiety attack.

His core belief was not our discovery—previous cognitive therapists had identified it, but former attempts at disputing it had not worked. No one had previously identified or challenged the historical roots of his belief, so they were still intact. We decided to change these roots in order to shift his contemporary belief.

Mark worked hard and energetically searched for the historical forerunners to his present irrational thought. We found the environmental trigger for these formative irrationalities.

- Age 2–6

    Critical event: Overprotected by mother.

    Irrational belief: Life is dangerous and I need someone to protect me. I can't handle this world by myself.

    Corrected belief: My mom overprotected me because of her own fears, not because of my supposed weaknesses. Life was no more dangerous for me than for anyone else. I can handle the world as effectively as others.

- Age 6–12

    Critical event: Spoiled.

    Irrational belief: Life should be as easy as it once was.

    Irrational belief: I shouldn't have to feel pain.

    Corrected belief: Because of my early distorted learning, I developed a false expectation that I should have my wishes fulfilled without much effort. This belief is not only false but is damaging to me. People have to work to get what they want. The sooner I learn this, the happier I will be.

- Age 12–16

    Critical event 1: Rejected by peers because he acted spoiled.

    Irrational belief: It's horrible if everybody doesn't like me.

    Irrational belief: If I am perfect I will be liked.

    Irrational belief: I need to control everything to be perfect.

    Corrective beliefs: The other kids didn't like me because I was a spoiled brat and I demanded that they treat me the way my overprotective mom did—they would have none of this. My perfectionism and attempt to control everyone was one of the causes of their rejection rather than a correction.

    Critical event 2: Saw a fellow student vomit in class and observed that his classmates rejected the student.

Irrational belief: People will reject me unless I control everything physical going on inside my body.

Corrective belief: No human being can control all of their physiological symptoms, many of which are instinctual. Attempting to do so causes huge problems; I am spending all my time and energy trying to control something that can't be controlled. People are far more likely to reject me as a control freak.

Critical event 3: Panicked about getting sick in a car during a cross-country trip. Started to fear panic itself.

Irrational belief: Now I must control everything psychological going on in my body so that people don't reject me.

Corrective belief: I am spending my life watching my mind work instead of living.

Critical event 4: Whenever he considered taking a plane trip he would get panicky.

Irrational belief: I won't be able to control my fear in a plane, and I won't be able to escape, therefore I will be trapped in an intolerable situation.

Corrective belief: So what if I get scared and embarrass myself? It would be better if I did that than spending my whole life trying to control these feelings.

Example 2: The Story of Ronald

Sometimes it is difficult to find the past critical event connected to the present emotion. The association may be obscurely linked.

For example, a client from Denver had anxiety that proved to be quite a mystery. Ronald was a middle-aged man who came to see me because he would occasionally have sudden and extremely powerful panic attacks. These attacks would occur once every four or five months, and the source couldn't be found. I made a careful list of all Ronald's previous anxiety attacks and then used functional analysis to gather an extensive list of possible causes or stimuli that happened right before he got anxious. The checklist included questions such as: Were you angry? Sexually frustrated? Were you having problems in your marriage? Had you changed your eating habits? Was there trouble at work? Had you been extremely tired or depressed? Were you thinking of something that had happened in your childhood?

There were more than 80 items on his list, and I had used this technique successfully with many other clients. Most often I had found one or more stimuli that always occurred right before the client got anxious, but would never occur when the client didn't get anxious. But I could find no associations for Ronald; there were no common triggers for his anxiety attacks.

I tried to help him anyway through relaxation training and some cognitive exercises, yet I knew that unless I found the specific association or exact stimuli, I couldn't effectively treat his anxiety. I was trying to use a shotgun when I needed a rifle.

Even though counseling wasn't solving his panic problem, Ronald continued therapy because it was helping him in other ways, and because he was curious as to whether we would ever be able to figure it all out. But it was difficult. He had his attacks so infrequently that it was hard to find the cues. Finally, I asked Ronald to stop the sessions until he had another attack and then to call—day or night, weekday or weekend—and come to my office.

One night several months later he phoned me late at night. He had just had one of his anxiety attacks. When Ronald came to the office, he was still anxious. Now at last, I had the anxiety sitting in front of me so I could observe it directly.

We reviewed everything that had happened during the day, from the time he had woken up to the time he felt the first pangs of fear. We explored his thoughts, feelings, remembrances, what he had eaten that day, and so on.

We still didn't find any triggers—nothing significant, no unusual traumas, frustrations, or conflicts—just an average day until the anxiety attack. We kept searching. Ronald had been watching TV, so I found a TV Guide and reviewed all the shows he had watched that day to see if one of them might have been a trigger, but we found nothing. He had read the morning paper so we reviewed the news stories of the day. Still nothing. We skimmed the sports section, the cartoons, the editorials, the advertisements—still zero.

Finally, right before I was about to throw the paper away, I noticed the daily weather forecast. It said an unusually high-pressure front would be coming through Denver at about ten o'clock in the evening. It struck me that this was the same time Ronald had become anxious. As a wild guess, I asked Ronald if he'd felt a change in the weather.

Ronald said, "Funny that you mention it, but I did. I had this eerie feeling right before the panic. I can't describe it, but it was like the pressure on my skin felt different—stronger or something."

"Have you had this sense of pressure before"?

He couldn't recall exact details, but he did remember feeling this sensation before.

Still not sure, I gave Ronald a homework assignment. I told him to go to the library and pull out the weather reports for each of the previous times he'd had his anxiety attacks. I asked him to try to find any common feature occurring in them all.

A couple of weeks later he contacted me. He was very excited, and said he'd found only one element common to all the situations. He'd discovered that before each of his anxiety attacks the barometric pressure had been unusually high and the number had been exactly the same on each of these days. Exactly!

It seemed strange. How could barometric pressure cause panic attacks? After some more detective work, we uncovered the explanation.

About 15 years earlier, a critical event had happened in Ronald's life. One day while at work, he had received a call from a local hospital informing him that his dad had been in an automobile accident and was in critical condition. He was told to come to the hospital quickly, that his father might not last long. He jumped into his car and rushed to the hospital, panic-stricken that he might not make it in time. One can guess what the weather was—an unusually high–pressure system was moving through Denver. By the time he had arrived at the hospital, it was too late. His father had died.

Strange as it may seem, the grief, anxiety, and guilt Ronald had about his father's dying were associated to the barometric pressure. He didn't recognize it, but his brain had connected the two events. Later on in life, long after the incident, his brain still held the pairing, so that every time the barometric pressure reached exactly the same level, it triggered a panic attack.

One may reasonably ask why the anxiety became connected to the barometric pressure rather than some other stimuli, like the temperature, the time of day, driving cars, accidents, hospitals, or anything else. We don't know. But something about the original incident made the barometric pressure most salient and most receptive to being paired.

Once we found the cause it would have been fairly easy to counter the effects by creating new associations to barometric pressure, but in Ronald's case we didn't have to do that to break the pairing. He didn't have to practice resynthesizing because he'd found the trigger, and the core of his anxiety was removed. This happens with many clients suffering from anxiety attacks. When Ronald realized the real trigger for his fear, it removed the thought, "I am getting anxious for no reason. There must be something seriously wrong with me." This thought is often a key companion to anxiety. Ronald no longer gets anxious when a certain pressure system moves through Denver.

This case is a good example of how any emotion can become associated with any critical event in unpredictable ways. Everything that the brain is aware of can be paired with any item surrounding a critical event. I have observed many stimuli that have become connected: fur, the color red, cloud shapes, acid rock music, full moons, the movie Citizen Kane, South American animals, taking a deep breath, books on astronomy, green bathrooms, having a full stomach, making love. In such cases it is useful to help the client find the connections to the critical event.

Comment

Many therapies explore the historical routes of present problems. CRT differs because of its emphasis on the history of clients' non-adaptive beliefs. We do not assume that it is necessary or useful to synthesize these histories with higher-level abstractions like ego states, psychosexual stages of development, fixation, unconscious archetypes, regression, or cathexis. Finding the historical origins of a present belief helps clients to see why they think as they do, thus enabling them to more readily shift the cognition.

Further Information

Guidano (1987, 1991) and Guidano and Liotti's comprehensive work (1983) explore the historical roots of dysfunctional beliefs. The development of PTSD is not only dependent on the severity of the traumatic critical event, but on the interpretation of why it happened. (Monat & Lazarus, 1991). Critical events may create assumptions about life that are too global to be useful, e.g., "I must never show any weakness" (Williams, 1996b).

RESYNTHESIZING LIFE THEMES
Principles

Critical life events not only create mistaken beliefs, they also help form life themes. These themes transform over time and have their own developmental history, just as organisms change physically. The power behind a life theme is assessed by tracing its development from the past. Life themes have a vertical depth. Like cognitive trees, they have long roots stretching back from the present into the distant past. It is useful for the therapist to dig up the roots of certain core beliefs in order to find the life theme behind them. To illustrate, a present perception of inferiority is diagrammed chronologically:

- *Present:* "I am inferior as a husband, father, and employer."
- *Recent past:* "I am not a terrific boyfriend or worker."
- *Adolescent:* "I am a lousy student, and girls don't like me."
- *Young adolescent:* "I stink at sports and other guys are a lot tougher than me.
- *Late childhood:* "I am a bad boy. My brother is better."
- *Early childhood:* "Mommy and Daddy don't like me."

In this example the client's present inferiority feelings are represented in the past. His earlier mistaken beliefs contribute to his present irrationality.

Method

1. Use the cognitive maps you have developed (see chapter 3) but make them longitudinal. Pick out each thought and trace its origins—how it has transformed into other beliefs, and how its representation has changed during different stages of the client's life.
2. What other thoughts, emotions, behaviors, or environmental triggers have become linked with the theme as it has developed? How have the misperceptions spread from one zone of a client's life to another?
3. Have your clients imagine what their life would have been like if they had perceived differently. Ask them to imagine how they would have acted if they hadn't had this distorted life theme.

Example: The Story of Mary

The most powerful example I can think of was the life theme of a client I will call Mary.

When Mary was young she was different from other girls. She was interested in studying philosophy while other girls played with Barbie dolls. Her grades in school were not good, and although her teachers thought she had potential, she kept answering questions in odd ways that the teachers judged as aberrant. Her friends of choice were older people until her parents pressed her to associate with people closer to her own age.

Mary didn't think like most people. She tried to explain why she believed certain things or why she thought so differently, but nobody really understood what she meant; she concluded that she was too vapid to explain things well. Most of the other girls rejected her and seemed embarrassed to be seen with her, so she spent much of her early life alone. Her parents worried and sent her to therapists who never found anything specifically wrong with her. She just didn't seem to fit in with her peers.

Mary was quite young when she realized that she was being rejected. She was sure it was because she was bird-brained. She didn't understand why others thought the way they did, and she hadn't met anyone who thought her way, so she concluded that she was a real idiot. Sometimes she thought she might be crazy, but she had read the *DSM* manuals, and knew that she didn't show the sufficient number of symptoms. She finally developed the life theme that she must be retarded in some way and that other people were simply smarter. This was the only explanation she could come up with.

She acted out this theme throughout much of her early life. She didn't attend college because she felt that college was only for bright people and she didn't want to embarrass herself. Her family didn't press her. They pushed college on her brothers, but believed that girls only went to college to meet husbands, and since she preferred reading philosophy to meeting boys, they saw no reason to spend their money. She took odd jobs that bored her very quickly, so she kept looking for others that might be more interesting. She never found one she liked, and concluded that she was too dull-witted to enjoy the work. She occasionally took some adult education classes at the local university, but received only average grades—she didn't seem able to give the answers the professors wanted; she answered essay questions in divergent ways.

Her relationships with men followed a similar pattern. She didn't act like other women; she didn't try to flatter men or boost their egos or wear seductive clothing. Most of the time she just wanted to talk, to find out what they thought about things. Most men just tried to get her into bed, and when she wouldn't play the seduction game they thought she was strange, so they usually left her for someone more traditionally feminine. Mary concluded that she was too lame-brained to attract men.

Because of all these experiences, Mary developed a core life theme about herself. It became her overriding philosophy, the glasses through which she perceived the world. At the base of this philosophy was one simple truth: *"I am stupid."* Since she concluded this over many years, her belief took on the strength of a religious dogma.

As she got older things didn't get any better for Mary. She never finished college. "Too harebrained," she thought to herself, but she continued to enroll in noncredit courses as a nondegree student. She would sneak into graduate-school lectures on philosophy when she could. She would hang around with the students after and try to open a conversation, but she found that most students were not interested in discussing what had been covered in class; they only were concerned with what grade they would receive on the next test. Those few that would talk about the subject would ignore Mary when they discovered she wasn't a real student and hadn't even earned an undergraduate degree.

Mary became more depressed about life and finally came to see me. She told me about her life and her problems. Most of what she showed me was how very sad she was because she was such a pudding head. I asked her some questions and encouraged her to express what she had read and what she had been thinking about.

I realized quite quickly that her life theme was truly distorted, and I tried various rationalistic cognitive techniques to help her, but she rejected them all. Clients hold on to life themes despite overwhelming evidence to the contrary.

Finally, out of frustration more than anything else, I decided on another tactic. I knew that it was risky, but if my guess about Mary was correct, it might work. I decided to give Mary a homework assignment, and I got her to promise that she would do it.

I told her that a world-famous woman professor was coming to town and going to offer a serious lecture on some matters of philosophy (I have disguised the actual discipline) in an area that interested her. She recognized the woman's work and agreed that the professor was brilliant. The lectures were by invitation only, and only local university professors and advanced doctorate students were allowed to attend, but I had a friend who was a professor of philosophy who could get her a ticket. Mary was grateful.

Then I added that there was a catch. I said that after lectures the professor usually conducted a question and answer period for the audience. During this time, no matter how nervous she was, she must ask the best question she could. In addition and most importantly, I wanted her to do something else. After the lectures the professor would often meet with some of the prominent local professors and advanced graduate students and invite them to her hotel, where they would discuss philosophical matters. I told Mary that she must do everything she could to be part of that group. "Be as assertive as you must but join the group."

She strenuously objected. She said she couldn't do it. How could she talk to this famous woman whose work she had admired for years? She would be surrounded by professors and she hadn't even finished college. I reminded her of her promise, and finally and very reluctantly she agreed.

I then ended the sessions and told Mary we would stop further counseling until after the lecture. She promised to call and tell what had happened.

About a month later she phoned and told me she had gone to the lecture and sat in the back. The place was crowded with professor types and graduate students. She recognized some of the professors, many of whom had written books and articles. The graduate students were some of the people she had seen when she audited the classes—they had been the most verbal and confident students.

She said that the lecture had been wonderful, and that during the question period afterwards she had been very nervous while waiting for a chance to ask her question. The professor answered most of the questions quickly and concisely. Mary asked her question, which was based upon an aspect of the professor's theory that she had thought about but hadn't been able to figure out. The professor looked at her and smiled, then answered the question in great detail, going on for at least twenty minutes. The answer was brilliant, and Mary listened intently to everything the professor said.

After the talk, Mary approached the stage to see the professor, who was talking with colleagues. Mary tried to nudge in but a professor blocked her. He told her something like, "Dr. _____ is very busy, young lady. She has a very tight schedule, is tired from her long flight and really needs to get away. So, we would appreciate it if you would leave." But Mary had insisted and finally had the opportunity to say hello. The professor recognized her and said, "Oh. You are the young lady who asked that excellent question, how can I help you?" Mary asked whether she could join the group of colleagues so that she could listen and learn more about the theories. She had almost begged. She promised not to be a bother—she just wanted to sit in the back and listen. One of the conference organizers overheard the conversation and said that there were already too many people, but the professor said, "Oh let her come, George. One more won't make any difference."

Mary went to the hotel suite along with about 10 university professors and graduate students. They all had coffee and doughnuts and talked about the professor's theories. Initially Mary didn't say much, but gradually she started to ask questions and then began to give voice to some of her own ideas. It got later and later and the other people started to make their apologies and leave. Finally the professor and Mary were left there alone. They talked until five o'clock in the morning, discussing vast, sweeping concepts. They used yellow pads to illustrate their points. They drank 10 cups of coffee. Mary said, "It was wonderful—the best thing that had ever happened in my life."

Right before the professor left she had asked Mary which graduate school she was attending. At this point Mary had become comfortable, so she decided to tell the truth. She told the professor that she was not in graduate school and that she hadn't even finished her undergraduate degree. This astounded the professor, but she gave Mary her home phone number and suggested that she call in a couple of weeks. The professor hinted that she might be able to help Mary.

This took place many years ago, and a lot has happened since then. The professor helped Mary complete her undergraduate degree very quickly by directing her to a college where she could pass classes by challenging the courses. She would take the final exams and if she answered the questions satisfactorily, she was given credit for the class. Later the professor got her into a good graduate school and helped her receive an assistantship so that she could afford to attend.

Mary has done very well. She completed her Ph.D. in record time, published many articles for professional journals, and even wrote a book. Her most recent work was reviewed as some of the most innovative in the field. For the first time in her life, Mary is content and happy.

Because of a series of early critical events, Mary had come to an incredibly erroneous conclusion about herself. She'd noticed early that she was different from others, and had concluded (as many children do) that this difference meant that she was inferior in some way. Her peers and teachers treated her this way, so she believed it herself.

In reality, the reason that Mary was so different was that she was a genius—one of these rare people that comes along only occasionally. She could see things in a clearer and more comprehensive way than the vast majority of us, but while she was brilliant about most things, she couldn't read herself at all. It may sound strange for someone to be so aware in some areas but totally blind in others, but this is often true of geniuses, and it was true of Mary.

Most people meeting Mary didn't recognize her ability because it takes talent to recognize genius. It takes excellent skill to recognize supreme skill. It takes a Haydn to recognize a Mozart. The professor who met Mary had the knowledge and understanding to recognize the extent of Mary's ability.

Comment

The way I tried to help Mary change her life theme was unorthodox. It was luck that the professor showed up at the right time. Life themes are the most powerful cognitions clients can have, and they will strongly defend them, damaging as they may be. We therapists need to use all of our skills and judgments to put a dent in them. Usually they are so well defended that rational argumentation will not work. Our best chance of helping our clients is to try to give them the right kind of experience so that they will discover the truth for themselves. By using the environment we facilitate clients' ability to prove to themselves whether their life themes are true. If you can arrange such a test for your clients you are fortunate.

Further Information

The importance of modifying a client's life themes has increased in recent years. Today, cognitive restructuring therapists spend more time working on clients' life themes than on present cognitions.

Schema-focused therapy has developed a similar system of modifying life themes that includes a life review and experiential, interpersonal, and behavioral techniques (McGinn & Young, 1996, pp. 196–200).

RESYNTHESIZING EARLY RECOLLECTIONS
Principles

An important principle in psychology is known as the *rule of primacy*. It means that clients pay more attention to their first impressions than to their later ones.

Many therapies attribute great significance to a client's first memory. For example, Adler (1964), Binder and Smokler (1980), Bruhn

(1990b), Edwards (1990), Last (1997), Mosak (1958,1969), and Olson (1979) employed clients' earliest recollections as an important ingredient in their therapies.

Cognitive restructuring uses a client's earliest memories to identify core beliefs, but without a psychodynamic theoretical framework. Frequently, the earliest memory identifies one of a client's lifelong beliefs. This belief probably didn't originate with the event, as usually only a whole series of experiences can do that, but the earliest event often unveils the existence of the belief during an early stage of a client's life.

Many mistaken beliefs that cause clients pain are rooted in these early personal histories. The damaging perceptions might have been implanted long before a client could process information in a rational manner, and during the years since that time, an entire pattern of thinking might have evolved based upon that mistaken beginning. A pattern of believing can be altered if the original mistaken belief has been discovered and replaced.

Method 1. Image Exercise

1. Have clients imagine a current situation where strong emotion occurs. Take some time on this. Help clients to use all their senses to make the scene vivid. When the scene is clear, ask them to focus on the core belief, gestalt, or theme.
2. Instruct your clients to focus on the first or earliest recollection they have of thinking a belief. Concentrate on the initial situation when the emotion developed. Have them imagine the scene again and visualize it clearly. It is helpful if your clients say the false belief to themselves in a child or adolescent voice.
3. For damaging beliefs, ask clients, "What was erroneous in your interpretation of this event? How did you misperceive it? What did you say to yourself that was untrue? Why was your interpretation mistaken? Who or what experiences taught you this misperception?"
4. Discuss with your clients that they are misjudging the present situation in the same way that they misjudged the earlier one.
5. Correct the earliest mistaken belief. Have clients imagine redoing the situation by thinking a useful, realistic thought instead of what was first believed. Ask them to imagine how they would have felt and how they would have acted differently if they had thought differently.

6. Finally, get your clients to picture their present difficulty differently. Correct the present mistaken belief just as the earlier one was corrected.

Example 1

The rule of primacy holds true for many of clients' earliest experiences. One important experience is a client's first mentor. Clients' first teachers who taught them some meaningful principle of life are always special. They may have learned from many other teachers since then, but there is a hallowed place in their memory for their first.

Clients' first attitudes also hold primacy. Santa Claus, the Easter bunny, and the tooth fairy may seem absurd, but they feel warm and close inside. First religious beliefs seem like the only true religion. Though the client may long since have become agnostic or rejected the old theology, in times of confusion they feel drawn back to their earlier faith.

A first achievement or accomplishment is another important experience. The time they won the ribbon for the three–legged race or scored the winning basket will take precedence over later, much greater accomplishments.

The first time they travel to a new and distant culture will often make this culture and these people forever special to them. One of my clients remembers her first trip to South America, during which she flew from Miami to Lima, Peru. The flight seemed to take forever, but when she arrived and walked around the large city square, she was enchanted with the strange–looking people wearing multicolored costumes and the unusually shaped buildings, some of which dated back to the conquistadors. Since that time, whenever she sees pictures of Lima or reads an article about Peru, she feel strangely invigorated and excited. Even her later knowledge that Peru is a very poor country with multiple social and political problems doesn't dampen her enthusiasm.

The first house that clients ever lived in may forever define what a house should be. A man who grew up in a three–story house made of stone never feels quite comfortable in brick houses or ranch–style wooden structures. Many people search desperately in Wyoming for colonial–styled houses or look for adobe haciendas in Maine. Some Australian clients quietly yearn for a house like one near the Murray river with gum trees, a verandah out the front, and kangaroos out the back. If they are searching outside Australia, their hope is forlorn. But for them and for most clients their first houses are the only real houses; anything else is considered an inferior substitute.

Similarly, clients' ideals of what a family is like often reflects the way their family was. The true definition of a man is often their father, the definition of a woman is their mother. A real marriage is what their parents had with each other even if it was defective.

They often consider a substantial job as the first one that gave them solid satisfaction. They may view other endeavors that are more profitable as merely lucrative hobbies.

Finally, the definition of true love is often based on the client's earliest romance, despite its having been short-lived or a poor match. They hold it in a special place in their memory that later, more important relationships don't assail.

These early experiences take on so much importance because they are fresh and new. Clients enter them with few frameworks to guide them, so their first experience becomes their first prototype, the model by which they judge all that comes later. When their early experiences are positive they give them a gentle reference point, a soft reminder of a safe place inside.

Example 2: The Story of Renee

Unfortunately the rule of primacy has a negative side. If early experiences are positive, they may serve as good models for later life. But when negative, they may cause lifelong mistakes in thinking. Early distorted learning may harden their perceptions into concrete that a lifetime of later experiences can't crack.

One client's story reveals how this happens.

Several years ago Renee reluctantly came to see me. He was from France and his company had recently transferred him to the United States. He was having a terrible time; he felt deeply homesick, couldn't find any fellow Frenchmen to talk to, and spent his evenings and weekends alone staring at the TV. His isolation was causing a deep depression, and he needed to get out of the house and start meeting people. I arranged a series of activities, carefully planned so that he could gradually develop some friendships in the U.S.

When the plan was presented to him he looked annoyed and asked just one question, "Will there be a lot of Yanks there?"

Taken aback, I said, "Well . . . er . . . yes. We are in the United States and this country has a tendency to be overrun with Yanks."

"Then," he said, "I won't go."

A curious answer since he was now living in the United States, so we explored why he felt this way about Americans. It turned out that his first experience with Americans had been very negative.

Renee grew up in a small town in the south of France; it was fairly isolated and far from the usual tourist routes. He had heard American music and seen American movies and TV shows, but he had never actually met an American.

One day he went to town with his father and saw a very fat man standing in the local hotel. The man was dressed in green baggy shorts and was wearing an orange shirt with prints of little yellow fishes all over it. He was shouting at a clerk behind the desk. He was apparently complaining about the room not having a color television and was demanding that the clerk find him one immediately. He yelled that France had the worst service he had ever seen, and that this kind of thing wouldn't be tolerated back home. While he was browbeating the clerk, his two pudgy children were running up and down the lobby pulling leaves off of the potted plants and climbing over the furniture while his obese wife looked on with a bored expression. Renee's father turned to him and said, "Those are Americans!"

Renee never forgot this first impression. It colored all of his subsequent contacts. When he saw other American tourists he remembered only those who looked and acted like the man in the lobby. Those who didn't, he assumed, were from Canada or some other place.

His selective perception picked out only those Americans who were egotistical, fat, noisy, and who spent their vacations insulting his country. As a result he learned to feel a repugnance for anyone and everything American. When his boss told him he had to work in the U.S., he had adamantly refused, but to keep from being fired he had reluctantly agreed.

The rule of primacy was explained to Renee, but he wasn't convinced. He still felt most Americans were of the loud, arrogant, and ugly variety. To challenge him I suggested that he go to some places and conduct a survey. "Even if you don't like the Americans there, at least complete the study. Determine how many are like the man in the lobby, and how many aren't."

A few months later he came back with the results. He had found some ugly Americans, but most of the time he'd met people very similar to his French friends back home. More surprisingly, he'd became close to a few Americans and spent some of his free time going to baseball games and parties with them. His loneliness was gone and his depression had lifted.

I said, "See? You were overgeneralizing about Americans." His response surprised me.

"No I wasn't!" he said. "I've just met those few Yanks who are the exception."

His prejudice continued and probably remains to this day. It shows that anyone can hold on to their first impression despite strong evidence to the contrary. But he had met some friends and didn't need my help anymore, so we finished our therapy.

On leaving he said, "You know for a Yank, you're okay." Maybe from his vantage point this was a great compliment, but I'm not so sure.

Method 2. Resynthesis Worksheet

The following worksheet may be used in the resynthesis process.

Resynthesis Worksheet

Present Situation_____

Emotional Response_____

Present Belief about Present Situation_____

_____

Early Recollection_____
(preformal situational events)

Emotional Response_____

Mistaken Early Belief_____

Corrected Early Belief_____

Corrected Present Belief_____

1. Use the client's master list of beliefs and have clients connect the beliefs to the situations in which they occurred. Each of these situations should be listed under "Present Situation" on the worksheet. The beliefs associated with each situation should be listed under "Present Belief."

2. Look for critical experiences the client had prior to or during early adolescence. First, identify the events. For very early events your clients may be able to recall only vague images, but even if they are only fragments of senses and impressions have your clients visualize them as clearly as possible. Record them on the worksheet.

3. Formulate into a sentence the mistaken belief that resulted from each of these events. Record those sentences on the worksheet.

4. After careful discussion with your client, correct each early thought. Record that information on the worksheet. The earlier mistaken

interpretation should be expunged by having your client discover the correct interpretation of the early events. Replace all early mistaken cognitions connected to the events.

5. Once the mistaken early irrationalities have been corrected, help the client to change present irrational thinking.

6. Have your clients regularly use the worksheet—finding mistaken beliefs, identifying their early origins, correcting the earlier misinterpretations, and then adopting a more functional belief as a guide to their present lives.

Example 1

Present situation: Client got anxious at party that many international students attended.

Present belief: People from other countries are dangerous.

Early situational event: Client was isolated from anybody not in the immediate family; was overprotected and not exposed to unusual environmental stimuli. She had never seen anyone who looked "different."

Mistaken early interpretation: Anything new or novel is dangerous.

Corrected early interpretation: The new and novel can be exciting and give me an opportunity to grow and expand. The new is no more dangerous than the known and familiar.

Corrected present belief: It is interesting to meet people from other countries; I have an opportunity to learn more about other cultures.

Example 2

Present situation: Client was so afraid of being alone in the evening that she surrounded herself with as many friends as possible so that she would always have someone to invite over.

Present belief: I am a very sociable person.

Early situational event: She had been abandoned by a parent when young.

Mistaken early interpretation: I will never allow myself to be abandoned again.

Corrected early interpretation: I am not a child anymore and I don't need a person's protection like I once did. I can survive alone, and don't need to be terrified about being by myself.

Corrected present belief: I no longer need to surround myself with 50 friends in order to protect myself from running out of people. I can pick a few close friends who really mean something to me.

Example 3

Present situation: Client would never undertake any task requiring patience, concentration, and persistence.

Present belief: Routine is boring.

Early situational event: As a child the client engaged in extensive day-dreams to make up for a socially impoverished early childhood.

Mistaken early interpretation: The only way to enrich one's life is through fantasy and imagination. Everyday activities are dull, drab, and gray.

Corrected early interpretation: Real life is at times drab and gray and at other times bright and colorful. Actual life is far more meaningful than fictional fantasies. True satisfaction can only come from engaging in the struggles, triumphs, and tragedies of real life, not by living in a fairy tale world of magic where fate controls all successes. Meaning comes from human beings striving against all odds to make things better, not from escaping into sanguine fantasies.

Corrected present belief: Concentration and persistence on various activities provide the foundation for making my life ultimately meaningful and enriching.

Comment

The emotional components of clients' first experiences are usually very strong. It is therefore important to search memories slowly. Have your clients imagine other early positive experiences to offset powerful negative feelings that may emerge.

The hypothesis behind this technique finds support in the work of such noted theorists as Piaget (1954). He argued that thoughts, themes, and beliefs accepted into the frontal lobe during the preoperational stage of brain development (ages 2–7) are likely to be based upon many kinds of logical errors. During the concrete operational stage (ages 7–11), the individual cannot abstract reality in terms of "as if" thinking, viewing problems concretely. Any misperceptions that accrue during these two stages of intellectual development will be stored in long-term memory, and will not be easily removed as the individual matures.

Assuming that this hypothesis is correct, it seems clear that early mistaken beliefs that were synthesized into clients' overall patterns of thought must be subsequently resynthesized if clients are to gain a healthier perspective on themselves and the world around them.

When done correctly, this technique can provide rapid, dramatic shifts in clients' perceptions. Psychodynamic therapists often use elements of this approach in their therapeutic practice. The cognitive restructuring approach differs both theoretically and in practice. This is because of the emphasis it places upon actively correcting the faulty life theme and because of its reliance upon the hypothesis that pre-operational and concrete beliefs are readily accessible to conscious manipulation. In our view the battle doesn't rage between the conscious and unconscious, or among repressed conflicts of the ego, superego, and id; rather, the conflict is between what is verifiably real and what was once spuriously learned.

Further Information

A very early example of using a client's earliest experience is Freud's famous case of Katharina (Breuer & Freud, 1937; Freud, 1933). His treatment of her anxiety symptoms (which revealed themselves in breathing difficulties) was straight cognitive therapy. Although he would later develop his psychodynamic theory, initially his treatment of this client was very similar to our cognitive resynthesis technique. His counseling leads were as follows.

Freud:

- "What are you complaining of?"
- "Describe to me how such a state of 'difficulty in breathing' feels."
- "When you have the attack, do you always think of the same thing?"
- "When did you first get them (anxiety attacks)?"
- "Fraulien Katharina, if you could now recall what went through your mind at the time that you got the first attack, what you thought at that time, it would help you."

Katharina recalled a scene where her uncle was making love to her cousin and she felt disgusted.

Freud then restructured this scene by saying that she was now a grown-up girl, knew all about these matters (sexual facts of life) and could now understand what was going on. Katherina answered, "Yes, now, certainly." The anxiety attacks ceased from this point on (Breuer & Freud, 1937).

Piaget's works are extensive (see Piaget, 1954, 1963, 1970, 1973, 1995; Montangero & Maurice-Naville, 1997).

For a discussion of early preformal recollections and their importance, see Mosak (1958, 1969). His research review demonstrates that preformal recollections reflect the basic client life themes. The most comprehensive review of preformal attitudes and their use in therapy is by Bruhn (1990a, 1990b), Edwards (1990), and Olson (1979).

RESYNTHESIZING FAMILY BELIEFS
Principles

Cognitive histories begin with a client's family. The family is the earliest source for a client's beliefs and a primary source throughout most of a client's life. Clients are brought up not only to act in certain ways, but also to think in certain ways. As children they trust that their parents are the soul possessors of truth. Parents seem so powerful to a small child that they conclude that mighty power is immediately translatable into mighty truth. While it is factual that parental power fades as clients get older (and with it clients' certainty of parental truth), their mothers' and fathers' beliefs will always hold a special place in their belief systems.

The family extends beyond a client's parents and can include brothers and sisters, grandparents, aunts and uncles, nieces, nephews, and cousins. All members of the family may hold the same central belief. The family theme may be, "We are special," or "We have a nasty little secret." This philosophy may be as much a family characteristic as the family's upturned nose, tendency towards flat feet, or red hair. Clients may have long since left their family of origin but still carry the attitude the family implanted.

Many clients don't see the significance of their family beliefs because they think that their own attitudes are considerably different from those of their parents. They are often mistaken. Clients holding opposite Bs from their parents may still have related cognitions. One may cause the other. For example, a family may have believed that social appearances are important. They may have instructed their son constantly about shining his shoes, wearing the right clothes, having his hair cut, cleaning his fingernails, etc. The son may believe the opposite. As soon as he left home he may have thrown away all of his parent-bought clothes and replaced them with grunge, let his hair go ratty and long, not cleaned his fingernails. He may have thought that he was clear of his family's influence, but he would be wrong. Whether he believes exactly as his family or exactly the opposite, the common element is that he is still reacting to his family. Mentally his family is still directing his choice of clothes. Whether we place a plus or minus sign next to his beliefs, his parents' cognitions still dominate him.

Another type of belief may also illustrate the importance of family beliefs. There is a type of cognition that is neither the same nor the opposite of the family's theme. It's a synergistic belief, a belief that acts in cooperation with the family's and the child's beliefs. Like pieces of a jigsaw, the two Bs may fit together. Families may train their members so that all of the individual Bs together form in a synergistic pattern. It becomes a family dance with everybody doing a slightly different step, but all steps are synchronized with each other. For example, Father plays the heavy and does a tango like—"Why are kids so irresponsible today? When I was a kid I didn't have a car until I was 25." Mom counters with a waltz, "Leave the kids alone. All their friends are allowed to use the car, so why can't they?" The son does a jive step, "I'm old enough to own my own car." And daughter tries a cha–cha by dancing into her bedroom crying, "Nobody lets me do anything around here."

Method

1. Make a graph of all the key people in your client's family. List their first names and ages and show the importance of their relationship to the client by using arrows. Be sure to include their parents, grandparents, aunts, uncles, or any other member that had a significant influence on them.
2. List the major beliefs, principles, values, and attitudes held by the people on the list. Look for beliefs shared by most of the members.
3. See if you can collapse these principles down to a few core beliefs.
4. How did the family teach each core attitude? How were members rewarded for believing in the principles or punished for not believing in them?
5. Describe how your client's family acts differently from other families based on the family's principles?
6. Compare the family's beliefs to the beliefs enumerated on your client's master list of beliefs. How many of them are related? Are they collateral—the same, the opposite, or synergistic?

Example

Probably the most intricate family dance and the best example of a synergistic B is the alcoholic shuffle. The whole family plays. Dad leads off by drinking every night. He loses four jobs in a year, gets picked up for three DUIs, and ends up in a detox unit. The rest of the family responds with carefully choreographed countersteps. Mom cleans up Dad's messes, bails him out of jail, and calls his boss to say he is sick again. Daughter blames Mom for being a rotten wife and applies for the job herself. The son feels ignored and tries to get attention by stealing cars and scoring cocaine while blaming Mom and Dad for being such rotten parents.

It's hard for the therapist to break up this dance because the partners have gotten so good at it. It can be a major problem in treatment. Many alcoholics are able to stop drinking when they are away from their families in an inpatient setting. But when they go back home, they start the dance again. Because Dad has stopped drinking the whole family gets out of step. Mom has no one to play nurse for anymore, so she feels lost and useless. Daughter can't play substitute wife anymore, and Son gets stuck with a cocaine habit that he can't blame on anyone but himself. Some families become so frustrated with the changes that the whole family tries to get Dad drinking again. From their point of view the dance had changed, and as bad as the old one was at least the family was familiar with the music and knew the steps.

Consequently, many families will subtly try to get Dad to drink again by leaving opened whisky bottles around the house or by accusing Dad of being worse when he's sober than he was drunk. Everybody wants to do the old alcoholic shuffle again. Sobriety had stopped the dance.

Comment

Your client may model after one family member rather than the whole family. In this instance. compare your client's beliefs with the model. The model may or may not be a parent. The key family member is the one most salient and important to your client.

Further Information

Dysfunctional cognitions in children are produced and maintained by the family system (Alexander, 1988; Kendall, 1991). Interventions with family system problems have been extensively discussed. Robert Taibbi has developed an extensive guided imagery exercise that resynthesizes family beliefs (Taibbi, 1998). Also see the following articles and books for a review of other cognitive techniques used in family therapy (Bedrosian & Bozicas, 1993; Ellis, 1991; Ellis et al., 1989; Munson, 1993; Reinecke, Dattilio, & Freeman, 1996; Schwebel & Fine, 1994).

SURVIVAL AND BELIEFS
Principles

If personal histories taught clients their beliefs, why do they pre-serve some beliefs but reject others? The total number of beliefs a client is exposed to is far greater than those that become part of their cognitive system. Or, to put it another way, why do some Bs last and become pandemic in a client's life while others fade away with just a whisper?

The simplest answer is that some beliefs are more helpful to clients than others. It's as if pragmatism is their teacher; pragmatism teaches clients throughout their lives to believe in certain things and to look at things in certain ways. If their own logic can't prove why they should believe as they do, then so much the worse for their logic. Their experiences have taught them these same principles over and over again.

Clients' beliefs emerge from the pragmatic interplay of forces that face them. Their beliefs are chosen to solve specific environmental and social problems they have encountered. The patterns and schemes they have of themselves and their world exist because they perceived that these attitudes would help them cope with the world. In many cases, possibly in most, these attitudes hurt rather than help them, but beliefs are selected for their perceived rather than their actual utility. It is very helpful for the therapist to explore the usefulness of a client's Bs along with their truth or falseness.

Method

1. Review your client's master list of beliefs
2. Help them to decide whether believing these thoughts improves their ability to solve specific survival or social problems.
3. If the beliefs don't help, assist them in planning a strategy to change them.
4. If the beliefs were once useful but aren't any longer, help the client see the change.

Example

I give a handout to some of my clients to explain how humanity has learned some of its beliefs (see page 302).

HANDOUT:
HOW HUMANITY LEARNED ITS BELIEFS

You may have learned some of your beliefs through a process of trial and error. Imagine two cave men, Zork and Mervine, living in the year one million B.C. It is late at night and both are sitting in a cave by the fire, huddling from the wind and glacier cold. Suddenly they hear a loud, furious roar outside the cave. Mervine's clear brain concludes that it is a saber-toothed tiger. He builds the fire higher and grabs his club. Zork, on the other hand, has a fanciful brain. He concludes that the sound is the disguised siren call of a voluptuous cavewoman. He puts on his new antelope skin, rubs bear grease in his hair and goes outside for some earthly pleasure. Mervine survives with his clear B brain, while Zork with his fanciful brain ends up in the stomach of the saber- toothed tiger. Scratch one fuzzy brain and one fanciful B.

Centuries of fanciful beliefs ending up in the tummies of tigers gradually selected for beliefs that are a little bit clearer. Over time, ancient humanity's brain developed less clouded Bs; science emerged from the blanket of intuitive superstitions, research replaced implicit authority, thinking emerged from blind dogma. It was no longer solely luck, authority, or revelation that formed your beliefs; it was a matter of survival.

Comment

In practice, your clients will be far less interested in how humanity learned to believe certain attitudes and far more interested in how they learned their own thoughts. A historical search as to when the beliefs were formed will help. You may find that originally the Bs were adaptive and helped the client cope with the environment they were in at the time. What you may need to do is to show your client that what was once adaptive and helpful at an earlier time is nonadaptive and harmful today.

If we accept the premise that clients choose beliefs because they are pragmatically adaptable, how can we explain the following clearly nonuseful acts?

1. Doing something that physically hurts the client, such as using crack cocaine, smoking, or drinking alcohol.
2. Engaging in activities that society punishes them for, such as committing felonies.
3. Sacrificing their self for another; for example, charging a machine-gun nest or running into a burning building to save a child.

What is the pragmatic payoff for these activities? According to pragmatic theory, people shouldn't do these things, but they do. Is something wrong with the theory?

Despite these examples, the theory is still correct. Our mistake is that we don't recognize the real payoffs for these behaviors. Seeing the rewards would help us to understand why clients keep behaving in these ways. Let's look at each of these examples more closely.

Doing things that hurt us (like taking crack cocaine) doesn't contradict the theory, because the pain comes much later, after the pleasure. Clients who drink too much or who use a damaging drug may seek the immediate reward and ignore the long-term consequences. The immediate reinforcement for many drugs is a thing called "the rush." Some clients are stimulus junkies who love the feeling of endorphins pumping in their brains. These clients seek a thrill, the same way some people enjoy roller coasters, driving fast, bungee jumping, or skydiving.

The difficulty is that the rush is temporary, lasting only a few minutes or hours. The cocaine addict eventually will crash and the alcoholic will start going through withdrawal, but despite the days of pain they know they will face, many clients choose the few minutes of pleasure. They may think that this time the pain won't happen, or they may simple ignore the pain because they want the pleasure so much.

If the payoff for chemical abuse is temporary pleasure, then what is the payoff for criminal activity? The rush? The rewards of intimidation? The financial gain?

All of the above and still more. One of the most surprising things about counseling criminals is what they often tell themselves about the crime they just committed. The majority of felons we work with don't think they did anything wrong. By this we don't mean that they insist they were innocent—almost everybody in jail claims innocence. What we mean is that even those who privately admit to having committed the crime deny that what they did was wrong even though it was against the law. Most convicted felons offered a guiltless, blameless reason for breaking the law. They have told me during my counseling interviews:

> "Everybody steals, but I had the bad luck to get caught."
>
> "She deserved to be bashed because she was such a bitch."
>
> "Those rich people in those big houses have all the money; I have none. I had the right to break in and take all I could."
>
> "I did the world a favor by killing the bastard."
>
> "I fenced the goods for my friend because I was just trying to help him."
>
> "I held up the store because I needed the money."
>
> "I took a swing at the cop because he was hassling me. I had the right."

I have counseled very few criminals who thought they were bad or guilty for what they did.

This is a human trait. Many people find it extremely difficult to think badly of themselves. Peoples' self–concepts require them to see themselves in the best possible light. They may have committed some horrible acts, but they will somehow justify them to themselves. For example, some multiple rapists think of themselves as agents of God punishing women for their licentious ways. In their eyes their acts were not only not evil, they were legitimately good: They were carrying out the will of God by removing evil women from the world. It appears that clients can rationalize any act if they try hard enough.

The pragmatic gain for many lawbreakers is not only the money they make, the rush they feel, or the frustration they express. It's also the positive feeling they get from their own convoluted rationalizations.

The ultimate consequence of their criminal act is punishment—imprisonment; and *this* they don't like. But punishment doesn't change their behavior—amazingly, they don't connect the punishment with the crime. I have asked prisoners in jail, "How did you end up in jail?" Few replied, "Because I violated the law." Instead, most answered, "Because Joe turned me in—that son of a bitch," or, "The cops found the crack in my car when they pulled me over for speeding," or, "The bitch screamed so loud after I hit her that the neighbors called the cops." When I ask them, "What could you do in the future to avoid ending up in prison again?" Instead of saying things like, "I shouldn't rob stores, deal cocaine, or assault my wife," they say, "I have to get rid of Joe!" "Don't speed when you have crack in the car!" or, "Get myself an old lady who doesn't scream so much."

It proves a point about punishment. For punishment to work, it's not enough for it to be strong. What's more important is that the person being punished sees the connection between his act and his punishment. Most lawbreakers don't see this connection. Because of their distorted thinking, they don't believe they did anything wrong, so there is no reason for them to stop their criminal behavior.

Finally, we are left with the third contradiction against beliefs being pragmatic, and this one seems most telling. What could possibly be the reward for those heroes and heroines who give up their lives, who sacrifice themselves for others?

In some cases it may be simple—admiration of humanity. "Isn't Mr. Smith a wonderful human being?" is a very powerful reinforcer if you are Mr. Smith. Even if only a few people watch a client's sacrifice, clients can imagine all of humanity applauding. How many young men have pictured their girlfriends' adoring gaze as they mentally imagined charging that machine-gun nest? That fact that the girlfriend is unlikely to think, "You are such a big, strong, wonderful hero," and more likely to believe, "I don't want to marry an idiot who charges machine guns," is irrelevant to the fantasy.

Further Information

Judith and Aaron Beck discuss how cognitions represent each individual's unique solutions to the problems of juggling inner pressure for survival and of battling external obstacles, threats, and demands (J. Beck, 1995; A. Beck, 1996).

Sociobiology, psychobiology, and psychoevolution discuss the adaptive function of certain beliefs, attitudes, and cognitions (see Lungwitz & Becker, 1993; Van Der Dennen & Falger, 1990).

Edward Wilson (1998) argues that biological utility is at the base (consilience) of social sciences, physical sciences, religion, philosophy, and the humanities.

ELEVEN

Practice Techniques

COGNITIVE THERAPY IS NOT PRIMARILY based on insight, because insight alone is insufficient; simply recognizing that a thought is irrational is usually not enough to change it. Many clients enter therapy knowing that their thoughts are illogical, and they are still unable to respond usefully when faced with strong environmental triggers. Some perceptual shifting techniques like transformation and bridging can produce rapid, one–trial learning shifts, but most others require repetition and practice.

Repetition is essential to countering. Most clients have little notion of how long a thought must be disputed to change it. If, for example, a client has repeated an irrational thought 100,000 times, disputing it for an hour or so will do little to reduce it. Yet most clients believe they should be able to remove a thought in a day or two, and certainly in no longer than a week. They think that because they know that the thought isn't true, they should be able to remove it easily. These clients forget that thoughts are habits, and like any other habit they accrue strength over the years. Just as clients can't learn to speak Spanish or to play a cello in a week, they can't counter their thinking instantaneously.

All of the techniques described in this chapter require a great deal of practice. How many repetitions are needed varies from client to client.

VISUAL PRACTICE
Principles

Counters can be memorized in the same way that foreign words are, repeated again and again until they can be used instantaneously. Don't use a counter that the client can't remember on the spot.

Memorizing counters speeds up the disputing process. Initially the client won't recall counters until after the irrational thought has come and gone, but with practice counters can become second nature, as shown below.

$$A - B - C_e \text{————————— time ————————— } D$$

A = Situation
B = Irrational Thought or Belief
C_e = Emotional Reaction
D = Disputing or Countering

With practice the counter moves backward in time, getting closer and closer to interrupting the irrational thought.

$$A - B - C_e \text{———————— } D$$
$$A - B - C_e \text{————— } D$$
$$A - B - C_e \text{—— } D$$

(C_e is now experienced as a flash of emotion, such as fear, lasting for about 30 seconds.)

When the client learns the counters extremely well, the disputing counters (Ds) will automatically occur between the A and B, preventing the negative emotion from arising.

$$A \text{———— } D$$

Method

1. Have the client make up a set of index cards. On one side of each card have the client write the irrational thought and rate how strongly the client believes it on a scale of 1 to 10.
2. On the other side of the card have the client write down as many counters as possible.

3. Tell the client to read the card several times every day, adding one counter each day. Record any change in belief level on the front of the card.
4. Reading the cards for 6 weeks generally reduces the strength of the client's belief by at least half.

AUDITORY PRACTICE
Principles

Since most clients report "hearing" their thoughts rather than "seeing" them, auditory memorization is often effective. This technique has the advantage that it can be practiced while the client is doing other things, such as washing the dishes, cleaning house, etc.

Method

1. Record on a cassette tape a list of the client's major irrational thoughts.
2. Leave a blank space on the tape after each thought. Instruct the client to counter or record counters to each thought on the tape.
3. Have the client listen to the tape and make up new counters daily.

Comment

Be sure to forewarn clients using this technique that the quality of their practice will vary; they'll have good days and bad ones. Like many other procedures, practice techniques show improvement of an elliptical nature. Since most clients expect their irrational beliefs to decrease steadily, they must be told to expect bad days in order to avoid discouragement.

Further Information

The reader will recognize the similarity of some of these practice techniques to Wolpe's desensitization methods (Wolpe, 1958; Wolpe et al., 1964), the difference being the addition of the cognitive component.

Other practice procedures can be found in the work of Ellis (1985, 1988a, 1995, 1998), Mahoney (1971, 1979,1993a), Mahoney and Thoresen (1974), Maultsby (1990), and Richardson (1967). Ellis (1998) has clients play their practice tapes to others who help make counters more vigorous and forceful. Further information about the card technique can be found in the works of Beck (1998), McGinn and Young (1996), and Young and Rygh (1994).

ROLE-PLAYING
Principles

One of the most common difficulties with cognitive therapy is that many clients learn to dispute their thoughts in a mechanical, uninvolved fashion. One of the best ways to counteract this problem is by role-playing, which is less rote and more realistic. Among other things, role-playing allows the client to practice in situations that are more akin to those they will encounter in real life.

In this technique clients are forced to assume the role of a therapist. This allows them to distance themselves both from their preoccupation and from the intensity of defending their old position in front of the therapists. They are forced to give more attention to the possible sources of their own misperceptions than they would otherwise.

Elsewhere in this book we have noted the passion with which clients cling to their mistaken beliefs, even when these beliefs cause them pain. They may even experience guilt if they allow themselves to be easily dislodged from their false perceptions. Sometimes their motivation is far more basic—clients simply do not want to appear to be "giving in" to the persuasive logic of their therapists. Role-playing is a technique that preserves clients' self-esteem, lowers their resistance to therapy (because the therapist assumes a passive, accepting attitude toward their damaging beliefs), and hones their practice skills so that they can better monitor their own attitudes and behaviors in the future.

Method

1. Use the client's master list of beliefs.
2. With the client's help, compile a companion list of arguments to these thoughts.
3. Role-play an argument between the rational and irrational thoughts in which the client takes the rational position and you, the therapist, play out the irrational argument.
4. Variations

a. The therapist plays the role of the person who originally taught the false belief to the client while the client argues against both the person and the belief.
b. Using the empty–chair technique, have the client play both sides—irrational belief and counters—arguing both for and against the core beliefs.
c. Help the client to dissect irrational beliefs into component parts, then role-play each part while the client counters. For example, the thought, "I could lose control and embarrass myself in front of others," has many components that can be role-played. The therapist could role-play the part of the client that wishes to be in control or that would be embarrassed, the client's anxiety, others observing the client's embarrassment, etc., as the client counters each component.
d. In most cases, it is best for the therapist to model the role-playing before the client attempts it.

Example 1: The Story of Lynn

Lynn was a client who was so afraid of flying that she hadn't been on a plane for 10 years. She had been referred to me by a behavioral therapist who had used traditional desensitization for the acrophobia. The treatment had been successful in that the client could imagine all of the items on her hierarchy without tension, but she still wouldn't get on a plane. The therapist had sent Lynn to see me with the hope that a cognitive component would take her over the last step.

Lynn learned the key components of cognitive therapy after a few sessions, but still actively resisted countering her irrational beliefs. She was willing to learn the intellectual components of cognitive therapy much as she had learned behavior therapy from the behavior therapist, but was recalcitrant in using this knowledge to help herself. Throughout each session she would argue against any direct suggestion or instruction. Unwilling to accept anyone else's advice, she believed that she should be able to solve her problems herself. I decided that role-playing would put her argumentative nature to good use, enabling her to argue against her own irrational thoughts. The following is an excerpt from one of my sessions with Lynn.

THERAPIST: I would like to do something a little bit different for this session. Instead of you telling me your irrational belief and me giving you the counters, let's reverse it. I'll argue for your beliefs and you argue against them, okay?

LYNN: I'm not sure I understand what you mean.

THERAPIST: Well, let's get started, and I think you'll get the idea.

LYNN: Okay.

THERAPIST: I think your fear of flying is quite sensible. It's a strange sensation to be in this huge lump of metal 30,000 feet in the sky. And if something goes wrong you can't pull over to the side and get off.

LYNN: Yeah! It is scary.

THERAPIST: No, I want you to argue against me.

LYNN: That's hard because I believe what you're saying.

THERAPIST: I know, but try arguing with me anyway.

LYNN: Well, nothing will happen, probably. It probably won't crash.

THERAPIST: Probably, probably, that's not very reassuring. Who wants to have his guts splattered all over Kansas because you misjudged a probability?

LYNN: There isn't much of a chance something bad will happen.

THERAPIST: Maybe not. But shouldn't you take every possible precaution?

LYNN: Like what?

THERAPIST: Like worrying, or not getting on planes, or freaking out once you do.

LYNN: I don't see how worrying would help in the least.

THERAPIST: If you worry, then at least you're prepared for the danger. You wouldn't want something to happen if you weren't ready.

LYNN: That's silly. Worrying won't keep the plane from crashing.

THERAPIST: Well, I guess that means you have to stay off planes.

LYNN: Then I'd have to stay in one place all my life.

THERAPIST: Nonsense. You could drive a car, take a bus, or even walk if you had to.

LYNN: That would take too long.

THERAPIST: Which do you want—to take a long time or get smashed like a pancake?

LYNN: Aw, come on! I'm not going to get smashed. Besides, cars and buses have more accidents than planes. And I could break a leg or something if I walked.

THERAPIST: Or get hit by a crashing plane.

LYNN: (Laughing) Yeah! I'd be safer in a plane. At least I would have metal around me and I wouldn't be caught out in the open.

THERAPIST: Still, planes are a lot scarier than other types of transportation.

LYNN: So what? Feeling scared isn't going to kill me. But car accidents or bus accidents could.

THERAPIST: Yeah, but you could embarrass yourself on the plane by showing fellow passengers that you're scared.

LYNN: Embarrass myself! Who cares about that? That's nothing compared to being trapped in the same place for the rest of my life. And all because I *couldn't* fly.

THERAPIST: You mean *wouldn't* fly!

LYNN: (*Pause*) Yeah! *Wouldn't!*

Example 2: The Story of Barton

The following transcript summarizes a portion of my exchange with Barton, a client who sought counseling because his close friends had been telling him for years that he didn't trust people enough; they had told him that he must be paranoid. This edited transcript is near the end of the role-playing session in which Barton and I had reversed roles.

THERAPIST: This thought that people can't be trusted is absolutely true. There are probably a thousand examples of your being taken advantage of by someone whom you had thought you could trust. It's best not to trust anybody, but to treat all people like they are trying to manipulate you, and to guard against their doing so.

BARTON: But some people have treated me fairly.

THERAPIST: For now! But just wait 'til the future

BARTON: What do I get for covering my ass all the time? No friends and lots of enemies.

THERAPIST: At least you won't be taken like you have been for the last 15 years.

BARTON: But that's a bad exchange. No friends, lots of enemies, and what do I get for all this protection? I can put a banner on my wall when I am dying alone and friendless. It will read, "HE NEVER LET ANYBODY TAKE ADVANTAGE OF HIM!" Big deal! It wouldn't be worth it.

THERAPIST: But if you let yourself get taken it will show everybody what a schmuck, what a weakling you are.

BARTON: It would only show that I win some and lose some, like everybody else. A real schmuck would be a guy who throws away all closeness just so somebody doesn't take advantage of him. Now, that would really be dumb!

THERAPIST: How could you have any self-esteem if you don't protect yourself from others?

BARTON: Do I have any self-esteem now, with my present attitude?

THERAPIST: That's because you have not done a very good job of
guarding.

BARTON: I don't know of anybody who guards more than I do, and
I've paid the price for it. I have no friends, no lover, and despite
all the guarding, some people are still able to take advantage of
me. It's not worth it anymore. Better I stop protecting all the time
and open up to people, and if I get hurt, then so what? It would
still be better than what I have now.

THERAPIST: You have a good point there. I can't argue against it.

Comment

Besides being a good treatment technique, role-playing can be used
to assess how solidly clients have incorporated their new beliefs.
Clients who have just memorized them will be unable to argue with
the therapist. They give up the argument quickly and agree with the
therapist. In the above examples, the clients demonstrated that they
understood the new beliefs—not just the words, but the counter philosophy behind them as well.

This technique can also be useful for clients who oppose the counselor's direction, particularly when this behavior seems to be part of
their social repertoire. Such clients are highly motivated to win an
argument, even if it means giving up their irrational thoughts. When
role-playing is used in this way it is a paradoxical technique. If client
and counselor do not switch roles, role-playing is a countering technique.

Further Information

The role-playing technique is a significant part of schema-focused
therapy (Bricker, Young, & Flanagan, 1993). The techniques mentioned
are a cognitive adaptation of some of the procedures developed by
gestalt therapists. The reader may find it useful to refer to some original sources, such as Fagan and Shepherd (1970), Feder and Ronall
(1980), Hatcher and Himelstein (1996), Mac Kewn (1996), Nevis (1993),
and the creator, Perls (1969a, 1969b, 1973).

Role-switching is used in many forms of psychotherapy (see
Corsini, 1957, 1981, 1998; Greenberg, 1974; Moreno & Zeleny, 1958).

ENVIRONMENTAL PRACTICE
Principles

Environmental practice is a technique that solidifies therapeutic gain by providing clients with an opportunity to practice cognitive changes in real–life situations. Hence, clients are urged to engage in the avoided behavior to prove that no harm will actually befall them. Repeated testing under the overt conditions while practicing cognitive techniques also helps clients realize that what has worked covertly will also work *in vivo.*

It is usually necessary for clients to try out their cognitive changes in real life. While some clients don't actually have to test their beliefs to become comfortable with them, most clients need to try them out. Eliminating their old beliefs totally by covert, cognitive means usually leaves the lingering thought, "Yes, but I haven't actually done it, yet" (e.g., get on the plane; ask her for a date; speak in public; take the test, etc.). For such clients, environmental practice is a valuable last step for all cognitive techniques.

Method

1. List the core beliefs connected to your client's problems.
2. Teach all aspects of covert, countering, perceptual shifting, or other cognitive techniques with these beliefs.
3. After discussing it with your client, develop a conclusive environmental test of the beliefs. For example, you could test the thought, "I could go crazy if I travel far from home" (the agoraphobic's fear) by suggesting your client travel 6 miles, then 7, then 15, etc. Develop a test for each irrational thought.
4. The client then actually performs the tests and records the results.

Example: The Story of John

John was a young man who entered therapy to remove his compulsive behaviors. Every day he performed 40 or 50 meaningless rituals to reduce anxiety. He had seen several other therapists but the frequency of his rituals had not been reduced.

He had made a lot of covert changes but hadn't actually reduced his rituals in his environment. We first identified what he said to himself immediately before performing the rituals and found many beliefs.

- If I don't do the rituals, some catastrophic thing will happen.
- Rituals protect me from danger.
- I must have people like and respect me.
- I must always be in control. I cannot let myself feel something that I don't control.
- I have the power to make myself feel anything I want.
- Rituals exercise this power.
- If I give up the power, I will be in great danger.

We then used hard and soft countering and perceptual shifting techniques to change his beliefs. He first practiced all the cognitive techniques covertly, we taped the sessions, and he practiced the techniques at home several times a week.

We then decided to try the techniques *in vivo*. The first environmental practice used a single–subject experimental design. He conducted a study with himself to compare the effects of doing the ritual versus doing a cognitive technique. He did the experiment for five weeks. We used an individual time series design.

$$01 \qquad Xn \qquad 02 \qquad 03$$
$$\underline{\hspace{4cm}}\text{time}\underline{\hspace{4cm}}$$

with 0s = self-rating of anxiety level on a 1–10 scale.
with 01 = his tension level immediately before he engaged in the ritual.
with 02 = his anxiety immediately after he either did the ritual or did some alternative treatment (Xs).
with 03 = his anxiety 15 minutes later.

The independent variable (Xn) stands for:

X–1. Doing the ritual.
X–2. Not doing the ritual.
X–3. Substituting relaxation for the ritual.
X–4. Finding the thoughts causing the anxiety preceding the ritual.
X–5. Objectively analyzing the truth or falseness of the thoughts.
X–6. Contradicting, challenging, and disputing his thoughts.
X–7. Switching to another ritual.
X–8. Finding the environmental trigger preceding the anxiety and ritual.
X–9. Imagining a relaxing scene.
X–10. Changing the visual components of the ritual.

X–11. Doing something behaviorally assertive in the situations.

X–12. Countering his fears when he doesn't do ritual.

Since John averaged 40 rituals a day before treatment, I told him to picture four or five times each day when he would record his anxiety and try to interrupt the ritual by doing something else (independent variable). Table 11.1 shows which interruption (Xn) helped most.

TABLE 11.1

Mean Self-ratings of Anxiety (10-0) During Different Time Periods (Os), in Different Experimental Conditions (Xs). N = 175 trials.

01	Xn	02	03	mean change (anxiety reduction)
3.75	1	0	0	–3.75
4.17	2	5	0	–1.67
3.67	3	1.8	3	–1.79
3.75	4 to 6	1.02	0	–2.73
3.50	8	1.05	0	–2.45
3.00	10	1.00	0	–2.00
4.00	11	.71	0	–3.29
3.00	12	1.00	0	–2.00

The study shows several important data: (a) His rituals reduced the anxiety more effectively than any other technique. That was why he was obsessive. (b) Whether he did the ritual or not, his anxiety left after 15 minutes, usually in a minute or two. (c) Besides doing the ritual, identifying and countering his thoughts reduced his anxiety the most (4 to 6 SUDS); finding the environmental triggers (8), and doing something assertive in the situation (11) also helped.

After the study we decided to try environmental practice. He was told to use his most effective intervention techniques to reduce the rituals; the procedure would take 85 days. Each day he was allotted a certain number of times he could engage in ritualistic behavior. He could not do rituals if he had fulfilled his daily allotment. When he approached his daily limit he was told to counter his thoughts, find the environmental CSs, and do something assertive instead of doing a ritual. He would monitor his practice with a hand counter. The following is a record of his environmental practice.

Day	Rituals Allowed	Rituals Used
1	40	26
2	39	23
3	38	34
4	37	26
5	36	30
6	35	22
7	34	21
8	33	28
7	32	17
8	31	17
9	30	14
10	29	13
11	28	19
12	27	19
13	26	14
14	25	23
15	24	17
16	23	15
17	22	16
18	21	21
19	20	14
20	19	15

The ritual behavior gradually reduced. This reduction continued.

31	9	10
32	8	9
33	7	8
34	6	8
35	5	6

At this point he was going over his daily limit so we shifted the approach. Each week he was allotted a maximum but decreasing number of rituals. If he went over his allotment one day he had to take it from the next day's allotment. Finally, on day 70, he engaged in no rituals.

70	2	0
71	2	1
72	2	2
73	2	0

74	1	0
75	1	1
76	1	0
77	1	0
78	1	0

We continued the practice until he consistently didn't do the rituals.

Comment

As the last step in CRT, we almost always have clients practice their techniques in real–life situations. Without this procedure most clients feel that they haven't really completed their work.

Further Information

Several authors have debated the necessity of environmental practice for cognitive techniques (see Bandura, 1977a, 1977b, 1982, 1984, 1995, 1996; Mahoney, 1993a; and Meichenbaum, 1993).

Other authors remark that environmental practice is the only necessary component for behavioral change and that working on cognitions may be superfluous (Hawkins, 1992; Hayes, 1995; Skinner, 1953, 1974, 1991).

Diary Research and Practice
Principles

All cognitive techniques share a major problem—the therapist does not know for certain that the procedures are going to work. Generally it is not bad to assume their efficacy, for they have been tested on thousands of clients at clinics throughout the world. But every new client entering therapy presents a special challenge, and we cannot be certain that a specific technique will be effective simply because it has helped others.

It's best to discover what works for a particular client in a specific situation through experimentation rather than by following a favorite technique or two. The easiest, most logical, or most clever counters may have helped hundreds of clients, and may even have had scores of books written about them, but what good are they if they don't help the client sitting in front of you?

The purpose of diary research is to help clients find and practice the most effective counters by experimentation.

Method

1. Have clients keep a record of all the techniques they have found effective in reducing anxiety or other negative emotions.
2. For each technique have clients record, on a series of 10–point scales: (a) the strength of the emotion before the technique, (b) the strength of the technique, (c) how long the technique was used, and (d) the strength of the emotion after using the technique.
3. The best techniques are those that remove a strong negative emotion. Clients should be especially careful to keep accurate records on those techniques that remove or reduce anxiety attacks or severe depressive episodes.
4. After a sufficient number of workable techniques have been gathered, have clients choose those that produced the greatest reductions in negative emotions. Next, instruct clients to develop a whole new series of techniques emphasizing the key points in previously successful procedures.
5. Have clients continue to refine these techniques based on trial and error. Eventually clients will develop some very powerful, effective techniques.
6. In many cases it is also useful to have clients recall all of the techniques they used throughout their lives when changing the same or similar thoughts. Often the techniques that worked especially well in the past will continue to work well in the future.

Example: The Story of David

Following are some excerpts from the technique diary of a client we will call David, a 31–year–old professional who had weekly anxiety attacks for several years. The trigger for these attacks was always the thought that he would go insane.

The attacks had started after a relative of David's was institutionalized for severe emotional difficulties. Although David had absolutely no symptoms of psychosis, he lived in mortal terror of becoming schizophrenic. He was stricken with anxiety whenever he was exposed to people, movies, or conversations that depicted or mentioned insanity or abnormal behavior of any kind. One year of psychoanalytic therapy and six months of behavioral desensitization had not reduced his anxiety.

David was unable to attend therapy on a regular basis so we decided he should use the diary technique, which can be done at home. He reported to me periodically by phone.

For one year he keep a careful record of all the techniques that were effective in reducing the severity of his anxiety attacks. Once a month he was to rate the effectiveness of each technique.

Based on his research David was able to develop increasingly effective techniques, significantly reducing the frequency and intensity of his anxiety attacks in one year's time. He continued the diary after we terminated his therapy. Three years later, he was entirely free of anxiety attacks.

Excerpts from David's Diary

(These are the most effective techniques he tried when he had anxiety attacks. The ratings of how effective they were are included.)

Technique No. 145. Look at your anxiety like this—it's just catastrophizing. Consider the troubles that others have, and how upset they deserve to be. Your problems are considerably less than theirs, but you catastrophize considerably more. (David rated the effectiveness of this technique at 2.4 on a scale of 10.)

No. 146. The fear you have now is the same one you had years ago. The only difference is that now you're calling this feeling crazy. (3.4/10)

No. 147. Look around at the reality. Ignore your emotions. (2.9/10)

No. 148. The flaw in me is a flaw in life. (1.9/10)

No. 149. Remember and retrace your history of catastrophizing. You are doing it right now. Stop it! (5.7/10)

No. 150. Don't try so hard to get rid of your emotions. The anxiety you feel isn't so terrible—and concentrating on it only makes it worse. So just wait for it to go away. Consider it as a cold—a temporary nuisance that doesn't really require much attention. (7.3/10)

No. 151. Become extremely assertive and goal-directed. (3.7/10)

No. 152. You are being super-dramatic again. Get real. (5.2/10)

No. 153. You have had over 300 anxiety attacks. Every single time you were afraid you were going crazy, but nothing has ever happened. So big deal! This is just another one. (8.1/10)

No. 154. You are anxious because you learned to be and you can unlearn it. (4.6/10)

No. 157. You can stand to be scared for a little while. You don't have to get rid of it, or get in a stew every time you feel a little bit upset. (4.1/10)

No. 158. You're getting anxious in this situation because you *think* you should get anxious. If you thought you should get anxious because you picked your nose, then picking your nose would make you anxious. (3.6/10)

No. 159. You have no alternative. If you are going to go crazy, then it's going to happen. You can't prevent it no matter what you do, so you might as well be as happy as you can in the meantime. Go ahead and enjoy life while you still can. (8.9/10)

No. 160. Grow up! Stop being a little baby! A little fear isn't going to kill you. (1.0/10)

No. 161. Give yourself a break! There's no point in blaming yourself for your fear. You didn't try to get it, so stop attacking yourself. (4.4/10)

When David was interviewed after he got over his anxiety, he said that two techniques ultimately removed his fear. The first was the idea that fear had nothing to do with being crazy; it was just a learned phobia. The second was that the purpose of human life is not simply to protect oneself from every conceivable threat. Ours is the dominant species on this planet because historically we have taken risks. There are no guarantees for any of us. One can see the origin of both of these ideas in David's diary.

An update on David: He hasn't had major anxiety for over 15 years now. In looking back at what he did to get rid of it, David now concludes that Number 159 in his dairy was the key. "You have no alternative. If you are going to go crazy, then it's going to happen. You can't prevent it no matter what you do, so you might as well be as happy as you can in the meantime. Go ahead and enjoy life while you still can. (8.9/10)."

David got himself to accept his anxiety. The acceptance was not just a verbal counter, but a firm, deep belief. He had been creating his own anxiety all along, yet demanding of himself that he get rid of it. He had been telling himself that it was absolutely terrible, horrible, and catastrophic that he had anxiety attacks, that having them showed a fundamental weakness, that he couldn't stand to live with them, and that he had to get rid of them at all costs. He finally told himself, "The hell with it. I have spent too much time in my life trying to get rid of this anxiety. I don't want to waste any more time. Tough shit that I have to live with anxiety attacks. I just will have to. Now let's move on." When he believed this, his anxiety attacks disappeared. Ellis is correct—when David removed his musterbation, he removed his fear.

Comment

This client found the diary highly beneficial, but it deserves mention that he had a strong background in psychology and read extensively in the area of cognitive/behavioral therapy throughout the year he was under treatment. Most clients need more help from their therapists.

Further Information

Ira Progoff (1977, 1992) has developed a comprehensive set of methods called intensive journal therapy, the use of diaries and journals in psychotherapy. His approach has a psychodynamic underpinning as opposed to our procedures.

GUIDED PRACTICE
Principles

Guided practice puts several major cognitive techniques together in the same exercise. Because cognitive therapy involves subtleties that clients often miss, it is best to guide them step by step through the various procedures, correcting mistakes as they occur. After several practice sessions clients usually master the techniques well enough to employ the unified procedures in real–life situations.

Method

1. Attach a biofeedback measure (GSR, EMG, or pulse rate) to your client. Observe the measure for five minutes to obtain a baseline reading.
2. Induce relaxation. Standard relaxation, hypnotism, deep breathing, pink or white noise, nature images, or biofeedback response reduction are appropriate. Allow the client to stabilize on the selected biofeedback measure before proceeding.
3. Prepare a hierarchy of upsetting scenes and have the client imagine the first item on the hierarchy.
4. Ask the client to tell you the belief causing the pain. Allow all the time needed on this step, until the client is able to articulate the belief in a core sentence or two.
5. Help the client find the philosophy underlying the surface

thought. Probing questions like, "So what if . . . ? What's so terrible if . . . ?" can be used to root out core beliefs.

6. Analyze each core belief and help the client decide whether it is useful or not useful.

7. If a core belief is not useful, help the client challenge and dispute the thought as deeply as possible, using all the evidence available to expose it as faulty. Continue this attack until the biofeedback measure shows a reduction in the painful emotion.

8. Repeat the exercise, speeding up the procedure until the client's biofeedback reading remains the same while the scene is being imagined.

9. Encourage the client to speak out loud during the entire proce-dure. This will enable you to assess the client's ability to counter and dispute.

10. Tape the session and have the client practice it 4 or 5 times a week for several weeks.

Example: The Story of Martin

The following transcript is an excerpt from a guided practice session with Martin, a 35–year–old professional man with multiple problems. Martin fluctuated between periods of anxiety and depression, had a history of drug and alcohol abuse, and avoided all major risk–taking behaviors.

After several sessions, we found Martin's core philosophy: He believed that everyone should respect him all the time, in every situ-ation imaginable. He panicked at the mere thought of rejection and felt deeply depressed when he experienced it. He had apparently learned his other–directed philosophy from an overly perfectionistic father, who had pushed for impossible achievements. As is true for many clients with this background, he felt he would never accomplish enough to gain his father's respect.

Martin constantly searched for respect. He became tense whenever he anticipated rejection and coped by increasing his perfectionist demands on himself, creating intense internal pressure. His anxiety would then accelerate into panic—which only produced more failure. Trapped in a vicious cycle, he would then redouble his demands on himself until the only way out was to turn to drugs and alcohol to soothe the pain.

Biofeedback techniques were used to teach Martin relaxation. A measure was used to read his skin conductivity. The unit has a skin resistance range of 5000 to 3,000,000 ohms, and a meter/tone resolution <0.2% of base resistance of O.sF(.OSC). Inputs consisted of external finger electrodes. Output was provided on a dual sensitivity meter graduated into 40 units, which could be switched to a sub/superior displacement of 40 additional units, creating an 80–unit range.

During the first 15 minutes of the session Martin practiced relaxation while being monitored for skin conductivity, producing a decrease of 35 units. He maintained this rate during a five–minute base reading period, after which the meter was reset at the central zero–displacement level.

The following is a transcript of the instructions I gave to Martin. The figures in parentheses are the amount of time elapsed, and increases (+) and decreases (–) in galvanic skin response (GSR).

I would like you to close your eyes and imagine the next scene in your hierarchy that causes anxiety. Imagine it as vividly as you can and use all of your senses until it is clearly in mind. When you see it, indicate this by slightly raising your finger. (43 seconds; +12)

(*Martin imagined himself at work. Because of a new promotion, he was now supervising 20 people he had worked with for several years as a colleague.*)

Very good. Now keep imagining the situation, but concentrate on what you are saying to yourself. Take your time, but focus on the first thought that pops into your head that's connected to your anxiety. Try to capture it and see if you can put it into a sentence. Indicate when you are ready. (23 seconds; +16)

Now, as we have discussed before, I want you to look underneath the surface. Imagine your thoughts are constructed like an upside–down pyramid. At the top the shallow beliefs sit, but the one on the bottom holds up all the rest. I want you to start moving down the pyramid till you find the core. Look at the first belief and ask yourself the question, "So what if . . . ?"

(*His first thought was that everybody would be very angry with him for being promoted over them.*)

I had him counter with, "So what if they are angry?"

I said, "Take all the time you need, but wait until you have an answer." (12 seconds)

"Then they wouldn't like or respect me."

"Now keep on asking yourself the question, 'So what if?' or 'Why?' Take your time until you have an answer, and move on to the next statement. Continue until you can find no further beliefs." (1 minute; +8)

(The most basic thought Martin discovered was, "It would be absolutely horrible if somebody didn't respect me.")

Keep imagining the same situation and keep repeating the thoughts to yourself until you are sure you can remember them. Indicate when you are done. (55 seconds; +8)

Take some more time just to relax. Make your muscles loose, limp and slack. (30 seconds; −8)

Keep relaxing but get some distance from yourself and start looking at each thought, one at a time. Make a coldly objective, nonemotional decision as to whether each thought is true or false, using all the techniques I have previously taught you. Take your time but be sure to make the most objective decision you can. (1¹/₂ minutes; +6)

(He decided that the first thought was true but that the next two were false.)

Imagine the situation again and picture thinking the first thought that you judged false. Keep doing this until it's clearly in mind. (54 seconds; +10)

Now attack, challenge, contradict that thought in every way you can. Convince yourself that it is false, using all the evidence you can find against it. Continue until you feel a definite lessening in the belief. Indicate when you are done. (4 minutes; +2).

Take the next belief you logically know is false but still aren't convinced of and do the same thing. Dispute it as hard as you can and keep doing it until you feel more convinced. (2¹/₂; −3).

Okay, now relax again. (45 seconds; −20)

Now just as a check, imagine the first scene again just as you had first imagined it. (98 seconds; −12).

We repeated the exercise twice more, increasing the speed during each repetition. When the test scene was presented the last time, Martin's GSR reading was −27, from the baseline relaxed state where it remained throughout the session. In later sessions, we used the same technique to reduce his anxiety about the other hierarchy items.

Comment

The guided practice approach is an extremely useful therapeutic technique. Almost all clients have practiced it during therapy. Much of

the research that helped establish key principles in cognitive restructuring therapy was gleaned from this technique. Without the guided
technique the therapist can never be sure the client knows how to
counter maladaptive beliefs. With it, the therapist can pinpoint and
correct a range of key problem areas.

Further Information

A form of guided countering called VCI has been discussed in five
previous works (Casey & Mc Mullin, 1976; Mc Mullin, 1986; Mc Mullin,
Assafi, & Chapman, 1978; Mc Mullin & Casey, 1975; and Mc Mullin &
Giles, 1981). Leuner (1969) has developed a whole form of psychotherapy based on guided imagery.

TWELVE

Adjuncts

IN THE PREVIOUS ELEVEN CHAPTERS we have focused upon cognitive restructuring techniques that therapists can use with most clients they encounter in their practice. This chapter focuses on specialized techniques therapists can use with more limited clinical populations.

"Crisis Cognitive Techniques" reviews some methods for helping clients who are in a crisis situation and don't have time to learn many of the basic procedures. "Treating Seriously Mentally Ill Patients" shows the specialized techniques used with chronically psychotic patients. "Handling Client Sabotage" discusses working with resistive clients who attempt to undercut their own therapeutic growth. "Cognitive Restructuring Therapy with Addicted Clients" offers a new perspective on counseling clients who are drug or alcohol dependent.

Finally, we finish the chapter with two sections aimed at helping the therapist. The first, "Cognitive Focusing," discusses a key principles underlying all effective cognitive techniques. The second, "Core Components of CRT," gives therapists a checklist of the necessary and sufficient conditions for therapeutic effectiveness.

CRISIS COGNITIVE THERAPY
Principles

Any mental health professional's immediate response to a client's crisis situation is to take whatever action seems appropriate to insure the client's physical and mental well-being until his or her condition stabilizes. Then and only then should other treatments be considered.

We take a cognitive approach to crises. The goal of this approach is to discover what thought has provoked the critical state. If clients in crisis have some background in cognitive techniques, an accelerated form of cognitive therapy can be used to stabilize their condition at a more comfortable level. If the client is new to cognitive therapy, counselors might try a marathon session or resort to traditional crisis–intervention approaches initially, then introduce cognitive fundamentals and techniques when stability has been achieved.

Following are four cognitive methods for helping clients in crisis.

Method 1. Quick Perceptual Shift

To help your client form a rapid perceptual shift, arrange all of the necessary components.

1. Clearly identify the core perception causing the crisis. Make certain that the client sees it clearly.
2. Point out the perception that would remove the crisis if the client believed it.
3. Do not reduce the client's tension level to zero by various ameliorative procedures. Some reduction may be necessary, but some negative emotions may motivate clients to make the shifts.
4. Search for the key bridge perceptions that can help carry clients from the old to the new perceptions (see chapter 9).The bridges should be an image, value, or belief firmly implanted in the clients' experiences. They should have a strong positive emotional valence. The bridges must come from the clients' experiences since time does not allow for creating new ones.
5. Confront all sidetracking the client may use to avoid the shift. Examine denials, alibis, excuses, sabotages, and evasions; press for the shift. You may wish to refer to the perceptual shift worksheet (Table 7.1) as a guide.

Method 2. Marathon Session

In a severe crisis, spend three or four hours teaching your client cognitive methods. Take no major breaks. Flood the client with countering techniques; repeat them until the client comprehends their use. The therapist should dispute the key damaging beliefs causing the crisis, concentrating on the here–and–now perceptions. Sometimes several therapists may work with one client, increasing the persuasiveness of the counters. As in other crisis intervention techniques, the therapist

presents an assured, self–confident manner to enhance the client's feelings of support. The therapist assumes control of the session and
actively directs the client's responses.

Method 3. Brief Cognitive Restructuring

Prepare a series of questions for your client to answer. Keep the
client focused on the content of the questions. Directly and actively
intervene to help your client develop effective responses. For example:

- What are you feeling at this moment?
- What situation are you in that surrounds your emotions?
- What are you telling yourself in this situation that is causing you to
  feel upset?
- What other thoughts are connected to this belief?
- Let's look at each thought right now and make a decision as to
  whether it is true or false. Be tough and hard–nosedly objective.
- If the thought is true, what constructive steps can you take *right
  now* to change, avoid, or cope with the situation?
- If the thought is false, what is the key untruth?
- What evidence do you have against it?
- What are your best arguments for disputing the thought?
- What practical method can you use right now to help convince
  yourself of the falseness of your thought?

Method 4. Other Cognitively Oriented Crisis Techniques

As in other crisis intervention methods, the cognitive therapist must
immediately intervene in an active, directive manner (Greenstone &
Leviton, 1979, 1980, 1983; Rosenbluh, 1974). Several CRT techniques can
be adapted to this style.

1. *Alternative attitudes and anticatastrophic thinking.* Show clients less dis-
   astrous alternatives to their fears.
2. *Coping statements.* Give your crisis clients a series of self–statements
   they can use to cope with the immediate crisis. For example: "Distressing but not dangerous." "Ignore trying to solve all your problems; just work on this one." "Spoil yourself right now." "This is not
   a question of sickness or guilt; it is a matter of finding a solution."
   "I will solve this just as I have solved the other crises in my life."

3. *Label shift.* Change negative labels like "bad," "sick," "nervous break-down," "going crazy" to neutral ones like "mistaken," "upset," "confused."
4. *Rational beliefs.* Direct much of your intervention toward helping clients form rational judgments of the crisis rather than correcting irrational ones.
5. *Objectifying.* Help clients separate the emotions that are connected to the crisis from the objective assessment of the crisis.
6. *Here and now.* Concentrate on present perceptions rather than their historical roots.
7. *Covert assertion.* Most clients behave passively in crisis. Teach them how to solve their problems assertively by practicing assertive coping images.
8. *Paradoxical methods.* In crisis situations avoid the use of paradoxical or complicated techniques. Clients are already confused, and such techniques may bewilder them more. Clients need procedures that are direct, simple, and easy to remember.

Comment

Crisis intervention aims at solving the immediate problem, not removing all maladaptive cognitions and behaviors. The therapist should work only with the perceptions that are exacerbating the present situation. Later, after the crisis is resolved, the therapist can work on the fundamental core beliefs that laid the groundwork for the crisis.

Further Information

There is only one reference I will provide for this chapter because it is the only one the reader will need. Frank Dattilio and Arthur Freeman have edited an excellent book about cognitive strategies in crisis intervention (Dattilio & Freeman, 1994). The book describes the theory, research, and practice of crisis intervention techniques for panic disorders, suicide, depression, rape, child sexual abuse, natural disasters, families in crisis, violence, and many others. Each chapter provides the reader with copious references.

TREATING SERIOUSLY MENTALLY ILL PATIENTS
Principles

There are three basic modes for using cognitive restructuring techniques with chronically psychotic patients. I will briefly mention the first two, and then spend the remainder of the chapter discussing the third.

Stress–reduction Model

Various cognitive therapists assert that critical life events interpreted through maladaptive cognitive schemas produce stress that, at least in part, elicits psychotic episodes. According to this theory, if stress is reduced, the frequency, intensity, and duration of patients' psychotic symptoms will also be reduced, even as the biological component remains unchanged. The various methods that therapists have employed to reduce patients' stress include: belief modifications to decrease hallucinations and delusions; verbal challenges to help patients control delusions; refocusing techniques to help patients to focus their attention toward other external and internal stimuli; reinterpretation, which helps patients reinterpret their psychotic experiences; coping skills, such as modeling, response prevention, and thought–stopping; teaching nondelusional responses to cued social situations; increasing self–esteem, reducing coexisting anxiety and depression, and teaching reality testing. Some of these techniques were developed for neurotic clients and have been transplanted for use with seriously mentally ill patient.

Rehabilitation of Cognitive Deficits Model

Cognitive and neuropsychological rehabilitation has recently become a target of research. The techniques aim at helping patients learn skills to reduce the cognitive deficits accompanying their disorders. Specific cognitive techniques have been developed to improve attention span, concentration, psychomotor speed, cognitive flexibility, learning, concept formation, auditory, cognitive sets, and memory. Many of the techniques were originally developed for brain–injured persons, but they have recently been adapted for psychotic patients (Jacobs, 1993).

Acceptance–integration Model

The acceptance–integration model emphasizes the biochemical basis of psychosis, but it does not assert the dominant importance of environmental stresses, critical life events, or cognitive deficits. Psychosis is considered a brain disease that needs to be dealt with like any other. The model supports the research compiled over the last 30 years suggesting biochemical etiologies for chronic mental illness. This research encompasses genetic origins suggested by twin studies, adoption studies, and molecular biology. It also includes findings on gross brain abnormalities, such as ventricular enlargement, cerebral asymmetry, soft neurological signs caused by an inadequate intrauterine environment, and aberrant biochemical pathways (Carson & Sanislow, 1993; Maher, 1988).

Implicit in the acceptance–integration model is that seriously mentally ill (SMI) patients have neurochemical deficiencies, and that traditional cognitive procedures developed primarily for neurotic clients are unlikely to significant impact them. Cognitive interventions may be of some help, but psychotherapeutic attempts such as stress reduction, delusions modification, or cognitive skill training are unlikely to affect patients' central problems because they are essentially biochemical.

Patient acceptance is the key psychotherapeutic postulate of the model. Patients need to acknowledge that they have a major biochemical disorder and to make adjustments in their lives to help them cope with the effects of the disorder. A common nonpsychiatric example often given is people who have diabetes—they can live reasonably normal lives as long as they accept that they have diabetes, take insulin as prescribed, and make adjustments in their diet and lifestyle. If diabetics deny having an illness they place themselves in severe danger. Likewise, SMI patients need to accept that they have a mental illness, take psychotropic medication, and make adjustments in their lives.

The greater the bioneurological disorder, the more SMI patients need to accept their condition. The goal of treatment is not just the process variable of reduced psychotic symptomatology (as is often true in the vulnerability–stress model) but rather the outcome goal of living in the least restrictive environment possible. The ideal outcome would be for patients to successfully integrate back into the community without the constant need for rehospitalization.

Method

1. Educate patients about their mental illness in a systematic, controlled fashion.
2. Aim to teach acceptance rather than reduce stress. Stress levels should not be reduced to zero; some stress provides a motivation to leave the hospital.

3. When the patients are ready, give them their diagnosis and tell them exactly why the professionals working with them have made the diagnosis.

4. Give each patient an 8–10–page manual written specifically for him or her that describes the illness, the possible causes, and specifically what needs to be done to cope with it (see figure 12.1).

5. Require patients to attend education classes on medications, mental illness, and how to recognize and manage symptoms.

6. Tell patients what beliefs are conducive to being released into the community and what attitudes are damaging and would keep them in the hospital. Use any cognitive approaches that will improve their rationality (Olevitch & Ellis, 1995).

7. Have patients who have accepted their illness and integrated into the community give testimonials about how they learned to cope with denial.

8. Do not confront patients' denial directly, but require them to learn about mental illness (Milton, Patwa, & Hafner, 1978). Explain that it is the patients' job while in the hospital to learn about mental illness and medications and that their release from the hospital will be in part dependent upon how well they learn the material.

9. Create a therapeutic community with a "cognitive milieu," to help enhance cognitive change (see Wright, 1996; and Wright, Thase, Beck, & Ludgate, 1993).

10. Many seriously mentally ill patients will vehemently reject any suggestion that they are mentally ill. Any direct attempt to change this cognition results in a strong reaction—they may walk out of treatment, verbally attack, or in some cases even physically assault the therapist.

We are experimenting with a technique that uses graduated shaped practice to reduce denial. We show the patient the reversible and hidden images illustrated in chapter 9, presenting them one at a time from easiest to hardest, in group or individual sessions. The procedure usually takes several weeks. We train patients to find the hidden images and reverse the ambiguous drawings.

During these sessions we mention nothing about mental illness or psychotic symptoms—we simply teach patients how to see the pictures.

We hypothesize that learning to see the images may help patients ultimately learn to see their illness because the same types of transformations are required. In both situations, patients must learn: (a) to accept help from others, (b) not to give up looking, (c) to try small changes first, (d) to practice hard, and (e) to keep trying to look at things in a new way. Once they succeed with the images, we gradually introduce their personal cognitions and teach them how to shift their thoughts.

Figure 12.1 depicts the first two pages of a manual we give to patients with schizoaffective disorder to educate them on their mental illness.

To John

*from your
Treatment Team*

COPING

WITH
SCHIZOAFFECTIVE
DISORDER

Bldg. J Maka Wili Wili

What Is
Schizoaffective

The "Schizo" part stands for Schizophrenia.

Some Symptoms of Schizophrenia

- Thought patterns become disorganized and illogical.
- The person often experiences hallucinations--they see or hear things that nobody else sees or hears.
- The sense of body boundaries deteriorates.
- Emotions become grossly inappropriate or flattened.
- The person may have delusions--believing in things that nobody else believes in and that are either realistically impossible or very implausible. There are several types:

  Grandiose = An exaggerated sense of one's importance, power, or knowledge.

  Persecutory = Believing that a person or group is conspiring against you.

  Somatic = Believing there is something wrong with your body when there isn't.

  Anosognosia = Being subjectively certain that you *don't* have a mental health problem, even though you have been in and out of mental hospitals for years and everyone around you (relatives, doctors, friends) know that you do.

FIGURE 12.1 Patient manual

Examples

Possibly the best examples of the beliefs of seriously mentally ill patients who have learned to accept their illnesses are the comments of two patients—Kelly and Randy (Mc Mullin, Samford, & Kline, 1996).

KELLY: I was diagnosed 15 years ago as having bipolar–II disorder . . . Like many professionals, I was very stubborn. I did not want to accept that I had, particularly, a serious problem. I denied my actual diagnosis of manic depression. I denied that for over a year, until it was beyond my control and I had to give in and be one of *those people* and take *that medicine*, which is called lithium (her emphasis). . . . I would like the public to realize that mental illness is an illness first and foremost. It's like diabetes, hypertension, and like those illnesses, I have to take a medication to stabilize the problem that's inherent in my illness.

RANDY: I have been diagnosed with schizoaffective disorder and I've been under doctors' care for over 30 years now. For many years I did not know I was ill. I did not realize that anything was wrong with me. I just felt I was different, but it certainly did not feel good being the way I was. . . . I did not like the idea of medication. It felt very uncomfortable for me, and it took me some more years of wandering around from place to place to discover that I *really* did have a problem that needed some medical attention and also some psychotherapy.

Comment

Insight and acceptance are complex concepts and can mean many things (Greenfeld, Strauss, Bowers, & Mandelkern, 1989). But the type of insight that allows seriously mentally ill patients to live in the community is something specific. Interviews with patients who were able to stay in their communities revealed that their acceptance of mental illness consisted of three parts: First, *internal*—they believed that their problem was biochemical and not just caused by a bad environment or bad training. Second, *global*—they accepted that their problem encompassed most aspects of their lives and was not just isolated to one part. Third, *stable*—they knew that their illness wouldn't go away in a few days, weeks, or months and that, barring a medical breakthrough, they would have to cope with it for the rest of their lives.

Martin Seligman found that individuals whose acceptance included these three components (internal, global, and stable) were at a greater risk for depression, particularly learned helplessness (Seligman, 1975, 1994, 1998). In his research these three factors were damaging, but in the present study they were helpful. Why the difference?

One answer is that different types of patients face different types of reality. Depressed patients often catastrophize their reality. They deny having control over events that they really can control. As Seligman and his colleagues point out, internal, stable and global attributions induce helplessness and contribute to giving up and not trying. The reality for the depressed patient is quite different from that of the seriously mentally ill patient, who often minimizes the extent of his or her illness. Seriously mentally ill patients have to face the harsh presence of their own biochemical disorder, which they can influence but not completely control. They are faced with this reality throughout their life.

Similarly, the attribution style, which is so helpful for the depressed patient, can be very damaging to the SMI patient. Attributing their mental illness to environmental factors (external) helps seriously mentally ill patient to believe that all they have to do is move, change their jobs, or get out of the hospital to make their psychotic symptoms disappear. Believing that their hallucinations and delusions are temporary (unstable) prompts them to refuse to take their medications when they leave the hospital because they hope that their symptoms will go away in a few days. Believing that their problem is small (specific) may keep their self-esteem intact, but it also keeps them from accepting that their mental illness compels some major life adjustments.

The exact nature of acceptance cognitions is speculative, but it appears that the core central theme is the denial of mental illness (see figure 12.2). Since most hospitalized patients don't believe they have serious problems, they see no reason to take medication. As one patient said, "I'm not sick, so I don't need any pills." They generally

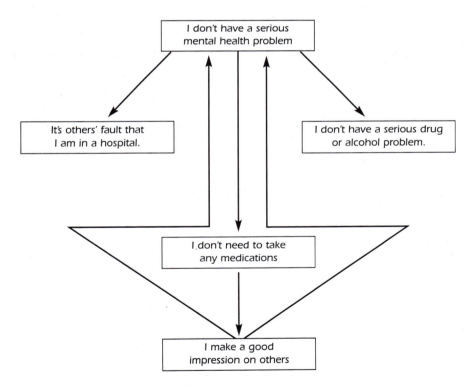

FIGURE 12.2 Core cognitions of rehospitalized psychotic patients

blame others—their families, the doctors, the courts—to create an explanation as to why they are in a psychiatric hospital: "The judge had it in for me"; "I didn't do anything wrong"; "I got a bum rap." These cognitions keep their self-esteem unrealistically high ("I make a great impression on others, and I don't have any faults") and feeds back into maintaining the denial of their mental illness ("Worthwhile people aren't crazy").

In contrast, patients in the community appear to have accepted their illness. They believe that they need medications to help them cope with their disorder. They realize that they are responsible for being in the hospital, usually because they stopped their medication. They have good self-esteem (I like myself) but it's conditional—" If I stop taking my medication I will become a not-very-nice person" (see figure 6.5, p. 191).

Further Information

Stress Reduction Model

Many stress reduction therapists call their theory the vulnerability-stress model (see Avison & Speechley, 1987; Birchwood & Tarrier, 1994; Brenner, 1989; Chadwick, Birchwood, & Trower, 1996; Kingdon & Turkington, 1991a, 1991b, 1994; Lukoff, Snyder, Ventura, & Nuechterlein, 1984; Nuechterlein & Dawson, 1984; Nuechterlein, Goldstein, & Ventura 1989; Perris, 1988, 1989, 1992; Perris, Nordstrom, & Troeng, 1992; Perris & Skagerlind, 1994; Zubin & Spring, 1977).

Rehabilitation of Cognitive Deficits

Neuropsychologists, occupational therapists, and rehabilitation specialists have been some of the major movers in the use of cognitive rehabilitation. See particularly the *Journal of Clinical and Experimental Neuropsychology, Journal of Clinical Neuropsychology, Neuropsychological Rehabilitation*, and *Cognitive Rehabilitation*.

One of the most important books in this area is Harvey Jacobs's text *Behavior Analysis Guidelines and Brain Injury Rehabilitation* (1993).

For more techniques see Benedict (1989), Cassidy, Easton, Capelli, Singer, and Bilodeau (1996), Jaeger, Berns, Tigner, and Douglas (1992), Spaulding, Sullivan, Weiler, Reed, Richardson, and Storzbach (1994), Stuve, Erickson, and Spaulding (1991).

Acceptance–integration Model

The emphasis I give this model comes from research that colleagues and I have done with the SMI population (see Mc Mullin, 1998). Although I recognize and accept that stress reduction and rehabilitation of cognitive deficits can be very helpful, I think that a majority of SMI patients could also benefit from the acceptance–integration model.

Although many other cognitive therapists have tended to ignore this model, there have been important exceptions. Hayes and Wilson have created a new therapy, acceptance and commitment therapy (ACT), based on patients accepting their illness and committing to cope with it. ACT suggests that emotional distress is caused by maladaptive experiential avoidance (Hayes, Strosahl, & Wilson, 1996; Hayes & Wilson, 1994).

McGlashan (1994) and McGlashan and Levy (1977) discuss the differences between acute psychotic patients who "seal–over" (deny) and those who integrate (assimilate) their psychotic experience. David (1990) describes acceptance of mental illness in terms of insight. He defines insight as the patients' ability to recognize that they are suffering from a mental illness and to reliably label their psychotic experiences in terms of the illness. Coursey (1989) recommends that psychotherapy be given to patients so that they have accurate information about the causes and prognosis of their disability. McEvoy, Apperson, et al. (1989) and McEvoy, Freter, et al. (1989) explore the relationship between insight and acute psychopathology. They found that patients who had good insight about their mental illness were significantly less likely to be rehospitalized. Drury used an acceptance component in his study. Part of his cognitive therapy was to help patients, "'To face up to' and integrate their illness rather than seeking refuge in their psychotic experiences" (Drury, Birchwood, Cochrane, & Macmillan, 1996, p. 595). He found that the cognitive therapy group had fewer residual symptoms after their acute psychotic episodes than the controls.

Possibly most prominent have been the acceptance therapies. Although originating from a behavioral rather than a cognitive frame of reference, acceptance and commitment therapy (Hayes, Strosahl, & Wilson, 1996) suggests that psychological distress often results from maladaptive experiential avoidance that includes cognitive elements. According to Wilson, Hayes, and Gifford (1997), psychopathology is in part caused by clients' efforts to reduce, escape, or avoid their problems.

HANDLING CLIENT SABOTAGES
Principles

James Randi, an internationally known magician and mystic debunker, offers to pay a sum of more than one million dollars to any person who can demonstrate the existence of paranormal powers under scientifically observable conditions. Since 1964 thousands of persons have applied for the prize and several hundred have made it through the initial screening; none has stood up to scientific scrutiny by passing his scientific tests. Randi is still prepared to give a check on the spot to anyone who can convince him of paranormal capabilities (Randi, 1982, 1989, 1995).

Randi describes those who have made claim to his prize as falling into one of two groups. First are the outright fakes—the snake–oil salesmen, the flimflam artists. They know that they are fakes and have tried to win the prize with sleight–of–hand tricks. Second are the true believers—a group far more interesting to therapists. These people actually believe that they have paranormal powers and are amazed when the experiment fails to prove it. Members of this second group suffer from what might be called, "self–sabotage." They have fooled themselves so completely that they believe they have powers that they don't. Many clients belong to this second group.

Paradoxically, self–sabotage clients are often very intelligent and quite well educated but they sabotage the therapeutic process. If one is even moderately objective it is silly to spend time and money going to a therapist and then to subtly undercut what the therapist is trying to do. Yet some very bright people engage in such behavior when they enter counseling. These clients don't do their homework, miss appointments, or use other self–defeating behaviors. These sabotages can be distinguished from other types of client problems only in that they must be treated *first*, because no progress will occur if the client is engaging in sabotage; the ability of the client to resist getting help is greater than the ability of the therapist to help.

Clients may use various types of sabotages:

- *Secondary Gain.* Environmental reinforcements anchor the client's beliefs. "It is easier not to change."
- *Social Support.* "People wouldn't like me if I changed."
- *Value Contradiction.* Not changing has a higher value in client's hierarchy. "It would be wrong to change."
- *Internal Consistency.* The old behavior is tied to so many other things

that changing it would require changing one's whole life. "It would cost too much to change."

- *Defense.* "It would be dangerous to change."
- *Competitive.* "I won't let anybody tell me what to do."
- *Dependency.* "If I change I won't need you anymore."
- *Magic Cure.* "I shouldn't have to work hard to change. It should happen quickly without a great deal of effort."
- *Motivation.* "I don't feel I have to shift. I can be happy without changing."
- *Denial.* "I understand everything you are telling me." (They don't.) "I will never understand anything you are telling me." (They will.)
- *Behavioral Sabotages.* Skipping sessions; arguing against every principle presented; doing no work in session but calling constantly during off hours; not paying fees; complaining about not being cured; jumping from one therapist to another every time they reach an arduous phase of counseling; complaining about all the therapists they have seen before you; seeing you only in crisis and discontinuing the minute the crisis is over.

Method 1. Counter Sabotage

After you and your clients have developed a list of counters to an irrational thought, ask clients to write down any sabotages or arguments against the counters that automatically occur to them. Next have them analyze these sabotages and dispute and challenge them before they attack the irrational thought (Giles, 1979; Loudis, personal communication, April 10, 1979).

Example

Irrational Thought: "I can't let people know who I am. I need to hide behind a social mask to protect myself."
Counter: "If I don't show who I am, no one can ever get close to me. I will always be alone."
Sabotage: "But they may reject me."
Counter: "They are rejecting me now because I am hiding behind a cardboard mockup of myself."
Sabotage: "Better they don't know me then that they dislike me."
Counter: "Better to give people a chance to like or dislike me than to assure their rejection by playing hide–and–seek with myself."

The counter sabotage process is continued until clients can no longer think of any sabotages to their counters.

Method 2. Preventing Sabotages

It is far better to undercut sabotages before clients resort to them. Once clients present their attitudes in public, they will defend them against attack. If it appears to you that a client is likely to sabotage therapy, in an early counseling session have your clients make a list of all the ways any person could sabotage counseling. Ask them to identify what particular method they would use if they ever decided to sabotage counseling. Then discuss why the sabotage would keep people from reaching their therapeutic goals.

This technique is usually introduced as follows:

> One of the things I have noticed after counseling clients for 25 years is that most clients have mixed feelings about therapy. Part of them wants to improve things in their lives and for this reason they come to therapy. But another part of them resists changing or worries about risking getting into a worse state than they are in now. It's like they have two tape–recorded voices in their brain, one shouting "Grow, change, be better," while the other shouts, "Be careful! You may get worse; let it be."
>
> I have also found that most clients have difficulty telling their therapist about these conflicting feelings, so they usually don't. Instead, they subtly sabotage the therapy and often try to convince themselves that they aren't doing so.
>
> I am going to give you some ways others have attempted to sabotage counseling. I would like you to add some more. If you were going to sabotage but you didn't want me to know it, what methods would you use?

Sabotaging may be more widespread than most therapists think. Graduate programs don't often discuss it, assuming that it is a rare occurrence, but whenever I have presented the concept of sabotage to my clients almost every one seems to know exactly what I am talking about.

Method 3. Finding Payoffs

List the client's sabotages separately. Hypothesize what positive or negative reinforcers (payoffs) are connected to them. Discuss these payoffs with your clients and help them discover other methods of getting the payoff. Help them discriminate between useful payoffs and destructive ones.

Their sabotage thoughts are like cognitive tricks that they play upon themselves. Beliefs such as, "I could lose control and go crazy," or "I must be better than all other people to be worthwhile," may not be solely mistaken perceptions arising out of poorly synthesized experiences. They may also reveal a kind of cognitive game that clients play in order to reap seeming rewards. Just as a con artist plays tricks on the public for external payoff, so clients may trick themselves for internal payoffs—to generate feelings of security or high self-esteem, to reduce anxiety, to empower someone else, or simply to spice up an otherwise boring existence.

Method 4. Exposing the Play

Other clients make counseling a dramatic play, a theatrical show, a performance in which the client is the performer and the therapist is the audience. Initially, clients may create the drama for external applause, but after years of practice they begin to play the role only for themselves, long after external payoffs have vanished.

Many cognitive approaches are not effective for clients who perform for the therapist, as they often view therapy as another arena for their performance. While these clients may pretend to work very hard at therapy they make little if any real progress. Sometimes they reveal their game playing with an inappropriate smile or a verbal slip. Sometimes they quit counseling altogether when the sessions get serious.

To free the client from a self-delusionary belief, it is necessary to expose their performance as an act and then to redirect their focus on the problem rather than the performance. To do this, look for the internal and external payoffs for the theatrical performer. Identify these to the client, then explain the negative effects that engaging in a performance has on their ability to achieve their goals. Teach your clients more-productive, more-effective ways to achieve their goals.

Example 1: The Story of Mika

Most clients are straightforward and visit cognitive therapists because they want help for personal problems, but occasionally a person asks for help for disingenuous reasons.

A case in point occurred with a woman named Mika from Sydney,

Australia, who sought out therapists simply because she liked to confound them. She was independently wealthy, hadn't worked for 15 years, and felt overwhelmingly bored. All she had to do in life was to search around for something interesting to do. She had been through the tennis, golf, and mahjong class circuit, and had taken all forms of strange Eastern meditations.

Finally she stumbled upon a new and more interesting thing to do. She would develop a weird, psychiatric ailment and go to different therapists pretending that she needed help. They, of course, couldn't help her since she only made up her problem, so she would leave and sadly say, "I was so much hoping that you could help me, but I see you can't. Oh my." The professionals felt upset; she felt triumphant.

After a while, however, she had performed her role so often that she came to believe it. She had learned to lie to herself, and had forgotten that she had made the whole thing up.

When she contacted a therapist, her beginning move was always the same. She called up in a terrified voice saying something like, "Doctor, you must help me! You are absolutely the only professional in Sydney who could possibly guide me through my horrible problem. I have heard such great things about you. I'm sure you're the only one who is smart enough to help. Please, please, make some room in your busy schedule. I'm on my last legs. Please. I will bless you, God will bless you, and I'll pay whatever you ask."

Well, with a gambit so expertly played, what professional could resist? Few! Since therapists are as subject to flattery as the next person, they usually said yes and swallowed her hook.

She then played her first session artistically. She presented a problem akin to multiple personalities, like the *Three Faces of Eve* or *Sibyl*. For one session she would come as Neurotic Mika, acting scared, depressed, confused, and passive. She cried, rung her hands and said, "Oh my! Oh my!" She sat with her head down and talked in a high-pitched whine. The next session she would walk in the room as Mika the Vamp, wearing a slinky dress and discussing in great detail her sexual encounters with rich and powerful men. She sounded suspiciously like Vivian Lee from *Gone with the Wind*. She even made passes at male doctors, which they, fortunately, dropped.

Before the middle sessions her therapists would eagerly anticipate whomever would show up next, and they weren't disappointed. Mika would come to the sessions dressed as a female version of Conan the Barbarian, speaking in short, guttural grunts and sprinkling her comments with four-letter words. The intent was obviously to shock her therapists, but the play was hard to carry off since your average psychologist is not intimately familiar with the dialogue of your average barbarian. She did as best she could, and a heroic effort it was.

Enough! Although therapists can be fooled many times by clients, their gullibility is not eternal. Accordingly, one experienced psychologist had had it, and began to confront her about her acting. He pointed out that it was not nice to fool your therapist. He told her that there are many people with real problems and that there aren't enough psychologists, so if she really didn't mind it would be nice if she made room for someone else. She strenuously rejected his suggestion, and mustering the combined power of her various personalities said: (Neurotic Mika) "I am much too nervous to leave," or (Vamp Mika) "Little old me playing a game? Why, fiddle dee dee," or (Barbaric Mika) "Fuck off! I pay; you listen!"

It was clear that the psychologist wasn't replying the way that her other therapists had. He hadn't gone on TV explaining the fascinating multiple personalities of Mika, or rushed to publish her case in a professional journal, probed into the ancient origins of these different personalities as some others had done. He was a disappointment to her, and she was about to consider finding a more appreciative audience, but the psychologist decided to try one last approach before ending the counseling. Maybe he could still parry her game and be of some small help. It occurred to him that a paradoxical approach might work, so he searched for a technique that would catch her off guard and that she would be unprepared to parry.

He realized that all of her previous therapists had treated her the same way and she had gotten used to it. They had all assumed that she was really one person with different personalities, and had all rejected her contention that she was three different people. All of them had insisted that either she was a deeply disturbed human being who had these multiple personalities inside her or an actress out to have some fun, which was his view. Either way, all had rejected the different personalities as being truly separate, while she pretended that she was three different people and vigorously countered any suggestion to the contrary. She claimed to have no recognition of the other personalities, but he wondered what would happen if a therapist took her at her word and pretended that each personality was in reality a different person.

Having no other ideas, he chose to treat her different personalities as separate people. He set up separate accounts for each of them, separate psychological testing sessions and separate homework assignments. He gave each personality different counseling appointments and billed each separately. This caused her some frustration, because when she called up as Neurotic Mika to change an appointment made by Vamp Mika the psychologist said that another client had scheduled the hour. She became even more annoyed when as Vamp Mika she was given the same arduous $1\frac{1}{2}$–hour–long psychological test that Neurotic Mika had already taken. When she hesitated to take it again, the psychologist asked, "What's the difficulty? You haven't taken this before have you? I know I've never given it to you." She was taken aback, but said, "No, of course not. It just looks long."

During a session with one of her characters he wouldn't let her refer to things that only the other personality could know. This became increasingly more frustrating to Mika because she needed to remember more and more about what each personality had told him. Finally he gave each personality extensive homework that would take an hour a day, and then at the next session he would go over the homework in great detail.

Soon the burden of maintaining three characters was too much for Mika. She was running out of energy so she tried one final gambit. She started to switch personalities in midsession. It was a nice try, but the psychologist learned to counter it by treating each character separately when they popped up. He pretended that each one had just arrived and that the other hadn't been there at all. So when the Vamp appeared she was asked, "How was your week?"—this after she had just finished explaining her week in great detail as Neurotic Mika. She was forced to come up with a whole new week of experiences to talk about.

The whole thing got to be too much work for Mika. At their last session she wasn't any particular personality, just Mika with all the different aspects that she really was anyway. With everybody there, together, they could talk straight. The psychologist told Mika that life is interesting only when we are struggling against some challenge. We can never be happy by making up phony challenges and phony plots; there are enough real problems for humanity to work on without creating counterfeit shams. For example, there's the environment, poverty, injustice, AIDS, cancer, prejudice, addictions, physical abuse, and all kinds of things that need some real work. The psychologist told her that she was bright, rich, and had a great deal of free time, and that she could make some real differences in some of these areas if she put her time and energy into them. He didn't call her on her multiple personality gambit, but she showed him she knew what he was talking about. She didn't admit to anything, but when she left she just said one word, "Thanks."

The last time the psychologist saw Mika she was appearing on a local TV station, speaking on behalf of saving the northern hairy-nosed wombat—or some such creature that was in danger of losing its habitat. All of Mika's personalities were there fighting for the wombat, and she seemed happy and content.

Example 2: The Story of Maurice

The following is an edited transcript of the opening session with Maurice, a very successful, attractive, divorced man in his thirties who had lots of women interested in him. Unfortunately, Maurice also had a history of ruined relationships, all of which ended the same way—with the woman leaving him for another man.

> MAURICE: I am in the same situation that I have been in many times before. It's always very painful and I need your help. . . . I am doing something wrong in my relationships. I get involved in a love relationship and it goes real well for a while, but then something starts happening: I get jealous, I get suspicious, I get manipulative, I get angry, I get childlike, and I start sabotaging the relationship. It always ends up the same—the woman gets disgusted and I get real hurt and feel real inferior.
>
> I have been going with a woman for about a year and a half now. She is a very attractive woman—bright, vivacious, spirited. She might be better than me, socially more popular, more gregarious. Men have always been interested in her. I think I feel inferior to her, and I am scared. She told me recently that she may be beginning to feel love towards another man. He is a macho type, rich, powerful, and has high–status friends. I am not. I am bright, creative, emotional—but I am not powerful.
>
> I could feel the pain and hurt in my gut when she said it. So as I often do in situations like this, I did a strange thing. I said, "Thank you for telling me; I really admire your honesty. Clearly there is only one thing to do in a situation like this. You must pursue the other relationship as hard as you can, you should

sleep with him; spend a lot of time with him and see what happens to your feelings towards him. See if you fall in love with him. And then, if you are, that will be it for us. If you're not, then we can go along as we were. I don't want to see you until you find out how you feel towards him." She protested, but I insisted that she should not see me until she makes up her mind. She said she loved me and wasn't sure about him and wanted to see me. I said, "Well, maybe we could, but we couldn't have any sex."

That's kind of a typical example of the problem I have. I do the opposite of what I want. I say and do things and I don't know why I do them. I keep doing things that go contrary to what would be to my advantage.

Even in the first session the client was beginning to see that he was engaging in some kind of self-sabotage. Later sessions revealed what this sabotage was about.

MAURICE: I play this martyr role with women. They hurt me or I get jealous but instead of yelling at them, I trick them. I pretend to be kind, wise, forgiving, interested only in their welfare. I show them that I will sacrifice myself for their happiness in true martyr fashion.

The game is really sickening. I say things like, "You go ahead and marry him. Be happy. I hope it works out. You are a wonderful person. I want to release you from me. I don't want to hold you down anymore.

It's totally bullshit. I don't believe a word of it. The payoff I get is twofold. First I get back at the woman for hurting me. I make her feel guilty, and she can't attack me back for being kind, caring and nice. Secondly, I fulfill my little heroic martyr image of myself by thinking what a terribly compassionate, kind, courageous man I am.

It took Maurice many more sessions to continue to explore the martyr self-sabotage. At times he would forget he was playing a role and act like a martyr again. But gradually he saw the performance and its damaging effects. He practiced being straight about his anger and started showing who he really was—a normal human being with fears, angers, and jealousy, not a sacrificial lamb for man—or woman—kind.

Comment

Clients will defend their beliefs angrily if they feel attacked, so it is best to build a good client–therapist rapport before exposing self-sabotage or role-playing. Moreover, if the therapist mistakes a real response for a dramatic sham, more guilt and confusion will be added to the client's already negative emotions.

Further Information

The name of the technique is taken from the title of Randi's (1982) book. Further readings in the area will give therapists more tools to deal with excessive self-deception in a variety of areas (see Franklin, 1994; Gardner, 1957, 1981, 1991; Holton, 1993; Kurtz, 1992; Randi, 1989, 1995). Also see the works of Carl Sagan—most relevant are: *The Demon-Haunted World: Science As a Candle in the Dark* (Sagan, 1995) and *Broca's Brain: Reflections on the Romance of Science* (Sagan, 1979). One magazine and its parent organization devotes itself to exposing flim-flam—*The Skeptical Inquirer: The Magazine for Science and Reason* and The Committee for the Scientific Investigation of Claim of the Paranormal, Buffalo, NY; http://www.csicop.org.

Social psychologists and sociologists have examined social performances, roles, and presentations. See the germinal work of Erving Goffman (1961, 1971, 1980, 1987).

One of the ways to distinguish the beginning therapist from the experienced therapist is the latter's use of paradoxical techniques. Raymond Corsini and Milton Erickson, two highly experienced therapists, use paradoxical methods extensively (see Corsini, 1957, 1981, 1994, 1998). Corsini is the editor for the encyclopedias of psychology (Corsini & Ozaki, 1984; Corsini & Wedding, 1987). Erickson's work can be found in many sources (Bandler & Grinder, 1996; Erickson, 1982; Erickson & Rossi, 1981; Havens, 1985; Lankton, 1990; Lankton & Lankton, 1983; Rossi, 1980; Rossi & Ryan, 1985).

COGNITIVE RESTRUCTURING THERAPY WITH ADDICTED CLIENTS

CO-AUTHORED WITH PATRICIA GEHLHAAR, D.PSY., SYDNEY, AUSTRALIA

Principles

Our brand of cognitive restructuring therapy makes a crucial distinction between the treatment of drug and alcohol abuse and the treatment of dependency. It views the causes, cognitions, and methods of treatment for both as not only different but in some ways quite opposite. Clients who abuse drugs (we include alcohol as a drug) can be treated with the standard cognitive techniques presented in this and other cognitive therapy books, but those who are seriously physically dependent require some major treatment adjustments.

Drug Abuse

The typical model for clients who abuse chemicals is negative reinforcement (see figure 12.3). They experience a negative emotion such as anxiety, fear, depression, or anger and discover that these feelings are reduced or eliminated when they use drugs (escape conditioning). After many repetitions they learn that they often don't experience the emotion if they take the drug first (avoidance conditioning). Chemically abusing clients often resort to drugs in response to life crises.

Drug abuse may be entirely learned. People are taught to use excessively by modeling others in their early environments whose drug use became connected to various external stimuli. The drug abuser often

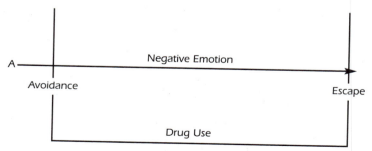

FIGURE 12.3 Negative reinforcement model for alcohol and drug abuse

shows premorbid psychological disorders such as antisocial behavior, poor impulse control, highly generalized anxiety or depression, and low frustration tolerance. They frequently have had a series of critical negative events (often sexual or physical abuse) occurring in childhood and adolescence.

The cognitive components of the abuse model consist of two elements. First, the initial cognitions may elicit negative emotions. If the therapist changes these cognitions, the negative emotions won't occur or will occur only at a reduced level. Therefore, clients will have less reason to escape or avoid (Clarke & Saunders, 1988; Gallant, 1987). Second, the cognitions may intervene between the stimulus (critical environmental event) (A) and the response (drug use) (C^b). Different cognitive therapists emphasize different key cognitions for the chemical abuser. Ellis stresses low frustration tolerance: "I can't stand feeling upset, and I must remove these feeling immediately by drugs" (Ellis, McInerney, DiGiuseppe, & Yeager, 1988, and Ellis personal communication, August 10, 1989). Aaron Beck emphasizes lack of coping skills: "I don't know how to handle this problem. If I take some drugs I can forget about it" (Beck, Wright, Newman, & Liese, 1993).

Drug–abusing clients benefit from cognitive therapy (REBT, cognitive restructuring, and cognitive–behavioral). Unlike dependent clients, they may learn to drink socially and may be good candidates for controlled–use programs.

Drug Dependency

Drug or alcohol dependency (figure 12.4) is an entirely different matter from drug abuse. Seriously chemically dependent clients do not use drugs simply to cope with negative emotions or stressful situations; they use drugs to remove the beginnings of withdrawal symptoms that their physical dependency has produced.

There is a strong physical component to clients' dependency. Ini-

FIGURE 12.4 Physical–dependency model for drug and alcohol addiction

tially, their physiological systems neutralize and eliminate alcohol or drugs so that they may recover quickly, but prolonged use puts more pressure on their systems. As dependent clients continue pumping alcohol or drugs into their system, their various organs—particularly their livers—spend more and more time trying to eliminate the drugs.

After their physiology becomes continually overloaded, an important event occurs. Their systems stop treating the drug as a foreign substance and start regarding the artificial chemicals as natural substances necessary for homeostasis. Chemically addicted clients have to use more and more of the drug to return to a feeling of normalcy. When the drug's presence falls below the level that their bodies demand they have to take in more in order to return to homeostasis. As one addict told me, "It's as if my body gave up fighting. While initially it said, 'Take this drug away, I don't want it.' Later it told me, 'I give in! You want drugs? You can have them! But now you're not only going to want them, you're going to need them!'"

Once addicts become physically dependent on drugs, they can never become independent. Drug–dependent clients cannot choose to use socially; they can only choose to stop. In order to cope with their illness they must not use at all. If they continue to take drugs, they will find they can't use enough to be satiated. Their bodies will crave the drugs more and more, and they will no longer be able to drink or use for pleasure or thrills, or to remove negative emotions. Their use will have become a physical compulsion driven by the hope that they can temporarily lessen their ever-worsening withdrawal symptoms. Unless they stop, they may drink or use drugs until they die.

Cognitive restructuring therapy, as opposed to cognitive therapy in general, hypothesizes a bimodal distribution for drug and alcohol problems (figure 12.5 and table 12.1).

The left side of the distribution represents abusers. Abusers often are neurotic, have premorbid personality disorders, little genetic or family history, fewer coping skills, low self–esteem, and low tolerance for frustration. Abuse clients often take drugs in order to relieve negative emotions that they feel they can't cope with. These clients can often be taught to control their drug use; cognitive psychotherapy, as well as other psychotherapies, can help these clients cope with their emotional problems without using drugs.

The right side of the distribution shows drug dependency. These clients show a strong genetic predisposition and usually have three or more relatives with a similar problem. They present a variety of premorbid personalities, coping skills, and frustration tolerances. Depen-

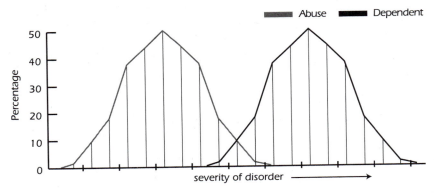

FIGURE 12.5 Bimodal distribution of alcohol and drug abuse and alcohol and drug dependency

dent clients use drugs in a great variety of trigger situations rather than just when they are stressed; they show grandiose denial, may have withdrawal symptoms, and have a high tolerance for their drug of choice. They usually do not benefit from traditional cognitive techniques but instead require the specialized cognitive therapy suggested below.

If the above analysis is correct it may appear that there is little the cognitive therapist can do to help dependent clients. While these

TABLE 12.1
Characteristics of Abuse and Dependency

ABUSE	*DEPENDENCY*
premorbid personality	varied premorbid personality
lack of concordance genetics	genetic predisposition
neurotic history	no consistent neurotic history
antisocial before use	antisocial after use
can learn controlled drinking	must abstain
fewer coping skills	varied coping skills
low self–esteem	grandiose self–esteem
low frustration tolerance	varied frustration tolerance
aversive S_d & CS preceding use	varied S_d & CS
no significant family history	significant family history
low tolerance for drugs	high tolerance
few withdrawal symptoms	many withdrawal symptoms

clients can never drink or use drugs in a controlled fashion, they can stop the progression of their addiction. Although they have failed many times, with help from the therapist using a specialized cognitive restructuring treatment, they can stop.

Because the treatment of abuse is described in a number of excellent publications (see Further Information), we will not repeat the procedures here. Instead, we will spend the remainder of this chapter discussing the unique treatment required for chemical dependency. The approach is called "cognitive confrontation," and it requires working on a totally different list of cognitions than most cognitive therapists are in the habit of using with drug abusers.

Assumptions for the Treatment of Drug and Alcohol Dependency

The reason that addicts and alcoholics are addicted to drugs is physical, but the reason that they take the drug is psychological. Addicts have learned to use and they can unlearn it. How? Observe the chart.

$$A \longrightarrow C$$
$$\text{Craving} \qquad\qquad \text{Using drugs or alcohol}$$

Before addicts use they have a craving for the drug. They may be strongly aware of it or they may not notice it at all, but it is there. The alcoholic craves alcohol so strongly and the heroin addict craves heroin so powerfully because the body notices a drop in its usual level of the drug; the addict feels the pressure to get the level back to the amount they had been taking. The cravings also get stronger when addicts experience situations in which they drank or used in the past, such as when they felt stress, were depressed, or had relationship or employment problems. Whenever one of these situations occurs, their craving increases.

The addicts' physical cravings are not the sole cause of their problem; it is not simply an A $\longrightarrow$ C theory as previously shown. Cravings alone do not equal drug intake. Not *all* alcoholics and addicts give in to their cravings. There are hundreds of thousands of chemically dependent clients around the world who have the same powerful cravings, the same frustrations, the same fights with their spouses, the same job stresses. Many of them have similar genetic histories but they don't use when they feel their cravings. A visit to some well established AA or NA meetings will reveal many chemically dependent people with 10 or more years of sobriety who have felt the craving hundreds of times but haven't picked up a drink or used a drug. If cravings cause use and all addicts have the cravings, why don't they all use or drink?

The answer is that the A ⟶ C theory is wrong. There is a missing element. The correct formula is:

$$A \xrightarrow{\hspace{3cm}} B \xrightarrow{\hspace{4cm}} C$$

A	B	C
Craving	Belief	Drug Use

As the formula shows, it is the B (what addicts and alcoholics say to themselves about their cravings) that causes them to use. The B can stand for many things: their *expectations* ("I'll stop after a couple of beers"), their *selected memories* ("What great times I used to have in the bar"), their *self talk* ("I need this to relax"), their *excuses* ("I really meant to stop"), *denial* ("I can manage my life perfectly well even though I use cocaine"), *overgeneralizations* ("Because I was once able to drink socially [20 years ago], I still can"), *false predictions* ("I know I can control my drinking or drugging in the future") Whatever they think, it is their thoughts about their cravings *rather than* the cravings themselves that cause them to take the drink or use the drug.

One of the major attitudes that needs to be changed is called the stimulation syndrome. Addicts, alcoholics, and other people who have addictions (such as gamblers) have developed a love affair with emotional extremes. Their addictions have caused them to spend much of their lives on an emotional roller coaster. Their emotions have ranged from ecstasy to despair, from grandiose self-confidence to suicidal depression, from blissful contentment to psychological terror. With all these mood swings, alcoholics and addicts have gotten used to "the rush." When they stop using, their mood gradually moves toward normal. This calming down would be a wonderful relief for the rest of us, but to the recovering addict calmness is experienced as a great emptiness. Life seems boring and flat. Since they have spent much of their lives in the pursuit of exaggerated emotions, they have a strong visceral discomfort with harmony and emotional balance. This attitude can be a major barrier in their recovery.

For example, an alcoholic client named Nigel had a pattern of going on and off the wagon. He would attend alcohol treatment programs, get sober for 6 months, improve his relationships, and start working again. With all aspects of his life running smoothly, he would start integrating disharmony by picking fights with his wife, committing petty crimes that got him in trouble with the law, and showing up late for work, thus putting his job in jeopardy. Finally he would end up drinking again, blaming his relapse on all of the trouble he was in. Why did he bother going through this whole charade?

He may have simply wanted to drink again and created all of his troubles to give him an excuse. But another reason is the stimulation syndrome. A lifetime of using and drinking caused Nigel to get used to a dramatic lifestyle of emotional highs and lows, a chronic cycle of crisis situations. He felt that he was only half alive unless he was struggling with one emotional crisis or another. Normal emotional feelings were unacceptable to him; he felt he was being emotionally deprived. He created problems to stir his life up again so he could feel "the rush."

Nigel's attitude was the real culprit. He believed that life was sup-posed to be a series of triumphs and tragedies, and when these stopped because of his recovery he felt he had to liven things up again. This belief led to his relapse.

Since addicts' beliefs produce their drug use, they have to change their thoughts in order to begin their recovery. No matter how strong their cravings, alcoholics and addicts *don't have to use.*

Method

1. Determine whether your client abuses drugs or is dependent on them. There are many possible ways to make this decision. There are standard screening tests, such as the MAST, CAGE, DQEAA and SADQ, but they all suffer from the same limitation of all paper–and–pencil tests have—the lack of candor in clients' responses.

The Langton test (figure 12.6) increases accuracy because it is based on a structured interview that allows the counselor to ask detailed fol-low–up questions. The test is given orally to clients and scored by the examiner. It can be given in groups or individually.

The Langton test is based on the *DSM-III, DSM-III-R, DSM-IV* and has two columns and four sections. For a diagnosis of dependency to be made the client must score in both columns.

Scoring. The total number of check marks are added for each column and summed into a grand total. Number of DUIs and family members with addiction problems are added to the score.

Results. The mean grand total for dependent clients is $X = 27.59$; SD $= 6.54$; $N = 321$ (cross–cultural sample from Australia, Washington

Name: _____   Date: _____

Langton Test

USE	TOLERANCE
☐ Weight problems, ulcer ☐ M.D. told you to cut down ☐ Daily use ☐ Binges lasting 2+ days ☐ Could not control ☐ Blackouts ☐ Failed to stop ☐ Early opener ☐ Other illnesses because of use	☐ Tolerance (Need for marked increase in amount of drug to get effect)

SOCIAL AND WORK	WITHDRAWALS
☐ Off work ☐ Driving accidents ☐ Other accidents ☐ Arrested in public places ☐ Arguments at home ☐ Violence—assaults, damage ☐ DUIs ☐ Lost job ☐ Divorced or separated ☐ Money worries ☐ Injuries ☐ No. of family members addicted	☐ Tremors ☐ Nausea & vomiting ☐ Malaise ☐ Tachycardia, sweating, + BP ☐ Anxiety ☐ Depression ☐ Rage ☐ Headaches ☐ Swelling—skin, face, legs ☐ Night terrors ☐ Delirium ☐ Dementia ☐ Hallucinations ☐ Delusions
Total =	Total =

FIGURE 12.6 The Langton Test for severe alcohol and drug dependency and scoring and interpretation procedures

State, and Hawaii). In the subcategories the mean number of checked items for patients are as follows: Pathological use—X = 8.27; SD = 2.24. Impaired Social or Work Functioning—X = 8.59; SD = 2.61. Tolerance = 98%. Withdrawal Symptoms—X = 7.86; SD = 3.49.

Interpretation. A score of 10 or less clearly puts clients into the abuse category, since less than 2% of dependent clients would achieve such a result (usually only young dependent clients beginning their drug use). A chemical abusing client usually reports one family member with an addiction problem, while a dependent client reports a mean of 5.03 (but there is a large standard deviation, SD = 4.83). No matter what the overall score, the client needs to present some signs of toler-ance or withdrawal symptoms (column 2) in order to achieve a diag-nosis of dependency.

Eighty–six percent of the alcoholic patients in the sample reported blackouts; 68% were separated or divorced because of their drinking; 63% had been charged with driving while intoxicated; 45% had been arrested for violent or assaultive behavior when drunk.

We found that one of the major discrimination questions is the clients' ability to control their drug use. Subjects were asked, "How many times were you able to limit your intake of drugs or alcohol when you tried to control your use?" The abuser client stated they could control their intake 98/100 while the dependent patient could only remember one time out of every 358. Many of the dependent clients said they had never bothered to try to limit their intake at all.

2. If your client scores in the dependent category, find the Bs that maintain this dependency.

Before you can change clients' thoughts about drugs or alcohol you need to have an accurate list of the core beliefs that may be intimately related to their use. After trying several lists we have discovered the following 42 beliefs to be most revealing; much of the therapy we do with chemically dependent clients is based on changing these 42 beliefs. We discovered these cognitions by using the following proce-dures.

Method. A large list of alcoholics' and addicts' self–statements was compiled by therapists with extensive clinical experience with chem-ical addiction. Each statement was converted to a strongly–agree to strongly–disagree Likert scale. The statements were then given to two large sample groups of chemically dependent clients. The first sample comprised clients who were still drinking or using (N = 285). The sec-ond sample included clients who were at various stages of their recov-ery, ranging from immediate, posttreatment, to over 10 years (N = 230).

Results. Forty–two beliefs distinguished the using from the recover-ing group of clients. These were incorporated into the Mc Mullin–Gehlhaar Addiction Attitude test (MGAA) (table 12.2). (The test is used for chemically dependent clients only. It *cannot* be used for clients who abuse drugs or alcohol because the appropriate answers would be dif-ferent for this population.)

Administration. It can be given in groups or individually. The MGAA is read to the clients, the items are explained, and any questions are

TABLE 12.2

Mc Mullin-Gehlhaar Addiction Attitude Test (MGAA)

Name:_____   Date:_____

CIRCLE WHAT YOU BELIEVE

1. I am not responsible for my drinking or drugging.
   Strongly Agree   Agree   Neutral   Disagree   Strongly Disagree

2. I can stop using through willpower alone.
   Strongly Agree   Agree   Neutral   Disagree   Strongly Disagree

3. A couple of drinks are good for me.
   Strongly Agree   Agree   Neutral   Disagree   Strongly Disagree

4. I can't stop, so why bother?
   Strongly Agree   Agree   Neutral   Disagree   Strongly Disagree

5. A little bit can't hurt me.
   Strongly Agree   Agree   Neutral   Disagree   Strongly Disagree

6. I need to use to have fun.
   Strongly Agree   Agree   Neutral   Disagree   Strongly Disagree

7. It's normal to use the amount I have used in the past.
   Strongly Agree   Agree   Neutral   Disagree   Strongly Disagree

8. Bad feelings (fear, sadness, anger, etc.) cause me to use too much.
   Strongly Agree   Agree   Neutral   Disagree   Strongly Disagree

9. The best way to stop feeling bad is to use.
   Strongly Agree   Agree   Neutral   Disagree   Strongly Disagree

10. Being high or drunk feels good.
    Strongly Agree   Agree   Neutral   Disagree   Strongly Disagree

11. I can handle my drugs better than others can.
    Strongly Agree   Agree   Neutral   Disagree   Strongly Disagree

12. I need the drug or drink to feel more self-confident.
    Strongly Agree   Agree   Neutral   Disagree   Strongly Disagree

13. Drugs are a good way to remove boredom.
    Strongly Agree   Agree   Neutral   Disagree   Strongly Disagree

14. I can cure my drug problem with a little self-discipline.
    Strongly Agree   Agree   Neutral   Disagree   Strongly Disagree

TABLE 12.2 (CONTINUED)
Mc Mullin-Gehlhaar Addiction Attitude Test (MGAA)

15. I can control my use if I try hard enough.
    Strongly Agree   *Agree*   *Neutral*   *Disagree*   *Strongly Disagree*

16. It's my fault that I am addicted.
    Strongly Agree   *Agree*   *Neutral*   *Disagree*   *Strongly Disagree*

17. Something inside of me takes over and makes me use chemicals.
    Strongly Agree   *Agree*   *Neutral*   *Disagree*   *Strongly Disagree*

18. Addiction is just a bad habit.
    Strongly Agree   *Agree*   *Neutral*   *Disagree*   *Strongly Disagree*

19. Outside catastrophes (losing a job, spouse leaving, being in a hospital) cause people to use drugs or to drink too much.
    Strongly Agree   *Agree*   *Neutral*   *Disagree*   *Strongly Disagree*

20. I can cope better with life by using chemicals.
    Strongly Agree   *Agree*   *Neutral*   *Disagree*   *Strongly Disagree*

21. Using drugs or drinking is a good way to get back at someone.
    Strongly Agree   *Agree*   *Neutral*   *Disagree*   *Strongly Disagree*

22. I have to give in to my craving.
    Strongly Agree   *Agree*   *Neutral*   *Disagree*   *Strongly Disagree*

23. You can be cured of addiction.
    Strongly Agree   *Agree*   *Neutral*   *Disagree*   *Strongly Disagree*

24. The best way to stop withdrawal symptoms is to take more drugs.
    Strongly Agree   *Agree*   *Neutral*   *Disagree*   *Strongly Disagree*

25. My drug problem or my drinking problem is not that serious.
    Strongly Agree   *Agree*   *Neutral*   *Disagree*   *Strongly Disagree*

26. I can always predict that I won't lose control over myself when I use.
    Strongly Agree   *Agree*   *Neutral*   *Disagree*   *Strongly Disagree*

27. I am a better lover when I am drunk or high.
    Strongly Agree   *Agree*   *Neutral*   *Disagree*   *Strongly Disagree*

28. Social pressure made me drink or use too much.
    Strongly Agree   *Agree*   *Neutral*   *Disagree*   *Strongly Disagree*

29. I need a drug or a drink to keep my emotions from overpowering me.
    Strongly Agree   *Agree*   *Neutral*   *Disagree*   *Strongly Disagree*

TABLE 12.2 (CONTINUED)
Mc Mullin-Gehlhaar Addiction Attitude Test (MGAA)

30. I can recover without help if I try hard enough.

    Strongly Agree   *Agree*   *Neutral*   *Disagree*   *Strongly Disagree*

31. I need a drink or a drug to feel better.

    Strongly Agree   *Agree*   *Neutral*   *Disagree*   *Strongly Disagree*

32. A person who works hard earns some drugs or a few drinks.

    Strongly Agree   *Agree*   *Neutral*   *Disagree*   *Strongly Disagree*

33. Using chemicals is a good way to escape from life's stresses.

    Strongly Agree   *Agree*   *Neutral*   *Disagree*   *Strongly Disagree*

34. I should be happy all the time.

    Strongly Agree   *Agree*   *Neutral*   *Disagree*   *Strongly Disagree*

35. I am not an addict or an alcoholic.

    Strongly Agree   *Agree*   *Neutral*   *Disagree*   *Strongly Disagree*

36. You can't tell me anything about my addiction that I don't know.

    Strongly Agree   *Agree*   *Neutral*   *Disagree*   *Strongly Disagree*

37. We should get what we want in life.

    Strongly Agree   *Agree*   *Neutral*   *Disagree*   *Strongly Disagree*

38. Being drunk or high uncovers an individual's real personality.

    Strongly Agree   *Agree*   *Neutral*   *Disagree*   *Strongly Disagree*

39. Psychological problems cause addiction.

    Strongly Agree   *Agree*   *Neutral*   *Disagree*   *Strongly Disagree*

40. The best way to handle problems is not to think about them.

    Strongly Agree   *Agree*   *Neutral*   *Disagree*   *Strongly Disagree*

41. I am more creative when I use or drink.

    Strongly Agree   *Agree*   *Neutral*   *Disagree*   *Strongly Disagree*

42. There are more important things in life to work on than my addiction.

    Strongly Agree   *Agree*   *Neutral*   *Disagree*   *Strongly Disagree* answered. Clients have the items in front of them and circle one of the five ratings after each item.

Scoring. Five points are given for "Strongly Agree" and one point for "Strongly Disagree." Unmarked items are scored as "Neutral" and are worth three points. Mean score for nonrecovering, alcohol and drug-dependent clients is X = 110.5; SD = 16.6. Recovering clients' scores varied depending upon the length of their recovery (see figure 12.7). The therapists can translate the raw scores into percentiles using the mean and standard deviation.

Interpretation. It's important to realize that the norm group of the MGAA is *clinical.* A score of 110 places the client at the 50th percentile of chronic drug- and alcohol-dependent clients. Of all drug and alcohol clients this group can be considered the most severe (Jellinek's gamma category, Jellinek, 1960). The average client in this group has been using drugs for many years, shows severe withdrawal symptoms, has numerous legal problems, and has attempted and failed in many previous drug treatment programs. The higher the score the more damaging the client's attitudes and the farther away from recovery the client is. The therapist can use the MGAA to determine how far a client has progressed in recovery (figure 12.7) by comparing the individual score to the mean of clients at different stages.

3. Go over the MGAA test results with your client and explain the core factors that keep clients drinking or using (see figure 3.4, p. 87 for a graphic representation of these factors).

Five factors have been abstracted from the test. When I explain them to clients I simplify the explanation by drawing an animal that describes each factor. I tell clients, "Let's see what type of animal you are telling yourself that keeps you drinking/using." (Look at the test.) "Ah yes. You are a fox."

Factor 1. The Fox

I can control my drinking or drugging anytime I wish. I have willpower over it. I can do it on my own without help. ("I am clever like a fox.")

Factor 2. The Lamb

I am not responsible for my use. The devil made me do it. Others are to blame. It's poor potty training. ("I am helpless as a lamb.")

Pre = immediately before beginning drug treatment.
Mid = halfway through inpatient drug treatment.
Post = immediately following inpatient treatment.

One year to 10+ = years of sobriety based on the client's
anniversary date. Please note that the lowest possible score
on the MGAA test is 42.

FIGURE 12.7 The mean MGAA scores for chronic drug- and alcohol-dependent clients at different times during their recovery

Factor 3. The Pig
It still feels good to use. I still like it. I am more creative.

Factor 4. The Ostrich
My use is not a big problem. It doesn't really hurt me. Nothing to
worry about.

Factor 5. The Butterfly
I need the drug to make me feel better. I can't cope with life without it. ("I am fragile like a butterfly.")

4. Use various cognitive therapy techniques to help clients change
   their maladaptive beliefs. Focus particularly on the items on the
   MGAA that clients strongly agreed with.

Group sessions and therapeutic classes that describe why the beliefs
are false are generally more effective than individual sessions. In addition, use manuals and pamphlets that discuss why the 42 beliefs are
false (see particularly Mc Mullin & Gehlhaar, 1990a). In outpatient

groups provide a mix of clients (some beginning recovery and some with a year or more of sobriety). The more experienced clients can model how to dispute some of the thoughts. Require AA and NA meetings because these organizations dispute similar beliefs.

*Example 1. Client Manual**

Beliefs
1. I am not responsible for my drinking or drugging
17. Something inside of me takes over and makes me use chemicals.

Example
Ian, one of our clients, heard our talk about drug addiction being a biochemical problem that he had probably inherited. He went home and told his wife that she was wrong to blame him for using, since it wasn't his fault in the first place.

Counter
Your dependency on drugs is physical, but your actual use is not. Taking a drink or a drug is a voluntary behavior. Nothing inside or outside of you *makes you* drink. You do it! You go into the pub, sit on the bar stool, look at the selection, order a drink, pay the bartender, lift up the glass, bring it to your lips, and swallow it. No craving, reflex, compulsion, emotion, conditioning, disease, or other factor makes you engage in this complex behavior. All of these things may incline you to drink, but ultimately it is you saying "yes" that starts the process. The devil doesn't make you do it. You are responsible! Only you can stop!

Beliefs
3. A couple of drinks are good for me.
5. A little bit can't hurt me.

Example
In one of our groups a client named Ted said that a doctor had told him that some alcohol was good for people. The doctor thought a couple of glasses would help him relax and thin his blood, making

---

*The following excepts are based on a manual we hand out to our addicted patients. (Mc Mullin & Gehlhaar, 1990a). Reprinted with permission of the authors.

him less likely to develop hardening of the arteries.

Although Ted wasn't in the habit of listening to medical advice, he had become highly enthusiastic about this lesson and had stored the information in the deepest recesses of his brain. He would dredge it up whenever he needed it (mostly when he was thirsty, which was most of the time), but he did the doctor one better. He reasoned that if two were good, then four would be better, eight would be terrific, sixteen would be outstanding, and so forth. Following that reasoning, Ted should have had the softest arteries and the most relaxed temperament of anyone on the planet. He didn't!

Counter

When was the last time you had just two drinks of anything?

Beliefs

14. I can cure my drug problem with a *little* self-discipline
15. I can control my use if I try hard enough

Example

Many hospitals offer intensive, inpatient treatment programs for alcoholics and addicts. We conduct two group–therapy sessions in the morning, two classes in the afternoon, and meetings in the evenings. The treatment runs for 6 days a week. Patients are allowed no distractions, holidays, or days off. They must concentrate fully on their recovery, and it's a lot of work. Over the years we have found some patients don't want to do the work; they think that a little self-discipline is all they need.

Counter

Chemical addiction is one of the most difficult problems you can have. Compared with some other troubles like phobias, depression, anxiety reactions, and the like, fewer people recover. Why? The answer is simple—you fight the treatment. Phobic and anxious patients are usually so miserable that they listen carefully, try to be honest, and do their homework religiously. But *not you* and *your fellow addicts!* You are likely to evade, distort, ignore, not listen, refuse to do the homework, and in general try every method you can think of to sabotage help.

You are more likely to sabotage *not* because you are inherently sicker, lazier, more dishonest, or less intelligent or worthwhile than others—you do it because of the nature of your addiction.

Being an addict is like having two tape–recorded messages in your brain. One tells you not to use. This is the message that got you to pick up our manual; it's your sensible, realistic side. But you have another tape; it comes from your craving for drugs. It tells you to use no matter what.

John, a client in one of our groups, gave a good description of his using message; he called it the lizard. It is the craving an addict has for a drug. He had read a story several years ago that described something like the following:

> A man died and went to Heaven. It was just as he had imagined, with golden gates and St. Peter sitting behind a desk in the front. Thousands of people milled around the gates trying to get in. But there was something different about them—all of them had a little lizard sitting on their shoulder, and all the lizards were hopping up and down and yelling in high squeaky voices into the ears of the people. They were saying things like: "You're in the wrong place, it's a trick, don't go near the man at the desk because he will try to trap you here. This place will hurt you; listen to me, I'm the only one on your side. I'm your friend, don't listen to anyone else, get out of here before it's too late." The man found that he also had a lizard that was shouting the same kinds of things. The man walked up to St. Peter and said, *"I* doubt if you will let me in. *I* have committed many sins that I'm sorry for so *I* am probably not good enough to get into heaven." But St. Peter said, "No worries. Everybody is a sinner. Anybody who wants to come in is allowed and is welcome. There is only one rule, but *I* can't tell you what it is; you have to find out for yourself." So the man started to walk though the gates. Halfway in he hit something. It was like an invisible shield and he couldn't get through. He kept on trying but had no luck, for he kept bumping against the shield. Finally he saw an angel on the other side, who pointed to a little sign on the top of the gate. It read: *Lizards must be restrained.* The man put a muzzle on his lizard and walked in.

All addicts and alcoholics are born with lizards on their shoulders. They usually have a father, mother, grandparent, uncle, or aunt who also had one on their shoulders. The lizard lies dormant until the person starts drinking or experimenting with drugs around the age of 14 or so; then the lizard springs to life. Initially it acts like a spoiled brat and screeches, "I want some dope. I want a drink." If it doesn't get what it wants it throws a temper tantrum and pleads and begs until it does. But the more the lizard is given a drug, the more it demands and yells for another, then another, then another.

As you get older and more experienced with the lizard you start telling it to shut up, because you remember what happened when you fed it before. But your lizard is smart and comes back in various disguises to fool you. Sometimes it dresses up as your mom (Mother lizard) and starts whispering things like: "Poor dear. I'm only trying to help you. You are all tensed up; you need some drugs to relax." Sometimes it disguises itself as a macho friend (Rambo lizard) and says "What are you some kind of wimp? Of course you can handle a couple of drinks. Stop being such a chicken shit!" Sometimes it clothes itself as a Shakespearean actor (Hamlet lizard) and makes a speech like. "Oh, life is such toil, pain and misery, we need some drugs to endure our meaningless fate." And sometimes your lizard gets really sneaky and appears disguised as a therapist (Sigmund Freud lizard). It tells you "Let's go into the pub, sit down and order a coke, just to show how strong we have gotten over the power of drugs." (For more lizard disguises, see Mc Mullin, Gehlhaar, & James, 1990.)

No matter what trick, con, flim–flam, or lie the lizard tells you, it wants just one thing—the drug—and it will keep pressuring you over and over again until it gets it.

You can never get rid of your lizard, but if you stop giving it drinks it will shrivel up and only rarely bother you. Ultimately you have to control it by never giving in; just a little discipline isn't going to do it. You do have the power, for you are stronger than your lizard. You must, however, see through its many disguises and catch it in its lies. The best way to stop a conning lizard is to know the con.

Belief
20. I can cope better with life by using chemicals

Example
Life had always been difficult for Bruce. His father had abandoned the family when he was three years old, and he had been pushed around by an alcoholic stepfather, two older brothers who used cocaine, and other bullies. Things didn't hurt so badly when he drank and used pills. Life seemed a little bit less overwhelming and a little more manageable with the chemicals.

Counter
If you look up the word "cope" in a dictionary, you will find it means "To contend, to strive, to struggle with." It comes from the old

French word "couper" which means "to strike a blow." In fact, the old definition of the word meant to engage in combat.

When you use alcohol or pills or drugs to handle life's problems you aren't coping with life. You aren't struggling, contending with difficulties, or striking a blow; you are doing the opposite. You are running away as fast as you can. Drinking and taking drugs is a yellow–bellied, chicken–hearted, cowardly way of facing life that does nothing to conquer problems. Using hides problems under a chemical security blanket.

To cope properly with life you must engage in combat. You must attack your problems and strike a blow against them. Sometimes you win, sometimes you lose, but you will be far stronger for having engaged in the battle. The biggest bully you have to fight is your own addiction. It is a powerful adversary. Stop trying to escape. Fight back!

Belief

26. I can always predict that I won't lose control over myself when I use.

Example

Roy listened to the stories other clients told in a group session. He heard how other alcoholics and addicts had assaulted loved ones, damaged property, and engaged in other outrageous behavior when they were drunk or high—things that they wouldn't have even thought about doing when they were clean or sober.

Yet Roy felt he was different. He was absolutely sure that no matter how high or drunk he got, he would never assault his wife, or abuse his kids, or generally lose control of his behavior.

Counter

Drugs and alcohol affect the parts of your brain that control your emotions and your primitive behaviors (the subcortical areas). Once the chemical gets into these areas you can't control yourself—in fact you won't even bother to try. No matter how horrible or stupid it may seem to you now, you could do literally anything when you are high, and you could spend the rest of your life trying to make amends for what you've done.

Over the years addicts and alcoholics have told us many stories about what they did when they were high or drunk. All of the following stories are true.

- A man who was high wandered across a railroad yard and decided to take a nap. He lay down with his feet across a track. A train came. He didn't even know what had happened until he found himself in a hospital with his feet bandaged. All of his toes had been cut off.
- A professional man had always wanted to travel. It was his life's dream but he had never made enough money to be able to afford it. Eventually, he applied to attend an overseas conference. His firm gave him a round–trip, nonnegotiable airline ticket and prepaid his accommodation. It was a once–in–a–lifetime opportunity because the financing was difficult to get. He went to the airport with his friends to have some farewell drinks in the VIP lounge, got drunk, and never made it to the plane. His funding was canceled and he never took his trip.
- An alcoholic from Sydney, Australia had an argument with his wife. He went down to the pub with the intention of drinking. He didn't remember anything after the first couple of drinks until he came out of a blackout 28 hours later. He found himself on a plane bound for Vancouver, Canada. He was flying at 35,000 feet somewhere past Tahiti. He had no idea how he got there, but he looked through his pockets and found a return ticket dated a week later. He had some Australian money, his passport, and some loose change. He had no idea whether he had any luggage with him so on arrival in Vancouver he checked at the luggage carousel. There he found only two things: his golf clubs and an extra pair of socks.
- A man had been charged on three separate occasions for driving under the influence. His license had been suspended for three years and he'd been given a good behavior bond with a warning that he would be imprisoned if he offended again. He was at work one day and had been drinking continuously. As the day progressed he became increasingly agitated about the staff pilfering goods from the firm. The more he drank the more convinced he became that it was his duty as foreman to report the thefts to the authorities. So he climbed into his car and drove to the local police station. Before he could say a word he was arrested, locked up, and his car impounded.
- A man was known to all his friends as a sensitive, compassionate person. They'd never heard him say an unkind word or seen him do an unkind action when sober. One day he went on a huge bender. He dragged himself onto a cargo ship out of San Francisco bound for Singapore. He didn't know why; he just did it. When he got there he wandered around for weeks in a total drunken stupor.

He finally found himself traveling on a train in India. He sat in third class, which on Indian trains means people hang all over the roofs and on the sides. He sat by an open window and the train started to pull out from the station. An Indian was running beside the train and leapt onto the side, grabbing the windowsill next to the man. The train picked up speed and the Indian signaled that he wanted to be pulled in. The man said to himself, "Wouldn't it be interesting to see the expression in a man's eyes right before he's about to die?" So he started to push the Indian out of the window. As the Indian begged to be pulled in, he put his hand on the stranger's head and pushed as hard as he could. The Indian loosened his grip, and finally was only holding on to the windowsill by his fingertips. The man slammed the window on the Indian's fingers and started to press down hard. Then, as suddenly as he'd started, he stopped, looked startled, and said to himself, "What am I doing?!" He opened the window and pulled in the man just in time.

Example 2. Therapist's Style

While in Australia I worked in a major public hospital for alcohol and drug addiction. There I met psychologist Patricia Gehlhaar, one of Australia's premier addiction therapists. We were counseling alcoholics who had relapsed. There are scores of books and programs that suggest causes for relapses but I asked Pat for her opinion. She said, "Hear how they describe their relapses. Listen to their language."
I took her advice and heard patients make statements like the following:

"I slipped."
"My AA meeting started to drop off."
"The booze tripped me up."
"I fell off the wagon."
"The bottle grabbed me."
"It caught up with me again."
"I got hooked."

I learned that Pat was right. Their language showed why they had relapsed and why they were susceptible to relapsing. Their words described attitudes of victimization and helplessness. Put all of their phrases together and one finds the common core theme: The patients looked at their lives as a series of *uncontrollable* events. Their phrases suggested that they thought they weren't responsible, that it wasn't their fault. Phrases like "I slipped," "I fell off the wagon," "It caught up with me," "I found myself in jail," and "My mother went and died on me," imply that something from the outside was controlling their lives. It's not that they had *chosen* to drink again, to get divorced, to commit a crime; it was that these kinds of things happened *to* them.

I listened some more and found that not only did they have the attitude that they weren't responsible for their relapses, but they also had the same attitude about life.

"I found myself unemployed." —from a client who'd had a half dozen warnings from his boss.
"The next minute I found myself divorced." —from a client who'd had chronic marital problems for five years.
"The train left without me." —from a client who was 20 minutes late.
"I discovered I was broke." —from an addict who made $1000 dollars a month but paid $800 in rent.
"I found myself in jail." —from a client who hadn't filed a tax return for 10 years.
"I started drinking again because I took my mother on a holiday, and she went and died on me."

This attitude was the key to their problem. As long as they felt that something external was controlling their lives and making all of these horrible things happen to them, they didn't have to take responsibility for their drug use or their lives. They could always escape responsibility by saying, "It wasn't my fault. The devil made me do it. Don't blame me, and don't expect me to do anything about it."

With an attitude like this a person could drink or use forever. Therefore it became crucial to change their language. But how?

After years of trying many different approaches with thousands of alcoholics and addicts, Pat Gehlhaar discovered her cognitive confrontation technique. It is an effective technique for the chronic, seriously dependent alcoholic or addict—those addicts who have a lifetime of using and drinking, who have been through multiple programs, who are at the terminal stages of their addiction. Her technique puts the patient in extreme cognitive dissonance by using paradox and irony. After being flooded with this approach for more than a week, few patients could maintain their excuses and denials; they were then open to making real progress in recovering from their addiction.

Here is an example of how Pat would handle a patient who had relapsed.

THERAPIST: So why did you start to drink again?

CLIENT: Well, my AA meetings started to drop off.

THERAPIST: Wait! Oh my God! What a terrifying experience! You mean to say that you were walking down the street one night to go to an AA meeting, you turned the corner, and suddenly the AA meeting disappeared in front of your very eyes? Dropped into a chasm or something? What a frightening thing that must have been for you.

CLIENT: Well no, ah . . . ah . . . ah. That's not what I mean. Ah . . . ah . . . Right before I drank again, the meetings started to get less . . . ah . . . you know what I mean, don't you?

THERAPIST: No, I don't! You mean they started to cancel meetings knowing that you were coming or something? Or you would show up and nobody would be there because they changed the location? What a nasty thing for AA to do to you.

CLIENT: Ah . . . ah . . . no, of course not! Ah . . . ah . . . oh, the hell with it! I stopped going to meetings!

THERAPIST: Oh, well! Okay, then—now, we have it straight. Now, exactly why did you feel you didn't need to go to meetings anymore?

Pat responded to other statements in similar ways. She would attack clients' language and force them to see exactly what they were thinking behind their words.

CLIENT: I slipped up and drank a beer.

THERAPIST: You didn't slip. That's what people do when they step on a banana peel. It wasn't an accident. You wanted one, so you got one.

CLIENT: I fell off the wagon.

THERAPIST: You didn't fall off; you jumped off.

And so it went. It didn't take Gehlhaar's clients long to stop saying things like, "I fell off, it tripped me up, the booze caught up with me, I found myself divorced, she went and died on me." Instead they started to say, "I decided to drink again," "I thought I didn't need AA," "I was fired because I didn't show up at work," "My mother died." And then an interesting thing happened. Not only did they start saying things the right way; they started to understand them in the right way. They realized that they were ultimately responsible for their relapses and for their lives, and that they and they alone could do something about them.

Comment

The differences between the two cognitive models of addiction are not as extreme as presented here. Our model accepts that emotions can be triggers (although not causes) of drug use, and the other model accepts that facilitating beliefs (permission to use drugs beliefs—i.e., our 42 beliefs) are likely to cause the client to succumb to urges (Liese & Franz, 1996).

The major difference between the two models is that we pay a great deal of attention to what clients say to themselves *after* they get a craving, not *before*. For seriously dependent clients the only thing necessary to develop a craving is time. The addict's body becomes accustomed to a certain level of the drug, and when this level is reduced a craving is set off. Dependent clients do not need to be anxious, depressed, bored, angry, frustrated, or in crisis to use; all they need is the craving.

A personal note. I am well aware of the reactions of some readers to the presentation of our cognitive treatment for the seriously chemically dependent patient. It would have been my reaction for the first 15 years of my career before having worked full-time in drug treatment programs, before I met Pat.

I had been using cognitive therapy for chemically abusing clients for years. It had been successful with many clients. Through most of the early part of my career I had *not* made a distinction between treating the abusing versus treating the seriously dependent client. Cognitive techniques were helpful with most of them.

But when I went to work in public drug and alcohol treatment hospitals, I found that the standard cognitive techniques that had worked before seemed to make these patients worse. The patients in the public hospitals were two standard deviations above the mean on the various chemical dependency tests. They had lost their families, their jobs, their financial resources, their physical health; many were homeless and living on the streets. When I tried to help these patients by reducing their negative emotions, it gave them an excuse to keep on using. They would say, "I am addicted because I have emotional problems. When I solve these problems, then and only then will I stop drinking." Pat taught them to think, "The hell with my emotional problems. I have them because I have been using and drinking for 20 years. First

I need to stop *now*! I'll worry about the other stuff later on."

The literature on drug and alcohol treatment doesn't often mention this population and doesn't often describe the cognitive confrontation that is necessary. I believe the reason for this is because many professionals who write the textbooks don't often see this type of patient. I hadn't until I worked in the Australian drug hospital. You don't see these patients in a college counseling center because they have long since dropped out of school. You don't see them in private practice because they have long ago run out of money and have used up all of their insurance. You don't see them in employer drug treatment programs because they were fired years ago. You don't see them in outpatient clinics because they have tried this route and failed many times before. The only place you find them is in a public hospital after they have been picked up on the street for their uncountable detoxes, with their livers almost gone.

One final note about the counselor style. This style is not for the faint-hearted or inexperienced therapist. It must be done correctly. Pat was a master and had more than 20 years' experience. For two years I observed many Pat "wannabes" who tried to duplicate her style but failed miserably. In one session Pat could totally destroy a patient's old cognitive system without destroying the patient. Her irony and paradoxical methods confronted the patient's thoughts rather than the patient; many imitators were unable to make this subtle but crucial distinction.

Many of the patients didn't like their cognitive systems being destroyed; some became angry and would even walk out of treatment saying, "I don't need to put up with this crap." But then something would happen that I've never seen with any other counselor. A few weeks or a few months later, the same patient would come back, demanding to see Pat. I interviewed these patients and asked them, "After what happened in the therapy sessions with Pat before, why did you specifically come back to see her?" They all told me the same type of thing:

> Yes, I was angry. I was angry because everything she told me was exactly and precisely correct, and I knew it! My only option was to get the hell out of there. But I also knew that the only counselor who could ever help me was her, because I couldn't fool her with all my bullshit. So when I was ready to do something about my problem, when I knew that I would die if I didn't stop using, I immediately knew who I had to see.

A few years ago Pat retired from full–time drug and alcohol coun-seling at the public hospital. At her retirement, thousands of recover-ing alcoholics and addicts from all over Australia and other countries showed their appreciation for all that she had done for them.

Further Information

The specific cognitive treatments for drug dependency presented in this chapter were created by the authors. Much of the material is taken from two books—Mc Mullin and Gehlhaar (1990a) and Mc Mullin, Gehlhaar, and James (1990). The graphs and the majority of the research come from Mc Mullin and Gehlhaar (1990b). The theory, research, and practice have been presented at several international conferences on the treatment of drug and alcohol dependency (Adam-son & Gehlhaar, 1989; Mc Mullin, 1990; Mc Mullin & Gehlhaar, 1990c). Other research support for this approach is provided by Blum (1990), Blum and Trachtenberg (1988), Bohman, Sigvardsson, and Cloninger (1981), Cloninger, Bohman, and Sigvardsson (1981), Deitrich (1988), Goodwin, Schulsinger, Hermansen, Guse, and Winokur (1973), Good-win, Schulsinger, Moller, Hermansen, Winokur, and Guse (1974), Lumeng, Murphy, McBride, and Li (1988). Schuckit (1984), and Schuckit and Vidamantas (1979).

The more traditional cognitive model is represented in many good books. Although in disagreement with some components of our model, Albert Ellis and his colleagues provide a therapist–friendly summary of REBT procedures with addicts and alcoholics (Ellis, 1989; Ellis & Velten, 1992; Ellis et al., 1988). Miller and Rollnick (1991) have some excellent motivational strategies and even accept that seriously dependent patients may require a cognitive intervention model simi-lar to Gehlhaar's (Miller, personal communication, December, 1989). Bruce Liese offers a comprehensive picture of present cognitive ther-apy, including the need to confront patients appropriately and effec-tively (Liese & Franz, 1996). Baer, Marlatt, and McMahon (1993), Beck et al. (1993), and Clarke and Saunders (1988) have some important principles for any therapist who wishes to use a cognitive therapy approach with chemical abuse clients.

COGNITIVE FOCUSING
Principles

In the first edition of this book, cognitive focusing was treated as an important but nonessential technique. Further experience with supervising beginning cognitive therapists, however, has shown that an element of focusing may be necessary for any cognitive intervention to be effective.

The essential feature of focusing is the ability of the therapist to stay in touch with the client's ongoing processing during the therapy session. Processing encompasses clients' feelings, automatic thoughts, images, emotions, attitudes or values, felt physical senses, meanings, or any other elements actually experienced during the session. If the therapist is constantly in touch with the clients' ongoing experiences, cognitive techniques will be on target and are likely to be effective. If the therapist is not, techniques will lack meaning for clients and the therapy sessions will deteriorate into meaningless intellectualization. It is hypothesized that process focusing is a necessary but not sufficient condition for all effective cognitive therapy.

Cognitive focusing is one of the most difficult aspects to learn—it involves many subtleties that require careful concentration on the part of the therapist. It is a procedure that takes practice (sometimes years); very experienced therapists do it well while beginning therapists may not be able to do it at all.

Method 1. General Focusing in Cognitive Therapy

1. Focus on the ongoing processing of your clients during the sessions. The difference between an experienced cognitive therapist and a beginner is that the experienced therapist uses the client's responses rather than the therapist's own agenda as the subject matter of the therapy.

2. Focus on not only *what* clients are telling you but also on *how* they are telling you. Pay close attention to their tones, expressions, emotions, postures, and other nonverbal cues.

3. When you make an intervention (e.g., ask a question, offer an interpretation, clarify a feeling, give an explanation, counter a thought), immediately focus on the client's verbal and nonverbal responses. Listen very carefully.

4. Follow your clients' responses rather than your original statement.

The client's responses will often reveal another underlying pattern or belief that is more fundamental to the problem you are examining.

5. Continue following ongoing responses wherever they lead. Clarify the cognition they are revealing (e.g., self–concept, attribution, self-instruction, expectation, conceptual focusing).

6. Help clients to pay attention to their ongoing experiences (e.g., therapist says, "I notice you are smiling"). Then help clients form the experience into a cognition (e.g., client says, "I am smiling because I think it's very funny he got so upset, because he keeps pretending to be so strong.")

7. When clients show confusion about what they mean, help them to focus on their own feelings until they can find the cognition that clarifies it.

8. Keep working on finding the cognition that connects to their felt meaning (e.g., "Yes, that's it!").

Example

One of the world's most experienced cognitive therapists is Albert Ellis. After five decades of working with all kinds of clients in individual and group sessions, he has probably accumulated close to a hundred thousand counseling hours (DiMattia & Lega, 1990).

If you listen to Ellis's many published taped counseling sessions or, even better, his video sessions, or, best of all, if you observe him in one of his many public sessions (tapes can be obtained from the Albert Ellis Institute for Rational Emotive Behavior Therapy in New York), you will notice the following characteristics:

- He focuses on the client intently. Though he may be before an audience of several hundred professionals, he is constantly observing what his client is saying, feeling, and showing him. (Professionals in the audience who whisper during his sessions do so at their own peril. More than a few have heard, "If the people in the back can't be quiet during this session, we will bring them up here to see what their problem may be.")

- He drops his agenda to follow the client's present experience. He follows a cognitive framework, but it is a framework based on where the client is rather than on where he is himself.

- He is a directive therapist, teaching, guiding, and instructing his client, but he immediately and quickly stops his comments when the client makes a statement.

- Although he may strongly and assertively attack a belief, he never attacks a client. He shows complete and total respect for the person.
- He takes clients as far as they are willing to go during the session, but doesn't try to push them to his end point before they are ready.
- He shifts directions instantaneously based on his clients' responses.
- He is honest and emotionally transparent. He doesn't hide behind a professional facade or pretend to be distant, removed and non-emotional. If a client asks him a question he gives an honest answer. For instance, a client might ask, "Well, what would *you* do in this situation?" Instead of replying, "You want to know what I think?" or "You feel uncomfortable deciding for yourself," or "We are talking about you, not me," Ellis will answer the client directly and honestly.

Method 2. One Specific Cognitive-focusing Procedure

1. Ask your clients to relax and ease any tautness in their muscles. Have them recline and close their eyes if they wish. (3 minutes)
2. Urge them to clear their minds and to focus inwardly while you set the scene for the exercise. If they haven't come to you with a specific problem, present them with an analogy to help uncover the major sources of their discomfort. An example of such an analogy follows:

   Imagine that you are sitting in a storeroom cluttered with boxes. In each box is one of your problems. Each problem has a different box and the largest boxes contain the largest problems.

   Now picture yourself moving the boxes one at a time into the corners of the room so that you can have space to sit down. From a relatively comfortable perch in the middle of the room, survey the boxes around you carefully. Pull out the box that you most want to open and open it.

   Lift the problem out of the box and look at it. Turn it from side to side so that you can see every aspect of it. Try to step outside yourself and watch your reactions to it.

3. Once clients have selected a problem from their "storeroom," ask them to focus on how they feel about that problem. For example, one of our clients reported feeling uncomfortable whenever she met her spouse's ex-wife. We asked her to focus on how she felt about these meetings. She tried to recreate the feeling in the

present rather than simply remembering what she felt.

4. Instruct your clients to focus on the overall emotion that best captures how they feel about the problem. This will be more difficult for some clients than for others, and it won't be easy for anyone. Many clients are conditioned in ways that prevent them from clarifying their feelings, either to themselves or to others. Feelings are usually composites rather than single entities, which could make it difficult for clients to easily sense one overall impression. Clients must subdue all of the self–squawking and jabbering that may be going on in their heads before they can recognize the overall emotion. In our example, after much effort, the client was able to label the emotion associated with meeting her husband's ex–wife as *anxiety*.

5. Once the overall emotion has been defined to your clients' satisfaction, involve them in a careful analysis of the various nuances and components of that feeling. Since feelings are usually composites, elements of anger, guilt, resentment, jealousy, etc., could be evident in and around the central emotion of anxiety.

6. Now have your clients recall in detail other similar situations in which they have felt that same emotion. ("Have you always reacted fearfully when you met his ex–wife? When you met someone else, like your mother–in–law or his ex–girlfriend? Describe those other situations. Tell me exactly how you see yourself feeling about each one of them.") Have your clients resonate the situations with the feelings so that you can confirm that there is an apparent "association" between the overall emotion (anxiety) and the meetings. The situations can be drawn from the past as well as from the present.

7. Most importantly, probe to determine what thoughts sparked the same emotion in each of these similar situations. In each instance determine what your clients have been saying to themselves. What meaning do they assign to these situations? Follow the trail suggested by each of these components to see if it leads to a mistaken core perception held by the client. In our example the following core perception emerged: "I am not as good as she is. When my husband sees us together he will realize he made a mistake leaving her for me."

8. Now try to help your clients switch the emotion. The first step is to ask them to focus on similar situations that did not incite the negative overall emotion. ("Was there ever a time when you met his ex–wife that was not upsetting to you? Describe how you felt

then.") Remind them not to simply recall what they experienced but to try to recreate the same feelings. (If your clients can only recall having the negative overall emotion, ask them to focus on how other people might feel in the same situations.)

9. Next, instruct your clients to focus on their thoughts, beliefs, or what they told themselves during these similar situations when the overall emotion was different. ("Describe how you thought on those occasions when you weren't anxious about meeting her.") Guide your clients through an analysis of these feelings. In our example, the resulting core perception that emerged was: "I feel sorry for her. She is a good person just like me. Not better or worse, just another human being that has had difficult times like myself. He is with me now, not her, but he still cares for her and I can accept his caring and learn to like her myself."

10. Finally, have your clients practice replacing the feelings that they had initially (steps #4 and #5) with the feelings in the other situations (step #8). The key to switching the emotions is switching the thoughts. Have your clients imagine the thoughts they had when they weren't anxious (step #9, rather than step #7). In our example, the client pictured believing that the ex–wife was a good person instead of thinking that her husband would regret the divorce. Depending upon the severity of the damaging preoccupation, expect this practice to continue for quite some time. Teach your clients how to practice this shifting technique at home using a variety of concrete examples from their own histories. The more they practice, the more proficient they will become at shifting from negative to positive emotions, and the more durable the positive shift will be.

Example: The Story of Lester

Lester, in his forties, was having a great deal of difficulty with his romantic relationships. He described diverse feelings in a very confused, discordant manner. Nevertheless, he was psychologically sophisticated and a professional writer. We used the storeroom analogy to help him focus on the central problem. The main components of the dialogue, which took an hour and a half, are summarized here.

LESTER: I see several big boxes. One has my problem of being jealous when the woman I am going out with shows interest in another man. Another problem is the inner conflict I feel of wanting to be very close to her but at the same time feeling "trapped" if I get too close. A third problem is my inability to hurt a woman whom I like as a person but don't particularly want as a mate. I can't seem to break off these relationships. Another box is the love–hate–fear–joy–anger conflict I have with a woman I have fallen in love with. The fifth box is my propensity to protect myself by always going out with several women at the same time, even though one is always special.

THERAPIST: Pull out one of the boxes from the corner—any one you wish—and put it in front of you. Open it up and lift the problem out of it. Just look at it. Get the feel of the whole problem. There are probably many aspects to it—too many to think of separately, so try to get the total feel of it. Look inside of yourself where you feel things and see what comes to you as you look at the problem. What comes up when you ask yourself "How does it feel now?" Just let the feeling come in whatever way it comes but don't go inside of it. Keep looking at it from the outside. (3 minutes)

LESTER: I pulled out the largest box, the love–hate–fear–joy–anger box. When I opened it I saw all these swelling emotions. It felt familiar, for I have seen this box many times before. I remember noticing that at different times there are different dominant emotions—sometimes the fear, other times the love, frequently the anger.

THERAPIST: What was your overall reaction to the problem?

LESTER: Confusion.

THERAPIST: Look for a label for your overall feeling, like "sticky," "tight," "confined." Keep focusing on the overall feeling and try different words or pictures until one clicks. (4 minutes)

LESTER: There is a feeling of great sadness and loneliness. It feels very empty. It also feels twisted—like all these emotions don't belong, like they come from somewhere else and have just attached themselves to the relationship. They are very old feelings, like they started long before I dated. Mostly though, I feel regret that they are there. They seem to be muddling what otherwise would be a clear pool of good feelings.

THERAPIST: Fine. Now I would like you to search for situations that are connected to these emotions. Find events in the present and one from the distant past. Keep focusing on your feelings until some situation occurs to you. Take each overall emotion one at a time, and wait until an event attaches itself to the emotion. (3 minutes)

LESTER: Every time I am with a woman I feel sad and lonely. I felt this same feeling when I was in grade school. I didn't fit in and I felt I didn't have any friends and nobody liked me. The twisted impression comes a day or two after I am with a woman. I remember feeling this many years ago when I fell in love for the first time. My feelings for her didn't seem quite real; they seemed kind of neurotic or something.

THERAPIST: Okay. Keep focusing on your emotions silently but this time look for the core belief that ties the past and present situations to your emotions. Take each feeling one at a time. (5 minutes)

LESTER: Yes, the sad and lonely feeling comes from the thought, "I am different from others. In some way I am separate from the rest of humanity. I am not like other people."

THERAPIST: And the twisted feeling? What thought makes you feel that the emotions are wrong and out of place?

LESTER: Yes, my thought is that feeling this way is sick and I must be inferior to other men.

THERAPIST: Can you tie the two thoughts together?

LESTER: I can begin to see what I am thinking. "I am different from the rest of humanity because I am sick." I thought this when I was in grade school, the different and inferior parts—but they turned to a feeling of being sick when I fell in love with my first girlfriend. Nowadays I don't feel this often, only when I start deeply caring for a woman.

THERAPIST: Very good work. Now let's try some shifting. I want you to focus on some different situations. Try to think of some times when you were with a woman but you felt calm, confident, and healthy.

LESTER: There have been lots of women I felt good with, but I never cared for them. If I fall in love with a woman then I get these bad feelings.

THERAPIST: All right. Then look for the times you have been with these women who you love when you haven't felt these emotions. Take your time and find several situations from the past and present.

LESTER: Well, there have been short periods of time, usually lasting only a few days, when I didn't feel them.

THERAPIST: Take some time now, silently with yourself, and focus on what you were feeling at these times. (3 minutes)

LESTER: I can feel it. Free! Not jealous. Happy to know them and to love them.

THERAPIST: Okay. What did you perceive during these times that you didn't perceive in the others? What did you say and believe differently? Be silent with yourself and see what comes up. (1 minute)

LESTER: I was thinking I didn't need them. I wanted them but I didn't have to have them. See, before, I felt these women I loved were my only contact with the rest of humanity. Without them I was totally alone. But at the other times I felt like I was a part of humanity, like I had my unique individuality but I was not alone. When I thought that way, my lovers were just people, not saviors there to rescue me from loneliness.

THERAPIST: Please continue.

LESTER: There are times when I am with the woman I love when I can see things clearly. These times only come occasionally, maybe for a day or so, and then I slip back into the old murky pool. It feels like I can see her as a separate individual, with her own struggles, triumphs, and tragedies. I don't think she only exists to make me feel good. It's like I lose myself during these times and see her as independent of me.

THERAPIST: Please stay with this feeling. Keep focusing on it. Now, try something. While being in the feeling, look back at the old feeling. View the old felt sense of being different, twisted, and sick from the perspective of your new feeling. (2 minutes)

LESTER: Oh my! The old feeling is not real. That's why I called it twisted. It is incredibly arrogant. What conceit and narcissism to believe that nature created me separately from others! It's like nature had two creations—everybody else in the world, and then me. That makes me as important as all the rest of humanity. I am so special I needed an independent genesis! It is a self–indulgent selfishness to demand that a woman give up herself to minister to my arrogant loneliness. Hell, we are all lonely; we are all trapped inside our own skins wishing to be part of a "we" rather than just an "I." My feeling of being different from all other people is just an exercise in cosmic vanity, an existential snobbery.

THERAPIST: Hold that perception. Tuck it away somewhere in a safe place. Call it up when your are staring at the big box of contradictory emotions. Pull it out when you are with the woman you love and are feeling angry, hurt, lonely, and hateful.

The sessions continued using cognitive focusing. Lester would kept moving among situations, feelings, and thoughts. When he was with his lover he practiced changing his perception that he was uniquely different and switched it to "I am part of humanity. I am not alone."

Comment

The term "focusing" is adapted from the work of the well-known Rogerian theorist Eugene Gendlin (1992a, 1992b, 1996a, 1996b). Some research indicates that focusing might be the active element in Rogerian therapy, producing high levels of client self-experiencing (Mc Mullin, 1972). But in the present context focusing means both less and more than what Gendlin describes; less because Gendlin has created a whole therapy based on the concept, focusing–oriented psychotherapy (Gendlin, 1996a), and more because he discusses cognitions only as a component of his procedures (Gendlin, 1996a, pp. 238–246), and believes that cognitive methods should be "occasional and brief" (Gendlin, 1996a, p. 246). We are not advocating the exact duplication of all of his procedures; our position is that cognitive focusing is at the very core of both his and our therapy.

To explain why focusing is so important it may be useful to briefly review the key theoretical assumption underlying cognitive restructuring therapy.

The central feature of cognitive therapy is to shift the core belief (B) that connects the environmental stimuli (A) to the emotional (C_e) and behavioral response (C_b). The focus is on the B, unlike other therapies that may direct attention to other elements. For instance, Rogerian therapy focuses on the C_e, assuming that if clients are in touch with their ongoing self–experiencing then they will grow and change in a positive direction. Behavioral therapies direct their attention at the A–C connection and aim to break down old associations or develop new ones. Psychodynamic therapy uncovers the original A–C_e experiences, believing that when these connections become conscious the associations between the two will weaken and then be broken.

Other therapies often criticize the cognitive approach because they view many Bs as either superfluous (behaviorism), intellectualizations (Rogerian), or defense mechanisms (psychodynamic). But these criticisms are based on a very narrow view of what a B is. They view Bs as words or language. If Bs are only words, then much of cognitive therapy would deteriorate into investigating rationalizations, intellectualizing, or language shifting, but a major theme of this book is that Bs are much more than language.

In the early part of this book we describe Bs as: expectations, selec-

tive memories, attributions, evaluations, life themes, inner philosophies, self-efficacy, and cognitive maps as well as other cognitive
processes. Bs can be grouped and described as *the way the brain organizes raw data into patterns*. So Bs are far more than words. Words and language are simply ways of communicating the patterns; they are not
the patterns themselves. Even if clients had no words to describe their
patterns (as is often true with young children), the patterns are still
there. The purpose of cognitive therapy is not to change the client's
language but to change the client's patterns.

The danger in the use of the specific focusing technique lies in
overmystifying the process. Focusing narrows clients' attention on
their emotions so that they can more easily identify the external triggers and intervening cognitions causing those emotions. The beliefs
that clients find are therefore more likely to be precise, and any cognitive change technique is more likely to be effective. The process is
not based, in our view, on getting in touch with hidden elements
inside one's subconscious or on repressed emotions that need to be
expunged; rather, it focuses clients' attention on specific, manageable
perceptions that can be usefully shifted.

Further Information

The theoretical, practical, and research basis for the focusing technique can be found in Gendlin's works (1962, 1964, 1967, 1969, 1981,
1991, 1992a, 1992b, 1996a, 1996b; Gendlin, Beebe, Cassues, Klein, &
Oberlander, 1968).

CORE COMPONENTS OF COGNITIVE RESTRUCTURING THERAPY: A CHECKLIST
Principles

Conducting cognitive therapy is both an art and a science. There are
thousand of procedures and techniques that need to be mastered, and
although the key principles connected with the science can be learned
quickly through an academic course or by reading a few good textbooks, it takes a lot longer to learn all the subtleties of the art. Having
supervised graduate students for over 25 years, I estimate that novi-
tiates should not do cognitive therapy independently, until they have
had two years' clinical experience; this time period allows for one

supervisory session a week to review their tapes and critique their counseling, and assumes that they are continuing their study outside the sessions.

Despite the diversity of skills that can be learned, there are a few key principles that therapists must teach their clients if cognitive therapy is to be effective. Following is a list of essential questions.

1. Can clients distinguish between situations, thoughts, and emotions or do they confuse the three? Remember that situations are an environmental variable outside the organism, thoughts are frontal–lobe processing, and emotions are subcortical feeling responses. (See chapter 1, "First Session: Teaching the Basic Formula.")

2. Do your clients believe that thoughts cause emotions, or do they still think that situations elicit feelings? There is no point in continuing a cognitive therapy if your clients continue to believe that outside physical events are causing their emotions. (See chapter 1, "Providing Evidence that Beliefs Produce Emotions.")

3. Have your clients found the core beliefs linked to their emotional responses? If the beliefs you are working with are irrelevant to the client's emotions then changing them will not remove the emotion. The first step in cognitive counseling of all types is to clearly identify the most basic belief that is causing the client problems. The beliefs that clients are aware of are usually only the surface thoughts; the therapist often needs to dig for several sessions before the core is uncovered. (See chapter 2, "Finding the Beliefs.")

4. Do the clients see the negative effects of their beliefs on their lives, or do they think that their thoughts are irrelevant to what they feel and how they act? (See chapter 1, "How Powerful Are Environmental Forces?")

5. Can the clients discern the interrelationship between one thought and another? Do they see that their fear in a grocery store is fundamentally the same as their fear in a restaurant, elevator, or conference room? Can they draw a cognitive map of these relationships? (See chapter 3, "Groups of Beliefs.")

6. Do they understand the need to analyze the usefulness or falseness of their beliefs or do they think that feeling something strongly establishes its validity? (See chapter 6, "Finding the Good Reason.")

7. Can they successfully analyze statements and make decisions as

to their usefulness or falseness? (See chapter 6, "Logical Analysis.")

8. Have they committed to the idea that if a thought is logically false it is useful to change it? (See chapter 6, "Utilitarian Counters.")

9. Are your clients willing to go against their beliefs? Have they developed the motivation to use various methods (countering, perceptual shifting, resynthesizing) to change them, or are they simply going through the motions without really wanting to work on anything? (See chapter 4, "Counterattacking," and "Forcing Choices.")

10. Have they practiced the techniques enough? (Some beliefs may take a year or more of practice.) Unfortunately, many clients believe in magic and think that one afternoon of disputing will make up for 15 years of believing an irrationality. Clients need to practice over a long period of time not rather than simply when they are in crisis. (See chapter 11, "Practice Techniques.")

11. Do they use the procedures mechanically or have they shown that they understand the underlying concept? (See chapter 8, "Transposing Images," and chapter 9, "Bridging.")

12. Have they modified your procedures so much that they have destroyed the active therapeutic element? Client creativity is to be encouraged but you need to make sure that the client doesn't change the technique so much that it becomes ineffective.

13. Do your clients recognize that therapists don't have the power to change beliefs and that only they have that power? Do they accept the counseling relationship as more of a teacher–student than that of a doctor and patient, or are they waiting for you to cure them?

14. Are the clients' perceptions of therapeutic efficacy so low that they expect the therapy to fail? The research on self-efficacy is rather strong on this point; if clients expect to fail they will often do subtle things to help make their prediction come true. (See chapter 2, "Self-Efficacy.")

15. Do they think that another approach or another therapist would help them more? They may not put any effort into your therapy if they feel it is second best. Suggest that they try the other approach first and then return to you if it proves ineffective.

16. Do clients complete their homework or do they only work during your therapy sessions? One hour engaged in the right direction does not offset 112 hours of working in the wrong direction. (See chapter 1, "Learning the Concepts.")

17. Are your techniques ineffectual because the client is sabotaging

them? (See chapter 12, "Handling Client Sabotages.")

18. Have you found that some of your clients have difficulty changing beliefs that are anchored to their personal or cultural histories? Changing these types of thoughts often evokes feelings of
guilt; you may be required to pull these beliefs out by the roots.
(See chapter 10, "Historical Resynthesis" and chapter 13, "Cross-
cultural Cognitive Therapy.")

19. Are there too many noncognitive factors interfering with your
techniques? Although your clients' central problems may be cognitive, in order to effectively work on them they need to have
both time and freedom from constant crisis in order to effectively
change their negative perceptions. Clients with severe marital
problems, physical illness, drug abuse issues, or who are not sure
of where their next meal is coming from are not in the right frame
of mind to work on their cognitive problems. In such situations it
is better to mitigate the crisis before you attempt traditional cognitive therapy. (See chapter 12, "Crisis Cognitive Therapy," "Treating Seriously Mentally Ill Patients," "Cognitive Restructuring
Therapy with Addicted Patients.")

Example

Psychotherapy has failures like any other profession, but professional therapists writing about their techniques often only show the
public their successful cases. In newspaper articles, books, journals,
and on talk shows, therapists talk about those people whom they have
helped. This creates the perception that we only succeed and never
fail, but we do fail more frequently than we wish or hope. Like a professional photographer, we throw away our bad prints in the dark-
room trashcan and show only our best prints to the public. It may
sometimes be useful to let people see our failures and why they happen.

There are some clients I can't help because I simply don't know
enough; other client problems may be incurable. A few years ago
there was a woman who lived across the country from me. She had
read some of my earlier books and liked what she'd read, so she flew
out to see me with the hope that I would be able to help her. I later
found out that she was a millionaire who constantly perused psychology books and journals. Whenever she read something she liked
she'd jump on a plane to visit the author. Before having seen me she
had visited many famous therapists across the country.

A few minutes into my first session with her I realized that she was chronically psychotic and that none of my psychotherapeutic techniques could cure her. There were techniques that could be used to help her, but she didn't want help; she wanted to be cured. She had taken all the new antipsychotic medications, but they hadn't produced any characterological changes. Unfortunately, she will probably only have her problem removed if there is a major biochemical breakthrough in the treatment of schizophrenia; in the meantime, she is probably still flying around to therapists who publish new books, hoping that they will provide her with an answer.

This case illustrates a problem peculiar to therapy. Although the public accepts that there are incurable diseases in medicine, such as terminal cancer or Hodgkins Disease, they don't accept that problems in psychology or psychiatry are incurable. Despite the public's denial, *there are clients with problems we can't fix.* When we work with these clients we can only teach them some skills, help them to accept their problem (see chapter 12, "Treating Seriously Mentally Ill Patients."), and make them as comfortable as possible, but the essence of their disorder will remain the same.

At other times we have the tools and the necessary knowledge, but are still not able to help because the client will not allow us. This is not their fault; they are not to blame, but they sabotage treatment.

One client was a convict. He was in prison for having committed murder, and would not be eligible for parole for many years. He suffered from extreme compulsive behavior including excessive hand washing, counting his steps when he walked in the exercise yard, and performing meaningless rituals for hours on end. There are many cognitive and behavioral techniques for such problems. There was a reasonable chance of helping him, but he wouldn't listen to anything I said. He was much too angry at the courts, the prison, the world, and himself to follow my instructions or even to want to.

The problem that our profession faces is captured by the old joke about therapists.

"How many psychologists does it take to change a light bulb?"

"Just one, but the light bulb has to want to be changed."

Many of my colleagues have found this concept to be true. Humans can choose to do something or not to. The combined persuasion of the best therapists in the world cannot budge a person who had decided not to change. We can plead with a person to practice a particular exercise three times a day for 10 weeks, but the person can always think, "No. I won't do it."

Of course sometimes we just fail, usually because we are either *too hard* or *too soft* on our clients. We are *too hard* when we put too much pressure on them and expect them to change too quickly or too much. Counseling is a form of encouraging growth, and the therapist is like a gardener. We can become impatient or frustrated and start to pull on the person to grow faster. Change and growth and healing take their own good time; they do not operate according to the dictates of either the doctor or patient. It is our responsibility as psychologists to weed peoples' garden in order to provide a fertile ground and then to wait for the blossom of change to appear.

In my experience, most therapists' mistakes arise from having been *too easy*. Beginning therapists make this mistake frequently, and untrained counselors do it all the time. Therapists are people, and are conditioned to feel sympathy for someone in pain. Beginning therapists don't see what's behind the pain, so they rush in and offer sympathy and try to rescue clients from their hurt. This makes clients feel better temporarily, and the therapist receives gratitude, letters of appreciation, and referrals.

Usually, however, this rescuing is a big mistake and ultimately hurts clients a great deal. The emotional pain that we human beings feel is a signal or sign that something is wrong. In a sense it is much like physical pain; it tells us that some body part is injured and needs our attention. The pain of a splinter in our foot tells us to look for the splinter, but if we quickly numb the pain we may leave behind too many splinters. Likewise, emotional pain motivates us to find its cause. When we remove the hurt we make it more difficult, and sometimes impossible, to find the root of our pain.

The best example of this type of mistake is treating the alcoholic person. Initially societies treated alcoholics with scorn and disgust because society assumed them to be moral degenerates. This tactic didn't work; alcoholics continued drinking just the same. Later society treated them as psychologically disturbed individuals who needed empathy and sympathy to boost their flagging self–confidence and to lessen the negative effects of their early childhood; alcoholics continued drinking just the same. Next society suggested that alcoholics had a medical disease and treated them as medical patients. Society gave them drugs to lessen their craving, but they kept drinking just the same.

Today we know that these approaches were mistakes, although some therapists would still disagree. These previous attempts enabled alcoholics to drink more by rescuing them and not allowing the natural consequence of their behavior to hit them; these treatments served as a buffer between the alcoholics' drinking and real-world consequences. To help alcoholics, therapists have found it best to confront them with the truth that they are hooked, that drink is destroying their families, their health, and their ability to be happy, and that the best way to turn their lives around is to admit to their addiction and stop all use. Often the only way some alcoholics can see this truth is to stew in their own messes until they perceive what a personal holocaust their drinking has produced.

Therapists have many failures that have saddened us, but we endure them because we remember those clients we were able to help. Most of the time our successes make up for our failures.

Further Information

With the advent of HMOs into the administration of mental health services, there has been increasing need to show the effectiveness of any brand of psychotherapy (Giles, 1993a, 1993b). The necessary and sufficient conditions for effective cognitive therapy have stood up well to these tests (Beck, 1995; Dobson, 1989; Elkin et al., 1989; Rachman, Rachman, & Eysenck, 1997; Shea et al., 1992).

THIRTEEN

Cross-cultural Cognitive Therapy

CLIENTS DON'T FORM THEIR beliefs in isolation. They compose them both from their own life experiences and by adopting attitudes from the broader belief system held by others around them. By looking at clients' affiliation groups, we usually discover that they share many core beliefs with their culture.

As a result, cultural awareness on the part of the therapist is central to cognitive therapy; the therapist must have an understanding of each client's culture in order to counsel effectively.

Culture determines many client cognitions: what they believe and what they reject; what they perceive and what they ignore; how much they are willing to share with a stranger outside the family; what relationship they will have with you, the caregiver; what values they will consider important; what style of therapy will be acceptable and what style they will reject out of hand; what they will consider as the possible causes of their emotional problems, and how much effort and what type of work they will be willing to put into their own therapy.

REFERENCE GROUPS
Principles

Clients can identify with the beliefs and attitudes of many different types of groups: cultures, races, subcultural groups, regions, language groups, national states, religious affiliations, and political parties. Because there are so many potential groups, it is hard to determine why clients adopt the Bs of one group over another. Sociologists offer an explanation called "reference group." It is not the group that people are born in, grew up in, or that other people think they are in; it is the group with which they identify. Thus, a client could be an upper–middle–class Irish Catholic from the east coast, and may have been brought up in a liberal, democratic household, but he may mentally identify with an ancient oriental ideology that he learned while studying Zen and kung fu. A reference group is the mental home that clients live in.

Method

1. Assemble a list of the groups that your client associates with or feels mentally part of.
2. How does your client model what the group teaches?
3. List the core beliefs of these groups—the Bs that separate them from other groups.
4. Compose a chart that shows the similarities between these group beliefs and the beliefs of your client.

Example 1. Xenophobia

A negative aspect about many reference groups is that they inspire fear of others outside their own group. This fear is associated with xenophobia; *xenon* is Greek for stranger, and *phobia* derives from the Greek *phobias*, meaning fear. Together they signify an exaggerated and persistent dread of or aversion to foreigners and strangers. Although it may seem a trivial fear, it is significant. Xenophobia is one of the most common cultural fears, and certainly one of the most damaging.

Our clients have reported many instances of being subjected to other people's xenophobia. East coast college students have been told, "You won't learn anything in the schools out west. Education out there is barbaric. There is no culture west of the Allegheny Mountains."

Our clients from the west have been told, "People from the east coast are intellectual snobs, pompous, stuffy, effete people who are totally disingenuous."

In the south, xenophobia takes the form of, "Damn Yankee carpetbaggers. Go back were you come from, if you know what's good for you," while northern clients are told that everybody in the south is a bigot, a hick, or a dumb redneck.

In Texas, our clients hear xenophobia expressed as Texas against the other 49 states, or "Tex'ns vs. the Feds," as they put it. In Colorado, many people dislike Texans, or flatlanders, as they call them (anybody not from mountainous terrain). In Washington and Oregon, some people have bumper stickers saying, "Out of Staters Go Home!" and visiting Californians are warned not to drive with California license plates.

Similar tales can be told of xenophobia involving country of origin, religion, political party—it can be found everywhere. As therapists we could discount clients' xenophobia as a normal pride for people like themselves, a natural nonpathological rooting for the home team. But monstrous damage may lurk inside this self-pride. The *others*, the *strangers*, the *foreigners*, the *"thems"* are perceived as evil, sinister, and malevolent. This produces an almost spiritual rejection of people who act and appear different. From this contempt spring the psychological roots of prejudice, bigotry, and discrimination that have caused the lion's share of misery on our planet. Helping clients to recognize xenophobia (their own and others') as a core fear can aid in creating a more fair-minded and becalmed belief system.

Example 2. Culturally Approved Diagnosis

The cultural reference group also teaches clients what types of emotional problems are acceptable to have. It may be acceptable to have an adjustment reaction to adult life but considerably less acceptable to have a sexual disorder or a major psychotic episode. The disorders that are culturally approved have changed throughout the years as each decade has produced its own diagnostic fads.

In the late sixties and early seventies many of our clients suffered from what can be called existential anxiety. They complained about the lack of meaning in life. They sought answers to questions like, "Why am I here? What is the purpose of life?" Many had lost trust in traditional institutions such as government, family, and religion, and had come to therapy because they felt bewildered—"drifting in a nonsensical cosmos," as some put it. As a result they often delved into mystical religions and cult groups to provide some sense of meaning.

In the middle and late seventies our clients complained of having relationship difficulties. Either their relationships weren't successful or they had no intimate relationships at all; clients complained of loneliness and lack of intimacy. As radical changes were occurring in male-female roles, clients were confused about what masculinity and femininity were, and their relationships suffered for this confusion.

In the early and middle eighties clients' problems changed again. Clients were less concerned about lack of meaning in life or lack of personal intimacy than they were about failing. "Wouldn't it be horrible if I wasn't successful?" They would ask. They were terrified of not owning the right kind of cars or not getting into the right M.B.A. programs. For these clients, success was interpreted as having money, power, and material goods.

In the nineties many of our clients were expressing a type of fear of disapproval; clients fear others won't like them; they are afraid their facade is not good enough and that people may see the real persons behind the mask. Some examples of their concerns are: "I may not impress others enough. I may embarrass myself. It would be terrible if people didn't approve of me and respect me."

When our clients are asked which of the following choices they prefer—knowledge or the appearance of knowledge; courage or the appearance of courage; achievement or the appearance of achievement; intimacy or the appearance of intimacy—a surprising number of people choose the appearances. They are embarrassed by this, but defend themselves by arguing, "What does it matter if you have these things but no one recognizes that you have them? You won't get any benefit from them."

Life revolves in cycles; in time, there may be a great increase in clients again seeking help for existential anxiety. They will complain about the lack of meaning in life. They will seek answers to questions like, "Why am I here? What is the purpose of life?" Many will have lost trust in traditional institutions such as government, family, and religion and come to therapy because they feel bewildered—drifting in a nonsensical cosmos. As a result they will delve into mystical religions and cult groups to provide some sense of meaning.

Comment

Many clients may turn their xenophobia against themselves. They blame themselves for being part of the "wrong" groups (ethnic, racial, class, gender, cultural, generation). Such rejection can create an internal war with devastating consequences.

The cognitive solution to xenophobia, whether it is directed outside against others, or inside against self, is to show that it is based on the logical fallacy of overgeneralization. Although cultural groups may have some common traits, the within–group variance is almost always as large as the variance between groups. Therefore saying that all Xs share a certain characteristic is a symptom of emotional conditioning rather than a statement of fact.

Not only do client problems run in fads but the most popular treatments also go in cycles. In the course of my practice I have seen the wax and wane of many treatments: transcendental meditation, primal scream, existential analysis, transactional analysis, neurolinguistic programming, Rolfing, EMDR, dialectics, and many others.

Further Information

The original and more complete version of the xenophobia issue can be found in my newspaper article (Mc Mullin, 1995).

The principle of ethnocentrism is a mainstay of sociological theory developed by one of the founding fathers of sociology, Graham Sumner, in 1906. The concept reveals itself in two ways: the proclivity for people to judge their own group as the reference for all other comparisons, and the disposition to believe that one's own reference group is superior to all others (Summer, 1906; Summer, Keller, & Davie, 1927). Marsella has done extensive work on ethnocentrism in particular and cross–cultural counseling in general (Marsella, 1984, 1997, 1998a, 1998b; Marsella, Friedman, Gerrity, & Scurfield, 1996).

CULTURAL CATEGORIES
Principles

The culture not only instructs clients on how to respond to people outside of their reference group, it also directs them on how to view themselves.

Clients maintain a certain self–deception about their culture's influence on them. They have difficulty recognizing that their culture taught them how to look at the world, and that their culture taught them to think of other cultures as alien, fouled–up, or muddled. They believe that the way their own culture sees the world is the way the world really is, that their culture has the only correct way of looking at life.

Example 1: Dyirbal Categories

Women, Fire and Dangerous Things, written by Lakoff (1985), shows how clients' views of the world are relative to their culture. The book is full of stories about the language of different societies, and it explains how language forces people to see and feel different things. A central story in the book is about the Dyirbal Australian aboriginal tribes—the book's title comes from this story.

In the Dyirbal language every noun is preceded by one of four categories, and in essence everything in the universe can be divided into these categories. Each category has a name: Bayi, Balan, Balam, or Bala. Whenever the Dyirbal name anything, they introduce it by identifying the category that the object falls under. These categories are more than linguistical; they also show how the speaker relates to the object, so that different emotions, behaviors, and values are associated with each group. For example, the culture categorizes the objects in figure 13.1.

Many westerners would classify these items into the following categories: (1) *Natural Phenomena*: rainbows, rivers, the sun, stars, the moon, and fire; (2) *Animals*: snakes, parrots, fireflies, hairy Mary grubs, crickets, honey, echidnas, kangaroos; (3) *Manmade Goods*: spears; (4) *Humans*: men, women. These groupings reflect Western logic rather than Dyirbal culture. The correct Dyirbal categories are:

Bayi: boomerangs, men, kangaroos, nonpoisonous snakes, rainbows, and the moon. This category often produces an animated, excited feeling in the listener.

Balan: rivers, women, poisonous snakes, stars, lightning bugs, fire, the sun, platypus, parrots, echidnas, spears, and the hairy Mary grub. Items in this category are often feared.

Balam: consumable items like honey, fruit, and edible leaves. *Balam* items are often desired.

Bala: anything not in the above three groupings. These items the Dyirbal will often feel neutral about.

Dyirbal people categorize in this way because of their culture. Men and the moon are in the first category because in Dyirbal mythology, the moon and the sun are husband and wife and men are descended from the moon. Since men use boomerangs to hunt kangaroos, both are placed here. Rainbows are included because the souls of men who die as heroes turn into rainbows.

Women and the sun are both in the second category because all women descend from the sun, which is considered female. Fire, poisonous snakes, and the hairy Mary grub sting like the sun so they are all included. Surprisingly, spears also fall into this category because this entire category includes the concept of dangerous things (thus the

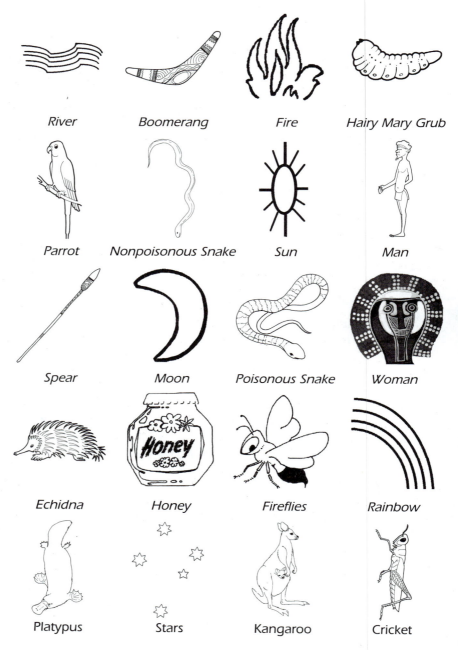

FIGURE 13.1 Objects classified in the Dyirbal language

title of the book—*Women, Fire, and Dangerous Things*). Rivers are included because water from rivers puts out fires. Stars and lightning bugs shine like the sun, so they are included. Parrots and many other birds are believed to be the spirits of human females. And crickets? In Dyirbal myth, crickets are old ladies.

Modern, industrialized Western logic would have difficulty explaining these categories. Understanding them at all requires that we set aside the logic system that we have been culturally born to. Even in attempting to do so, most Westerners would still think the categories are cockeyed, the product of primitive, uneducated brains. Many would incorrectly believe that the categories are just primitive superstitions, that ours are the only correct ones.

There are no natural or correct categories. Theirs are as good as ours. Ours seem correct to us because we grew up in our own culture and we think our view of the world is the only natural one. The same is true of the Dyirbal.

Herein lies the great insight in Lakoff's book and the reason it can be so important to therapists. There are no natural or correct ways of looking at the world. Clients have learned to perceive things in certain ways because their culture has taught them to do so. Because different societies teach different categories, there are no a priori or necessary groupings—there is no natural way of looking at things; all culturally dictated categories are arbitrary. Clients' cultures, their societies, and languages all teach them how to view things.

The language that clients use is metaphorical in nature. In other words, they understand one experience by comparing it to another. These metaphors are cultural and reveal some of the most fundamental values of the society they live in. Clients' metaphors tell them what to see, how to cope with the world, and how to interact with other people. Often clients upset themselves unnecessarily by implicitly accepting an outdated metaphor that misrepresents them. Some words, such as bipolar, manic with catatonic features, bulimia nervosa, or paranoid schizophrenic, can haunt clients for the rest of their lives.

It is important that we as therapists help clients to examine the core categories that reside at the base of their cognitions and to understand that there are other ways of looking at the world and themselves (Duhl, 1983).

Method

1. Have your clients pick a personal trait they feel most upset about.
2. Look in a good thesaurus and collect all of the metaphors associ-

ated with this trait. Pay particular attention to slang expressions.
3. See whether the metaphorical descriptions accurately describe your
   clients' problems or whether they are simply cultural anachronisms.

Example 2: One Client's Categories

One of my clients picked the word "inferior" as his central trait. He looked the word up in a thesaurus and picked the following phrases as the most accurate description of his feelings.

Came up short	Lightweight
Lower than	Lowly
Under	Less than
Small potatoes	Puny
Bargain basement	Two–bit
Small time	Mickey mouse

This client associated "inferior" with the metaphor of shortness and smallness because he perceived that the size of a man is associated with his ability to defend and protect women; his culture had taught him that a small or short male is less capable of doing this. This metaphor was countered by helping him recognize that the invention of the bow and arrow, the slingshot, guns, bombs, automatic weapons, and nuclear bombs have blurred the importance of male size to a great extent. His favorite counter phrase was, "I will protect you from those nasty nuclear weapons, my dear."

Example 3: Another Client's Categories

A client in Melbourne, Australia, was an agoraphobic who suffered constant panic attacks that caused her to hide in her house and not travel. This client, whom I'll call Martha, had not traveled beyond a half–mile radius of her house for 10 years. Her grandchildren lived in another state, and she only saw them on those rare occasions when the whole family could afford to visit her.

After a few sessions we found the particular cognition that was the cause of Martha's panics. She believed that the emotions of anger and stress were dangerous, and so to protect herself from these feelings she had created a narrow emotional safety zone. If her emotions ever rose above the zone, she would panic. To cope she had to hide in her house and avoid all situations that might produce these feelings.

What was difficult to determine was why she believed this thought.

Why did she view feeling anger and stress as so dangerous? We could find no traumatic event in her history that could have caused such fear, but Lakoff's book provided a clue. It suggested that she might have simply categorized these emotions as dangerous because of her cultural background. Her culture may have labeled these feelings in such a way that she associated danger with them.

To explore this idea she described in detail everything she had been taught about feeling emotions such as anger, fear, stress, sadness, rage, or terror.

She had grown up in an upper–class British family, and had attended private prep schools based on the continental model. In her culture it was considered low class to show any feelings strongly. Displays of emotion were considered petty bourgeois and indicated a lack of breeding. These are the synonyms she had learned describing strong emotions:

Anxiety: losing control, on tender–hooks, out of one's head, hysterical, berserk; shaking like a leaf, overwhelmed, about to explode, falling to pieces

Anger: blowing your top, losing it, exploding, flipping your wig, freaking out, having a fit, hitting the ceiling, having a hemorrhage, blowing a gasket

These were more than just phrases; they were the ways she viewed emotions, and they prescribe how she would experience having these feelings. Like the example of the Dyirbal, the core categories prescribe the glasses through which she saw the affective world. They were basic reflexive reactions that Martha had learned from the time she was young, and she did not believe that emotions could be perceived in any other way.

Her definitions show how she categorized emotions—she perceived them as energies inside containers. Anxiety and anger were the energy, while her body was the container, and if emotional pressure became too strong, the container could explode. Descriptions like, "falling to pieces, exploding, blowing a gasket, hitting the ceiling," demonstrated her perception. She was afraid of emotionally exploding, so whenever she felt the slightest fear or anger she became terrified that the feeling would build to an uncontrollable level and she would go insane or have a nervous breakdown. In her mind she would only be protected if she kept these emotions in a narrow safety zone; she had to control her environment completely to keep her emotions from growing.

To help Martha we had to change the way her language categorized her emotions. If we changed her metaphor, maybe we could remove her panics.

I told her that human beings don't have gaskets that can be blown. Nobody hits ceilings, and the tops of our heads don't explode when we get upset. This description is just an old metaphor from a time when people were unenlightened about human emotions or human physiology. A more useful way to look at her emotions was to think of an electrical circuit. Either the switch is on or it is off, but the energy doesn't build up inside of her any more than the energy builds inside a television when she shuts it off. She didn't have to fear her emotions; she just had to feel them.

It wasn't easy to change Martha's language. These categories were part of her basic model of the world, so she held on to them tightly. Other people were constantly reinforcing her perceptions by suggesting, "You should let your anger out before you explode," or "Don't let jealously built up inside of you or you could crack."

Over time she was able to change her language. She shifted her frame of reference and started to see emotions differently. When she accomplished this, her panics left. She accepted fear and anger as a normal human process—distressing at times, but not dangerous. She started to extend her emotional safety zone so that she could experience the full range of her emotional life. It took time, but over many months she shifted her categories and felt more and more while fearing her feelings less and less. She started to cross her one–mile territory; the last I heard she has been visiting her grandchildren regularly.

Comment

If we accept Lakoff's concept that there are no natural categories, it follows that one cultural view is not naturally superior to another. As therapists we need to maintain cultural–relative positions and not reject our client's view simply because it is different from our own. We do, however, have the obligation to show our clients that although their categories may be equally "true or false" they may not be equally useful to them. Ultimately the client will decide which view is most helpful.

Further Information

Lakoff has written several major works that discuss his concepts in detail (Lakoff, 1983, 1985, 1990; Lakoff, Taylor, Arakawa, & Lyotard, 1997).

Semin and Fiedler have explored the functions of linguistic categories on people's behaviors (Semin & Fiedler, 1988, 1989, 1991).

The ability of a culture's evaluations to create emotions in members has been studied extensively (see Kitayama & Markus, 1994; Marsella, 1984; Marsella, Friedman, Gerrity, & Scurfield, 1996; Russell, Manstead, Wallenkamp, & Fernandez-Dolls, 1995; Scherer, 1997).

CULTURAL BELIEFS
Principles

Behind many client problems are a few core beliefs and a few key attitudes that cause most of the damage. Over the years cross-cultural researchers have gathered lists of these beliefs and have found that many of them originate from the cultures that clients grow up in. If therapists are to understand why some beliefs are so damaging, we first need to understand the cultures that give birth to them.

People all over the world share certain superstitions. These beliefs are not confined to one country or one culture; therapists hear these distortions wherever they travel. No one group is more or less rational, healthy, or enlightened than another because of their beliefs; all cultures have these distortions. The only difference among them is that different cultures have different types of superstitions.

A major source of cultural superstitions is attribution theory—the explanations that a culture gives to explain why people act the way they do. Different cultures develop different explanations. When clients search for an explanation for their own or others' behavior they usually choose the culture's attribution first. For example, United States culture has offered a variety of explanations for why people engage in certain behaviors. Here are a few that have been suggested:

Behavior	*Attribution*
homeless	laziness
criminal acts	low self-esteem
colds	lack of vitamin C
insanity	bad parenting
AIDS	God's punishment

Method 1

1. Give clients the following survey and ask them to rate their answers on a Likert scale from "Strongly Agree" to "Strongly Disagree."

   - I must have everybody like me.
   - Making mistakes is terrible.
   - My emotions can't be controlled.
   - I should be terribly worried about threatening situations.
   - Self–discipline is too hard to achieve.
   - I *must* depend on others.
   - My childhood will always dominate me.
   - I can't stand the way others act.
   - Every problem has a perfect solution.
   - I should be better than others.
   - If others criticize me, I must have done something wrong.
   - I can't change what I think.
   - I should do everything perfectly.
   - I have to help everyone who needs it.
   - I must never show any weakness.
   - Healthy people don't get upset.
   - There is one true love.
   - I should never hurt anyone, even by accident.
   - There is a magic cure for my problems.
   - Strong people don't ask for help.
   - I can do things only when I'm in the mood.
   - I am always in the spotlight.
   - It's others' responsibility to solve my problems.
   - People ought to do what I wish.
   - Giving up is the best policy.
   - I need to be sure to decide.
   - Change is unnatural.
   - Knowing how my problems got started when I was young is essential to solving them.
   - Everybody should trust me.
   - I should be happy all the time.
   - There is a secret, terrible part of me that controls me.
   - Working on my problems will hurt me.
   - The world ought to be fair.
   - I am not responsible for my behavior.
   - It is always best not to be genuine.

- It is dangerous to feel emotions.
- People shouldn't act the way they do.

2. Review your clients' answers and ask them where they learned the belief. Try to help them find the exact cultural source for each belief they agree or strongly agree with.

Example

One particular cultural fiction that seems to cause a great deal of problems for many clients is the "one true love" fantasy. Relationships are difficult enough, but they become almost impossible to navigate when a client's only map is a cultural fable. One of the oldest fables about love comes from the orient. Many clients have described a version of this tale.

The tale describes how men and women were not separate creatures in ancient times, but were combined in a single human being. One day an evil demon became angry with God, and magically split the human soul into two parts—male and female. He then hurled these divided parts into the north wind, scattering them across the earth. From that time on all men and women had to spend the rest of their lives trying to find their missing half. There was only one ideal, one perfect match for each person. If they found their missing half, their one true love, they would become whole again and eternally blissful. If not, they would forever wander the world searching—forlorn and inconsolable.

This fable teaches a damaging moral and causes worlds of problems between men and women. Many couples reject good potential mates because they find a faint blemish in them. In their minds their one true love can have no flaws. They can go through scores of relationships looking for the perfect mate, and may reject promising partners simply because of an imperfection. When they discover the futility of their search, they may find out that it's too late to find anyone at all.

The fable may also underlie some marital problems. In some cultures over half of the marriages ultimately end up in divorce. Typically these relationships start out well. A young man and young women date each other and fall in love. Initially everything is romantic and exciting but then after a few years the relationship loses its excitement; the couple gets bored and they become disillusioned.

While there may be many reasons marriages break down—loss of novelty, sexual boredom, in–law problems, financial insecurity, loss of an extended family system, easy divorce, infidelity and so on—

the fable may lurk behind many of these failures.

The reason that this belief is so damaging is that it teaches the young to expect a lot from marriage—a perfect union, one true love, becoming whole and complete.

The fable has spread to all cultures, with the only difference lying in the definition of "perfect." An American may define perfection in a marriage as wealth and high status, while an Australian may mean companionship. To a Pacific Islander a perfect marriage may refer to serenity and babies, while many other cultures may expect permanent romance.

Expectations climb mountains while reality sits there trying to put on its socks. The reality of marriage crashes down on the "one true love" fable: the American couple hits an economic recession; the Australian wife encounters male "mateism"; the Pacific Islander discovers that it is folly to mention serenity and babies in the same sentence.

The fable has spawned many other superstitions. Among them are:

- In order to be happy, you need your spouse to love you all the time.
- When your spouse makes a mistake you should criticize and blame them.
- In a good marriage you will only have sexual desires for your spouse.
- You should be concerned and upset when your marriage is not ideal.
- The spouse causes marital problems.
- Successful marriages should solve or at least greatly reduce the emotional problems you had before you married.
- Loving each other is all you need to have a good marriage.
- You should love steadily all the time.
- A good spouse puts up with any problem their partner has—alcoholism, bad temper, etc.
- Simultaneous orgasms are necessary for a good sex life.
- When your spouse treats you badly, it's your fault for not being a good enough partner.
- It is good for the partners to be totally emotionally dependent on each other.
- Good marriages don't have major problems.
- Your partner should know your needs and desires without having to ask.
- If you love each other enough, you shouldn't have to work on your relationship.

- Spouses must act the way their partners want them to act in order to have a happy marriage.
- Love is a mysterious thing and no one knows what it is.
- Children always make a marriage happier.
- If you never argue, it means you have a good marriage.
- Love and marriage go together.
- When the romantic feelings fade it means there is something wrong with the marriage.
- In good marriages couples do everything together.

So what can clients do to improve their intimate relationships? I often tell them it's best to remember what James Cagney said on the occasion of his fiftieth wedding anniversary. The press had noted that it was unusual for a marriage to last fifty years, particularly in Hollywood, where long-lasting fidelity is uncommon. When reporters asked him why his marriage was so successful, Cagney answered simply, "We didn't expect too much."

Method 2

1. Focus on a client's particular A–C situation.
2. Discover what he or she believes is the cause of the problem in the situation.
3. Help your client find the source of the attribution. Did it come from the culture or is it based on the client's own experience?
4. Describe how another culture might attribute a different cause in the same situation.

Example

Some attributions are crucial to a culture. Among them is the attribution about who is to blame when something goes wrong. There are several possible cultural explanations.

Self vs. Others

"Was I the cause or was someone else responsible?" The answer to this question may determine whether a client will go through life with guilt. In certain cultures, children of divorced parents often misattribute the cause of the divorce and conclude that they were the cause. From an adult point of view the child's misinterpretation is astounding, but from the child's view it is quite natural. One client thought he had caused his parents to divorce because he hadn't kept his room clean. Another remembered thinking her mom left because she was continually soiling her dresses.

Though the attributions in this example are not necessarily culturally inspired, they are pertinent because they demonstrate that the attributions that clients assign when they are children don't change when they become adults. Once a conclusion is reached at an early age, it is tucked away and considered to be a basic truth, not subject to further review. The result is that mature, intelligent adults can be running corporations and raising their families, but still thinking in the dark recesses of their brains that they were rotten kids and that their messed-up rooms caused their parents' divorce.

Human vs. Environmental

People from other countries are often perplexed as to why there are so many lawsuits in America. They ask why we sue so much.

The answer is complex. There are many economic and social reasons, but another answer may be an American cultural attribution.

When bad things happen, the American culture often attributes the cause to human error. There seems to be a core attribution that someone has to be to blame. Not *something*, but *someone*. Many Americans do not accept accidents, bad luck, acts of God, or an individual's bad judgments as acceptable causes. The belief is that natural accidents don't happen. If something bad occurs there must be some human being or group of human beings who caused it or who should have prevented it from happening. Many people may sue primarily to confirm this core belief about themselves and the world. Some recent law suits confirm this view.

- There was a flood in Oahu, Hawaii due to some heavy torrential rains. Some houses were destroyed and an elderly man died. His wife sued the local council for damages.
- A basketball fan sued the coach of his local professional team because the team was having a losing session.
- A woman in Florida sued the community because she hurt her retina looking at a partial eclipse of the sun. She said the local papers should have warned her.
- Several parents have sued record companies because their children were psychologically damaged (one committed suicide) after listening to rock music.
- Several people have sued tobacco companies because they smoked cigarettes for 40 years and ended up getting cancer.

- Anytime an operation doesn't work or a medical treatment fails, physicians are vulnerable to a malpractice suit.
- A man drinks too much in a bar and gets into an auto accident, but sues the bartender for serving him the drinks.
- People in California sued the local council because they were attacked by a mountain lion.
- In Colorado some skiers skied out of bounds, then sued the ski resort because of an avalanche.

The American cultural attribution that someone is always to blame is a relatively recent development. Prior to the present century, many Americans accepted that bad things *can* happen by accident. It would be difficult to imagine a pioneer farmer suing because his crops failed or because his daughter contracted small pox and the country doctor couldn't help. Even if the mechanisms for suing had been as comprehensive then as they are now, the farmer would have felt it immoral to blame and take money from others for his own misfortunes.

But the world has changed. Many Americans no longer believe that a fickle and powerful nature constantly surrounds them. They switched their belief about the power of nature and the power of humanity, and now assume that any catastrophe or misfortune occurring in their lives is manmade rather than natural. There are no longer acts of God; if something bad happens, some person is to blame. Because of this culturally driven attribution, instead of cursing the gods, people now curse humanity, and they have a way of fighting back—they sue.

Comment

A client's cultural beliefs are rarely challenged directly. Instead the therapist usually helps the client identify the cultural source of the cognitions and then allows them to decide how useful the belief is.

One of the most important cultural beliefs is religion. It essential that the therapist is familiar with the religious perspective of the client and incorporates this viewpoint in counseling (see Cox, 1973; Nielsen, & Ellis, 1994). It is also crucial that clergy and religious workers be familiar with psychotherapeutic procedures. For the best guidance in this area see particularly the work of Dr. Andrew Weaver (Koenig & Weaver, 1997, 1998; Weaver, Koenig, & Roe, 1998; Weaver, Preston, & Jerome, 1999).

Further Information

I originally published the client attitude survey in Mc Mullin & Casey (1975).

A major resource for all therapists working with clients from different cultures is the *Intercultural Press*, P.O. Box 700, Yarmouth, ME 04096. It provides textbooks, manuals, books, and articles that teach multicultural awareness, cross-cultural learning, cultural adaptability and multiculturalism. Of particular interest are those guidebooks that describe the cultural perspectives and attributions of different societies. They are written for Westerners by authors who are aware of the attitudes, values and beliefs because they are native to, or have lived in, the culture. For example, *Understanding Arabs: A Guide for Westerners; Good Neighbors: Communicating with the Mexicans; Considering Filipinos; Spain is Different; Exploring the Greek Mosaic; Border Crossings: American Interactions with Israelis; A Fair Go for All: Australian and American Interactions; From Da to Yes: Understanding East Europeans; Encountering the Chinese; From Nyet to Da: Understanding the Russians.* All these and many more may be purchased at the Intercultural Press.

COUNSELING IN DIFFERENT CULTURES
Principles

Textbooks that instruct therapists on how to counsel clients often appear admirable. They present techniques in a neat, clean, logical manner. But clients are more complex than our theories about them, so in actual practice many techniques that may look good in a textbook can fail when applied to real people.

Many of these slips between theory and practice occur when working with clients from different cultures. Despite admonitions that counseling techniques should work anywhere, many therapists have discovered that counseling techniques are not universally effective. To their surprise they have found that they needed to adapt their techniques when working with people from different countries, or even when counseling clients from different parts of the United States.

Method

1. Cognitive therapy is based on helping clients change their beliefs, and beliefs are highly influenced by the clients' culture. To help

clients, therapists need to become intimately familiar with the client's culture.

2. Become familiar with the art, music, and literature of the culture.
3. Be particularly versed in the cultural stories, fables, and fairy tales (see next section).
4. Talk with therapists who have worked with clients in the culture.
5. Make adaptations to your techniques necessary to fit the cultural needs.

Example

My first job in Australia was as a psychologist in the major public drug and alcohol hospital near Sydney. Patients came for treatment from all over Australia. Those from the outback were homespun country–folk, genuine, kind, straightforward, but untutored in recognizing certain psychological aspects of themselves. Those who came from Australian cities like Sydney, Melbourne, or Brisbane were more verbal and more educated; they intellectualized their problems more and had more difficulty accepting help.

All of the psychologists at the hospital conducted therapy in groups. Usually 12 or more patients were crowded into a small room with few windows and poor ventilation; in the summer it became quite hot. We all sat in chairs, in a circle, staring at each other for an hour and a half several times a day, 6 days a week.

The early sessions went something like this:

SYDNEY MAN: I want to say something.

YANK COUNSELOR: Go ahead, Colin.

(*Some grumbling from men from the outback*)

SYDNEY MAN: I demand that we all do our part in picking up on the ward. My job is to clean up the loo before group therapy, and everybody else is making such a mess; I almost don't have time to get here.

(*Loud noisy outburst from some other people. You could hear, "There he goes whining again." Arguments ensued and people were shouting back and forth.*)

YANK COUNSELOR: Colin has his chance to talk, please let him do so.

(*Grumbling from others asking why did they have to listen to me again.*)

SYDNEY MAN: They snore too much and don't wash enough and . . .

NORTHERN TERRITORY MAN: (*interrupting*) Bloody puff. I guess we're suppose to use perfume and wear bloody pink panties too.

SYDNEY MAN: (*addressing Yank counselor*) Are you going to let them say that to me, Yank? I thought we're supposed to observe some rules in here.

(*Grumbling from some others; someone says, Pommy puff; everyone is talking at once.*)

YANK COUNSELOR: Colin can talk now and the others will get their chance later.

(*I spoke in my quietest, calmest, most unruffled voice. General pandemonium breaks loose.*)

MELBOURNE MAN: Some of these yahoos don't wash enough. They have been here for two weeks and I never seen any of them wash.

OUTBACK MAN: Eh, mate? Spending your time peaking into bloke's showers again, eh?

(*General laughter from the country men, strenuous objections from the city people, everybody talking at the top of their voices.*)

BRISBANE MAN: What's the outback word for foreplay? . . . Shearing!

(*All the city people start laughing hysterically while the country men make threatening remarks and raise their fists.*)

SNOWY MOUNTAIN MAN: Hell, everybody stinks in here.

(*The storm erupts again. Yells of approval from the city folks, and laughter from the outback men saying, "We will show you who stinks and who doesn't."*)

Somebody said, "Why do we have to room with sheep–poking swag men anyway?" Another said, "Why do I have to be in this damn hospital in the first place since what's wrong with having a couple of schooners of beer anyway."

The room erupted with catcalls and laughter again and a man from Bendigo said he hadn't stopped at only two beers since he was 10. I interrupted in my calmest manner saying, "We shouldn't all try to talk at once."

Everybody kept on shouting at each other despite my request, and I heard someone in the back of the room say under the din of noise, "Why do we have to have a bloody Yank as a drug counselor anyway?"

Then someone said the food stunk and this opened up further complaining with people shouting back and forth.

That session was supposed to be a lecture about the biochemical components of addiction. I had been trying to give this lecture for several sessions but had never been able to.

The tempest of sounds cycling around the room stood in stark contrast to the drug counseling groups I had run in America—there the process had gone quite well. One could be democratic and let anybody talk who wanted to. There wasn't much of a problem with noise, most people were polite and stayed on the topic. The therapist's job was to facilitate the group and guide the people in a therapeutic direction. One could be nondirective without forcing one's views on anybody. Mostly, the therapist simply reflected the group's feelings or quietly asked gentle questions for them to think about. It all had seemed to go along so smoothly and softly and quietly. But this! What was this?

Group after group, the sessions would be the same. The noise in all the groups was constant. Complaints and epithets were thrown at everybody about everything. Despite it all I kept my cool. I stayed empathetic, facilitative, and continued to employ all the techniques that I had been taught and had found effective with Americans. But after a while this constant din started to build up, and during one session, I'd had it. It was a hot day and a particularly noisy session when I suddenly stood up and shouted something like:

Shut up. Everybody, Shut up! It doesn't matter who smells, who snores, or how bad the food is. All your whining is just so much koala crap, dingo dung, and platypus piss. You are just drunks and junkies, who are here because you have messed up your lives so badly that somebody had to throw you into this hospital. This is not the Sheraton Hilton hotel. We are not a goddamn country club. You are not here to have a rest or to enjoy yourself or to smell sweet. You are here to get sober. You have only a few weeks to learn, so you don't have time to waste complaining about everything under the goddamn sun. I don't give a kangaroo's ass whether you are from Sydney or Bourke or any other place. There are no high–class drunks or junkies in here; you are all the same. You are running out of goddamn time to save your lives, so you better start listening *right now*, before I get moved to the point of annoyance.

Had this been said during a group session in the United States, the patients might have physically attacked, or at the least they may have stood up and walked out saying they wouldn't let anyone talk to them in this way. Probably they would have walked down to the director's office en masse and complained about how unprofessional I had been and how I had cursed at them. The director would have called me into his office and would have either fired me, suspended me, or required me to apologize to each client in person. A complaint would probably have been filed with the state drug and alcohol licensing board. But here, in this Australian group, an amazing thing happened. They all turned around, looked at me, and got quiet. They didn't curse back or act offended, or have a "nobody–can–talk to–me–like–that" expression on their faces. They sat expectantly, looked at me and waited for what I was going to say next. I took my opportunity and said something like,

> Ah . . . well . . . that's better . . . eh. Well now, the reason you are . . . er . . . addicted is that you all have this biochemical predisposition that you probably inherited . . . ahem . . . which means your bodies can't handle these chemicals like other people. Now the way it works is like this . . .

I then went to the blackboard and started drawing diagrams of brains, endorphins, and neurons. They sat up and listened attentively; some even took out little notebooks and copied my drawings. Amazing!

My outburst worked here because the culture in Australia is considerably different from that in the United States. While Americans may be more physically violent and quicker to take physical action when wronged or insulted, they are less prone toward verbal aggression. You can hear Australians say things most Americans wouldn't think of saying. But what would have been fighting words in the United States were just words to Australians. Australians tolerate verbal aggression far more than Americans, but they are far less tolerant of physical abuse. As they say there, "Words? No worries, mate."

Empathy and positive regard had worked in the United States, but had laid an egg in Australia. In Australia a therapist is an authority figure and so is expected to *act* like one. The group members assumed that an authority would act dominant, critical, and forceful. Anything less would be considered wimpy and would result in a loss of respect. Because I was a Yank, the people gave me a small break, but my U.S. counseling style wasn't effective. Not until I spoke up, challenged them, and confronted them, did they become willing to listen to me. Had I done this in the United States I might have been punched out or sued. But in Australia my behavior was considered appropriate and expected. Because of my outburst, I had earned their respect and the right to be listened to.

The point of this story is also one of the points of this chapter. Professional counselors don't simply apply abstract theories to disembodied peoples' problems—they attempt to help people, and those people are born and raised in a culture. The culture doesn't only provide languages, esthetics, or customs to the clients; it also gives them the metaphors through which they interpret everything around them. To counsel anyone effectively you have to immerse yourself in their culture so that you can see the world through their eyes.

Comment

I don't recommend my outburst. I have included it to demonstrate that the relationship between a client and a mental health professional is idiomatic to the specific culture. It is the culture that defines what the social roles of doctor and patient should be, and different cultures have different role expectations. The therapist cannot transplant the client–counselor relationship he learned in New York to east Texas, Hawaii, or Sydney, Australia. If we are to be effective therapists, we had best learn the relationship idiom allowed us within the local culture.

One of the main idioms all therapists must learn when counseling in other cultures is language and expression of the culture. I have found that understanding a client's language can be a big problem.

Many years ago I saw a client from east Texas. He was a young adolescent boy who had been born and raised in the local area. His minister had sent him for therapy because he was depressed about losing his girlfriend. He lived with his family in the backwoods of east Texas and had never been to a town before. The counseling office was on the second floor of a two-story, college administration building, but he refused to go up stairs. He said he had never been on a second floor before, and didn't understand why everybody didn't fall through. The counseling sessions were conducted on the campus lawn.

His first words were unusual. He said something like, "I'm been laid pretty low because of sufferins. Chawin–up ain't my meat, but the pard notions ye to be a fixen me."

I remember being horrified. All these years of schooling to become a psychologist, and I hadn't a clue as to what he had just said. How could we counsel together? With practice, however, I learned, so I can now translate his comment: "I have been depressed because of the pain of losing my girlfriend. I am not very good at talking about such things, but my minister believes you may be able to help me."

After having mastered the local idiom, I moved and was counseling people who spoke in a totally different parlance—the southern Georgia–northern Florida vernacular. After struggling with these dialects for a while, I found myself counseling clients from West Virginia who have a lilting twang, and then clients from remote Rocky Mountain regions who spoke in a guttural shorthand. It took me years to understand all of these idioms adequately.

At last, after years of seeing clients from all over the United States, I felt I had learned enough to have a reasonable chance of understanding most American dialects. But when I went to counsel in Australia, I was thrown into confusion and puzzlement again. I had picked an English–speaking country, thinking that clients and therapists would benefit from speaking the same language. But what I found was that Australian English is worlds different from the American version.

Then I traveled to Hawaii. Hawaii has a mix of several interesting dialects. The big island isn't like Oahu, where Honolulu is. It's more like a third–world, Pacific–Basin country. The locals are kind, gentle people, but they speak a combination of Hawaiian and pidgin English difficult for the outsider to understand. A client who was a cocaine addict sent by his probation officer said at our first session, "How's it . . . bummahs man. We got come haole de kine place from now? What you say brah? Fo' real? Eh?"

After a year of studying several dialects of pigeon English, I finally could translate, " How are you . . . This is unfortunate news. Do I have to attend counseling sessions at the office of a Caucasian therapist regularly? Am I interpreting the situation correctly? Is this true?"

Later I learned to answer in kind, "Yeah. . . . You got come, brah."

I believe that many therapists make mistakes that are not based on misdiagnosis or lack of skill, but are instead based on failure to know the particular idioms that the client is using, or failure to communicate to the client in an idiom that they can understand.

Further Information

There are many good works on the application of cognitive–behavior therapy in different cultures (see Ivey, Ivey, & Simek–Morgan, 1993; Hays, 1995; Pedersen, 1991; and Wehrly, 1995).

The relationship between therapist and client is highly determined by culture (Okpaku, 1998). For example, until recently doctors in Japan didn't tell patients their diagnosis, nor did they ask for informed consent for treatment. It seems the culture has had an unquestioned trust in doctors and there was no reason to consult the patient about such matters (Kimura, 1998; Reich, 1998). In China interfering with a suicide attempt may be considered culturally improper, because in some instances suicide is an obligation (Qui, 1998). In many cultures the therapists could not begin treatment without the full consent of the family or the person responsible for your client (Koenig & Gates, 1998).

The *Intercultural Press* (P.O. Box 700, Yarmouth, ME 04096) is an excellent resource for all therapists working in different cultures.

CULTURAL STORIES AND FABLES
Principles

One of the best ways to find the core themes of a culture is to become familiar with its favorite stories, art, and music. Throughout recorded history, values, insights, principles, and human pitfalls to guard against have been conveyed to each new generation through the medium of fables, fairy tales, nursery rhymes, folk music, and indigenous art. We all remember the stories and songs we heard when young; the morals conveyed by them, whether true or false, profound or silly, have found their way into our value systems. In these same stories the therapist will find a culture's ideals: the cultural hero, the main cultural adversary, the core value the story is honoring, the attitude the story is condemning. Notice how the fable reinforces the good value while punishing the wrong one. (Usually bad things happen to the hero and heroine when they follow noncultural values, such as cowardliness, antisocial actions, or overly independent thinking. Good things happen after the hero or heroine decides to conform to the prevailing social values.)

Cognitive restructuring therapy recognizes that there is a role for these stories in helping clients assume a more adaptive perspective on their lives. Cultural stories, fables, fairy tales, analogies, and metaphors in art, literature, and music are valuable means of communicating some of the complex subtleties of life to certain clients.

In using the storytelling technique, the therapist has the option of either concocting his own stories by drawing upon his own life experiences or by making use of the cultural stories through existing media, including the published works of popular poets and magazine and book writers. The stories thus used may be long or short, funny or serious. There are only two essential requirements for the use of this technique: (1) The story must be relevant to the circumstances of each client, and (2) the story must contain within it at least the essence of a bridge between the client's old, damaging belief and a new, preferred belief.

Method

1. Synthesize the client's core beliefs into a story. Each story should consist of the major situations the client has faced, the major emotional responses, and, most importantly, the principal themes or attitudes, noting especially those that are false or negative.
2. The therapist should then make up a story to explain how and why any evident false themes developed, and how they negatively changed the client's life.
3. Halfway through the story, the therapist should switch the themes toward a more rational, useful perception. Attach this new perception to a value higher in the client's hierarchy. Identify the positive changes that occur to the main characters in the story because of the new perception.

The story can be a fable, fairy tale, or extended metaphor, depending upon what genre seems most useful in persuading a particular client. Prepare the story ahead of time and have the client tape it, so that the client can refer to it when needed.

Example

When I worked on the Big Island of Hawaii, I needed to make some radical changes in the way I conducted psychotherapy. I had to learn to adjust to the island culture.

The Big Island is an unusual society. It's a gentle culture. The spirit of aloha permeates much of the society and is particularly evident in the local Hawaiians born there. Useful in other places, formal classes with didactic instruction are too harsh and would violate the spirit of the culture. What *does* work is a thing called *talking story*, which is a part of their local culture. On the Big Island many locals sit around and convey ideas by making up stories. They tell these tales in a conversational, relaxed manner. They make up long stories that have full descriptions of the local environment and numerous details about the people, but hidden away inside each story is a little principle or a small maxim.

To a haole (foreigner from a Western culture) these stories seem pointless. They appear to ramble on without purpose or direction, and the meaning of the story is hidden away among layers of unnecessary descriptive detail. Westerners want the stories to get to the point. Haoles wish the storyteller would go to a blackboard and diagram the idea behind the story.

But to the native Big Islander talking directly about ideas out of context is missing the point. They wisely suggest that all ideas and abstractions come from people, and that people all live in a place, and these people come from a long line of ancestors who have lived in this place. Therefore, all ideas, concepts, maxims, and principles come from people, who come from ancestors, who come from the land.

To native Hawaiians, drawing abstractions on blackboards would be a sacrilege, because the concepts are dissected from the total environment from which ideas come. They object to this dissection, much as they object to medicating depression separate from the person who is depressed. Hawaiians prefer a more holistic approach, and suggest that such dissection ignores the fact that the depressed person is a person who lives in a family, and that the family lives in a society, and that the society lives in the natural environment.

In order to work with people on the islands, I needed to learn to sit around and talk story with them. So instead of diagramming my ideas on a blackboard as I have done on the mainland, on the Big Island I incorporated various ideas and principles into fables and tales. Whenever possible I used Hawaiian legends, which I found have a storehouse of useful stories.

Here is one. It teaches people to challenge their superstitions and face their fears.

The Cove of Black Pearls

In ancient times, long before Captain Cook came to the islands, there was a tiny cove near Humuhumu Point. It is gone now, for Mauna Loa has long since reclaimed what is hers, but long ago it was there. It was a sheltered cove around a promontory that kept the open ocean out. A small, green–black sand beach with a tall coconut grove bound it on one side, and on the other side a steep wall of lava rose for hundreds of feet.

The water inside this cove was unusual and nowhere else was there water like it. It had a dark emerald hue, crystal clear to the bed 30 feet below. At the deepest part of the cove's bed lived oysters. They were not found anywhere else. Some of the oysters had pearls of the most exquisite sort. They were perfectly round and had a black turquoise hue. They had a luster so deep and rich that they created an iridescent beam of turquoise, emerald, and purple coming from deep within the pearl. No one had ever seen their like.

There were kamahamas who lived in a small village near the cove above the lava cliffs. They would climb down into the cove and dive for the pearls. Since the pearls were so beautiful and unique, the natives traded them to the other islands and the village became prosperous—all shared in the wealth of the pearls.

But one day the goddess Pele got angry and sent lava from Mauna Loa to engulf the cove. She sent broad rivers of fire from the southwest rift zone, down the slopes of the volcano, over the overhanging cliffs, and cascading down into the cove. The sea cooled the flaming rivers and encapsulated the cove in a dome of petrified lava. A mountain of impenetrable molten rock hid the cove beneath.

Without the pearls the villagers soon lost their wealth and became poor and destitute. But they passed the story of the cove from father to son for generations. In this way they kept alive the memory of the cove of black pearls.

Several hundred years later the people still told the story of the pearls, but they had long since forgotten the location of the cove.

One day a young boy was traveling to the sacred City of Refuge up the coast, but he decided to take another route. He walked across a lava dome and noticed a crevasse. The wind and sea of hundreds of years had worn away a hole in the lava. He was curious, so he stuck his torch into the crevasse and looked inside. There appeared to be a large cave underneath with ocean water flowing in from the bottom. It was a small hole, but he managed with difficulty to climb inside. At the bottom he found the green–black sand beach. The walls of the cave were honeycombed with eaves where one torrent of fire after another had rolled down in the ancient times. On one side he saw the burned–down coconut grove and the holes in the lava where the tree trunks had once stood. The lava retained the imprint of the bark from when the trees had fallen upon the burning river, and a perfect impression of every branch and leaf was stamped in the frozen lava. But what caused him to gaze in amazement and wonder were the flashes of lights on the ceiling. Reflected off the walls of the cave were brilliant flashes of turquoise, glistening dots of purple intermingled with emerald.

He lowered his torch to the green–black sand beneath his feet and saw what was causing the reflection. Stretching out before him in the sand were hundreds of black pearls casting iridescent beams of turquoise, emerald, and purple off the walls of the cave. Immediately he knew where he was. He knew that after all these centuries he had discovered the lost cove of black pearls. He excitedly grabbed all the pearls he could, hid them in his clothes and rushed to the City of Refuge. He ran by the city's huge, twenty–foot–wide, stone walls into the oblong square of the three ancient temples. There he entered the sacred sanctuary of the priests of Lono and spread out the pearls for the priests to see.

Initially the priests were ecstatic. Finding the pearls would bring prosperity back to the island and they would be rich. But then they started to worry. If the people heard that the black pearls had been found, they would all rush to the cove, take the pearls, and leave little for the priests. They couldn't keep the discovery secret since they would be trading the pearls to the other islands. What could they do?

They thought about it for many days until finally the high priest found a solution that all of the priests agreed was a perfect plan. They would make the cave *taboo*.

The priests told the boy that the cave was now taboo. They said that he had desecrated the cove of black pearls and that Pele had sent evil menehunes to guard the cove. They explained if anyone now entered the cave, the menehunes would possess the person's body and cause it to explode. They told him that only the priests of Lono were sanctified enough to resist the taboo, and only they could enter the cove.

The boy stayed away from the cave along with all the other villagers. The priests got richer and the people got poorer.

After a year or more, the boy started to get curious. He didn't care about the pearls, but being a boy he became more and more interested in the menehunes. He had never seen one before and wondered about what they looked like and how they could make things explode. So one day he decided to ask the priests. He went back to the City of Refuge and asked the high priest of

Lono what menehunes looked like. The priest told him that menehunes were invisible and that nobody could see them.

"Then how do you know they are there?" asked the boy. The high priest got angry and told the boy to go away. They said if he ever entered the cave again the menehunes would get inside him and make him explode, and that then he would know well enough that there were menehunes and what they could do to him.

But the boy wasn't satisfied. He kept thinking about the menehunes, and exploding, and the cove of black pearls. One moonlit night his curiosity got the best of him. He grabbed a wild piglet he had snared and crept to the cave. Gradually he lowered the pig down onto the beach and waited for it to explode, but it didn't. It kept squealing and running back and forth across the green–black sand. He waited and waited, but still the pig didn't explode. Finally he decided to take a chance and climb down himself. Terrified, he climbed into the cave and looked around. He kept waiting to explode, yet he never did. After a while he grabbed some black pearls and the pig and ran home. He showed the pearls to the villagers, told them about the cove and told them what the priests of Lono had done.

The people realized there was no taboo and that their priests were lying to them. They discovered that the priests' teachings were only superstitions aimed at keeping the people poor. The priests had held the fattest offices in the land, had been rich and powerful, had stood even above the chiefs, but now they were shown to be frauds, impostors, and fakes.

So, the people gathered and rose up in a mighty mass against the priests of Lono. After a great battle, all the priests were slain and their influence was removed from the islands.

The story was helpful to many clients. Anxious clients from the Big Island understood the moral: *Challenge your superstitions.* When this principle was explained using other methods, they hadn't understood—the manner of explaining was too foreign to them—but when I conveyed the message through this story, they understood and benefited from the lesson.

Comment

Ideally, an appropriate story or fairy tale should come rolling "trippingly off the tongue" of the therapist at exactly the right moment during a session. However, therapists who lack that particular kind of creativity can still make effective use of this technique. Those who cannot devise an appropriate story will simply have to devote more time and energy to planning in advance how best to interweave stories from some other source into their overall strategy for effecting a perceptual shift in a particular client.

Nothing, however, will replace the hard work the therapists need to put in to become intimately familiar with the cultures of their clients.

Further Information

Since psychotherapy began, counselors have been using stories to convey psychological concepts in ways that clients could understand, but little research has been undertaken to determine the effectiveness of such interweaving. Some exceptions have been: Lazarus (1971, 1989, 1995), and particularly the imagery and fantasy work of Singer (1974, 1976, 1995), Singer and Pope (1978), Sheikh and Shaffer (1979), and Sheikh (1983a, 1983b). Donnelly and Dumas (1997), Martin, Cummings, and Hallberg (1992), McCurry and Hayes (1992), and Siegelman (1990) have explored the importance of analogies and metaphors in therapeutic situations.

Milton Erickson is one of the best-known therapeutic storytellers. See Bandler and Grinder (1996), Erickson (1982), Havens (1985), and Lankton and Lankton (1983) for some examples.

For other therapeutic use of fantasy see Duhl (1983), Gordon (1978), Leuner (1969), Shorr (1972, 1974), and symbolic modeling of Bandura and Barab (1973).

The fantasy literature of different societies often reveals the core attitudes and values of cultures. There are some good fantasy anthologies from different countries: New Guinea (Gillison, 1993), Scottish, (Manlove, 1997), Celtic (Yeats, 1990), Dutch (Huijing, 1994), Portuguese (De Quieroz, 1995), Polish (Powaga, 1997), British (Stableford, 1993), Jewish (Neugroschel, 1997), Hungarian (Ivaldi Cdtud, 1995).

The therapist will also find a culture's mythology a useful storehouse of cultural cognitions. For a general review of folklore and fables see Smith (1995). For the stories and fables of the South Pacific see the *Mana*, a multivolume journal of language and literature of oceania (*Mana*, 1980). Norse mythology can be found in the *Prose Edda* from Icelandic translations (Young, 1954). Australian myths are recorded in *Aboriginal Myths: Tales of the Dreamtime* by Reed (1978). Hawaiian myths, oral traditions, and historical tales are reported by

Fornander (1996). Fables about the origin of the universe and the origins of man can be found in Philip Freund (1965), *Myths of Creation*. Bulfinch's classic work on more famous mythologies is a great source of cultural themes (see *Bulfinch's Mythology:* "Age of Fable," "The Age of Chivalry," "Legends of Charlemagne"). In addition, review *King Arthur and His Knights; The Mabinogeon, Beowulf, Religion and Folklore of Northern India* (Crooke, 1926), and that of Scotland (Dalyell, 1935).

FOURTEEN

Philosophical Underpinnings

THIS LAST CHAPTER STATES EXPLICITLY what has only been implicit in the rest of the book—the philosophical foundations underlying the practice of cognitive restructuring therapy.

In the two sections that follow I offer a brief and sometimes personal discussion of two philosophical principles. The first, "What is Rational to Clients?" uses the law of parsimony to help clients to discover which of their beliefs are preferable over other beliefs. The second, "What is Real to Clients?" discusses using pragmatism to help clients to sort through their different views of reality.

WHAT IS RATIONAL TO CLIENTS?
Principles

Ever since cognitive therapy began many years ago, cognitive therapists have been accused of indoctrinating clients with their own view of what is rational. The legitimate questions being asked include: Why should the client accept the philosophy of the therapist? What makes the therapist's view of what is true or false any more valid than the client's? Is the claim of the rightness of the therapist's view based on academic authority, professional consensus, intuition, divine revelation, scientific imperialism, rationalism, or some other philosophical foundation?

Cognitive restructuring therapy has an answer to these questions. The therapist's judgment of the truth or falseness of a client's belief is based on *the law of parsimony*.

I explain to my clients that the law of parsimony is one of the most useful tools available to help them determine the validity of their beliefs. At its most basic, the law means that, all things being equal, the simplest explanation is the best. A small book on philosophy—*The Web of Belief* by Quine and Ullian (1978)—explains the principle well. It describes the law of parsimony in great detail and gives many common everyday examples that demonstrate its power. I give my clients one example from the book.

> Imagine that one afternoon you get into your tan '99 Subaru wagon and drive to the supermarket. You park next to the shopping cart stall and go into the store. An hour later you return pushing a cart full of groceries. You look where you parked your car and see a tan '99 Subaru wagon. What do you conclude?

The answer is so obvious that most clients don't see the point of the question. They conclude that it is *their* car, the same car that they left in that very parking spot. Clients ask, "What else could it be?" I answer that it really could be a great number of other things. Someone might have stolen their car and then parked another tan '99 Subaru wagon in its place. The client could be imagining the car, or it could be a holograph of their car, or it could be a VW bug disguised to look like their car. After a few of these examples, the clients see the point; it is only their imagination that limits what it *could* be.

The difficulty is in determining what logic clients and the rest of us use to reflexively assert that it is our car and not one of the alternatives. Authority? There is no authority telling us it's our car. Consensus? The people in the parking lot did not vote to determine whether it is our car. Divine revelation? Most people would doubt that God would be concerned about where we parked our car. Scientific empiricism? No controlled experiment was conducted to scientifically prove that it is our car sitting there.

With all of those alternatives available, we simply automatically assumed that it was our car. What makes us so certain of the correctness of our answer that we don't even consider the other possibilities?

Clients usually tell us that they use their logic, their reasoning. They assume that it's their car because it is the most probable explanation. They have gone to the store 99 times before and have always found their car where they left it, so they assume that this time will be the same as the previous 99; this answer has the highest probability. Most clients admit that the other explanations are possible, but the probabilities are so unlikely that they don't need to consider them. Logic dictates that they pick the most probable answer.

This explanation may be mistaken. Many philosophers, starting with Hume and ending in the present day with Popper, assert other-wise. They suggest that just because something has happened a million times before there is no guarantee and no probability that the next time the same thing will happen again, that just because the sun has risen every other day is no guarantee that it will rise tomorrow. They point out that there is no logical connection between tomorrow's sunrise and all the previous sunrises; each are independent events.

Thinking that independent events are connected in some mystical way is referred to as the gambler's fallacy, and many clients make it; it is the belief that one chance event influences the next chance event. For instance, we know that the probability of getting heads when we flip a coin is fifty percent. We also know that the probability of getting a head the next time we flip the coin is the same fifty percent. It doesn't matter how many heads we get in a row, a hundred or a thousand, the probability for the coin landing on heads remains fifty percent each time we flip the coin. But many clients think that probabilities build up, and that the coin almost knows that after a hundred results of heads it is supposed to land as a tail pretty soon; the impetus for a tail gets stronger and stronger. But this is absurd. Coins aren't good at remembering.

A client's car is no smarter than a coin. It doesn't remember that it was in the parking lot 99 times before. It doesn't know whether it is a holograph or a negative hallucination or if it has been replaced by an identical car.

Many modern philosophers are convinced that we can't prove concepts like cause and effect, probability, or chance. If they are right, it is difficult to determine why humans automatically assume that the car they find in their parking spot is their car. They have no good reason for assuming it's their car despite the fact that they make this assumption all the time and without question.

This entire discussion strikes many clients as absurd. They suggest that nobody would think of these other options, and that everybody would conclude that the car they see is their car. They claim it is obvious, and it is, but the reason it's obvious is explained by the law of parsimony. This law, though usually unnamed and unidentified, is so ingrained in all of us that in situations like our example clients pick the simplest, clearest, least complex explanation without a second thought. They immediately assume that it's their car and don't consider the alternatives. They use the law of parsimony a thousand times every day, and they do it so automatically that they aren't even aware of it.

But it is this same law of parsimony that clients often suspend when judging their own damaging beliefs and attitudes. One of our biggest jobs as cognitive therapists is to help clients reapply the law that they use so constantly for exterior events to themselves.

Method

1. When clients are looking for an explanation for their behavior, help them find the *simplest* explanation first.

    The "simplest" means the most familiar or most ordinary explanation. For example, if a client squeezes his toothpaste and nothing comes out he could conclude that the laws of physics have been mysteriously suspended for his tube of toothpaste, that for this moment in time and space the second law of thermodynamics—for every action there is a reaction—doesn't hold. As we have seen, the fact that the toothpaste has always come out before is no guarantee that it will come out this time. The law of parsimony causes us to reject this notion out of hand—we don't even consider it. Instead we conclude that something is stopping up the end of the tube or that the tube is out of toothpaste.

2. Help your clients find the *easiest* conclusion.

    The law of parsimony also tells us to search for the answer that requires the least energy. The car analogy is a good example. The interpretation of what we see in the parking lot that requires the least amount of energy is that it is our car. It would take a great deal of energy to remove our car and substitute a holograph, or to steal it and replace it with another one of exactly the same year, model, and color. Our brain picks the explanation that requires the least amount of effort.

3. Help your clients pick the *least* complex answer.

    The interpretation that is least complicated is preferable to entangled explanations. For example, a Freudian theorist might suggest that women are afraid of snakes because snakes represent the male organ, and that those women who have repressed their sexual feelings will develop a phobia about anything that symbolically can be associated with the penis. This is a very complex explanation. It is much less complex to think that women (and people in general) are afraid of snakes because being bitten by a poisonous snake can kill us. To the rejoinder, "Why then are people afraid of nonpoisonous snakes?" the answer is that it is often difficult to tell the difference between the one and the other.

Example: The Story of Bob

If a client totally rejects all the components of parsimony he or she can have serious mental health problems; one of the more severe of these is paranoia. A client named Bob came to see me with an extensive paranoid delusion. He believed that units of the Irish Republican Army were out to make him go crazy and then kill him. This was a peculiar delusion because Bob wasn't Irish, had no connection with Ireland or the Irish, and wasn't a supporter of anti–IRA groups, but somehow he had gotten it into his head that the IRA had targeted him as an enemy. There was absolutely no evidence whatsoever that anybody disliked him—much less hated him enough to kill him.

Like most simple paranoid patients, Bob was not a generally insane man. He was quite bright, had a good, high–paying job, a wife and family. He didn't have a history of panic reactions or anxiety and he wasn't on drugs. He had a normal history in every way. The only event preceding his paranoia was a problem with his wife that had produced a moderate depression. Immediately after his depression had begun he'd developed his paranoia.

When I interviewed Bob he seemed perfectly normal. He was logical and rational throughout most of the interview, but near the end he asked me whether I was Irish. The referral agency had *not* informed me of the particular nature of his delusion, so I cheerfully answered, "Why yes. My grandfather Edward Ryan came over from Ireland in the 1890s." At that point, Bob stood up with a crazed look in his eye. He gagged and bolted out of the room with a look of horror about him. I thought, "Oh well . . . another satisfied customer."

I later found out what had happened and realized that I couldn't work with Bob again, so I conducted the therapy through one of my Jewish supervisees who had no connection to Ireland. The therapy was interesting. Bob could not be persuaded from his delusion and was totally unable to use even the slightest aspect of the law of parsimony. Instead, he would interpret all events in terms of his delusion. If a red–haired man walked past him on the street carrying a package, Bob was sure that he was from the IRA and that the package was a bomb. He refused to shop in any store that had "Mac" or "Mc" or "O" in its name. If he saw a green car he would break into a cold sweat, certain that it was an IRA patrol. When the networks broadcast a

Notre Dame football game he was sure that the IRA was sending him coded messages through the announcers telling him that his time was up.

When the therapist argued against Bob's nonparsimonious interpretations, Bob would counter with, "You are not aware of the international Irish conspiracy. If you were, you would see the reasonableness of my view." He could not perceive even the easiest components of parsimony, and therefore could not be persuaded from his views.

The difficulty in working with Bob and people like him is that the law of parsimony is based on a feeling, not on logic or reasoning, and this feeling is grounded on the concept of basic trust. At times we all need to trust our spontaneous, parsimonious, perceptions of events. Once this trust is removed because of emotional trauma or some kind of brain injury, the perception of parsimony disappears and it's very difficult to get it back.

I wish that I could report that Bob was cured by some dramatic, profound technique, but he wasn't. He left the center after having switched from an IRA conspiracy to a Jewish conspiracy, and since the other therapist was Jewish, well . . . you know what happened. Maybe we had misread him and he was really paranoid about psychologists—we aren't sure.

A colleague of mine has successfully used a paradoxical approach to counsel some clients like Bob who have lost their ability to apply the law of parsimony. In his approach the therapist becomes more unparsimonious than his clients—he out-paranoid the paranoia. In discussing Bob's case, he told me that he might have handled Bob by telling him something like this.

> The IRA is just a front group for the Jewish conspiracy. And behind them is the black conspiracy, which joined with the Chinese communists after they combined with the Mafia and Latinos. The cover organization for the movement is the National Organization for Women in conjunction with the Daughters of the American Revolution. They are all financed by the Save the Whales foundation. Of course the whole thing is run by those 10 WASP bankers in New York who everybody knows run everything anyway.
>
> If you really want to protect yourself you must guard against all these groups. Now that I think about it, that won't work either

because they all know that you'll be on the lookout for them, so they will come in the disguises that you would least expect. Be particularly careful about old ladies because that would be a great disguise. Also be aware of people from Kansas, Iowa, or any of the midwestern states because you wouldn't normally suspect them, which makes them highly suspect. Of course the Irish and the Jews are from the east, so keep an eye on Easterners. And in the west they have the Latinos so give Westerners a wide birth. All foreigners are suspicious because you don't really know where they are from.

Ah, Bob what the hell. There are so many people from so many places who could do you in that you can't protect yourself no matter what you do. Looks like they are going to get you for sure. Why try to protect yourself anymore? You might as well have the best life that you can until the inevitable happens, right? So let's see if I can help you be as happy as you can until the end comes. Since you're going to die anyway, why not enjoy your life until then. . . .

Now let's see now, What can we do to make your present life happier? . . .

Humm . . . We will have to work on that. OK, Bob?

By the way, how's your wife?"

Comment

The rule of parsimony does not mean that all unfamiliar, high-energy, complex explanations are wrong; the rule only means that clients should pick the simplest explanation first, and choose complex, unusual answers only if the simplest one doesn't fit the facts.

Further Information

Many philosophers have discussed the law of parsimony. Possibly the best presentation is by Quine and Ullian (1978). Also see Quine (1987). Historically, the law is known as "Occam's razor," coming from William of Occam, or Ockham, a 14th–century English Franciscan theologian who said exactly, "It is vain to do with more what can be done with fewer" (quoted by Bertrand Russell, 1945).

WHAT IS REAL TO CLIENTS?
Principles

The philosophical origins of cognitive restructuring therapy are similar to the origins of psychology and psychiatry in general. There has been a dichotomy between what could be called the material and the mentalistic traditions. On the material side there is the view that the human body, the human brain, and the human nervous systems are physical objects in space that are subject to the same mechanical laws that control other material bodies. They have size and mass and weight; they can be perceived directly by outside observers; they can be measured; and most importantly they operate deterministically in a cause–and–effect sequence. Radical behaviorism, medical psychology, and neuropsychology have all harkened back to the philosophical materialism of Thomas Hobbes and the realism of John Locke.

Behaviorist therapists such as Cautela took behavioral methods such as extinction, reinforcement, and conditioning and placed them in the mind of the subject by adding the prefix "covert." Thus, early in cognitive therapy we applied techniques such as covert conditioning, covert desensitization, and covert avoidance. Despite being covert, these techniques still operated in the material world with mechanical laws, and were subject to determinism and cause–and–effect relationships.

The second tradition, mentalism, has had an equally long and colorful history. Using the word "mind" rather than "brain" and emphasizing concepts such as volition, choice, responsibility, purpose, knowing, and believing, adherents to this tradition describe phenomena that are not in space, not subject to mechanical laws, and not viewable by external observation. Coming from the mentalistic philosophy and idealism of Plato, George Berkeley, and Emanual Kant, another group of early cognitive therapists came from the humanistic, Rogerian, or existential schools. To these therapists freedom of choice, rational decision making, and being responsible for one's own behavior were key principles in psychotherapy.

Cognitive therapy, like psychology in general, has been trapped in the material/mentalistic dualism throughout its history. The problem of reconciling the two traditions has always been the same, and the crux of the problem can be stated through questions such as, "How can minds influence bodies?" "How can mental concepts like choice and purpose be described in physical terms such as neurosynapses, chemical transmitters, or endocrine secretions? How can one explain physical concepts, such as cause and effect, in terms of mental concepts, such as choice, decision, and purpose?

This discussion is not simply a philosophical abstraction, but actually comes into play when the therapist has to testify in a courtroom as to whether clients intended to commit crimes, knew what they were doing, were competent to stand trial, or were incompetent because of psychosis, insanity, emotional trauma, or drug addiction.

The key problem in explaining the interaction between the mental and the physical world has been most succinctly stated by the modern philosopher, Gilbert Ryle. Ryle described the problem with his famous phrase, the dogma of the Ghost in the Machine (Ryle, 1949, p. 15–16). The ghost in Ryle's machine, like volition inside a human being, is an immaterial object. It has no size, weight, or dimension. It can go through walls and doors and can float above the ground because it is not subject to physical laws such as gravity. But the machine, like the human body, is entirely physical, and subject to all the laws and forces that all material objects are subject to. How can a ghost affect a machine? How can our will affect our actions? If the ghost tries to throw a lever or press a button on the machine, its ghostly hand goes right through it, touching no lever and pressing no button.

In cognitive therapy we take this conundrum to mean, "How do clients change their thoughts? How do clients get themselves to believe one thought and reject another? What does *believe* mean? Is shifting beliefs simply a matter of mechanical repetition and reinforcement, or do choice and commitment have something to do with changing an internal state such as cognitions?"

The predicament about how can a ghost affect a machine is the same predicament about cognitive therapy. How can clients change their thoughts? Even if one substitutes mind for ghost or body for machine, or substitutes choosing, believing, and intending for mind, or neurotransmitters, cortical and subcortical brain regions for body, the problem remains the same.

Since it is impossible for the ghost to manipulate the machine, is it not impossible for clients to change their thoughts? But clients do change their thoughts all the time so there must be something wrong with the theory, and there is.

Ryle suggests that the dichotomy between mind and matter doesn't exist and that therefore the problem of interface disappears. Humanity does not live in two parallel worlds, one material and the other mental, or where one is subject to mechanistic forces and involuntary causes and effects and the other is subject to volition, choice, purpose, and responsibility. The two descriptions are simply different ways of accounting for human beings. It is not that one description is true and the other is false, nor is it true that one is more useful than the other; each is useful in its own sphere. When prescribing medication for a seriously psychotic patient it is useful to look at the physical—the biochemical interactions and the entire chain of chemical causes and effects. But when counseling a client about life decisions, it is useful to look at the mental—the process of decision making, life purposes, and choosing. Ryle's statement best summarizes the answer: "Men are not machines, not even ghost–ridden machines. They are men—a tautology which is sometimes worth remembering" (Ryle, 1949, p. 81).

Example

I will make the final example in this book, my most personal example. It concerns how I came to accept the philosophy expressed above.

> We dance round in a ring and suppose,
> But the Secret sits in the middle and knows.
> —*Robert Frost (Lathem, 1975, p. 362)*

Despite years of study in psychology, as well as philosophy and science, my understanding of the complexity of human nature didn't come from any of my books, research, or years of education. It came from a personal source—*my father.* It happened this way.

My dad has been gone for many years now, but I still think of him often. He was an architect, the type who loved the art far more than the tech. He loved art so much that he engaged in a family ritual that we kids hated; every other Sunday or so he would pile the entire family into our car, Old Bettsy, and drive to some art show or museum to see a new exhibit. He told mom that it would be good for us kids, that it would make us cultured or something, but he really just wanted to see the show himself and liked having company along.

Preteen kids are less than enthusiastic about musty art museums, and we were no exception, so we sabotaged the excursions in every way we could, but one show came along that we couldn't get out of. A Van Gogh exhibition was touring the country and had arrived at the Philadelphia Art Museum, so when the next Sunday came around we were poured into Old Bettsy and taken to see it.

When we arrived at the museum I spent most of my time trying to find something interesting to do, touching the medieval armor and looking at the crossbows. When I couldn't avoid it any longer, I went inside to see the exhibit.

As I walked around looking at the Van Gogh paintings, I immediately disliked them. To my 10–year–old eyes they looked silly. The flowers didn't look like flowers and the farm had colors that no farm has ever had. Taken together the paintings didn't look real to me; they didn't show what people see when they look at things. I concluded that Van Gogh could *not* draw.

Near the end of the exhibit there was a painting off by itself in a place of honor. Standing in front of it was a group of admiring adults; my dad was among them. I was curious about what these grownups thought was so special, so I stood behind them and looked. It was a painting of a night scene, with a large sky overlooking a small village. The sky was a dark rich blue; the village below was sketched in outline. But the most surprising thing about the painting were the stars. They weren't dots of light, but huge golden spirals spinning in the sky. They dominated and overwhelmed the painting.

I stared at it for some time but still had the same reaction I'd had for the others—it didn't look real. Stars don't look like that; they are dots of light, not spirals, and the color of the sky was too blue, the texture too grainy. The whole thing looked as if it had been painted with a shovel rather than a brush.

I wanted to move on and find something else to do, but then I stopped for a moment. My dad and the other adults were still admiring the painting, and I remember thinking, "Maybe I'm wrong; if everybody saw what I saw, nobody would go to these exhibits. But they do. Maybe they see something I don't see. After all, I'm only a kid. What do I know? If somebody is missing something, it's probably me."

So I stayed and tried to comprehend what my dad saw by mimicking the way that he was looking at it. If he stood with his weight on one leg, stroked his chin and said, "Um–hum," then I did the same. But it didn't work. I kept on thinking the same thing—a sloppy painting, inaccurate, unreal, poorly drawn. Maybe other 10–year–olds could have appreciated its beauty; maybe other boys were more sensitive, insightful, artistic, or profound, but I wasn't; I was just a typical 10–year–old kid, and I saw nothing.

Then my dad asked me whether I liked it, and I knew I was stuck. If I said what I felt, "I think it's dumb," I would have caused a big problem. Dad and the other adults would have regarded me as a stupid, bratty kid who shouldn't be allowed into these exhibitions anyway, and far more importantly, my dad would have been embarrassed. He would have gotten angry, said, "The hell with it," and dragged us all home. Mom would have been hurt because the family outing was ruined, and my brother and sisters would have yelled at me for upsetting Mom and Dad and ruining their day. They would have demanded that I be left home the next time, and, although I disliked museums, I disliked being left out of the family even more. All this flashed through my mind in a split second. Suddenly I blurted out, "I like it . . . very impressive . . . nice colors." Not a profound critique of this famous painting, but the best that I could do at the time. My dad seemed satisfied; the day was saved.

I forgot all about the painting for many years, until I lived in Colorado. To escape the petty hassles of city life I would sometimes drive into the mountains by myself late at night and just lie in a mountain meadow looking up at the stars. Around midnight in the high country, the stars shine brilliantly because the air is so thin and the city lights are so far away. The sky is full of thousands of stars that appear to envelop the earth. When looking up at the sky from a high mountain pass, I was always conscious of how big the cosmos is and how small we little human beings are.

One evening I was lying in my meadow looking at the stars when Van Gogh's picture popped into my mind. Suddenly, after 20 years, I understood what the picture meant, why my dad had liked it so, why it was such a famous painting. Van Gogh's *Starry Night* captured the feeling of that moment, a feeling that I couldn't have understood at 10 but that I could now. Van Gogh had painted a human being's emotions of wonder and awe of the night sky.

Why was the picture understandable on that mountain meadow, but not before? A lot had happened in the 20 years since I had first seen it. Astronomy had caught my interest, and black holes, gaseous nebula, and the immensity of the universe had impressed me. I had studied philosophy and done a lot of thinking about human nature and about our place in the cosmos, why we are here and how small our earth is. So when I looked at the stars in the mountain meadow I looked at them with new eyes and saw life in a way far beyond what I could have seen at 10. Technically, they were the same stars, but they didn't feel the same. The stars I saw in the mountains of Colorado felt far more like Van Gogh's stars than the stars I had seen when I was

10. They were huge spinning galaxies, made up of millions of stars and planets and probably full of teaming life, not just little dots in the sky.

What is human reality? Which is the true picture of the sky: the view of a 10–year–old boy or the view of *Starry Night*? What is the true nature of ourselves and our clients—the mechanistic, deterministic side, or the freedom and responsibility side? When young, I would have said, "Stars are dots, and people are people. What you see is what you get." But as I got older and thought more and learned and felt more, I realized, "Stars are the universe, and people are made of star stuff. What you see is what your understanding enables you to see."

Human nature is not simple. It exists in many layers that change, move, and develop constantly. The top layer is one of simple appearance—what we see when we look, what I saw when I was 10. The bottom layer is one of deep meaning and understanding—what Van Gogh painted, what we feel on a mountain meadow, what we notice about our own nature. Our experience of living in the world forges this layer. The astronomer sees spiral galaxies, quasars, pulsars, black holes, and stellar mechanics. The astrologer sees constellations and cosmic deterministic forces influencing human nature. The ship's captain sees meridians of longitude and latitude. The minister sees the creative power of God guiding humanity. In the bottom layer, we don't see what we get; we get what we see.

So, which is the real sky, and what is our true nature?

All of them. It simply depends upon the way we look at it.

After all my years of counseling with my fellow human beings, I try to remember that there are many layers of human nature, and I strive to understand the layers that my clients are experiencing. I know that some clients are trapped on the surface and need to go deeper to feel happier. There are no right or wrong layers, but there are more helpful and less helpful ways to look at things. When I counsel clients who see only dots in the night sky, I attempt to show them that hidden inside the dots are swirling, multicolored galaxies dancing in the starry night.

Comment

The reader does not have to share the author's philosophical underpinnings to practice the cognitive therapy expressed in this book. Cognitive restructuring therapy is a large enough tent to encompass differing views.

Further Information

The reader will have his or her own favorite philosophical sources. Some of mine are: Bertrand Russell, *A History of Western Philosophy* (1945) and *The Basic Writing of Bertrand Russell* (1961); John Stuart Mill, *Philosophy of Scientific Method* (Mill, 1950); Quine and Ullian, *The Web of Belief* (1978); Gordon Ryle, *The Concept of Mind* (1949); Wilson, *Language and the Pursuit of Truth* (1967); and Wilson, *Thinking with Concepts*

Bibliography

Ackerman, R. (1965). *Theories of knowledge: A critical introduction.* New York: McGraw–Hill.

Adamson, B., & Gehlhaar, P. (1989). Cognitive structures in recovery from alcohol dependence: An examination of sex differences. Assisi, Italy: *Eighth International Congress on Personal Construct Psychology.*

Adler, A. (1964). The individual psychology of Alfred Adler: A systematic presentation in selections from his writings. New York: Harper & Row.

Alberti, R. (1987). *The professional edition of your perfect right: A manual for assertive trainers.* San Luis Obispo, CA: Impact Publishing.

Alberti, R. (1990). *A manual for assertiveness trainers: With 1995 supplement.* San Luis Obispo, CA: Impact Publishing.

Alberti, R., & Emmons, M. (1995). *Your perfect right: A guide to assertive living.* San Luis Obispo, CA: Impact Books.

Alexander, P. (1988). The therapeutic implications of family cognitions and constructs. *Journal of Cognitive Psychotherapy, 2,* 219–236.

Alford, B., & Beck, A. (1997). *The integrative power of cognitive therapy.* New York: Guilford.

Alford, B., Beck, A., Freeman, A., & Wright, F. (1990). Brief focused cognitive therapy of panic disorder. *Psychotherapy, 27*(2), 230–234.

Anderson, J. (1980). *Cognitive psychology and its implications.* San Francisco: Freeman.

Anderson, J. (1994). *Eye illusions.* New York: Modern Publishing.

Arnold, M. (1960). *Emotion and personality.* (Vols. 1–2). New York: Columbia University Press.

Aronson, E. (1980). *The social animal.* San Francisco: Freeman.

Ascher, L., & Cautela, J. (1972). Covert negative reinforcement: An experimental test. *Journal of Behavior Therapy and Experimental Psychiatry, 3,* 1–5.

Ascher, L., & Cautela, J. (1974). An experimental study of covert extinction. *Journal of Behavior Therapy and Experimental Psychiatry, 5,* 233–238.

Attneave, F. (1968). Triangles as ambiguous figures. *The American Journal of Psychology, 81.*

Aubut, L., & Ladouceur, R. (1978). Modification of self-esteem by covert positive reinforcement. *Psychological Reports, 42*, 1305–1306.

Avison, W., & Speechley, K. (1987). The discharged psychiatric patient: A review of social, social–psychological, and psychiatric correlates of outcome. *American Journal of Psychiatry. 144*(1), 10–18.

Ayer, A. (1952). *Language, truth and logic.* New York: Dover.

Ayer, A. (1984). *Philosophy in the twentieth century.* New York: Vintage.

Ayer, A., (1988). *The problem of knowledge.* New York: Penguin.

Azrin, N., Huchinson, R., & Hake, D. (1967). Attack, avoidance, and escape reactions to aversive shock. *Journal of the Experimental Analysis of Behavior, 10*, 131–148.

Baer, J., Marlatt, G., & Mc Mahon (Eds.) (1993). *Addictive behaviors across the life span.* Newbury Park, CA: Sage.

Bajtelsmit, J., & Gershman, L. (1976). Covert positive reinforcement: Efficacy and conceptualization. *Journal of Behavior Therapy and Experimental Psychiatry, 7*, 207–212.

Baker, S., & Kirsch, I. (1991). Expectancy mediators of pain perception and tolerance. *Journal of Personality and Social Psychology, 61*(3), 504–510.

Bakker, T. (1982). *Run to the roar.* Harrison, AR: New Leaf Press.

Banaji, M., & Prentice, D. (1994). The self in social contexts. *Annual Review of Psychology, 45*, 297–332.

Bandler, R. (1992). *Magic in action.* Cupertino, CA: Meta Publications.

Bandler, R. (1996). *Persuasion engineering.* Cupertino, CA: Meta Publications.

Bandler, R., & Grinder, J. (1979). *Frogs into princes.* Moab, UT: Real People Press.

Bandler, R., & Grinder, J. (1996). *Patterns of the hypnotic techniques of Milton H. Erickson, M.D.* Cupertino, CA: Metamorphous Press.

Bandura, A. (1977a). *Social learning theory.* Englewood Cliffs, NJ: Prentice-Hall.

Bandura, A. (1977b). Self-efficacy: Toward a unifying theory of behavior change. *Psychological Review, 84*, 191–215.

Bandura, A. (1978). Reflections on self efficacy. In S. Rachman (Ed.), *Advances in behaviour research and therapy* (Vol. 1). Oxford: Pergamon Press.

Bandura, A. (1982). Self-efficacy mechanism in human agency. *American Psychologist, 37*, 122–147.

Bandura, A. (1984). Recycling misconceptions of perceived self–efficacy. *Cognitive Therapy and Research, 8*, 231–255.

Bandura, A. (Ed.) (1995). *Self-efficacy in changing societies.* New York: Cambridge University Press.

Bandura, A. (1996). Ontological and epistemological terrains revisited. *Journal of Behavior Therapy and Experimental Psychiatry, 27* (4), 323–345.

Bandura, A. (1997). *Self-efficacy: The exercise of control.* New York: Freeman.

Bandura, A., Adams, N., Hardy, A., & Howells, G. (1980). Tests of the generality of self–efficacy theory. *Cognitive Therapy and Research, 4*, 39–66.

Bandura, A., & Barab, P. (1973). Process governing disinhibitory effects through symbolic modeling. *Journal of Abnormal Psychology, 82*, 1–9.

Bandura, A., Reese, L., & Adams, N. (1982). Microanalysis of actions and fear arousal as a function of differential levels of perceived self–efficacy. *Journal of Personality and Social Psychology, 43*, 5–21.

Bandura, A., & Schunk, D. H. (1981). Cultivating competence, self–efficacy, and intrinsic interest through proximal self–motivation. *Journal of Personality and Social Psychology, 41*, 586–598.

Barlow, D., Agras, W., Leitenberg, H., Callahan, E., & Moore, R. (1972). The contribution of therapeutic instructions to covert sensitization. *Behavior Research and Therapy, 10*, 411–415.

Barlow, D., Leitenberg, H., & Agras, W. (1969). Experimental control of sexual deviation through manipulation of the noxious scene in covert sensitization. *Journal of Abnormal Psychology, 74*, 596–601.

Barlow, D., Reynolds, E., & Agras, W. (1973). Gender identity change in a transsexual. *Archives of General Psychiatry, 28*, 569–576.

Barry, D. (1994). *The world according to Dave Barry*. New York: Random House.

Barry, D. (1996). *Dave Barry in cyberspace*. New York: Crown Publishers.

Barry, D. (1997). *Dave Barry is from Mars and Venus*. New York: Crown.

Baumbacher, G. (1989). Signal anxiety and panic attacks. *Psychotherapy. 26*, 75–80.

Beatty, J., & Legewie, H. (Eds.) (1977). *Biofeedback and behavior.* New York: Plenum.

Beck, A. (1967). *Depression: Clinical, experimental, and theoretical aspects.* New York: Hoeber.

Beck, A. (1975). *Depression: Causes and treatment.* Philadelphia, PA: University of Pennsylvania.

Beck, A. (1993). *Cognitive therapy and the emotional disorders.* New York:American Library Trade.

Beck, A. (1996). Beyond belief: A theory of modes, personality, and psychopathology. In P. Salkovskis (Ed.), *Frontiers of cognitive therapy* (pp. 1–25). New York: Guilford.

Beck, A., Emery, G., & Greenberg, R. (1985). *Anxiety disorders and phobias: A cognitive perspective.* New York: Basic Books.

Beck, A., Freeman, A., & Associates (1990). *Cognitive therapy of personality disorders.* New York: Guilford.

Beck, A., Rush, A, Shaw, B., & Emery, G. (1979). *Cognitive therapy of depression.* New York: Guilford.

Beck, A., Wright, F., Newman, C., & Liese, B. (1993). *Cognitive therapy of substance abuse.* New York: Guilford.

Beck, J. (1995). *Cognitive therapy: Basics and beyond.* New York: Guilford.

Beck, J. (1996). Cognitive therapy of personality disorders. In P. Salkovskis (Ed.), *Frontiers of cognitive therapy* (pp. 165–181). New York: Guilford.

Beck, J. (1998). Changing core beliefs: Use of the core belief worksheet. In H. Rosenthal (Ed.), *Favorite counseling and therapy techniques.* Washington DC: Accelerated Development.

Beck, J. G., & Zebb, B. J. (1994). Behavioral assessment and treatment of panic disorder: Current status, future directions. *Behavior Therapy, 25*, 581–611.

Bedrosian, R., & Bozicas, G. (1993). *Treating family of origins problems: A cognitive approach.* New York: Guilford.

Bellezza, F., & Hoyt, S. (1992). The self-reference effect and mental cueing. *Social Cognition, 10,* 51–78.

Benedict, R. (1989). The effectiveness of cognitive remediation strategies for victims of traumatic head–injury: A review of the literature. *Clinical Psychology Review, 9,* 605–626.

Berger, J. (1977). *Ways of seeing.* New York: Penguin.

Berne, E. (1961). *Transactional analysis in psychotherapy: A systematic individual and social psychiatry.* New York: Grove Press.

Berne, E. (1964). *Games people play; The psychology of human relationships.* New York: Grove Press.

Bernstein, M., & Barker, W. (1989). *The search for Bridey Murphy.* New York: Doubleday.

Beyerstein, B. (1985). The myth of alpha consciousness. *The Skeptical Inquirer, 10,* Fall.

Binder, J., & Smokler, I. (1980). Early memories: A technical aid to focusing in time–limited dynamic psychotherapy. *Psychotherapy: Theory, Research and Practice, 17,* 52–62.

Birchwood, M., & Tarrier, N. (1994). *The psychological management of schizophrenia.* Chichester: Wiley.

Bistline, J., Jaremko, M., & Sobleman, S. (1980). The relative contributions of covert reinforcement and cognitive restructuring to test anxiety reduction. *Journal of Clinical Psychology, 36,* 723–728.

Block, J., & Yuker, H. (1989). *Can you believe your eyes?* New York: Gardner Press.

Blum, K. (1990). The "alcoholic" gene: DNA research may prove major breakthrough in search for genetic link (pamphlet). Houston, Texas: Neuro Genesis. Also published in *Professional Counselor,* Sept.–Oct., 1990.

Blum, K., & Trachtenberg, M. (1988). Alcoholism: Scientific basis of a neuropsychogenetic disease. *International Journal of the Addictions, 23*(8), 781–796.

Bobbitt, Linda. (1989). *A test of attributional equivalence classes.* Dissertation, University of Kansas.

Bohman, M., Sigvardsson, S., & Cloninger, R. (1981). Maternal inheritance of alcohol abuse: Cross–fostering analysis of adopted women. *Archives of General Psychiatry, 38,* 965–969.

Botwinick, J. (1961). Husband and father–in–law: A reversible figure. *American Journal of Psychology, 74,* 312–313.

Boudewyns, P., & Shipley, R. (1983). *Flooding and implosive therapy: Direct therapeutic exposure in clinical practice.* New York: Plenum.

Bowler, P. (1986). *The true believers.* North Ryde, Australia: Methuen Australia Pty.

Bradley, D., & Petry, H. (1977). Organizational determinants of subjective contour. *American Journal of Psychology, 90,* 253–262.

Brehm, J. (1966). *A theory of psychological reactance.* New York: Academic Press.

Brehm, J., Snres, L., Sensenig, J., & Shaban, J. (1966). The attractiveness of an eliminated choice alternative. *Journal of Experimental Social Psychology, 2,* 301–313.

Brenner, H. (1989). The treatment of basic psychological dysfunctions from a systemic point of view. *British Journal of Psychiatry, 155* (Suppl. 5), 74–83.

Breuer, J., & Freud, S. (translated by A. Brill). (1937). *Studies in hysteria: Miss Katharina.* New York: Nervous & Mental Disease Publishing Company.

Bricker, D., Young, J., & Flanagan, C. (1993). Schema-focused cognitive therapy: A comprehensive framework for characterological problems. In K. Kuehlwein & H. Rosen (Eds.), *Cognitive therapies in action* (pp. 88–125). San Francisco: Jossey-Bass.

Bromley, D. (1977). Natural language and the development of the self. In H. Howe, Jr. (Ed.) *Nebraska Symposium on Motivation, 25,* Lincoln, NB: University of Nebraska Press.

Brown, B. (1974). *New mind, new body.* New York: Harper & Row.

Brown, C. W., & Ghiselli, E. (1955). *Scientific method in psychology.* New York: McGraw-Hill.

Brownell, K., Hayes, S., & Barlow, D. (1977). Patterns of appropriate and deviant sexual arousal: The behavioral treatment of multiple sexual deviation. *Journal of Consulting and Clinical Psychology, 45,* 1144–1155.

Bruhn, A. (1990a). Cognitive-perceptual theory and the projective use of autobiographical memory. *Journal of Personality Assessment, 55,* 95–114.

Bruhn, A. (1990b). *Earliest childhood memories: Theory and application to clinical practice.* (Vol. 1). New York: Praeger.

Bruner, J., Goodnow, J., & Austin, G. (1956). *A study of thinking.* New York: Wiley.

Brunn, A., & Hedberg, A. (1974). Covert positive reinforcement as a treatment procedure for obesity. *Journal of Community Psychology, 2,* 117–119.

Buchanan, G., & Seligman, M. (1995). *Explanatory style.* Hillsdale, NJ: Erlbaum.

Bugelski, B. (1970). Words and things and images. *American Psychologist, 25,* 1002–1012.

Buglione, S., DeVito, A., & Mulloy, J. (1990). Traditional group therapy and computer-administered treatment for test anxiety. *Anxiety Research, 3,* 33–39.

Bulfinch, T. *Bulfinch's mythology: The age of fable; the age of chivalry; legends of Charlemagne.* New York: Thomas Y. Crowell.

Burns, D. (1980). *Feeling good: The new mood therapy.* New York: Morrow.

Burns, D. (1989). *The feeling good handbook.* New York: Penguin.

Butler, P. (1992). *Self-assertion for women.* Revised edition. San Francisco: Harper.

Cameron, N. (1963). *Personality development and psychopathology: A dynamic approach.* Boston: Houghton Mifflin.

Cannon, W. (1998). Hypnotically enhanced interactive cognitive rehearsal. In H. Rosenthal (Ed.), *Favorite counseling and therapy techniques*. Washington, DC: Accelerated Development.

Carlson, J., & Seifert, R. (1994). *Clinical applied psychophysiology*. New York: Plenum.

Carson, R., & Sanislow III, C. (1993). The Schizophrenias. In P. Sutker & H. Adams, *Comprehensive handbook of psychopathology*. New York: Plenum.

Casey, B., & Mc Mullin, R. (1976). *Cognitive restructuring therapy package*. Lakewood, Colorado: Counseling Research Institute.

Casey, B., & Mc Mullin, R. (1985). *Cognitive restructuring therapy package. 2nd Ed.* Lakewood, Colorado: Counseling Research Institute.

Cassidy, J., Easton, M., Capelli, C., Singer, A., & Bilodeau, A. (1996). Cognitive remediation of persons with severe and persistent mental illness. *Psychiatric Quarterly. 67*, 4, 313–321.

Cautela, J. (1966). Treatment of compulsive behavior by covert sensitization. *Psychological Record, 16*, 33–41.

Cautela, J. (1967). Covert sensitization. *Psychological Record, 20*, 459–468.

Cautela, J. (1970). Covert reinforcement. *Behavior Therapy, 1*, 33–50.

Cautela, J. (1971a). Covert extinction. *Behavior Therapy, 2*, 192–200.

Cautela, J. (1971b). Covert conditioning. In A. Jacobs, & L. Sachs (Eds.). *The psychology of private events: Perspectives on covert response systems*. New York: Academic Press.

Chadwick, P., Birchwood, M., & Trower, P. (1996). *Cognitive therapy for delusions, voices and paranoia*. Chichester: Wiley.

Chandler, G., Burck, H., Sampson, J., & Wray, R. (1988). The effectiveness of a generic computer program for systematic desensitization. *Computers in Human Behavior, 4*, 339–346.

Chemtob, C., Hamada, R., Novaco, R., & Gross, D. (1997). Cognitive– behavioral treatment for severe anger in post traumatic stress disorder. *Journal of Counseling and Clinical Psychology, 65* (1), 184–189.

Cheng, P., & Novick, L. (1990). A probabilistic contrast model of causal induction. *Journal of Personality and Social Psychology, 58*, 545–567.

Cipher, D., & Fernandez, E. (1997). Expectancy variables predicting tolerance and avoidance of pain in chronic pain patients. *Behaviour Research and Therapy, 35* (5), 437–444.

Clark, J., & Jackson, J. (1983). *Hypnosis and behavior therapy*. New York: Springe.

Clarke, J., & Saunders, J. (1988). *Alcoholism and problem drinking: Theories and treatment*. Sydney, Australia: Pergamon.

Cloitre, M., Shear, K., Cancienne, J., & Zeitlin, S. (1994). Implicit and explicit memory for catastrophic associations to bodily sensation words in panic disorder. *Cognitive Therapy and Research, 18*, 225–240.

Cloninger, R., Bohman, M., & Sigvardsson, S. (1981). Inheritance of alcohol abuse: Cross–fostering analysis of adopted men. *Archives of General Psychiatry, 38*, 861–868.

Coleman, V. (1998). Lifeline. In H. Rosenthal (Ed.), *Favorite counseling and therapy techniques*. Washington, DC: Accelerated Development.

Corrigan, R. (1992). The relationship between causal attributions and judgments of the typicality of events described by sentences. *British Journal of Social Psychology, 31,* 351–368.

Corsini, R. (1957). *Methods of group psychotherapy.* New York: McGraw–HIll.

Corsini, R. (Ed.) (1981). *Handbook of innovative psychotherapies.* New York: Wiley.

Corsini, R. (1994). *Current psychotherapies.* (5th edition). Itaska, IL: F.E. Peacock Publishing.

Corsini, R. (1998). Turning the tables on the client: Making the client the counselor. In H. Rosenthal (Ed.), *Favorite counseling and therapy techniques.* Washington, DC: Accelerated Development.

Corsini, R., & Ozaki, B. (Eds.) (1984). *Encyclopedia of psychology* (Vol. 1–4). New York: Wiley.

Corsini, R., & Wedding, D. (1987). *Encyclopedia of psychology.* Canada: John Wiley and Sons.

Coursey, R. (1989). Psychotherapy with persons suffering from schizophrenia: The need for a new agenda. *Schizophrenia Bulletin, 15* (3), 349–353.

Cox, R. (Ed.). (1973). *Religious systems and psychotherapy.* Springfield, IL: Charles Thomas.

Cox, R. (1998). The use of symbols and rituals in psychotherapy. In H. Rosenthal (Ed.), *Favorite counseling and therapy techniques.* Washington, DC: Accelerated Development.

Crooke, W. (1926). *Religion and folklore of Northern India.* Oxford: Oxford University.

Csikszentmihalyi, M., & Beattie, O. (1979). Life themes: A theoretical and empirical exploration of their origins and effects. *Journal of Humanistic Psychology, 19,* 45–63.

Dallenbach, K. (1951). A puzzle-picture with a new principle of concealment. *American Journal of Psychology, 64,* 431–433.

Dalyell, J. (1835). *The darker superstitions of Scotland.* Glasgow.

Damasio, A. (1994). *Descartes' error: Emotion, reason, and the human brain.* New York: G.P. Putnam's Sons.

Dattilio, F. (1998). The SAEB system (symptoms, automatic thoughts, emotions, and behavior) in the treatment and conceptualization of panic attacks. In H. Rosenthal (Ed.), *Favorite counseling and therapy techniques.* Washington DC: Accelerated Development.

Dattilio, F. & Freeman, A. (1994). *Cognitive-behavioral strategies in crisis intervention.* New York: Guilford.

David, A. (1990). Insight and psychosis. *British Journal of Psychiatry, 156,* 798–808.

Davidson, P. (1997). *Adagio: Music for relaxation.* New York: Healing Arts Video.

Davis, K., & Moore, W. (1945). Some principles of stratification. *American Sociological, 10,* 242–249.

Deitrich, R. (1988). Genetics of alcoholism: An overview. *Australia Drug and Alcohol Review, 7,* 5–7.

De Quieroz, E. (1995). *Dedalus book of Portuguese fantasy.* New York: Hippocrene Books.

de Villiers, P. (1974). The law of effect and avoidance: A quantitative relation between response rate and shock frequency reduction. *Journal of the Experimental Analysis of Behavior, 21,* 223–235.

Dewey, J. (1886). *Psychology.* New York: Harper.

Dewey, J. (1920). *Reconstruction in philosophy.* New York: Henry Holt.

Dilts, R., Grinder, J., Bandler, R., DeLozier, J., & Cameron–Bandler, L. (1979). *Neuro-linguistic programming 1.* Cupertino, CA: Metal.

DiMattia, D., & Lega, L. (1990). *Will the real Albert Ellis please stand up?* New York: Institute for Rational–Emotive Therapy.

Dobson, K. (1989). A meta–analysis of the efficacy of cognitive therapy for depression. *Journal of Consulting and Clinical Psychology, 57,* 414–419.

Dobson, K., & Kendall, P. (Eds.) (1993). *Psychopathology and cognition.* San Diego: Academic Press.

Donnelly, C., & Dumas, J. (1997). Use of analogies in therapeutic situations: An analog study. *Psychotherapy, 34*(2), Summer, 124–132.

Drury, V., Birchwood, M., Cochrane, R., & Macmillan, F. (1996). Cognitive therapy and recovery from acute psychosis: A controlled trial. *British Journal of Psychiatry, 169,* 593–601.

Duhl, B. (1983). *From the inside out and other metaphors.* New York: Brunner/Mazel.

Dunlap, K. (1932). *Habits: Their making and unmaking.* New York: Liveright.

Dyer, W. (1993). *Your erroneous zones.* Reprint edition. New York: Harper Mass Market Paperbacks.

Edwards, D. (1990). Cognitive therapy and the restructuring of early memories through guided imagery. *Journal of Cognitive Psychotherapy, 4,* 33–50.

Elkin, I., Shea, T., Watkins, J., Imber, S., Sotsky, S., Collins, J., Glass, D., Pilkonis, P., Leber, W., Docherty, J., Fiester, S., & Parloff, M. (1989). NIMH Treatment of Depression Collaborative Research Program. *Archives of General Psychiatry, 46,* 971–982.

Ellis, A. (1962). *Reason and emotion in psychotherapy.* New York: Lyle Stuart.

Ellis, A. (1971). *Growth through reason: Verbatim cases in rational-emotive therapy.* Hollywood, CA: Wilshire Books.

Ellis, A. (1973). *Humanistic psychotherapy: The rational-emotive approach.* New York: Julian Press.

Ellis, A. (1974) *Techniques for disputing irrational beliefs (DIB'S).* New York: Institute for Rational Living, Inc.

Ellis, A. 1975). The rational–emotive approach to sex therapy. *Counseling Psychologist, 5,* 14–22.

Ellis, A. (1985). *Overcoming resistance: Rational-emotive therapy with difficult clients.* New York: Springer.

Ellis, A. (1988a). *How to stubbornly refuse to make yourself miserable about anything—yes, anything!* Melbourne, Australia: The Macmillan Company of Australia.

Ellis, A. (1988b). Are there "rationalist" and "constructivist" camps of the cognitive therapies? A response to Michael Mahoney. *Cognitive Behaviorist, 10*(2), 13–17.

Ellis, A. (1991). Rational–emotive family therapy. In A. Horne & M. Ohlsen (Eds.), *Family counseling and therapy* (pp. 302–328). Itasca, IL: Peacock.

Ellis, A. (1995). *Better, deeper, and more enduring brief therapy : The rational emotive behavior therapy approach.* New York: Brunner/Mazel.

Ellis, A. (1996). *Reason and emotion in psychotherapy: A comprehensive method of treating human disturbance.* (Revised). New York: Citadel.

Ellis, A. (1998). Vigorous disputing of irrational beliefs in rational–emotive behavior therapy (REBT). In H. Rosenthal (Ed.), *Favorite counseling and therapy techniques.* Washington, DC: Accelerated Development.

Ellis, A., & Abrahms, E. (1978). *Brief psychotherapy in medical and health practice.* New York: Springer.

Ellis, A., & Dryden, W. (1996). *The practice of rational emotive behavior therapy.* New York: Springer.

Ellis, A., Gordon, J., Neenan, M., & Palmer, S. (1996). *Stress counseling: A rational emotive behavioral approach.* New York: Cassell.

Ellis, A., & Grieger, R. (Eds.) (1977). *Handbook of rational-emotive therapy.* New York: Springer.

Ellis, A., & Harper, R. (1961). *A guide to rational living.* Hollywood, CA: Wilshire Books.

Ellis, A., & Harper, R. (1971). *A guide to successful marriage.* Hollywood, CA: Wilshire Books.

Ellis, A., & Harper, R. (1975). *A new guide to rational living (2nd ed.).* Hollywood, CA: Wilshire Books.

Ellis, A., & Harper, R. (1998). *A guide to rational living. (3rd ed.).* Hollywood, CA: Wilshire Books.

Ellis, A., & Lange, A. (1995). *How to keep people from pushing your buttons.* New York: Birch Lane.

Ellis, A., McInerney, J., DiGiuseppe, R., & Yeager, R. (1988). *Rational-emotive therapy with alcoholics and substance abusers.* New York: Pergamon.

Ellis, A., Sichel, J., Yeager, R., DiMattia, D., & DiGiuseppe, R. (1989). *Rational-emotive couples therapy.* Boston: Allyn & Bacon.

Ellis, A., & Tafrate, R. (1997). *How to control your anger before it controls you.* New York: Birch Lane Press.

Ellis, A., & Velten, E. (1992). *Rational steps to quitting alcohol.* Fort Lee, NJ: Barricade Books.

Ellis, A., & Whiteley, J. (Eds.) (1979). *Theoretical and empirical foundations of rational-emotive therapy.* Monterey, CA: Brooks/Cole.

Ellis, A., Wolfe, J., & Moseley, S. (1966) *How to raise an emotionally healthy, happy child.* Hollywood, CA: Wilshire Books.

Ellis, A., & Yeager, R. (1989). *Why some therapies don't work: The dangers of transpersonal psychology.* New York: Prometheus.

Ellis, W. (1939). *A source book of gestalt psychology.* New York: Harcourt, Brace and Co.

Engum, E., Miller, F., & Meredith, R. (1980). An analysis of three parameters of covert positive reinforcement. *Journal of Clinical Psychology, 36,* 301–309.

Erickson, M. (1982). *My voice will go with you: The teaching tales of Milton H. Erickson M.D.* (S. Rosen, ed.). New York: Norton.

Erickson, M., & Rossi, E. (1981). *Experiencing hypnosis: Therapeutic approaches to altered states.* New York: Irvington.

Escher, M. (1971). *The graphic work of M.C. Escher.* New York: Ballantine.

Fagan, M., & Shepherd, I. (1970). *Gestalt therapy now.* Palo Alto, CA: Science & Behavior Books.

Farber, I. (1963). The things people say to themselves. *American Psychologist, 18,* 187–197.

Fearnside, W., & Holther, W. (1959). *Fallacy: The counterfeit of argument.* Englewood Cliffs, NJ: Prentice–Hall.

Feder, B., & Ronall, R. (Eds.) (1980). *Beyond the hot seat: Gestalt approaches to group.* New York: Brunner/Mazel.

Fernberger, S. (1950). An early example of a "hidden–figure" picture. *American Journal Psychology, 63,* 448–449.

Festinger, L. (1957). *A theory of cognitive dissonance.* Stanford, CA: Stanford University Press.

Festinger, L. (1964). *Conflict, decision, and dissonance.* Stanford, CA: Stanford University Press.

Fishbein, M., & Ajzen, 1. (1975). *Belief, attitude, intention, and behavior.* Reading, MA: Addison–Wesley.

Fisher, G. (1967). Measuring ambiguity. *American Journal of Psychology, 80,* 541–557.

Fisher, G. (1968). Ambiguity of form: Old and new. *Perception and Psychophysics, 3,*189.

Flannery, R. (1972). A laboratory analogue of two covert reinforcement procedures. *Journal of Behavior Therapy and Experimental Psychiatry, 3,* 171–177.

Flemming, D. (1967). Attitude: The history of a concept. *Perspectives in American History, 1,* 287–365.

Foree, D., & Lo Lordo, V. (1975). Stimulus–reinforcer interactions in the pigeon: The role of electric shock and the avoidance contingency. *Journal of Experimental Psychology: Animal Behavior Processes, 104,* 39–46.

Fornander, A. (1996). *Ancient history of the Hawaiian people.* Honolulu, HI: Mutual Publishing.

Fowles, D. (1993). Biological variables in psychopathology: A psychobiological perspective. In P. Sutker & H. Adams, *Comprehensive handbook of psychopathology.* New York: Plenum Press.

Foy, D. (Ed.) (1992). *Treating PTSD: Cognitive-behavioral strategies.* New York: Guilford.

Frankl, V. (1959). *From deathcamp to existentialism.* Boston: Beacon Press.

Frankl, V. (1972). The feeling of meaninglessness: A challenge to psychotherapy. *American Journal of Psychoanalysis, 32,* 85–89.

Frankl, V. (1977). *The doctor and the soul: From psychotherapy to logotherapy.* New York: Knopf.

Frankl, V. (1978). *Psychotherapy and existentialism.* New York: Simon & Schuster.

Frankl, V. (1980). *Man's search for meaning: An introduction to logotherapy.* New York: Simon & Schuster.

Franklin, R. (1994). *Overcoming the myth of self-worth: Reason and fallacy in what you say to yourself.* Appleton, WI: R. L. Franklin.

Free, M. (1999). Cognitive therapy in groups: Guidelines & resources for practice. Brisbane, Australia: John Wiley & Sons.

Freeman, A. (1993). A psychosocial approach for conceptualizing schematic development for cognitive therapy. In K. Kuhlwein & H. Rosen (Eds.), *Cognitive therapies in action: Evolving innovative practice.* San Francisco: Jossey–Bass.

Freeman, A. (1994). *Depression: A cognitive therapy approach—a viewer's manual.* (Video). New York: New Bridge Communications.

Freeman, A., & Dattilio, F. (Eds.) (1992) *Comprehensive casebook of cognitive therapy.* New York: Plenum Press.

Freeman, A., & Dewolf, R. (1993). *The 10 dumbest mistakes smart people make and how to avoid them: Simple and sure techniques for gaining greater control of your life.* New York: Harper Perennial.

Freeman, A., Dewolf, R., & Beck, A. (1992). *Woulda, coulda, shoulda: Overcoming regrets, mistakes, and missed opportunities.* New York: Harper Perennial Library.

Freeman, A., & Eimer, B. (1998). *Pain management psychotherapy: A practical guide.* New York: John Wiley & Sons.

Freeman, A., Pretzer, J., Fleming, B., & Simon, K. (1990). *Clinical application of cognitive therapy.* New York: Plenum Press.

Freeman, A., & Reinecke, M. (1993). *Cognitive therapy of suicidal behavior.* New York: Springer.

Freeman, A., Simon, K., Beutler, L., & Arkowitz, H. (Eds.) (1989). *Comprehensive handbook of cognitive therapy.* New York: Plenum Press.

Freud, S. (1933). New introductory lectures on psychoanalysis. *The Standard Edition of the Complete Psychological Works* (Vol. xxii), J. Strachey (Trans. and Ed.). New York: Norton.

Freund, P. (1965). *Myths of creation.* New York: Washington Square Press.

Frijda, N., Markam, S., Sato, K., & Wiers, R. (1995). Emotions and emotion words. In J. Russell, Jose–Miguel Fernandez-Dols, & Manstead, A. (Eds.) *Everyday conceptions of emotions: An introduction to the psychology, anthropology and linguistics of emotion.* Dordrecht, the Netherlands: Kluwer Academic.

Fujita, C. (1986). *Morita therapy: A psychotherapeutic system for neurosis.* Tokyo: Igaku–Shoin Medical Publishing.

Gallant, D. (1987). *Alcoholism: A guide to diagnosis, intervention, and treatment.* New York: Norton.

Garcia, J., & Koelling, R. (1966). The relation of cue to consequence in avoidance learning. *Psychonomic Science, 4,* 123–124.

Gardner, M. (1957). *Fads and fallacies.* New York: Dover.

Gardner, M. (1981). *Science: Good, bad and bogus.* Buffalo, NY: Prometheus Books.

Gardner, M. (1991). *The new age: Notes of a fringe watcher.* Buffalo, NY: Prometheus.

Gendlin, E. (1962). *Experiencing and the creation of meaning: A philosophical and psychological approach to the subjective.* New York: The Free Press of Glencoe.

Gendlin, E. (1964). A theory of personality change. In P. Worchel & D. Byrne (Eds.), *Personality change.* New York: Wiley.

Gendlin, E. (1967). Focusing ability in psychotherapy, personality and creativity. In J. Shlien (Ed.), *Research in psychotherapy* (Vol.3). Washington, DC: American Psychological Association.

Gendlin, E. (1969). *Focusing. Psychotherapy: Theory, Research, and Practice, 6,* 4–15.

Gendlin, E. (1981). *Focusing.* New York: Everest House.

Gendlin, E. (1991). On emotion in therapy. In J. Safran & L. Greenberg (Eds.) *Emotion, psychotherapy, and change* (pp. 255–279). New York: Guilford.

Gendlin, E. (1992a). The primacy of the body, not the primacy of perception. *Man and World, 25,* 341–353.

Gendlin, E. (1992b). The wider role of bodily sense in thought and language. In M. Sheets–Johnstone (Ed.), *Giving the body its due* (pp. 192–207). Albany: State University of New York Press.

Gendlin, E. (1996a). *Focusing-oriented psychotherapy : A manual of the experiential method.* New York: Guilford.

Gendlin, E. (1996b). The use of focusing in therapy. In J. Zeig (Ed.), *The evolution of psychotherapy.* New York: Brunner/Mazel.

Gendlin, E., Beebe, J., Cassues, J., Klein, M., & Oberlander, M. (1968). Focusing ability in psychotherapy, personality and creativity. *Research in Psychotherapy, 3,* 217–241.

Gholson, B. (1980). *The cognitive-developmental basis of human learning: Studies in hypothesis testing.* New York: Academic Press.

Giles, T. (1979). Some principles of intervention in the absence of therapeutic alliance. *Transactional Analysis Journal, 9,* 294–296.

Giles, T. (Ed). (1993a). *Handbook of effective psychotherapy.* New York: Plenum.

Giles, T. (1993b). *Managed mental health care: A guide for practitioners, employers, and hospital administrators.* Boston: Allyn & Bacon.

Gillison, G. (1993). *Between culture and fantasy: A New Guinea highlands mythology.* Chicago: University of Chicago Press.

Glasser, W. (1989). *Control theory in the practice of reality therapy.* New York: HarperCollins.

Glasser, W. (1998). Reality therapy and choice theory. In H. Rosenthal (Ed.). *Favorite counseling and therapy techniques.* Washington, DC: Accelerated Development.

Goffman, E. (1961). *Encounters.* Indianapolis: Bobbs Merrill.

Goffman, E. (1971). *The presentation of self in everyday life.* New York: Basic Books.

Goffman, E. (1980). *Forms of talk.* Philadelphia: University of Pennsylvania Press.

Goffman E. (1987). *Asylums: Essays on the social situation of mental patients and other inmates.* New York: Penguin.

Goldfried, M. (1971). Systematic desensitization as training in self–control. *Journal of Consulting and Clinical Psychology, 37,* 228–234.

Goleman, D. (1977). *The varieties of the meditative experience.* New York: Dutton.

Goodwin, D., Schulsinger, F., Hermansen, L., Guse, S., & Winokur, G. (1973). Alcohol problems in adoptees raised apart from alcoholic biological parents. *Archives of General Psychiatry, 28,* 238–45.

Goodwin, D., Schulsinger, F., Moller, N., Hermansen, L., Winokur, G., & Guse, S. (1974). Drinking problems in adopted and non–adopted sons of alcoholics. *Archives of General Psychiatry, 31,* 164–69.

Gordon, D. (1978). *Therapeutic metaphors.* Cupertino, CA: Metal.

Gotestam, K., & Melin, L. (1974). Covert extinction of amphetamine addiction. *Behavior Therapy, 5,* 90–92.

Gould, R., Clum, G., & Shapiro, D. (1993). The use of bibliotherapy in the treatment of panic: A preliminary investigation. *Behavior Therapy, 24,* 241–252.

Graham, S., & Folkes, V. (1990). *Attribution theory: Application to achievement, mental health and interpersonal conflict.* Hillsdale, NJ: Erlbaum.

Greenberg, L. (Ed.) (1974). *Psychodrama: Theory and therapy.* New York: Behavioral Publications.

Greenfeld, D., Strauss, J., Bowers. M., & Mandelkern, M. (1989). Insight and interpretation of illness in recovery from psychosis. *Schizophrenia Bulletin, 15*(2), 245–252.

Greenstone, J., & Leviton, S. (1979). *The crisis intervention: A handbook for interveners* (Vol. 1) Dallas: Crisis Management Workshops.

Greenstone, J., & Leviton, S. (1980). *The crisis intervener's handbook* (Vol. 2). Dallas: Rothschild.

Greenstone, J., & Leviton, S. (1983). *Crisis intervention: A handbook for interveners.* Dubuque, IA: Kendall–Hunt.

Gregory, R. (1977). *Eye and brain: The psychology of seeing.* New York: World University Library.

Gregory, R. (1987). *The Oxford companion to the mind.* Oxford: Oxford University Press.

Grinder, J., & Bandler, R. (1975). *The structure of magic, 1.* Palo Alto: Science and Behavior Books.

Grinder, J., & Bandler, R. (1982). *Reframing: Neuro-linguisuc programming and the transformation of meaning.* Moab, UT: Real People Press.

Grof, S. (1975). *Realms of the human unconscious: Observations from LSD research.* New York: Viking Press.

Grof, S. (1980). Realms of the human unconscious: Observations from LSD research. In R. Walsh & F. Vaughan (Eds.), *Beyond ego: Transpersonal dimensions in psychology.* Los Angeles: Tarcher.

Guidano, V. (1987). *Complexity of the self: A developmental approach to psychopathology and therapy.* New York: Guilford.

Guidano, V. (1991). *The self in process: Toward a post-rationalist cognitive therapy.* New York: Guilford.

Guidano, V., & Liotti, G. (1983). *Cognitive processes and emotional disorders: A structural approach to psychotherapy.* New York: Guilford.

Haaga, D., Dyck, M., & Ernst, D. (1991). Empirical status of cognitive theory of depression. *Psychological Bulletin, 110,* 215–236.

Hatcher, C., & Himelstein, P. (Ed.) (1996). *The handbook of gestalt therapy.* New York: Jason Aronson.

Hauck, P. (1967). *The rational management of children.* New York: Libra Publishers.

Hauck, P. (1980) *Brief counseling with RET.* Philadelphia, PA: Westminster Press.

Hauck, P. (1991). *How to get the most out of life.* Louisville, KY: Westminster John Knox Press.

Hauck, P. (1992). *Overcoming the rating game: Beyond self-love, beyond self-esteem.* Louisville, KY: Westminster John Knox Press.

Hauck, P. (1994). *Overcoming the rating game: Beyond self-love, beyond self-esteem.* Louisville, KY: Westminster John Knox Press.

Hauck, P. (1998). Assertion strategies. In H. Rosenthal (Ed.), *Favorite counseling and therapy techniques.* Washington, DC: Accelerated Development.

Havens, R. (Ed.) (1985). *The wisdom of Milton H. Erickson.* New York: Irvington.

Hawkins, R. (1992). Self–efficacy: A predictor but not a cause of behavior. *Journal of Behavior Therapy and Experimental Psychiatry, 23,* 251–256.

Hayes, S. (1995). Why cognitions are not causes. *The Behavior Therapist, 18,* 59–60.

Hayes, S., Brownell, K., & Barlow, D. (1978). The use of self–administered covert sensitization in the treatment of exhibitionism and sadism. *Behavior Therapy, 9,* 283–289.

Hayes, S., Strosahl, K., & Wilson, K. (1996). *Acceptance and commitment therapy: Understanding and treating human suffering.* New York: Guilford.

Hayes, S., & Wilson, K. (1994). Acceptance and commitment therapy: Altering the verbal support for experiential avoidance. *The Behavior Analyst, 17,* 289–303.

Hayes, S., Wilson, K., Gifford, E., Follette, V., & Strosahl, K. (1996). Experimental avoidance and behavioral disorders: A functional dimensional approach to diagnosis and treatment. *Journal of Consulting and Clinical Psychology.*

Haygood, R., & Bourne, L. (1965). Attribute and rule learning aspects of conceptual behavior. *Psychological Review, 72,* 175–195.

Hays, P. (1995). Multicultural applications of cognitive–behavior therapy. *Professional Psychology: Research and Practice, 26(3),* 309–315.

Heimberg, R., & Juster, H. (1995). Cognitive–behavioral treatments: Literature review. In R. Heimberg, M. Liebowitz, D. Hope, & F. Schneier, *Social phobia: Diagnosis, assessment, and treatment* (pp. 261–309). New York: Guilford.

Herrnstein, R. (1969). Method and theory in the study of avoidance. *Psychological Review, 76,* 49–69.

Hineline, P., & Rachlin, H. (1969). Escape and avoidance of shock by pigeons pecking a key. *Journal of the Experimental Analysis of Behavior, 12,* 533–538.

Hobson, A., & McCarley, R. (1977). The brain as a dream state generator: An activation synthesis hypothesis of the dream process. *American Journal of Psychiatry, 134*(12), 1335–1348.

Holton, G. (1993). *Science and anti-science.* Cambridge: Harvard University Press.

Homme, L. (1965). Perspectives in psychology: XXIV control of coverants, the operants mind. *The Psychological Record, 15,* 501–511.

Hoogduin, K., de Haan, E., Schaap, C., & Arts, W. (1987). Exposure and response prevention in patients with obsessions. *Acta Psychiatrica Belgica, 87,* 640–653.

Horibuchi, S. (Ed.) (1994a). *Stereogram.* San Francisco, CA: Cadence Books.

Horibuchi, S. (Ed.) (1994b). *Super Stereogram.* San Francisco, CA: Cadence Books.

Hovland, C., & Janis, I. (1959). *Personality and persuasibility.* New Haven: Yale University Press.

Huijing, R. (1994). *The Dedalus book of Dutch fantasy.* New York: Hippocrene Books.

Hull, C. (1943). *Principles of behavior.* New York: Appleton–Century–Crofts.

Ivaldi Cdtud, A. (1995). *Hungarian fantasy.* (CD Audio). New York: Tudor Records.

Ivey, A., Ivey, M., & Simek–Morgan, L. (1993). *Counseling and psychotherapy: A multicultural perspective.* Boston: Allyn & Bacon.

Jacobs, H. (1993). *Behavior analysis guidelines and brain injury rehabilitation: People, principles, and programs.* Gaithersburg, Maryland: Aspen Publishers.

Jacobson, E. (1974). *Progressive relaxation.* Chicago: University of Chicago Press.

Jaeger, J., Berns, S., Tigner, A., & Douglas, E. (1992). Remediation of neuropsychological deficits in psychiatric populations: Rationale and methodological considerations. *Psychopharmacological Bulletin, 28,* 367–390.

Jamison, C., & Scogin, F. (1995). Outcome of cognitive bibliotherapy with depressed adults. *Journal of Consulting and Clinical Psychology, 63,* 644–650.

Jellinek, E. (1960). *The disease concept of alcoholism.* New Haven: Hillhouse Press.

Johnson, D. (1972). *A systematic introduction to the psychology of thinking.* New York: Harper and Row.

Joyce, K. (1994). *Astounding optical illusions.* New York: Sterling.

Kamin, L. (1956). Effects of termination of the CS and avoidance of the US on avoidance learning. *Journal of Comparative and Physiological Psychology, 49,* 420–424.

Kamin, L., Brimer, C., & Black, A. (1963). Conditioned suppression as a monitor of fear of the CS in the course of avoidance training. *Journal of Comparative and Physiological Psychology, 56,* 497–501.

Kazdin, A., & Smith, G. (1979). Covert conditioning: A review and evaluation. *Advances in Behavior Research and Therapy, 2,* 57–98.

Keenan, J., Golding, J., & Brown, P. (1992). Factors controlling the advantage of self–reference over other–reference. *Social Cognition, 10,* 79–94.

Kelleher, R. (1966). Conditioned reinforcement in second order schedules. *Journal of the Experimental Analysis of Behavior, 9,* 475–485.

Kelley, H. (1972). *Causal schemata and the attribution process.* Morristown, NJ: General Learning Press.

Kelly, G. (1955). *The psychology of personal constructs.* New York: Norton, 1955.

Kelly, G. (1980). A psychology of the optimal man. In A. Landfield & L. Leitner (Eds.), *Personal construct psychology: Psychotherapy and personality.* New York: Wiley.

Kendall, P. (Ed.) (1991). *Child and adolescent therapy: Cognitive-behavioral procedures.* New York: Guilford.

Kimura, R. (1998). Death and dying in Japan. In *Bioethics in the coming millennium.* Honolulu, HI: 1998 Bioethics Conference, St. Francis Medical Center.

Kingdon, D., & Turkington, D. (1991a). Preliminary report: The use of cognitive behavior and a normalizing rationale in schizophrenia. *Journal of Nervous and Mental Disease, 179,* 207–211.

Kingdon, D., & Turkington, D. (1991b). A role for cognitive therapy in schizophrenia? (Editorial). *Social Psychiatry & Psychiatric Epidemiology, 26,* 101–103.

Kingdon, D., & Turkington, D. (1994). *Cognitive-behavioral therapy of schizophrenia.* New York: Guilford.

Kitayama, S., & Markus, H. (1994). *Emotion and culture: Empirical studies of mutual influence.* Washington, DC: American Psychological Association.

Klemke, E. (Ed.) (1983). *Contemporary analytic and linguistic philosophies.* Buffalo, New York: Prometheus Books.

Klinger, E. (1980). Therapy and the flow of thought. In J. Shorr, G. Sobel, P. Robin, & J. Connella (Eds.), *Imagery: Its many dimensions and applications.* New York: Plenum.

Koenig, H., & Gates, W. (1998). Understanding cultural differences in caring for dying patients. In *Bioethics in the coming millennium* (pp. 71–81), Honolulu, HI: 1998 Bioethics Conference, St. Francis Medical Center.

Koenig, H., & Weaver, A., (Eds.) (1997). *Counseling troubled older adults: A handbook for pastors and religious caregivers.* Nashville, TN: Abingdon Press.

Koenig, H., & Weaver, A., (1998). *Pastoral care of older adults (creative pastoral care and counseling series).* Minneapolis, MN: Fortress Press.

Korchin, S. (1976). *Modern clinical psychology.* New York: Basic Books.

Kosslyn, S. (1980). *Image and mind.* Cambridge, MA: Harvard University Press.

Kosslyn, S., & Pomerantz, J. (1977). Imagery, propositions, and the form of internal representations. *Cognitive Psychology, 9,* 52–76.

Kroger, W., & Fezler, W. (1976). *Hypnosis and behavior modification: Imagery con-*

ditioning. Philadelphia: Lippincott.

Krop, H., Calhoon, B., & Verrier, R. (1971). Modification of the "self-concept" of emotionally disturbed children by covert reinforcement. *Behavior Therapy, 2*, 201–204.

Kurtz, P. (1992). *The new skepticism: Inquiry and reliable knowledge*. Buffalo, NY: Prometheus Books.

Ladouceur, R. (1974). An experimental test of the learning paradigm of covert positive reinforcement in deconditioning anxiety. *Journal of Behavior Therapy and Experimental Psychiatry, 5*, 3–6.

Ladouceur, R. (1977). Rationale of covert reinforcement: Additional evidence. *Psychological Reports, 41*, 547–550.

Lakoff, G. (1983). *Metaphors we live by*. Chicago: University of Chicago Press.

Lakoff, G. (1985). *Women, fire and dangerous things*. Chicago: University of Chicago Press.

Lakoff, G. (1990). *Women, fire and dangerous things*. (Reprint Ed.) Chicago: University of Chicago Press.

Lakoff, G., Taylor, M., Arakawa, & Lyotard, J., (1997). *Reversible destiny*. Chicago: University of Chicago Press.

Langacker, R. (1972). *Fundamentals of linguistic analysis*. New York: Harcourt Brace Jovanovich.

Lankton, S. (1990). *The broader implications of Ericksonian therapy*. New York: Ericksonian Monographs.

Lankton, S., & Lankton, C. (1983). *The answer within: A clinical framework of Ericksonian hypnotherapy*. New York: Brunner/Mazel.

Last, J. (1997). The clinical utilization of early childhood memories. *American Journal of Psychotherapy, 51*(3), Summer.

Lathem, E. (Ed.). (1975). *The Poetry of Robert Frost: The collected poems, complete and unabridged*. New York: Henry Holt and Company.

Lavigna, G. (1986). *Alternatives to punishment: Solving behavior problems with nonaversive strategies*. New York: Irvington Publications.

Lazarus, A. (1971). *Behavior therapy and beyond*. New York: McGraw–Hill.

Lazarus, A. (1977). *In the minds eye: The power of imagery for personal enrichment*. New York: Rawson.

Lazarus, A. (1981). *The practice of multimodal therapy*. New York: McGraw–Hill.

Lazarus, A. (1982). *Personal enrichment through imagery* (cassette recordings). New York: BMA Audio Cassettes/Guilford Publications.

Lazarus, A. (1989). *The practice of multimodal therapy*. Baltimore, MD: John Hopkins University Press.

Lazarus, A. (1995). *Casebook of multimodal therapy*. New York: Guilford.

Lazarus, A. (1997). *Brief but comprehensive psychotherapy: The multimodal way*. New York: Springer Publications.

Lazarus, A. (1998). Time tripping. In H. Rosenthal (Ed.), *Favorite counseling and therapy techniques*. Washington, DC: Accelerated Development.

Lazarus, A., Kanner, A., & Folkman, S. (1980). Emotions: A cognitive phenomenological analysis. In R. Plutchik & H. Kellerman (Eds.), *Theory of emotions*. New York: Academic Press.

Lazarus, A., & Lazarus, N. (1997). *The 60-second shrink: 101 strategies for staying sane in a crazy world.* San Luis Obispo, CA: Impact Publications.

Leuner, H. (1969). Guided affective imagery (GAI): A method of intensive psychotherapy. *American Journal of Psychotherapy, 23,* 4–22.

Liese, B., & Franz, R. (1996). Treating substance use disorders with cognitive therapy: Lessons learned and implications for the future. In P. Salkovskis (Ed.), *Frontiers of cognitive therapy* (pp. 470–508). New York: Guilford.

Litt, M. (1988). Self–efficacy and perceived control: Cognitive mediators of pain tolerance. *Journal of Personality and Social Psychology, 54*(1), 149–160.

Lohr, J., Kleinknecht, R., Tolin, D., & Barrett, R. (1995). The empirical status of the clinical application of eye movement desensitization and reprocessing. *Journal of Behavior Therapy and Experimental Psychiatry, 26,* 4.

Low, A. (1952). *Mental health through will-training.* Boston: Christopher.

Lukoff, D., Snyder, K., Ventura, J., & Nuechterlein, K., (1984). Life events, familial stress, and coping in the developmental course of schizophrenia. *Schizophrenia Bulletin, 10,* 258–292.

Lumeng et al., (1988). Behavioural and biochemical correlates of alcohol drinking preference: Studies on the selectively bred P and NP rats. *Australian Drug and Alcohol Review, 7,* 17–20.

Lundh, L., & Ost, L. (1997). Explicit and implicit memory bias in social phobia: The role of subdiagnostic type. *Behaviour Research and Therapy, 35*(4), 305–317.

Lungwitz, H., & Becker, R. (1993). *Psychobiology and cognitive therapy of the neuroses.* Boston: Birkhauser.

Lynn, S., & Kirsch, K. (1996). *Casebook of clinical hypnosis.* Washington, DC: American Psychological Association.

Mach, E. (1959). *The analysis of sensations and the relation of the physical to the psychical.* Mineola, NY: Dover.

Mac Kewn, J. (1996). *Developing gestalt counseling.* New York: Saga Publishing.

MacLeod, C., & McLaughlin, K. (1995). Implicit and explicit memory bias in anxiety: A conceptual replication. *Behaviour Research and Therapy, 33,* 1–14.

Magic Eye (1994a). *Magic eye: A new way of looking at the world.* Kansas City, MO: Andrews and Mc Meel.

Magic Eye (1994b). *Magic eye II: Now you see it.* Kansas City, MO: Andrews and Mc Meel.

Maher, B. (1988). Anomalous experience and delusional thinking: The logic of explanations. In T. Oltmanns & B. Maher (Eds.), *Delusional Beliefs.* New York: Wiley–Interscience.

Mahoney, M. (1971). The self–management of covert behavior: A case study. *Behavior Therapy, 2,* 575–578.

Mahoney, M. (1979). Cognitive skills and athletic performance. In P. Kendall & S. Hollon, *Cognitive-behavioral interventions: Theory, research, and procedures.* New York: Academic Press.

Mahoney, M. (1988). Constructive metatheory: II. Implications for psychotherapy. *International Journal of Personal Construct Psychology*, *1*, 299–315.

Mahoney, M. (1991). *Human change processes: The scientific foundations of psychotherapy*. New York: Basic Books.

Mahoney, M. (1993a). *The bodily self: A guide to integrating the head and body in psychotherapy*. New York: Guilford.

Mahoney, M. (1993b). Theoretical developments in the cognitive psychotherapies. *Journal of Consulting and Clinical Psychology*, *61*, 187–193.

Mahoney, M. (Ed.) (1994). *Cognitive and constructive psychotherapies: Theory, research, and practice*. New York: Springer.

Mahoney, M., & Arnkoff, D. (1978). Cognitive and self-control therapies. In S. Garfield & A. Bergin (Eds.), *Handbook of psychotherapy and behavior change*. New York: Wiley.

Mahoney, M., & Thoresen, C. (1974). *Self-control: Power to the person*. Monterey, CA: Brooks Cole.

Mahoney, M., Thoresen, C., & Danaher, B. (1972). Covert behavior modification: An experimental analogue. *Journal of Behavior Therapy and Experimental Psychiatry*, *3*, 7–14.

Mana: A South Pacific journal of language and literature. (1980 to present). Suva, Fiji: South Pacific Creative Arts Society, Mana Publications.

Manlove, C. (1997). *An anthology of Scottish fantasy literature*. New York: Polygon.

Marsella, A. (1984). *Cultural conceptions of mental health and therapy*. Boston: Kluwer Academic Publishers.

Marsella, A. (1997). Challenges to cultural diversity in Hawaii. *Peace and Policy*, *2*, 24–30.

Marsella, A. (1998a). Urbanization, mental health, and social development. *American Psychologist*, *53*, 624–634.

Marsella, A., (1998b). Toward a "Global–community psychology." *American Psychologist*, *53*(12), 1282–1292.

Marsella, A., Friedman, M., Gerrity, E. Scurfield, R. (Eds.) (1996). *Ethnocultural aspects of post traumatic stress disorder: Issues, research and clinical applications*. Washington, DC: American Psychological Association.

Marshall, W., Gauthier, J., & Gordon, A. (1979). The current status of flooding therapy. In M. Hersen, R. Eisler, & P. Miller (Eds.), *Progress in behavior modification* (p. 7). New York: Academic Press.

Martin, J., Cummings, A., & Hallberg, E., (1992). Therapists' intentional use of metaphor: Memorability, clinical impact, and possible epistemic/motivational functions. *Journal of Consulting and Clinical Psychology*, *60*, 143–145.

Martin, L. (1914). Ueber die Abhangigkeit vi-queller Vorstellungsbilder vom Denken, *Zsch. f. Psychol.*, *70*, 214.

Maultsby, M. (1971). Rational emotive imagery. *Rational Living*, *6*, 22–26.

Maultsby, M. (1976). *Help yourself to happiness through rational self-counseling*. Boston: Esplanade Institute for Rational Living.

Maultsby, M. (1984). *Rational behavior therapy.* Englewood Cliffs, NJ: Prentice-Hall.

Maultsby, M. (1990). *Rational behavior therapy: The self-help psychotherapy.* New York: Tangram Books.

Maultsby, M., & Ellis, A. (1974). *Techniques for using rational-emotive imagery (REI).* New York: Institute for Rational Living.

May, R. (1953). *Man's search for meaning.* New York: Norton.

May, R. (Ed.) (1981). *Existential psychology.* New York: Random House.

McCurry, S., & Hayes, S. (1992). Clinical and experimental perspectives on metaphorical talk. *Clinical Psychology Review, 12,* 763–785.

McEvoy, J., Apperson, L., Appelbaum, P., Ortlip, P., Brecosky, J., Hammill, K., Geller, J., & Roth, L. (1989). Insight in schizophrenia: Its relationship to acute psychopathology. *Journal of Nervous and Mental Disease, 177*(1), 43–47.

McEvoy, J., Freter, S., Everett, G., Geller, J., Appelbaum, P., Apperson, L., & Roth, L., (1989). Insight and the clinical outcome of schizophrenic patients. *The Journal of Nervous and Mental Disease, 177*(1), 48–51.

McGinn, L. (1997). Interview: Albert Ellis on rational emotive behavior therapy. *American Journal of Psychotherapy, 51*(3), Summer, 309–316.

McGinn, L., & Young, J. (1996). Schema–focused therapy. In P. Salkovskis (Ed.), *Frontiers of cognitive therapy* (pp. 182–207). New York: Guilford.

McGlashan, T. (1994). What has become of the psychotherapy of schizo-phrenia? *Acta Psychiatr. Scand. 90* (suppl 384), 147–152.

McGlashan T., & Levy, S. (1977). Sealing–over in a therapeutic community. *Psychiatry, 40,* 55–65.

Mc Mullin, R. (1972). Effects of counselor focusing on client self–experi-encing under low attitudinal conditions. *Journal of Counseling Psychology, 19*(4), 282–285.

Mc Mullin, R. (1986). *Handbook of cognitive therapy techniques.* New York: Norton.

Mc Mullin, R. (1990, June). Massed cognitive flooding with alcohol and drug dependency. Keystone, Colorado: *World Congress on Mental Health Counseling.*

Mc Mullin, R. (1995, July 4). Racism is our fear of strangers: Xenophobia and racism. *Honolulu Advertiser.*

Mc Mullin, R. (1998). *Make sense: A guide to cognitive restructuring therapy for inpatients.* Kaneohe, Hawaii: Hawaii State Hospital.

Mc Mullin, R. (1999). Unpublished survey of third and fourth grade students. Honolulu, HI.

Mc Mullin, R., Assafi, I., & Chapman, S. (1978). *Straight talk to parents: Cognitive restructuring for families.* Brookvale, Australia: F. S. Symes (dis.), and Kaneohe, HI: Counseling Research Institute.

Mc Mullin, R., & Casey, B. (1975). *Talk sense to yourself: A guide to cognitive restructuring therapy.* New York: Institute for Rational Emotive Therapy (dis.), and Kaneohe, HI: Counseling Research Institute.

Mc Mullin, R., Casey, B., & Navas, J. (trans.) (1979). *Hablese con sentido a si*

mismo. Juan, Puerto Rico: Centro Caribeno de Estudios Postgradua-
dos.

Mc Mullin, R., & Gehlhaar, P. (1990a) *Thinking & drinking: An expose of drinkers'
distorted beliefs. A cognitive approach to alcohol dependency*. Wheelers Hill,
Victoria, Australia: Marlin Pub. Ltd.

Mc Mullin, R., & Gehlhaar, P. (1990b) (unpublished). Research on omega
alcoholism. Surry Hills, Australia: The Langton Centre.

Mc Mullin, R., & Gehlhaar, P. (1990c, February). Two forms of cognitive
therapy with severe chronic alcohol dependent clients. Sydney, Australia: Fifth International Conference on Treatment of Addictive Behaviors.

Mc Mullin, R., Gehlhaar, P., & James, C. (1990). *The lizard: Our craving for alcohol*. 22 Sandstone Crescent, Tascott, NSW 2250 Australia: Sauria Publications Ltd.

Mc Mullin, R., & Giles, T. (1981). *Cognitive-behavior therapy: A restructuring
approach*. New York: Grune & Stratton.

Mc Mullin, R., Samford, J., & Kline, A. (1996). Patients' unedited film transcript. From J. Samford (Producer), R. Mc Mullin (Director), & L.
Jerome (Executive Producer). *Myths of Madness*. (Film). Available from
Hawaii Psychological Research Consortium, Department of Psychology, Hawaii State Hospital, Kaneohe, Hawaii.

McNally, R., Foa, E., & Donnell, C. (1989). Memory bias for anxiety information in patients with panic disorders. *Cognition and Emotion, 3*, 27–
44.

Meichenbaum, D. (1975). A self–instructional approach to stress management: A propose stress inoculation training. In I. Sarason & C. Spielberger (Eds.), *Stress and anxiety* (Vol. 2). New York: Wiley.

Meichenbaum, D. (1977). *Cognitive-behavior modification: An integrative approach*.
New York: Plenum.

Meichenbaum, D. (1985). *Stress inoculation training: A clinical guidebook*. Old
Tappan, NJ: Allyn & Bacon.

Meichenbaum, D. (1993). Changing conceptions of cognitive behavior
modification: Retrospect and prospect. *Journal of Consulting and Clinical
Psychology, 61*, 292–204.

Meichenbaum, D. (1994). *A clinical handbook/practical therapist manual for assess-
ing and treating adults with post-traumatic stress disorder (PTSD)*. Waterloo,
ON: Institute Press.

Meichenbaum, D., & Deffenbacher, J. (1988). Stress inoculation training. *The
Counseling Psychologist, 16*, 69–90.

Meichenbaum, D., & Genest, M. (1983). *Pain and behavioral medicine*. New
York: Guilford.

Meichenbaum, D., & Turk, D. (1987). *Facilitating treatment adherence: A practitioner's guidebook*. New York: Plenum Press.

Mill, J. S. (1950). *Philosophy of scientific method*. New York: Hafner Publishing.

Mill, J. S. (1988). *Utilitarianism*. Indianapolis, Indiana: Hackett.

Miller, N., & Campbell, D. (1959). Recency and primacy in persuasion as a function of the timing of speeches and measurement. *Journal of Abnormal and Social Psychology, 59,* 1–9.

Miller, W., & Rollnick, S. (1991). *Motivational interviewing: Preparing people to change addictive behavior.* New York: Guilford.

Milliner, C., & Grinder, J. (1990). *Framework for excellence: A resource manual for NLP.* Santa Crux, CA: Grinder Delozier & Associates.

Milton, F., Patwa, V., & Hafner, J. (1978). Confrontation vs. belief modification in persistently deluded patients. *British Journal of Medical Psychology, 51,* 127–130.

Monat, A., & Lazarus, R. (Eds.) (1991). *Stress and coping: An anthology (3rd ed.).* New York: Columbia University Press.

Montangero, J., & Maurice–Naville, D., (1997). *Piaget or the advance of knowledge.* Hillsdale, NJ: Erlbaum.

Moreno, J., & Zeleny, L. (1958). Role theory and sociodrama. In J. Roucek (Ed.), *Contemporary sociology.* New York: Philosophical Library.

Morita, M., & Kondo, A. (1998). Morita therapy and the true nature of anxiety–based disorders (shinkeishitsu). New York: State University of New York Press.

Morowitz, H., & Singer, J. (1995). *The mind, the brain, and complex adaptive systems: Proceedings.* New York: Addison–Wesley.

Mosak, H. (1958). Early recollections as a projective technique. *Journal of Projective Techniques, 22,* 302–311.

Mosak, H. (1969). Early recollections: Evaluation of some recent research. *Journal of Individual Psychology, 25,* 56–63.

Mowrer, O., & Lamoreaux, R. (1946). Fear as an intervening variable in avoidance conditioning. *Journal of Comparative Psychology, 369,* 29–50.

Munitz, M. (1981). *Contemporary analytic philosophy.* New York: Macmillan.

Munson, C. (1993). Cognitive family therapy. In D. Granvold (Ed.), *Cognitive and behavioral treatment: Methods and applications* (pp. 202–221). Pacific Grove, CA: Brooks/Cole.

Nagel, E. (Ed.) (1950). *John Stuart Mill's philosophy of scientific method.* New York: Hafner.

Neimeyer, R. (1993). An appraisal of constructivist psychotherapies. *Journal of Consulting and Clinical Psychology, 61,* 221–234.

Neimeyer, R., & Feixas, G. (1990). The role of homework and skill acquisition in the outcome of cognitive therapy for depression. *Behavior Therapy, 21*(3), 281–292.

Neimeyer, R. Mahoney, M., & Murphy, L. (Eds.) (1996). *Constructivism in psychotherapy.* Washington, DC: American Psychological Association.

Neugroschel, J. (1997). *Great tales of Jewish fantasy and the occult.* New York: Penguin.

Neukrug, E. (1998). Support and challenge: Use of metaphor as a higher level empathic response. In H. Rosenthal (Ed.), *Favorite counseling and therapy techniques.* Washington, DC: Accelerated Development.

Nevis, E. (Ed.) (1993). *Gestalt therapy: Perspectives and applications.* Cleveland, OH: Gestalt Institute of Cleveland Press.

Newhall, S. (1952). Hidden cow puzzle–picture. *American Journal of Psychology, 65*, 110.

Newman, M., Kenardy, J., Herman, S., & Taylor, C. (1997). Comparison of palmtop–computer–assisted brief cognitive–behavioral treatment to cognitive–behavioral treatment for panic disorder. *Journal of Consulting and Clinical Psychology, 65*(1), 178–183.

Nielsen, S., & Ellis, A. (1994). A discussion with Albert Ellis: Reason, emotion and religion. *Journal of Psychology and Christianity, 13*(4), 327–341.

Nisbett, R., & Ross, L. (1980). *Human inference: Strategies and shortcomings of social judgment*. Englewood Cliffs, NJ: Prentice–Hall.

Nuechterlein, K., & Dawson, M. E. (1984). Informational processing and attentional functioning in the developmental course of schizophrenic disorders. *Schizophrenia Bulletin, 10*, 160–203.

Nuechterlein, K., Goldstein, M., & Ventura, J. (1989). Patient environment relationships in schizophrenia: Informational processing, communication deviance, autonomic arousal, and stressful life events. *British Journal of Psychiatry, 155* (Suppl. 5), 84–89.

O'Donohue, W. (1997). *Learning and behavior therapy*. Boston: Allyn & Bacon.

Okpaku, S. (Ed.) (1998) *Clinical methods in transcultural psychiatry.* Washington, DC: American Psychiatric Press.

Olevitch, B., & Ellis, A. (1995). *Using cognitive approaches with the seriously mentally ill: Dialogue across the barrier*. Westport, CT: Praeger.

Olson, H. (1979). *Early recollections: Their use in diagnosis and psychotherapy*. Springfield, IL: Thomas.

Orne, M., & Paskewitz, D. (1973). Visual effects on alpha feedback training. *Science, 181*, 361–363.

Ost, L., & Westling, B. (1995). Applied relaxation vs. cognitive therapy in the treatment of panic disorder. *Behaviour Research and Therapy, 33*, 145–158.

Paris, C., & Casey, B. (1983). *Project you: A manual of rational assertiveness training*. Hollywood, CA: Wilshire Book.

Pavlov, I. (1928). *Lectures on conditioned reflexes*. New York: International Publishers.

Pavlov, 1. (1960). *Conditioned reflexes*. New York: Dover.

Pedersen, P. (1991). Multiculturalism as a generic approach to counseling. *Journal of Counseling and Development, 70*, 6–12.

Perls, F. (1969a) *Gestalt therapy verbatim*. Lafayette, CA: Real People Press.

Perls, F. (1969b). *In and out the garbage pail*. Lafayette, CA: Real People Press.

Perls, F. (1973) *The Gestalt approach*. Palo Alto, CA: Science & Behavior Books.

Perris, C. (1988). Intensive cognitive–behavioural psychotherapy with patients suffering from schizophrenic, psychotic or post–psychotic syndrome: Theoretical and practical aspects. In C. Perris, I. Blackburn, & H. Perris (Eds.), *Cognitive psychotherapy: Theory and practice* (pp. 324–375). Berlin: Springer–Verlag.

Perris, C. (1989). *Cognitive therapy with schizophrenic patients*. New York: Guilford.

Perris, C. (1992). Integrating psychotherapeutic strategies in the treatment of young, severely disturbed patients. *Journal of Cognitive Psychotherapy, 6*, 205–220.

Perris, C., Nordstrom, G. & Troeng, L. (1992). Schizophrenic disorders. In A. Freeman & F. M. Dattilio (Eds.), *Comprehensive casebook of cognitive therapy* (pp. 313–330). New York: Plenum Press.

Perris, C., & Skagerlind, L. (1994). Schizophrenia. In F. Dattilio & A. Freeman (Eds.), *Cognitive-behavioral strategies in crisis intervention* (pp. 104–118). New York: Guilford.

Petersen, C., Maier, S., & Seligman, M. (1995). *Learned helplessness: A theory for the age of personal control.* Oxford: Oxford University Press.

Petty, R., & Cacioppo, J. (1981). *Attitudes and persuasion: Classic and contemporary approaches.* Dubuque, IA: Brown.

Piaget, J. (1954). *The construction of reality in the child.* New York: Basic Books.

Piaget, J. (1963). *The origins of intelligence in children.* New York: Norton.

Piaget, J. (1970). *Structuralism.* New York: Harper & Row.

Piaget, J. (1973). *The child and reality: Problems of genetic psychology.* New York: Grossman.

Piaget, J. (1995). *The essential Piaget.* New York: Jason Aronson.

Plotkin, W. (1979). The alpha experience revisited: Biofeedback in the transformation of psychological state. *Psychological Bulletin, 86*, 1132–1148.

Plutchik, R. (1980). *Emotions: A psychoevolutionary synthesis.* New York: Harper & Row.

Popper, K. (1959). *The logic of scientific discovery.* New York: Basic Books.

Porter, P. (1954). Another puzzle-picture. *American Journal of Psychology, 67*, 550–551.

Powaga, W. (1997). *The Dedalus book of Polish fantasy.* New York: Hippocrene Books.

Premack, D. (1965). Reinforcement theory. In D. Levine (Ed.), *Nebraska Symposium on Motivation.* Lincoln, NB: University of Nebraska Press.

Progoff, I. (1977). *At a journal workshop.* New York: Dialogue House Library.

Progoff, I. (1992). *At a journal workshop: Writing to access the power of the unconscious and evoke creative ability.* (Revised edition). New York: J. P. Tarcher.

Qiu, R. (1998). Dying in China. In *Bioethics in the coming millennium.* Honolulu, HI: 1998 Bioethics Conference, St. Francis Medical Center.

Quine, W. (1987). *Quiddities: An intermittently philosophical dictionary.* Cambridge, Massachusetts: Harvard University Press.

Quine, W., & Ullian J. (1978). *The web of belief* (2nd ed.). New York: Random House.

Rabhn, J. (1974). Public attitudes toward mental illness: A review of the literature. *Schizophrenia Bulletin, 10*, 9–33.

Rachman, S. (1997). A cognitive theory of obsessions. *Behavior Research and Therapy, 35*, 793–802.

Rachman, S., Rachman, J., & Eysenck, H. (1997). *The best of behaviour research and therapy.* New York: Pergamon Press.

Randi, J. (1982). *Flim-flam: Psychics, ESP, unicorns and other delusions.* Buffalo, NY: Prometheus Books.

Randi, J. (1989). *The faith healers.* Buffalo, NY: Prometheus Books.

Randi, J. (1995). *An encyclopedia of claims, frauds, and hoaxes of the occult and supernatural.* New York: St. Martin's Press.

Ray, W., & Ravizza, R. (1981). *Methods toward a science of behavior and experience.* Belmont, CA: Wadsworth.

Reed, A. (1978). *Aboriginal myths: Tales of the dreamtime.* Frenchs Forest, NSW, Australia: A. H. Reed.

Rees, S., & Graham, R. (1991). *Assertion training: How to be who you really are.* London: Routledge.

Reich, W. (Ed.) (1998). *The ethics of sex and genetics: Selections from the five-volume MacMillan encyclopedia of bioethics, Rev. Ed.* New York: Simon & Schuster Macmillan.

Reinecke, M., Dattilio, F., & Freeman, A. (Eds.) (1996). *Casebook of cognitive-behavior therapy with children and adolescents.* New York: Guilford.

Relaxation Company. (1996). *Art of relaxation: 10 year collection.* (CDs). New York: Relaxation Co.

Rescorla, R. (1967). Pavlovian conditioning and its proper control procedures. *Psychological Review, 74,* 71–80.

Rescorla, R. (1969). Pavlovian conditioned inhibition. *Psychological Bulletin, 72,* 77–92.

Reynolds, D. (1976). *Morita psychotherapy.* Berkeley, CA: University of California Press.

Reynolds, D. (1981). Morita therapy. In R. Corsini (Ed.), *Handbook of innovative psychotherapies.* New York: Wiley.

Rhue, J. (1993). *Handbook of clinical hypnosis.* Washington, DC: American Psychological Association.

Richardson, A. (1967). Mental practice: A review and discussion (Part 1 & 2). *Research Quarterly, 38,* 95–107, 263–273.

Richardson, A. (1969). *Mental imagery.* New York: Springer.

Richie, B. (1951). Can reinforcement theory account for avoidance? *Psychological Review, 58,* 382–386.

Rizley, R., & Rescorla, R. (1972). Associations in higher order conditioning and sensory preconditioning. *Journal of Comparative and Physiological Psychology, 81,* 1–11.

Rogers, C. R. (1951). *Client-centered therapy: Its current practice, implications, and therapy.* Boston: Houghton Mifflin.

Rogers, C. R. (1959). A theory of therapy, personality, and interpersonal relationships developed in the client–centered framework. In S. Koch (Ed.), *Psychology: A study of science: Vol. 3. Formulations of the person and the social context.* New York: McGraw–Hill.

Rogers, T., Kuiper, N., & Kirker, W. (1977). Self–reference and the encoding of personal information. *Journal of Personality and Social Psychology, 35,* 677–688.

Rokeach, M. (1964). *The three Christs of Ypsilanti: A psychological study.* New York: Knopf.

Rokeach, M. (1968). *Beliefs, attitudes, and values.* San Francisco: Jossey–Bass.

Rokeach, M. (1973). *The nature of human values.* New York: Free Press/Macmillan.

Rokeach, M. (Ed.) (1979). *Understanding human values: Individual and societal.* New York: Free Press/Macmillan.

Rosenbluh, E. (1974). *Techniques of crisis intervention.* New York: Behavioral Science Service.

Rossi, E. (Ed.) (1980). *The collected papers of Milton H. Erickson on hypnosis* (Vols. 1–4). New York: Irvington.

Rossi, E., & Ryan, M. (Eds.) (1985). *Life reframing in hypnosis: The seminars, works and lectures of Milton H. Erickson.* New York: Irvington.

Rudolph, U., & Forsterling, F. (1997). The psychological causality implicit in verbs: A review. *Psychological Bulletin, 121*(2), 192–218.

Rumor, V. (Exec. Producer) (1994). *Magic eye: The video.* Nashville, TN: Cascom International Inc.

Russell, B. (1945). *A history of western philosophy.* New York: Simon and Schuster.

Russell, B. (1957). *Why I am not a Christian and other essays on religion and related subjects.* New York: Simon and Schuster.

Russell, B. (1961). *The basic writings of Bertrand Russell.* New York: Simon and Schuster.

Russell, J., Manstead, A., Wallenkamp, J., & Fernandez–Dolls, J. (Eds.), (1995). *Everyday conceptions of emotions: An introduction to the psychology, anthropology and linguistics of emotion.* Dordrecht, the Netherlands: Kluwer Academic.

Ryle, G. (1949). *The concept of mind.* Chicago: University of Chicago Press.

Ryle, G. (1957). *The revolution in philosophy.* London: Macmillan.

Ryle, G. (1960). *Dilemmas.* London: Cambridge University Press.

Safren, A., Juster, H., & Heimberg, R. (1997). Clients' expectancies and their relationship to pretreatment symptomatology and outcome of cognitive–behavioral group treatment for social phobia. *Journal of Counseling and Clinical Psychology, 65*, 694–698.

Sagan, C. (1979). *Broca's brain: Reflections on the romance of science.* New York: Ballantine Books.

Sagan, C. (1995). *The demon-haunted world: Science as a candle in the dark.* New York: Random House.

Salkovskis, P. (Ed.) (1996). *Frontiers of cognitive therapy.* New York: Guilford.

Salkovskis, P., Richards, C., & Forrester, G. (1995). The relationship between obsessional problems and intrusive thoughts. *Behavioral and Cognitive Psychotherapy, 23*, 281–299.

Sandry, M. (1992). *Ideas that make you feel.* (Computer Software). New York: Albert Ellis Institute.

Santrock, J., Minnett, A., & Campbell, B. (1994). *The authoritative guide to self-help books.* New York: Guilford.

Sargant, W. (1996). *Battle for the mind: A physiology of conversion and brain-washing.* (Reprint edition) New York: Harper and Row.

Schachter, S. (1966). The interaction of cognitive and physiological determinants in emotional state. In C. D. Spielberger (Ed.), *Anxiety and
behavior*. New York: Academic Press.

Schachter, S., & Gazzaniga, M. (Eds.) (1989). *Extending psychological frontiers:
Selected works of Leon Festinger*. New York: Russell Sage Foundation.

Schachter, S., & Singer, J. (1962). Cognitive, social and physiological determinants of emotional state. *Psychological Review, 69*, 379–399.

Schauss, S., Chase, P., & Hawkins, R. (1997). Environment–behavior relations, behavior therapy and the process of persuasion and attitude
change. *Journal of Behavior Therapy and Experimental Psychiatry, 28*(1), 31–
40.

Scherer, K. (1997). The role of culture in emotion–antecedent appraisal.
Journal of Personality and Social Psychology, 73(5), 902–922.

Schuckit, M. (1984). Prospective markers for alcoholism. In D. Goodwin, K.
Van Dusen, & S. Mednick (Eds.), *Longitudinal research in alcoholism* (pp.
147–163). Boston: Kluwer–Nijhoff.

Schuckit, M., & Vidamantas, R. (1979). Ethanol injection: Differences in
blood acetaldehyde concentrations in relatives of alcoholics and
controls. *Science, 203*, 54–55.

Schwartz, B. (1978). *Psychology of learning and behavior*. New York: Norton.

Schwartz, G. (1973). Biofeedback as therapy: Some theoretical and practical issues. *American Psychologist, 28*, 666–673.

Schwartz, M. (1995). *Biofeedback: A practitioner's guide* (2nd ed). New York:
Guilford.

Schwarzer, R. (Ed.) (1992). *Self-efficacy: Thought control of action*. Washington,
DC: Hemisphere.

Schwebel, A., & Fine, M. (1994). *Understanding and helping families: A cognitive-
behavioral approach*. Hillsdale, NJ: Erlbaum.

Scogin, F., Jamison, C., & Davis, N. (1990). A two-year follow-up of the
effects of bibliotherapy for depressed older adults. *Journal of Consulting and Clinical Psychology, 58*, 665–667.

Scott, D., & Leonard, C. (1978). Modification of pain threshold by the covert
reinforcer procedure and a cognitive strategy. *The Psychological Record,
28*, 49–57.

Scott, D., & Rosenstiel, A. (1975). Covert positive reinforcement studies:
Review, critique guidelines. *Psychotherapy: Theory, Research and Practice,
12*, 374–384.

Seligman, M. (1975). *Helplessness: On depression, development, and death*. San
Francisco: Freeman.

Seligman, M. (1994). *What you can change & what you can't: The ultimate guide to
self-improvement*. New York: Knopf.

Seligman, M. (1996). *The optimistic child: A proven program to safeguard children
against depression & build lifelong resilience*. New York: HarperCollins.

Seligman, M. (1998). *Learned optimism*. New York: Pocket Books.

Seligman, M., & Johnson, J. (1973). A cognitive theory of avoidance learning. In F. Mc Guigan & D. Lumsden (Eds.), *Contemporary approaches to*

conditioning and learning. Washington, DC: Winston-Wiley.

Seligman, M., Reivich, K., Jaycox, L., & Gillham, J. (1995). *The optimistic child: A revolutionary program that safeguards children against depression & builds lifelong resilience*. New York: Houghton Mifflin Company.

Selmi, P., Klein, M., Greist, J., Sorrell, S., & Erdman, H. (1990). Computer-administered cognitive–behavioral therapy for depression. *American Journal of Psychiatry, 147*, 51–56.

Semin, G., & Fiedler, K. (1988). The cognitive functions of linguistic categories in describing persons: Social cognition and language. *Journal of Personality and Social Psychology, 54*, 558–568.

Semin, G., & Fiedler, K. (1989). Relocating attributional phenomena within a language–cognition interface: The case of actors' and observers' perspectives. *European Journal of Social Psychology, 19*, 491–508.

Semin, G., & Fiedler, K. (1991). The linguistic category model, its bases, applications and range. In W. Stroebe & M. Hewstone (Eds.), *European review of social psychology* (Vol. 2, pp. 1–30). Chichester, England: Wiley.

Shapiro, F. (1995). *Eye movement desensitization and reprocessing: Basic principles, protocols, and procedures*. New York: Guilford.

Shapiro, F. (1998). *EMDR: The breakthrough therapy for overcoming anxiety, stress, and trauma*. New York: Basic Books.

Shea, T., Elkin, I., Imber, S., Sotsky, S., Watkins, J., Collins, J., Pilkonis, P., Beckham, E., Glass, D., Dolan, R., & Parloff, M. (1992). Course of depressive symptoms over follow–up: Findings from the National Institute of Mental Health Treatment of Depression Collaborative Research Program. *Archives of General Psychiatry, 49*, 782–787.

Sheikh, A. (Ed.) (1983a). *Imagery: Current theory, research and application*. New York: Wiley.

Sheikh, A. (Ed.) (1983b). *Imagination and healing*. New York: Baywood.

Sheikh, A., & Shaffer, J. (Eds.) (1979). *The potential of fantasy and imagination*. New York: Brandon House.

Shorr, J. (1972). *Psycho-imagination therapy: The integration of phenomenology and imagination*. New York: Intercontinental.

Shorr, J. (1974). *Psychotherapy through imagery*. New York: Intercontinental

Sidman, M. (1953). Two temporal parameters of the maintenance of avoidance behavior in the white rat. *Journal of Comparative and Physiological Psychology, 46*, 253–261.

Sidman, M. (1966). Avoidance behavior. In W. Honig (Ed.), *Operant behavior: Areas of research and application*. New York: Appleton–Century–Crofts.

Siegelman, E. (1990). *Metaphor and meaning in psychotherapy*. New York: Guilford.

Simkins, L. (1982). Biofeedback: Clinically valid or oversold. *Psychological Record, 32*, 3–17.

Simon, J. (1978). *Basic research methods in social science*. New York: Random House.

Singer, J. (1974). *Imagery and daydream methods in psychotherapy and behavior modification*. New York: Academic Press.

Singer, J. (1976). *Daydreaming and fantasy*. London: Allen & Unwin.

Singer, J. (Ed.) (1995). *Repression and dissociation: Implications for personality theory, psychopathology and health*. Chicago: University of Chicago Press.

Singer, J., & Pope, K. (Eds.) (1978). *The power of human imagination*. New York: Plenum.

Skinner, B. F. (1953). *Science and human behavior*. New York: Free Press.

Skinner, B. F. (1974). *About behaviorism*. New York: Knopf.

Skinner, B. F. (1991). *Beyond freedom and dignity*. (Reissue edition). New York: Bantam Books.

Smith, J. C. (1990). *Cognitive-behavioral relaxation training: A new system of strategies for treatment and assessment*. New York: Springer.

Smith, M., Bruner, J., & White, R. (1956). *Opinions and personality*. New York: Wiley.

Smith, N., Floyd, M., Scogin, F., & Jamison, C. (1997). Three-year follow-up of bibliotherapy for depression. *Journal of Consulting and Clinical Psychology. 65*, 324–327.

Smith, R. (1995). *Folklore fable & fantasy*. Lakeville, MN: Galde Press.

Sober-Ain, L., & Kidd, R. (1984). Fostering changes in self-blame: Belief about causality. *Cognitive Theory and Research, 8*, 121–138.

Sokolov, E. (1963). *Perception and the conditioned reflex*. New York: Macmillan.

Solomon, R. (1964). Punishment. *American Psychologist, 19*, 239–253.

Solomon, R., & Wynne, L. (1954). Traumatic avoidance learning: The principles of anxiety conservation and partial irreversibility. *Psychological Review, 61*, 353–385.

Solomon, R., & Wynne, L. (1956). Traumatic avoidance learning: Acquisition in normal dogs. *Psychological Monographs, 67*, Whole No. 354.

Spangler, D., Simons, A., Monroe, S., & Thase, M. (1997). Response to cognitive-behavioral therapy in depression: Effects of pretreatment cognitive dysfunction and life stress. *Journal of Consulting and Clinical Psychology, 65*(4), 568–575.

Spaulding, W., Sullivan, M., Weiler, M., Reed, D., Richardson, C., & Storzbach, D. (1994). Changing cognitive functioning in rehabilitation of schizophrenia. *Acta Psychiatrica Scandinavica*. 116–124.

Spielberger, C., & DeNike, L. (1966). Descriptive behaviorism versus cognitive theory in verbal operant conditions. *Psychological Review, 73*, 306–326.

Sprague de Camp, L. (1983). *The fringe of the unknown*. Buffalo, NY: Prometheus Books.

Stableford, B. (1993). *The Dedalus book of British fantasy*. New York: Hippocrene Books.

Stampfl, T., & Levis, D. (1967). Essentials of implosive therapy: A learning theory-based psychodynamic behavioral therapy. *Journal of Abnormal Psychology, 72*, 496–503.

Steam, J. (1976). *The power of alpha thinking: Miracle of the mind*. New York: Signet.

Stein, M. (Ed.) (1995). *Social phobia: Clinical and research perspectives*. Washington, DC: American Psychiatric Press.

Steiner, S., & Dince, W. (1981). Biofeedback efficacy studies: A critique of critiques. *Biofeedback and Self-Regulation, 6,* 275–287.

Sternbach, R. (1987). *Mastering pain: A twelve step program for coping with chronic pain.* New York: Putnam.

Stubbs, D., & Cohen, S. (1972). Second order schedules: Comparison of different procedures for scheduling paired and non-paired brief stimuli. *Journal of the Experimental Analysis of Behavior, 18,* 403–413.

Stuve, P., Erickson, R., & Spaulding, W. (1991). Cognitive rehabilitation: The next step in psychiatric rehabilitation. *Psychosocial Rehabilitation Journal, 15*(1), 9–26.

Suinn, R., & Richardson, F. (1971). Anxiety management training: A non-specific behavior therapy program for anxiety control. *Behavior Therapy, 2,* 498–510.

Summer, W. G. (1906). *Folkways.* New York: Ginn.

Summer, W. G., Keller, A., & Davie, M. (1927). *The science of society.* New Haven: Yale University Press.

Sutcliffe, J. (1994). *The complete book of relaxation techniques.* New York: People's Medical Society.

Symons, C., & Johnson, B. (1997). The self-reference effect in memory: A meta-analysis. *Psychological Bulletin, 121*(3), 371–394.

Szasz, T. (1960). The myth of mental illness. *American Psychologist, 15,* 113–118.

Szasz, T. (1970a). *Ideology and insanity: Essays on the psychiatric dehumanization of man.* Garden City, NY: Anchor Books.

Szasz, T. (1970b). *The manufacture of madness.* New York: Harper & Row.

Szasz, T. (1978). *The myth of psychotherapy.* Garden City, NY: Doubleday.

Taibbi, R. (1998). Life–play fantasy exercise. In H. Rosenthal (Ed.), *Favorite counseling and therapy techniques.* Washington, DC: Accelerated Development.

Taylor, F. S. (1963). *A short history of science & scientific thought.* New York: Norton.

Taylor, S., & Fiske, S. (1975). Point of view: Perception of causality. *Journal of Personality and Social Psychology, 32,* 439–445.

Teasdale, J. (1978). Self–efficacy: Toward a unifying theory of behavior change? *Advances in Behaviour Research and Therapy, 1,* 211–215.

Teasdale, J. (1993). Emotion and two kinds of meaning: Cognitive therapy and applied cognitive science. *Behaviour Research and Therapy, 31,* 339–354.

Teasdale, J. (1996). Clinically relevant theory: Integrating clinical insight with cognitive science. In P. Salkovskis (Ed.), *Frontiers of cognitive therapy* (pp. 26–47). New York: Guilford.

Teasdale, J., & Barnard, P. (1993). *Affect, cognition and change: Re-modeling depressive thought.* Hove, UK: Erlbaum.

Thorpe, G., & Olson, S. (1997). *Behavior therapy: Concepts, procedures, and applications.* Boston: Allyn & Bacon.

Torrey, E. (1972). *The mind game: Witch doctors and psychiatrists.* New York: Bantam.

Trabasso, T., & Bower, G. (1968). *Attention in learning: Theory and research*. New York: Wiley.

Turkat, I., & Adams, H. (1982). Covert positive reinforcement and pain modification of efficacy and theory. *Journal of Psychosomatic Research, 26*, 191–201.

Turner, L., & Solomon, R. (1962). Human traumatic avoidance learning: Theory and experiments on the operant–respondent distinction and failure to learn. *Psychological Monographs, 76*, Whole No. 559.

Twain, Mark (1906). *The stolen white elephant*. London: Chatto & Windus.

Twain, Mark (1916). *The mysterious stranger and other stories*. New York: Harper & Brothers.

Twain, Mark (1962). De Voto, B. (Ed.). *Letters from the earth*. New York: Harper & Roe.

Twain, Mark (1963). Neider, C. (Ed.). *The complete essays of Mark Twain*. Garden City, NY: Doubleday.

Twain, Mark (1972a). Anderson, F. (Ed.). *A pen warmed-up in hell*. New York: Harper & Roe.

Twain, Mark (1972b). Smith, J. (Ed.). *Mark Twain: On man and beast*. Westport, CT: Lawrence Hill & Co.

Twain, Mark (1980). Tuckey, J. (Ed.). *The devil's race-track: Mark Twain's great dark writings*. Berkeley, CA: University of California Press.

Udolf, R. (1992). *Handbook of hypnosis for professionals*. New York: Jason Aronson.

Ullmann, L., & Krasner, L. (1965). *Case studies in behavior modification*. New York: Holt, Rinehart and Winston.

Ullmann, L., & Krasner, L. (1969). *A psychological approach to abnormal behavior*. Englewood Cliffs, NJ: Prentice-Hall.

Urmson, J. (1950). *Philosophical analysis*. Oxford: Clarendon Press.

Van Der Dennen, J., & Falger, V. (1990). *Sociobiology and conflict: Evolutionary perspectives on competition, cooperation, violence and warfare*. New York: Chapman & Hall.

Warner, W., & Lunt, P. (1973). *The Status System of a Modern Community* Westport, CT: Greenwood Publishing Group.

Watkins, J. (1976). Ego states and the problem of responsibility: A psychological analysis of the Patty Hearst case. *Journal of Psychiatry and Law*. Winter, 471–489.

Watkins, J. (1978). Ego states and the problem of responsibility II. The case of Patrima W. *Journal of Psychiatry and Law*, Winter, 519–535.

Watkins, J., & Watkins, H. (1980). Ego states and hidden observers. *Journal of Altered States of Consciousness, 5*, 3–18.

Watkins, J., & Watkins, H. (1981). Ego-state therapy. In R. Corsini (Ed.), *Handbook of innovated psychotherapies*. New York: Wiley.

Watson, P., & Johnson-Laird, P. (1972). *Psychology of reasoning: Structure and content*, Cambridge, MA: Harvard University Press.

Weaver, A., Koenig, H., & Roe, P. (Eds.) (1998). *Reflections on aging and spiritual growth*. Nashville, TN: Abingdon Press.

Weaver, A., Preston, J., & Jerome, L. (1999). *Counseling troubled teens and their families: A handbook for clergy and youth workers.* Nashville, TN: Abingdon Press.

Wehrly, B. (1995). *Pathways to multicultural counseling competence: A developmental journey.* Pacific Grove, CA: Brooks/Cole.

Wehrly, B. (1998). Bibliotherapy. In H. Rosenthal (Ed.), *Favorite counseling and therapy techniques.* Washington, DC: Accelerated Development.

Weimer, W., & Palermo, D. (1974). *Cognition and the symbolic processes.* Hilldale, NJ: Erlbaum.

Weiss, J., Glazer, H., Pohorecky, L., Brick, J., & Miller, N. (1975). Effects of chronic exposure to stressors on avoidance–escape behavior and on brain norepinephrine. *Psychosomatic Medicine, 37,* 522–534.

Wever, E. (1927). Figure and ground in the visual perception of form. *American Journal Psychology, 38,* 196.

Whitehead, A. (1967). *Science and the modern world.* New York: The Free Press.

Whittal, M., & Goetsch, V. (1997). The impact of panic expectancy and social demand on agoraphobic avoidance. *Behavior Research and Therapy, 35*(9), 813–821.

Wicklund, R., & Brehm, J. (1976). *Perspectives on cognitive dissonance.* Hillsdale, NJ: Erlbaum.

Wilde, J. (1998). Rational–emotive imagery (REI). In H. Rosenthal (Ed.), *Favorite counseling and therapy techniques.* Washington, DC: Accelerated Development.

Williams, J. (1996a). Depression and the specificity of autobiographical memory. In D. Rubin (Ed.), *Remembering our past: Studies in autobiographical memory* (pp. 244–270). Cambridge, UK: Cambridge University Press.

Williams, J. (1996b). Memory processes in psychotherapy. In P. Salkovskis (Ed.), *Frontiers of cognitive therapy* (pp. 97–113). New York: Guilford.

Wilson, E. (1998). *Consilience: The unity of knowledge.* New York: Alfred A. Knopf.

Wilson, J. (1963). *Thinking with concepts.* London: Cambridge University Press.

Wilson, J. (1967). *Language and the pursuit of truth.* London: Cambridge University.

Wilson, K., Hayes, S., & Gifford, E. (1997). Cognition in behavior therapy: Agreements and differences. *Journal of Behavioral Therapy and Experimental Psychiatry, 28*(1), 53–63.

Wolpe, J. (1958). *Psychotherapy by reciprocal inhibition.* Stanford, CA: Stanford University.

Wolpe, J. (1969). *The practice of behavior therapy.* New York: Pergamon Press.

Wolpe, J. (1973). *The practice of behavior therapy* (2nd ed.). New York: Pergamon.

Wolpe, J. (1978). Cognition and causation in human behavior and its therapy. *American Psychologist, 33,* 437–446.

Wolpe, J. (1981a). The dichotomy between classical conditioned and cognitively learned anxiety. *Journal of Behavioral Therapy and Experimental Psychiatry, 12,* 35–42.

Wolpe, J. (1981b). Perception as a function of conditioning. *The Pavlovian Journal of Biological Science, 16,* 70–76.

Wolpe, J., Lande, S., McNally, R., & Schotte, D. (1985). Differentiation between classically conditioned and cognitively based neurotic fears: Two pilot studies. *Journal of Behavioral Therapy and Experimental Psychiatry, 16,* 287–293.

Wolpe, J., & Lazarus, A. (1967). *Behavior therapy techniques.* London: Pergamon Press.

Wolpe, J., Salter, A., & Reyna, L. (Eds.) (1964). *The conditioning therapies: The challenge in psychotherapy.* New York: Holt, Rinehart & Winston.

Worsick, D. (1994). *Henry's gift: The magic eye.* Kansas City, MO: Andrews and McMeel.

Wright, J. (1996). Inpatient Cognitive Therapy. In P. Salkovskis (Ed.), *Frontiers of cognitive therapy.* New York: Guilford.

Wright, J., Thase, M., Beck, A., & Ludgate, J. (Eds.) (1993). *Cognitive therapy with inpatients: Developing a cognitive milieu.* New York: Guilford.

Yeats, W. (1990). *The Celtic twilight: Myth, fantasy and folklore.* New York: Prism Press Ltd.

Young, J. (1954). *The prose edda of Snorri Sturlusion: Tales from Norse mythology.* Berkeley, CA: University of California Press.

Young, J., (1992). *Schema conceptualization form.* New York: Cognitive Therapy Center of New York.

Young, J. (1994). *Cognitive therapy for personality disorders: A schema-focused approach.* Sarasota, FL: Professional Resource Press.

Young, J., Beck, A., & Weinberger, A. (1993). Depression. In D. Barlow (Ed.), *Clinical handbook of psychological disorders* (pp. 240–277). New York: Guilford.

Young, J., & Rygh, J. (1994). *Reinventing your life.* New York: Plume.

Zaffuto, A. (1974). *Alpha-genics: How to use your brain waves to improve your life.* New York: Warner Paperback.

Zimmer–Hart, C., & Rescorla, R. (1974). Extinction of Pavlovian conditioned inhibition. *Journal of Comparative and Physiological Psychology, 86,* 837–845.

Zubin, J., & Spring, B. (1977). Vulnerability—A new view of schizophrenia. *Journal of Abnormal Psychology, 86,* 103–126.

Subject Index

Author Index